BEHIND
CLOSED DOORS

Irving Scholar

BEHIND CLOSED DOORS

Dreams and Nightmares at Spurs

IRVING SCHOLAR
with MIHIR BOSE

ANDRE DEUTSCH

First published in Great Britain 1992 by
André Deutsch Limited
105-106 Great Russell Street WC1B 3LJ

Copyright © 1992 by Irving Scholar
and Mihir Bose

The authors have asserted their moral rights

ISBN 0 233 98824 6

Printed in Great Britain by
St Edmundsbury Press, Bury St Edmunds, Suffolk

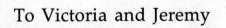

To Victoria and Jeremy

CONTENTS

ILLUSTRATIONS

Frontispiece: the author

PREFACE

by Mihir Bose

We may get the government we deserve, but do football clubs get the chairmen they deserve? Certainly it would be hard to deny that English football deserves better leaders. For all the romanticism that the game has traditionally generated in this country, and the media hype that now accompanies almost every football match, English football seems stuck in a time-warp that is really quite bizarre.

Indeed, if a visitor from America – let alone the proverbial Martian - were to come to our shores to look into a game whose world championship is going to be held in their country in 1994, they would conclude that English football has done what American sociologists have failed to do for almost thirty years. In America, black kids are bussed to white neighbourhoods so that they can profit from better-quality schools there. On Saturday afternoons in England, affluent, well-off whites drive their carefully groomed cars into grim inner-city areas that their fathers and grandfathers struggled to get out of, and which are now populated by the ethnics – blacks, Asians, Greeks – in order to watch their favourite football team. Half that team may be composed of black players, but only a handful of spectators in the stadium will be black.

What is more the English whites are so keen to see their team that they put up with almost any privation. They will circle for hours round the stadium to find a car parking space (there being no proper car parks). They are prepared to go without their favourite beers for the duration of the match (unless they go in the executive boxes). They will even agree to be frisked by security staff and the police as if they were potential criminals, and if they are away supporters to stay locked inside the ground for up to half an hour after the match has finished before they are considered safe enough to be let out on the street again. Why would any man – and football is still a man's game – want to go through such experiences, and all for the sake of watching ninety minutes of pretty awful football?

The answer is that in a world where almost everything is open to doubt, and every institution, including the monarchy, is subject to a corrosive scrutiny, English football clubs provide an oasis of stability. Neville Cardus once wrote that if everything about England was destroyed – her laws, customs, constitution – but if a copy of the laws of cricket remained, then an eternal Englishness could be recreated. Similarly, a football supporter must feel that whatever else happens in his life, as long as his club and the ground it plays on remains, then something of the past is retained.

Nothing else can explain why the English football fan has remained so resistant to change. In Italy football may be a religion, but the clubs can happily share grounds, yet even in England's capital city, Charlton's being forced to share a ground can mean many supporters swearing never to see the club unless it returns to its decrepit, desolate but beloved Valley. But then English football, unlike say English cricket, has that intense tribal feeling that convinces supporters that the opposition is always the enemy.

Given this blinkered commitment, it is hardly surprising that a government minister attacked in the media for various acts of omission and commission can go to his favourite football ground and be hailed as a conquering hero – less than two weeks before he has to resign from the Cabinet. Or that the Chairman of a football club can hold a Press conference in an expensive hotel to announce that he is having an affair with a woman not his wife.

Set against this background, how are we to judge Irving Scholar's stewardship of Tottenham Hotspur? The Spurs fanzine *Spur* recently called him rich, devious and naïve. Rich he certainly is, naïve he may have been – but devious, no. That Irving Scholar made mistakes one cannot doubt, but his greatest fault has been to love Tottenham and football to excess. His crime was to be too enthusiastic for change in a world which sees all change as the devil's work and all ideas for reform as a disguised attempt to grab money.

Now you may decide, in the tradition of Miss Mandy Rice Davies, that I would say that. After all, I have taken Irving's shilling and helped him write the book. But this is a view shared by others with a reputation both in football and the media. Jeff Randall, City Editor of the *Sunday Times*, had one of his most brilliant coups when he revealed Irving Scholar's dealings with Robert Maxwell, which were a prelude to what Irving calls his 'nightmare year' at Tottenham. Jeff's exposé of him brought him into intimate contact with all the players involved in that saga, not many of whom he respects, but of Scholar he says: 'One thing I must say about Irving. In all that time he never told me a lie. He always told me the truth. Also he was the first one to tell me that, perhaps, Maxwell was in trouble. Long before anybody else had guessed that.' Alex Fynn, who has specialised in football books dealing with recent changes in the game, may not have always seen eye to eye with Irving Scholar, but he acknowledges that Scholar was a football visionary who was, perhaps, a little ahead of his time.

If this has echoes of Alf Ramsey's description of Martin Peters – 'ten years ahead of his time' – this may explain why Scholar eventually failed. He was always pushing against the tide, and the tide in football always runs against change. But, perhaps, the deeper reason for the way the Scholar story has turned out is that the man himself is just not ruthless enough. I have learnt a lot while working with him on this book, but one of the principal lessons is that, despite his image, Irving Scholar finds it difficult to draw blood. Indeed, working with him I was reminded of Enoch Powell's famous story of the time the Conservatives were deciding on a successor to Harold Macmillan. The natural choice should have been Rab Butler, but Macmillan recommended Alex Douglas-Home, and Powell, Iain Macleod and a few others opposed to him gathered round Butler begging him not to serve under Douglas-Home. Had he listened to them, Douglas-Home would almost certainly not have become Prime Minister. As Powell picturesquely recalls, Butler was given the sword but he asked: 'If I use it will it draw blood?' When Enoch and the group assured him that the use of the sword does indeed draw blood, Butler shrank from it and Alex Douglas-Home became Prime Minister.

In the course of researching and writing this book with Irving, he has shown a similar inability to draw blood. There has been no dearth of stories - this man would have been a compulsive and engaging story-teller in the age before television and radio – but the stories tend to carry almost no malice, and therefore no sharp bite. So this book shows a surprising degree of good will to almost everyone in football. There are, as you shall see, exceptions to this, but like Rab Butler, Irving Scholar would rather not use the sword if it means spilling blood. Others in football are not quite so scrupulous. But then, says Scholar, he would rather sleep at night.

Contrary to popular myth, Irving does not see his decade at Spurs as a tragedy. After all why should he? He arrived in 1982 with the FA Cup in the Trophy Room, and departed in 1991 with the FA Cup in the Trophy Room. He invested a lot of money in buying the club, and got more money back when he left. And in between, he found himself at the centre of one of the most remarkable decades in English football history. If there was pain towards the end, the early years were full of pleasure and anticipation of change, and Irving clearly revelled in it. True, as with Thomas Carlyle writing his study of Oliver Cromwell, doing this book with Irving has meant having to dig it out from under a mountain of dead dogs, a huge load of calumny and oblivion. And in one respect Irving has hampered his own story by being almost entirely reticent about his personal life. Despite this, what emerges is a story of love and enthusiasm and a man of honour and energy, even if the energy was not always understood and was sometimes misdirected.

1 | THE ORPHANED DAY

'Victory has a hundred fathers, but defeat is an orphan.'

On the afternoon of 18 May 1991, as Gary Mabbutt raised the FA Cup above his shoulders and joyously displayed it to the whole of Wembley, I should have felt like the proudest of fathers. Tottenham had won the Cup for a record eighth time, and what is more it had preserved a unique Tottenham history. Ever since the start of this century a year ending with a one – 1901, 1921, 1951, 1961, 1971, 1981 – had seen Tottenham win a major trophy: either the League Championship, the League Cup, or, more often, the FA Cup. 1991 had preserved that slice of White Hart Lane history that all Tottenham fans loved. Now as Chairman I felt elated, but somehow there was a very hollow feeling within me.

But then it had been that kind of day, that kind of year: a day which had begun with a princess convincing me we could win the Cup and ended with my ex-wife having to restrain me from resigning the chairmanship of the club that very night at a celebration dinner. Looking back, perhaps it was not that unusual a day, for it seemed to sum up my nine years in charge of Tottenham Hotspur: a time of highs and lows, with the lows pressing hard upon the highs. So it was on that Cup Final day.

Club chairmen are no different from supporters. As Colin Welland has said, partisan sport-watching is terrible; the odd moment of bliss – and no bliss could have been purer than when Tottenham beat Liverpool at Anfield after seventy-two years – costing years of frayed nerves and black moods. FA Cup Finals provide a microcosm of that contrast, and in 1987, when Spurs lost to Coventry, I had experienced both the exhilaration and the despair. But 1991 was different.

As I arrived early that morning at Wembley I felt curiously detached. I desperately wanted Tottenham to win the Cup, but I knew this was going to be my last day of involvement with the club, and I was determined to enjoy it. The FA Cup Final is one of those marvellous occasions, like Wimbledon or the Lord's Test Match, which the English do so well. It marks the day when the English game, after a long, hard season, finally comes together in one symbolic moment: fair play, sportsmanship and the chance for the underdog to humble the mightiest all get a chance to find expression. In 1901, when Tottenham first won the Cup, they were a Southern League side, but in one of the great Cup upsets of all time they beat Sheffield United to become the first, and so far the only non-League club to win the trophy. Every football supporter who has seen his team play in a Cup Final at Wembley goes through a tumult of emotion. No one ever goes to Wembley not believing that their team is going to win.

All the same, that day in May it was difficult to divorce myself from what had gone before. Certainly no team in the history of the FA Cup has ever come to the Final with such a baggage of publicity and speculation as Tottenham was carrying. The previous nine months had seen the club's financial predicament debated first in the business sections and then spread over all the sports pages. Terry Venables, the Manager who was going to lead the team out on to the Wembley turf, was himself trying to buy the club from me, and the match itself was billed as the make-or-break match for Tottenham Hotspur. If Spurs won, a lucrative European season stretched ahead and substantial cash receipts would ease the debt; if they lost it could condemn the club to financial ruin – or so the Press speculated. To cap it all, the match itself was seen as a symbolic moment for Paul Gascoigne, the most charismatic figure in English football. He was bound for Lazio in Rome, and this match was meant to be his farewell before he left for Italy to become a millionaire.

Amidst all this, as Chairman of the club, but not of the plc where the debts had been accumulated, I had been painted in the Press as the arch-villain, the man responsible for Tottenham's financial problems and supposedly still trying to hold on to it by seeking to sell Gascoigne and prevent Terry Venables from taking over. The real truth was a different story. First, I had been stalling for months by imposing many conditions that would make Gascoigne's transfer to Lazio impossible. Second, I had agreed terms to sell my interest to Terry Venables on several occasions, but each time he had failed to honour his part of the bargain by not coming up with the money. His latest attempt was the night before, using a mutual friend as a go-between.

That Friday morning I had a meeting arranged with the Chairman of Tottenham plc, Nat Solomon, and Mel Stein, Gascoigne's agent. The meeting had been fixed a few days before, and it had to do with the decisive character of the Gascoigne transfer. I had made it clear to the board from the very outset, for something like seven or eight months, that if Gascoigne was sold then I would leave the club, and without hesitation. The reason was that I didn't think it was right that the football club should be responsible for financing debts not of its making. Player sales should be approached on the basis of whether it was right for the club and the team, not whether it suited the bank. I'd tried everything to delay the transfer, and although the Gascoigne contract had been signed by Solomon at the end of April, through that meeting on Friday I had finally come to terms with the fact that the transfer had now become inevitable.

Lazio had sent in the completion papers, and the contract with them was conditional upon Gascoigne agreeing. I had asked Mel Stein a couple of weeks before: 'What will it take to keep Gazza?' The terms Stein gave were staggering: 'If you want him to stay then you'll have to guarantee him a minimum of £2 million net after tax over the first year, plus a large annual salary on top of that.'

At the meeting Stein approached me and said: 'Are you able to present a package now that will stop Gascoigne signing?' I said: 'Unfortunately the chances of that now are virtually nil.' Stein wanted to take the contract to Gascoigne and get him to sign that day. I told Nat: 'Let me tell you something. What you don't understand is that it would be totally and utterly wrong for anybody to sign anything prior to the Cup Final. It will be wrong for you to sign it and it will be wrong for the player to sign anything. For heaven's sake let him concentrate on the Cup Final.'

But as I left the meeting I knew Gascoigne was going. Only the formalities were left: the medical examination, and Gascoigne finally agreeing terms and signing.

The evening before your club is playing in the Cup Final brings a wonderful sense of expectancy and anticipatory thrill – an almost indescribable feeling. You're looking forward to the sight of the famous twin towers as you approach Wembley, the walk up Olympic Way, the quite unique atmosphere before the Final with the singing and the chanting, the presentation of the teams to the Duke and Duchess of Kent, and then the game itself. If your team wins the Cup it will crown a memorable day. That Friday evening such thoughts of joy were very far from my mind. I returned to my office after meeting Mel Stein and Nat Solomon feeling very depressed. Gascoigne, the player I had helped bring to White Hart Lane, was going. I had always said that if Gascoigne went, so would I, and suddenly that evening it seemed that the moment had come.

Terry Venables, who had been trying to buy the club and was on the third or fourth deal with me – or as Robert Maxwell put it memorably, 'trying yet another pair of knickers' – now came up with a proposal. At about 4.30 in the afternoon Philip Green, Chairman of Amber Day, and a mutual friend of both Terry and myself, rang to say that Terry finally had the money to buy my holding in Tottenham. 'Philip,' I said, 'I'm quite prepared to deal, and Terry can have my shares for 80 pence. But if he manages to keep Gascoigne at the club then he can have them for 70 pence.'

Call it a gesture if you like, but I was prepared to put effectively around £270,000 into a fighting fund to try and keep Gascoigne at the club. It meant a very great deal to me.

Soon after my talk with Philip Green the lawyers and advisers got to work. Terry was with the team at the Royal Lancaster Hotel, a favourite bolt-hole for him before important matches, and I went off to have a drink with some friends. Through the evening my solicitor Peter Robinson was in contact by telephone. But as with so many other negotiations I'd had with Venables, this one broke down as well. At about 10 o'clock, after numerous telephone calls, it emerged that Venables could not deliver a straightforward deal. I had told Philip Green that I wanted a simple unconditional transaction, based on the price I had agreed with Terry. Now Terry wanted 'certain comforts from the Midland Bank', the bankers to the company, and as this made it a conditional deal my solicitor finally rang them to say that we could not proceed.

Less than twelve hours later I was at Wembley, experiencing with full force the cliché that the head is different from the heart.

My heart was full of Tottenham's unique club history and of the desire and the need to win the Cup, particularly after the traumatic year we had been through. I knew that to the bookmakers and nation at large we were probably not the favourites. Under Terry, we had only ever beaten one First Division side in an FA cup tie, and that was Arsenal in the semi-final a few weeks before. Our opponents were Nottingham Forest, managed by Brian Clough, who despite all his honours had never won the FA Cup. He had become the Stanley Mathews of his age, and the nation seemed to will its favourite football son to win the Cup. Yet if my heart rooted for the players my head was full of all the tumult that had gone before. As I watched and took part in the day, arranged with almost military precision by the FA, it was as if I was half there – and half somewhere else.

I tried hard to savour the moment. I was delighted to see John Major there, the most genuine politician I have come across during my involvement with football. In 1987, the previous occasion when I had been there as Chairman of the club, Margaret Thatcher was one of the guests. She had no interest in football, and I can well remember her surprise and distress when the match went into extra time and she had to stay and watch for another half an hour. Her husband Denis broke the convention that in the Royal Box you're not supposed to smoke by puffing away and stubbing his dog-ends out on the floor. But this time there was a rapport with Major which was quite marvellous. In the first half I sat next to him, and whilst I teased him about his great love, Chelsea, he was almost avuncular as he, appreciating some of the tension I was going through, kept saying: 'Relax, relax, I've just got this feeling that your team is going to win today.'

One other person had told me that we were going to win that day, and her words meant a lot. The Duchess of Kent. I had first met her during the 1987 Final and realised that she was both keen on football and a great authority. Then she had told me that she always watched a match whenever it was on television, and if she couldn't watch it live, she would record it and see it later. I could not help smiling as she said this, for I am not only, as my friends say, a nut about football, I also have an enormous video collection going back many years, covering many hundreds of matches.

In 1987 I had been surprised and impressed by the Duchess's knowledge of the individual players. When she came and shook hands with the President of Coventry City, who was standing next to me with his wife, she recited the names of Coventry players, and talked especially about Dave Bennett, who had such a profound effect on us that day. It had proved a lucky omen for them, and as we met up again I asked her: 'Who do you think is going to win?' She had a quick look around her, as if to make sure she wasn't being indiscreet, and then she smiled and said: 'I've got a feeling it is going to be your day.'

But this was another sort of day, another sort of Cup Final, and the pettiness, backbiting and sheer bloody-mindedness that had frustrated me through the year were never far from the surface. The Duchess of Kent had spoken to me at the lunch – a light summer lunch of salmon and boiled potatoes – but soon after it was finished I was back with the intrigue at Tottenham. Like all Cup Final teams we were given only a small allocation for the Royal Box. Paul Bobroff, the other major shareholder, had a ticket with his wife, as did the club's Vice-Chairman, Douglas Alexiou, and his wife. However this meant leaving out Nat Solomon who, along with the rest of the Tottenham board, was sitting very near the Royal Box, but not inside.

After lunch Nat Solomon's wife approached me and without much ado said in a tone that could not be mistaken: 'I think it's a disgrace that Nat's not sitting in the Royal Box.' This was hardly the moment to raise such a subject, but I tried to be polite and said: 'I'm terribly sorry but we just don't have enough tickets.' Half an hour before the game, as we were getting ready to be shepherded into the Royal Box, she approached me again, pointed to my twelve-year-old son who was standing next to me, and said: 'Well, he must be sitting in the Royal Box next to you. Why doesn't Nat have his ticket?'

By this time I was getting pretty nettled by her line of enquiry and couldn't restrain my response. 'Whatever makes you think that? If you must know, Jeremy is not actually sitting in the Royal Box. He's standing next to me at this moment but he's going to be sitting elsewhere.' My sharpness of tone quietened her and then I said: 'This is hardly the time and place to raise such trifling subjects. Listen, we are about to play one of the most momentous matches in our history. Do you think we could possibly discuss this some other time?' She marched off, obviously rather gruntled, and my ex-wife Roberta, who has not always admired everything I've done, said: 'What a delicate way you handled that!'

Nat Solomon had joined the company only a few months before, in mid-January, as a paid Executive Chairman of the plc on the recommendation of Brown Shipley, the company's merchant bankers. He had been a lifelong Spurs supporter, but there were other directors of much longer service who would have been more entitled to a seat in the Royal Box. This was not untypical behaviour on his part. Immediately on joining the club, he was pestering people about his ticket entitlement for home and away matches, and he never seemed satisfied with his allocation.

However, for the first time that day, probably for the first time since the July Sunday when I'd gone to see Robert Maxwell to try to organise a Rights issue for Tottenham Hotspur, football completely took over from my other worries. I sat next to John Major in the first half and we could revel in the occasion like two old, committed, football fans.

There was enough happening on the field to keep us completely glued. Within seventeen minutes of the start of the match Paul Gascoigne was being stretchered off, having badly damaged his knee ligaments in a terrible tackle. I must say I didn't realise quite how bad Gascoigne's foul was – it took the television replay to show that. Yet even before the foul I had felt that Gascoigne must have been wound up especially for this match. Later I was to learn that Venables had turned the key in the young player to get him psyched up for the occasion. The moment he went down I knew he was badly injured. John Major tried to reassure me and said: 'No, no, he's going to get up.' But I knew Paul and I knew that there are certain players that stay down only when something is wrong – if Paul went down and it was nothing very serious he would get up in a flash.

We went a goal behind when Nottingham Forest scored from the free kick resulting directly from the Gascoigne incident, but I still felt confident that it was going to end up our day. My heart went out to Gascoigne as he was stretchered along the touchline and replaced by Nayim, a particular favourite of mine. Even when Lineker missed a penalty, which I have to say I anticipated (the moment flashed across my mind when he missed the previous penalty he had taken for Tottenham a few weeks earlier), my spirits remained high. I felt that we were beginning to take the game more and more to Nottingham Forest, and apart from a scare when Erik Thorstvedt made a timely save at the feet of Crosby, we seemed to be taking a firm grip on the match. This was in marked contrast to 1987. There Clive Allen had scored in the first few minutes and I had felt we would either beat Coventry by four goals or be beaten. Sometimes a team scoring too early has the handicap of staying in front. Now I felt the team coming together, growing stronger in adversity.

Nobody symbolised us more than Paul Stewart. Both Gascoigne and Stewart had been signed at the same time and, as often happens, they developed a sort of bonding, as if they were children who had joined school on the same day. Halfway through the season circumstances compelled us to move Stewart to midfield in a match against Luton after we were reduced to nine men by the referee. This proved a revelation. Now, with Gascoigne's departure, he seemed to take over the leadership on the field. I'd always had a soft spot for Stewart. If Gascoigne had all the glory at Tottenham, Stewart had the knocks. For a time he had been the target of abuse from the very critical White Hart Lane crowd, and I felt they were being more than a touch unfair.

As I watched him leading Spurs back into the match I thought back to the night when Stewart had come on as substitute against Liverpool, just over a year before. As he was warming up on the touch-line to get on the field a section of the Spurs supporters booed him. It is a terrible thing for any player of any club to be booed at home by his own supporters and my heart went out to him. As luck would have it that night he headed the only goal of the game and ended Liverpool's long unbeaten run, and I thought of all the supporters after the match who must have said to their friends: 'I told you he was a good player!' I could not help thinking of his first match for us against Manchester United. In the last minute he went running down the right, got well inside the penalty area and was bundled down by Lee Sharp. Stewart himself took the penalty and hit the bar. If that penalty had been a few inches lower Stewart's whole career at White Hart Lane might have been very different. He was very much a confidence player.

At half-time the Duchess of Kent further encouraged me. She came up to me and said: 'Don't worry, you're definitely going to come back into the game. I think you're going to win.' And sure enough we did, and it was Paul Stewart who scored. The moment he hit the ball with his right foot I knew it was a goal, and although the Royal Box encourages the convention that nobody is partisan I could not help but leap out of my seat with both arms punching the air. Prince Charles, who had taken a sceptical view of things so far, turned to me and said: 'You look a bit happy don't you?' The Duchess of Kent just leant forward and looked at me down the line of seats in the Royal Box and said in a voice that was almost a scream of delight: 'I told you you'd score.'

After that, we seemed to grow as Nottingham Forest faded. Just at the beginning of extra time, Princess Diana, who had sat very cool and collected through the entire afternoon, and been very diplomatic to my persistent questions about who would win, turned to me and said: 'I think you're going to win, you know.' Five minutes later, in a copy of the Coventry match – but with us getting the luck this time – Des Walker put the ball in his own net and Princess Diana smiled.

Then as the final whistle blew and Gary Mabbutt climbed the thirty-nine steps to take the Cup, the Duchess of Kent turned round to me, presenting a beaming face, and slowly, very carefully, she winked.

Later on in the dressing room, my first thought was for Paul Stewart. After I had congratulated Terry Venables and the players I went and sat next to him. He was sitting down very quietly and looking at his medal as if it was an object from outer space. Then he said slowly: 'You know, when I was a boy I dreamt of playing in a Cup Final – and I have. When I was a boy I also dreamt I would score in a Cup Final – and I've done that as well. In the three years I've had at Tottenham, all those slagging-offs; today it's been all worth it.' And with that he held out his medal in his hand, like a knight who had discovered the holy grail. I felt for him; it was his goal at his old stamping ground, Blackpool, that had started us on our way in the third round, and his sweet strike and never-say-die attitude that had pulled us back into the match.

During the Final the late Bill Fox, then President of the Football League and Chairman of Blackburn Rovers, had sat in the Royal Box just behind me. Fox, a true Lancastrian, had spent his honeymoon at White Hart Lane watching his favourite team lose to Tottenham Hotspur. As Stewart scored he nudged me in the back and said: 'It takes a good Lancastrian to score a goal for a London club.' Stewart had been one of those signings much criticised by the tabloid Press, particularly the price tag of £1.5 million – except they'd always said it was £1.7 million – but now I was sure every Tottenham fan felt that he was worth every penny.

Then as the stadium emptied, creating an eerie feeling after the noise and tumult of the day, I led the directors back across the pitch towards the Royal Box and Banqueting Room. Suddenly Frank Sinclair, who was on the board at the time and had been going to Tottenham since the Thirties, said: 'I think he should thank us.'

'What are you saying?'

'I think he should thank us,' Frank repeated.

'Frank, I don't understand.'

'Terry Venables.'

'I don't follow what you're saying, Frank.'

'Think about it, we won the Cup today.'

'Yes.'

'Well, if we had done or been able to do what Terry wanted, which was to spend probably about £3 or 4 million during the season, for sure the money would have been spent. Equally, the team wouldn't have been the same. In other words he would have brought in new players. The question you've got to ask yourself, Irving, is if he would have changed the team, would we have won the Cup? We've won the Cup with the same team and he couldn't have done much better than that!'

What Frank was trying to say was that the chequebook was often Terry Venables's worst enemy. As we shall see, he had been presented with it when he arrived at Spurs, yet his best period had come when circumstances had forced us to lock it away.

It was an interesting point Frank made, but already the magic that the football had produced was fading. As I came out of the dressing room into the tunnel I was grabbed by David Davies from the BBC. He wanted to know about Gascoigne, what the injury meant for his transfer to Lazio, and a story that had been in the *Sun* that week that the directors were preparing to sell Lineker.

I had learned from the physio that Gascoigne's injury was very serious and that he had snapped his knee ligaments. I had seen over the years that the injuries which terminate a player's career are mainly to do with the knee. Broken legs are broken bones and they heal. Knee injuries are much more complicated, and I was vividly aware of what had happened to Danny Thomas a few years previously. I was convinced that the injury had scuppered any contract with Lazio, as it was conditional on a medical and there was no chance of Gascoigne passing it. The

Lineker story when it had emerged three days before the Final had made me very angry. It simply wasn't true. It seemed to be part of the dark forces that surrounded the club, and I wanted to talk to Davies about it, but that was not the time nor the occasion and I just said: 'Do you think that the directors who have the best interests of the club at heart would put out a story about the sale of their leading goal-scorer, just four days before the Cup Final? Whoever put that story out did not have the best interests of Tottenham at heart.' I stalked away, but the demons that had surrounded me and the club for much of the year had returned, even in what was the sweetest moment of our season.

I felt this with even greater force at the celebration dinner at the Hilton a few hours later. There were plenty of smiling faces there, plenty to celebrate. We were in the ballroom of the Hilton, and Terry, holding the Cup aloft, led in the team as if he were a Roman Emperor returning from the conquest of Gaul. I was very pleased that, after nearly two decades of being described as England's best tactical soccer brain, he had finally won his first major English trophy. Funny what an effect victory has on people. Terry was immediately embraced by a Spurs supporter who not long before had told me that I ought to get rid of him as he would never win anything at Tottenham.

There was Gary Lineker, with his heavily expectant wife, Michelle, proudly displaying his medal – the first major domestic honour that Lineker had won. There was Pat Van Den Hauwe, who had twice received losing medals with Everton and had, at last, been a winner. There was Gary Mabbutt. His own goal in 1987 had given Coventry the Cup; now he was the captain of the victorious team. And there was Paul Stewart's father, a good, honest Lancastrian, happy and proud for his son. But as I smiled, shook hands, patted the players and congratulated them, and felt happy for the supporters, in my heart there was an emptiness that I just could not fill.

What a contrast this was to 1987. Then we had gone back to White Hart Lane for the post-match celebrations feeling very flat. A huge marquee had been erected on the ground for the festivities, but we'd gone out as favourites against Coventry and come back with the losers' medals. Everybody behaved as though they had just lost somebody near and dear to them. At the appointed time I got up and said: 'Look, I know all of you are feeling very dispirited, but remember there are something like 2,000 teams who play in the FA Cup. And today each of them would give anything to change places with us.' As I said this there was an almighty cheer. Everybody snapped out of their depression and the whole evening came alive. But in 1991 while everybody cheered, somehow I felt low.

I knew Monday morning would bring the same round of meetings and the same endless discussions about how we could salvage Tottenham from the depths of its financial problem. For almost ten months now the board had struggled to find a solution, and in the process I had been made the villain. I had been libelled by the *Daily Mail* over my intentions about selling Gascoigne, and in an article for which they later apologised in print, the *Daily Express* had announced in 36-point headlines:

'CLEAR OFF SCHOLAR'

The Press campaign had been merciless. It seemed that everything that had gone wrong at the club was my fault. I didn't then, and do not now, deny joint responsibility as a board member of the plc until my resignation, but the villainy attributed to me was absurd. You couldn't pick up a paper at one stage without seeing my name in print, or more often a haggard-looking photograph of me, against a damning headline – damning me and damning the club.

Now, as I watched the players and supporters celebrate, I felt drained. The callous Press campaign had worn me down to where I felt very, very tired. What was worse was the effect this was having on my family. Clive James has said that *Private Eye* has the knack of writing cruel stories about fathers that can send their children home from school in tears. You can only imagine what my son Jeremy felt as his schoolmates read endless back-page smears about Scholar the man who had ruined Tottenham and was refusing to do anything to repair the damage. It seemed the Press had taken sides, and cast me as the villain. Indeed, in the Wembley tunnel as I approached one journalist he had said: 'In these things you have to take sides, and I'm afraid I have taken the other side.'

Ten years before, when Tottenham won the FA Cup with that magnificent goal by Ricky Villa – quite the most marvellous Cup-winning goal Wembley had ever seen – I had joined in the celebrations with a rapture and an unrestrained glee that I just could not summon this time. What was the point of being the Chairman of my favourite football club if I could not revel in one of their greatest footballing moments? I had not bought into

Tottenham Hotspur to make money. I had made that elsewhere and long ago. I saw football as a world I enjoyed, and I was willing to back that enjoyment and enthusiasm with time and money. But the last year had so soured me that now I felt there was no point in going on. I had stopped enjoying it, and when that happens it is time to go. Football is a sport. It is supposed to give you pleasure and enjoyment. All I seemed to be getting was aggravation.

I turned to my ex-wife, Roberta, and said that it was customary for me to say a few words at the dinner. After I thanked the players for their tremendous efforts throughout a difficult season, and the supporters for their faith, I said I would announce my resignation as Chairman of the club. She understood my frustrations, but advised very strongly against any immediate action. It wasn't the time or the place. It is not often that I can be persuaded to change my mind – my self-belief and self-confidence are well known – but I listened to Roberta. I'm glad I did. I let the dinner go on, but I did not make a speech. At about 11.15 I said my farewells and quietly left.

At home I watched the recorded highlights of the game, and for those few minutes the cares and worries slipped away. Then as the credits rolled on the heaviness that had been a part of me for the last few months came back. The next day Tottenham would follow the tradition and display the Cup in the streets of North London. As a young supporter I had often gone to such parades, and I vividly remembered the magical moment of May 1961, when Danny Blanchflower's brilliant team paraded the Cup and the League through the teeming streets of London. Tottenham were the first team this century to do the Double, and Blanchflower and his men holding the two trophies symbolised a unique moment of greatness. Now as Chairman I could take pride of place in our parade. But I had no heart for it. The enjoyment and the pleasure belonged to other people, everyone but me. I felt a bit like Gatsby in the Scott Fitzgerald story. Having seen the green light at the end of Daisy's dock, 'he had come a long way to this blue lawn, and his dream must have seemed so close that he could hardly fail to grasp it.' I had grasped my dream. But now I was about to wake up to the cold Monday morning reality: endless meetings, boring minutes, countless sessions with lawyers, and unending Press speculation about the future of Tottenham Hotspur.

It was concern for that future that had brought me into the

club. I had not only seen the green light at the end of Daisy's dock, I had actually entered the dock. But now, like Gatsby, I was beginning to realise that the dream was behind me.

2

BUYING THE DREAM

'But there is one thing. The directors can't stop you buying the shares.'
— Robin Potts, barrister.

Football fans can never be counted amongst the 'don't knows' of the opinion polls: everyone has an opinion. These may differ greatly, but all fans are convinced that their opinion is right.

The small group of friends that I had been going with to watch Tottenham away and home for many years were not very different. We were just an ordinary bunch brought together by our common love and devotion to Spurs. We didn't mix socially, but every other Saturday they would turn up on my doorstep to start a journey to wherever Tottenham were playing. We were very committed, even though there was very little to be excited about on the field in the mid to late Seventies apart from the wonderful signing of Ossie Ardiles and Ricky Villa, and the discovery of Glenn Hoddle. We kept on going week in and week out.

Our disenchantment arose from the fact that for a long time, the Spurs board had a reputation for meanness. They had not really competed with the other major clubs in the transfer market since Bill Nicholson resigned as Manager in 1974. The directors were a very old-fashioned group and many people took the view that they would rather the team played behind closed doors.

I think this was a little unfair, but I was aware of the many rumours that the board would not pay the going rate for players' salaries. This, it was said, was making it harder and harder for the club to sign the top-quality stars that Tottenham and its supporters deserved. *The Glory Game*, Hunter Davies's book which had provided an in-depth insight into the board of directors, confirmed this view, depicting the directors as a rather dull lot, out of touch with the supporters and jealously guarding their inheritance.

The glacial unity of the board melted when in 1980 the Chairman, Sidney Wale, suddenly resigned and was replaced by Arthur Richardson. This was hardly a move to youth – Richardson was seventy-five years old and had been on the board for almost twenty years. Rumour had it that before Richardson became involved at Spurs he was a season ticket holder at Arsenal. Later on it transpired that there had been a boardroom coup and the directors had moved a vote of no-confidence in the Chairman.

A Tottenham board without Wale seemed unthinkable. He was then the largest single shareholder in the company, with a holding of around 14 per cent, the remaining directors holding about 5 per cent. Appointed a director in 1957, he had become Chairman in 1969 following the death of his father, Fred. Fred had been on the board since 1944 and had once said: 'Anyone paying £200,000 for a player is barmy.' Ironically, it was Sidney Wale who sanctioned the first £200,000 transfer in 1970 when Martin Peters joined Spurs, with the great Jimmy Greaves going to Upton Park as part of the deal. Sidney appeared the classic football director: an accountant by profession, he had gone on to become managing director of a nuts and bolts firm before retiring.

The boardroom coup surrounded Wale's reluctance to authorise the proposed rebuilding of the West Stand, which had originally been built in 1908, the same year as Spurs joined the Football League. The old stand had provided me with wonderful memories. It had wooden floorboards, and whenever Spurs gained a corner in a big match, the fans would stamp their feet in unison and make a tremendous noise. Unfortunately, the stand had reached the end of its lifespan and stories had been circulating that it was in danger of losing its Fire Certificate.

Nothing generates as much passion and chaos in football as the rebuilding of stands. The history of English football is littered with clubs rebuilding stands and inviting ruin. Burnley had rebuilt its main stand and ended up sliding from the First Division to the Fourth. Wolves, the pioneers of the mid to late

Fifties, had also suffered disastrously. Just before Tottenham embarked on their project, there was the chilling example of Chelsea, whose redevelopment had led to the loss of control by the Mears family, who had originally built Stamford Bridge in 1905. The club was effectively run by an administrator on behalf of Barclays Bank for several years, before passing into the hands of the current owner, Ken Bates, for £1 in 1982.

Eventually Tottenham announced its intention to rebuild the old stand, and there was an artist's impression on the back page of the *Evening Standard*. It was estimated the cost would be in the region of £3.5 million. I was then in the middle of a number of commercial rebuilding projects in London and the south-east of England, and my immediate reaction was that the Spurs board had got their sums wrong.

Soon after, the Tottenham directors invited quite a number of people along to the Chanticleer restaurant next to the ground, to unveil plans for the proposed new development. I went along and for the first time met Arthur Richardson. Richardson explained that there would be seventy-two executive boxes, and the board hoped to sell them in advance. Three-year leases at £10,000 per annum were being offered, with full payment of £30,000 up front, and the board hoped that all seventy-two boxes would be leased, even before a brick was laid. If they succeeded in leasing all the boxes then it would go a long way towards meeting their budgeted costs.

I came away thinking their targets were optimistic and feeling convinced that to meet the cost of rebuilding, season ticket prices would have to rise very substantially. Spurs had always been afraid of pricing themselves out of the market, and even in the mid-1970s they were still charging in the region of £20 per annum for a seated season ticket in the old West Stand. However, I noticed after the Chanticleer meeting that a number of people signed up to pay in advance for executive boxes. Perhaps the board were lulled into a false sense of security by this.

A few days after the meeting I wrote a long letter to Arthur Richardson offering to help, but there was no response. At this stage I had no thought of taking over Tottenham. Ideas of buying into the club were far from my mind. All I wanted was to be involved in any small way, just as any supporter would. Before the stand redevelopment, my main interest in the old stand had been to move my season ticket when possible so that I got closer to the centre and nearer the front. I finally ended up in Block

J, Row K, which for me provided one of the best views in the ground. Now, I just felt that with my property experience I could be of some use to the board. But clearly they did not feel the need for any outside expertise.

A few months later Balfour Beatty, the contractors who were building the stand, won a competitive tender for a building contract from my own company: an industrial estate in west London. They hosted a lunch a couple of weeks prior to the FA Cup Final of 1981, at which both Arthur Richardson and I were amongst the guests, and we sat opposite each other. I could not help asking him if he had ever received my letter. He confirmed that he had, and not surprisingly appeared a trifle embarrassed, because he had not even had the courtesy to acknowledge it. Despite this, we parted on fairly friendly terms, although the next time we met it was not to be so amicable.

This came about in September 1981, when Spurs' Annual General Meeting of shareholders was held. At that time, like all football clubs apart from Nottingham Forest, Tottenham were a Limited Company with the shares rarely changing hands. A barrister friend of mine, Peter Leaver, the proud owner of one share, had asked me if I would like to attend as a proxy on behalf of someone else. The meeting was again held in the Chanticleer, but with only about fifty people present and in a much smaller room on the first floor. It was a low-key affair, and I had seen very few of the people attending before. As is the normal procedure, the accounts for the previous season 1980/81 were presented to the shareholders, the auditors were re-appointed, and the Chairman read out a brief prepared statement on the general state of the company.

The Spurs board clearly did not anticipate any problems at the meeting. In May, Spurs had won the FA Cup, maintaining the club's tradition of winning a trophy when the year ended with a '1'. What is more, a 3-2 victory over Manchester City in a replay had been fashioned by one of the greatest goals ever seen in a Cup Final. An amazing dribble and shot by the Argentinian Ricky Villa saw Spurs back in their rightful position of competing in Europe for the first time since 1974. However, I was determined to raise questions about the stand, but when I raised my hand Arthur Richardson objected. He knew I was not a shareholder, and felt I was not entitled to ask questions. It required the intervention of the solicitors to confirm that as a proxy for a shareholder, I did have the same right to speak and ask questions as any registered share-holder.

The stand was due to be completed within a few months, and Richardson assured me that progress was on schedule and the cost was in the region of the budgeted £3.5 million. But what would be the effect of this expenditure on the team? Would the Manager, Keith Burkinshaw, have the money to buy new players to improve the Cup-winning team? Richardson assured me that the bank had full confidence in the board and that no problems were foreseen. However, as I gently pushed Richardson, it became evident that the mood of self-congratulation which had prevailed so far, came with a tinge of anxiety. Several other shareholders began to raise questions about the stand, which quite agitated Richardson, and he became rather flushed.

The most significant thing happened after the meeting was over. As I was preparing to leave, Keith Burkinshaw made straight for me and said: 'You know you haven't been told the complete truth.'

'You're right,' I said. 'I don't think I have.'

I could see that Burkinshaw was intrigued by this, and he went on to say: 'Do you know I can't sign any new players, and the team does need strengthening in a couple of places.' It was obvious that there was no love lost, on his part, with the board.

'That must create a big problem for you, Keith,' I said sympathetically.

No one in football had quite squared the circle to build a new stand and improve the team. As I went away from the meeting, I began to think that despite Richardson's paternalistic assurances, Spurs seemed to be heading for a lot of trouble. What could I do, or anyone else for that matter?

In the great tradition of football stories, the solution came to me as I drove up with my usual friends to Leeds to see Spurs play in a League match. It was a typical journey away from home that I had done on countless occasions previously, where the talk all the way there and back covered just one subject, my favourite – football. This time I was a little quieter than usual. The AGM had greatly concerned me, and by the time I got home that evening, I had decided on a strategy to do something about it. I didn't say anything to my friends about what I had in mind.

The first thing to do was to get a full Company Search on Tottenham, which would give the Articles of Association (rules of the company), copies of the accounts, and a full list of shareholders. They proved to be my Christmas present that year, and I spent all my spare time wading through them. What first struck me was the number of women shareholders; they must have inherited them from their husbands or fathers, or so I thought, and I assumed they would have no interest in Spurs as a football club. I could have written a letter to the shareholders simply saying that I was interested in buying their shares, but I thought they must have received scores of such letters over the years, and like estate agent circulars, they would end up in the bin.

What I needed to do was to make them face a decision on whether they would sell or not, by inducing them with a hard cash offer. I decided to write offering £250 per share for anyone holding between one and twenty shares, £150 for anyone owning between twenty and fifty, and £100 per share for anyone holding more than fifty shares, and enclosed a stamped addressed envelope.

The response was immediate and gratifying. As I returned to work following the Christmas break, I found a letter from a Mrs Powell of West Sussex. She had inherited twelve shares on the death of her husband and she readily accepted my offer. The next morning there was a letter from a branch of Lloyds Bank in Devon, confirming that a lady client holding seven shares had instructed them to accept the offer. These may seem very small pickings, but I had to start somewhere and I was dealing with a Company with only 4,892 shares in issue. When the company was formed in 1898 in order to turn professional, 8,000 shares were offered to the public at £1 each. By 1905, only 4,892 had been sold, and the remainder were withdrawn. The existing shares were in the hands of between five and six hundred individuals, some 360 of whom only held one share each. Reflecting the appeal of the club, they were spread far and wide, including the United States and Australia.

Whilst I was growing confident that I could pick up small bundles of shares, there was one enormous obstacle to overcome: Article 14 of the Articles of Association. These were the rules that governed the Company and that made the Spurs board the cosy closed shop that it was. This Article gave the directors the right, without having to give any reason whatsoever, not to recognise the registration of shares to anyone they did not approve of. Those willing to sell were given the impression that the shares were of little value due to this right of veto. Over the years I had heard of a number of supporters who had tried to buy shares, but very few had ever succeeded. If they had, it was only for one or two shares.

The Articles were first written in the early 1930s and were tested in court in 1935, setting a precedent in English law. Commonly known as Berry v. Tottenham Hotspur, the case concerned a certain Hubert Berry. Berry was highly critical of the board at the time and feared that this new Article was likely to develop into the closed shop it ultimately became. He decided to test it by transferring one share to James Arthur Stewart. The directors refused to recognise the transfer, Berry took them to court and the directors won, giving them an unassailable veto. If I was to achieve anything, I clearly had to do better than Mr Berry.

My solicitor, Lawrie Heller of Berwin Leighton, a well-known City firm, put me in touch with a colleague of his, Jonathan Metliss, who specialised in company law. I had known Jonathan for nearly twenty years; he was a keen football supporter and understood my excitement and enthusiasm. I pointed out to him that this was far more important to me than any property deal, but there was a big problem concerning the Articles of the company. He would have to crack Article 14, and a copy was sent by hand at once for his professional view.

Jonathan suggested that we meet with a barrister as soon as possible to receive an opinion on the legality of Article 14, bearing in mind that nearly fifty years had passed since Berry had challenged the Tottenham board. A few days later a conference was arranged near the Law Courts. Jonathan and I were ushered in to meet the barrister, Robin Potts. He had a copy of the Articles of Association and had been sent a brief résumé of the background. Potts began by remarking that he had advised on a number of cases involving football clubs and directors and found it hard to understand why people became so emotional about it. He went on to say that he had given the matter some considerable thought and, unfortunately, had come to the conclusion that Article 14 was still good law.

My heart sank. There had been new Companies Act legislation in 1980, concerning oppression of minority shareholders, and I had been sure the situation fell within this sphere. When a shareholder is not allowed to sell his investment to a willing buyer and the directors of the company refuse to sanction the sale without having to give a reason, surely the shareholder is being oppressed? Potts replied that the piece of legislation I mentioned had not yet been tested, and it would be some time before it was.

Then, just as I felt that there was nothing to be done, he gave me an unexpected ray of hope. 'But, Mr Scholar,' said Potts, 'one important thing I must point out is that whilst the directors have the power to stop anyone being recognised as a new shareholder, they can't prevent a sale taking place.' 'What do you mean?' I said, quite confused by his reasoning. 'The point I'm getting to is that they cannot stop you buying the shares,' said Potts. As he said this, he smiled. 'What your solicitor must do now is draw up a Deed of Trust, effectively giving you legal ownership, and get the current shareholders to give you an irrevocable undertaking to name you as their proxy and always carry out your wishes in relation to the shares bought by you and any matters relating to them.' He wished me luck, aware perhaps that he had inflicted the most grievous damage on the closed world of the Tottenham board.

As I left the chambers I felt like a knight of the Round Table who had found the holy grail. Potts's words, 'they cannot stop you buying the shares', kept ringing in my head, and I knew I had found the secret key to unlock the stubborn Spurs board. Even at this stage, I had no thoughts of a takeover. What I was attempting to do was to buy enough shares to bring a little influence to bear. Perhaps at the very best, I might get a seat on the board.

Jonathan prepared the paperwork along the lines suggested by Robin Potts, and there was by now a steady trickle of replies from Spurs shareholders, accepting my offer. I was extremely surprised to find that very few of the shareholders had ever been approached before. Now I decided to broaden my scope, and sent out a further batch of letters. I had prepared lists giving the shareholding structure of the company; the largest twenty holders, the next twenty, and so on, and I was beginning to memorise shareholders' names and the size of their holdings. I had never done anything like this before, and although I had been involved in deals worth many millions of pounds, this was quite the most exciting and interesting venture I had ever embarked upon.

The one person I was very keen to contact was a Mrs Elsie Berry, who I suspected was the widow of Hubert. She had changed addresses a couple of times, and chasing her was a bit like a detective story. By this time, in March 1982, a few days after Spurs had lost to Liverpool in the first Milk Cup Final at Wembley, I had left England to live and work in Monaco. Paul Wayne, an old and trusted friend, acted as my Dr Watson in London, whilst I played the somewhat more remote Sherlock Holmes, abroad. It was not until June that, out of sheer persistence, Paul finally traced Elsie Berry to an address in the Midlands. Was she the widow of Hubert, and would she sell? She held 297 shares and was the third biggest shareholder in the company, with a holding of around 6 per cent.

Ten days after Paul wrote to her, she replied. Elsie was indeed the widow of Hubert, but before she would make a decision on whether to sell, she wanted us to tell her the full story. So far we had been very cagey about telling people why we wanted to buy the shares, simply stating that I was a very keen supporter eager to become a shareholder, which was true. However, Mrs Berry was such an integral part of the plan's success that I decided Paul should openly answer any questions she might have.

He pointed out to Mrs Berry my concern over the financial pitfalls the club was getting itself into, and that with her holding, there was a very good chance of being able to bring pressure to bear. Her response was extraordinary. 'I agree to sell,' she said, 'and I hope you succeed. My dear late husband will be dancing in his grave if you do.' She told Paul stories of how her husband had been the thorn in the side of the Spurs board during the 1930s, but had been thwarted in his efforts for change by the infamous Article 14. 'Good luck' were her parting words. For Elsie May Berry, revenge was strong and very sweet, albeit forty-seven years later.

Mrs Berry's agreement had certainly boosted my confidence, and suddenly there was great momentum. Following this purchase, I became the company's largest single shareholder with more than 800 shares, overtaking Sidney Wale who had 734. As far as the board were concerned, due to Article 14, none of these transactions had appeared on the share register, and therefore I simply didn't exist.

Only one person reneged after having verbally agreed to sell. This was a man who asked for the money to be transferred to a branch of the National Westminster Bank who would hold it as stake-holders, pending his signature on the documents. Before he would sell he wanted to talk to me personally. He seemed a harmless enough chap, then suddenly he asked: 'Are you a regular churchgoer?' It took me a while to realise that the question was somewhat loaded. I replied: 'Yes.' It went through my mind that it might not be his Church, but having been brought up in a religious manner, I saw no problem. He accepted my answer and agreed to deal with the documentation.

After a couple of weeks, when he had still not signed the papers and I could not get hold of him, I contacted his bank, to no avail. Eventually, after a month, I managed to catch him by telephone, but by then he had changed his mind.

The board had become aware of what I was attempting, and my purchases were now beginning to rattle Arthur Richardson and the directors. I discovered that Richardson had obtained a copy of the documents being used to effect the purchases, and had consulted the club's solicitors for advice on whether they could stop me. The lawyer's opinion was that I had been very well briefed and was not breaking any rules of the company. Richardson was furious.

I had never approached Sidney Wale, believing he would not be ready to dispose of his interest, but at the beginning of September, out of the blue, Paul Wayne received a call that was to completely change the picture. It came from Geoffrey Jones, who had been Club Secretary under Wale's chairmanship, but was now working for a firm of estate agents in Tottenham. He asked Paul when I was next going to be in London, and a meeting was arranged at the Churchill Hotel in Portman Square a couple of weeks later at 4 pm. I was intrigued.

Jones, a meticulous, precise man, arrived on the dot. When we talked I quickly realised why, after so many years of service, he was no longer at White Hart Lane. There was no love lost between him and Arthur Richardson. He made no secret of his admiration for Sidney Wale, and for some considerable time we spoke about our common love: Tottenham Hotspur. As the conversation proceeded, I could sense that Jones wanted to say something but couldn't quite bring himself to it. Finally, at about ten to six, I said to him that I would have to leave soon, as I had a dinner appointment at 7.30 pm. Jones paused, took a long breath and looking at me hard, said: 'I have to tell you that Sidney Wale is a bit surprised that he hasn't received a letter from you.' His words seemed to hang in the air of the Churchill Hotel. It was clear that Jones was acting as an emissary from Wale, and I told him: 'I haven't written to him because I didn't think he would be interested in selling, but if I'm wrong I would be delighted to hear from him. Why doesn't he give Paul Wayne a ring?' I gave him Paul's number and we prepared to part.

I liked Geoffrey and felt sorry for him. Tottenham had been his life for so long, but now he was out. As I stood up to leave, he wished me luck and said something which has haunted me down the years. 'Never get carried away by football. It will lift you into the clouds one minute and kick you up the backside the next.'

I was about to be lifted into the clouds, but the kick in the backside would take some years to materialise.

Although I had not written to Sidney Wale, I had met him and even had something of an argument with him while he was still the club Chairman. That was about fourteen months earlier, the night after Spurs had beaten Swindon in an FA Cup replay. There had been a dinner for supporters near the ground, followed by a question and answer session with Jack Taylor, the international referee, acting as Master of Ceremonies. Sidney Wale sat on the top table alongside Keith Burkinshaw, Steve Perryman the Club captain, and John Pratt, who was still playing at the time.

I was seated at a table right near the front, and it quickly became clear that the top table was in for a torrid evening. Spurs had recently sold Alfie Conn, a great favourite with the crowd at White Hart Lane, and the clear feeling of the supporters was that the Spurs board was fully living up to its reputation of being too mean to spend money on the players that were needed. It wasn't very long before this that Trevor Francis had been signed by Nottingham Forest, becoming the first £1 million player, and there had been much Press speculation that Spurs might buy Aston Villa's Scottish International, Andy Gray. However, the thought of spending £1.5 million on one player clearly appalled Sidney Wale; it was more than Spurs took at the gate in an entire season. As the questions became more heated, Wale kept on pleading poverty.

One supporter asked: 'Surely Spurs are a big club, and if Southampton can sign Kevin Keegan, why is it that Tottenham have such difficulty in signing the big names?' Wale replied that the answer was to do with the wage structure, but this could hardly pacify the supporters, especially when John Pratt honestly confessed that he would have no gripe should big-name players earn more than him.

I finally stood up to ask: 'Mr Wale, you have spent all evening telling us that you are short of money. You have supporters here, as you've seen, who care very much for this great club, and would be prepared to help you. Why not give them a chance by issuing the unissued shares in the company?' To me, the question was not particularly difficult, but Sidney Wale went white and just couldn't or wouldn't answer. I wanted to follow up with another, but Jack Taylor intervened saying that other people should be given a chance. My question had clearly caused a stir.

After the question-and-answer session had ended, the evening became far more informal, and as I was chatting to my friends at the table someone tapped me on the shoulder. I turned round to find Sidney Wale. 'Can I have a word?', he asked. 'Certainly,' I replied, and stood up. He pointed out it was not possible to take up my suggestion. 'I don't agree with you,' I told him, 'but I do understand your reasons for not wanting to follow it through. It could weaken your and the board's hold on the club, and might even see you removed. Still, even if you don't do that, why don't you raise the entrance prices in line with Arsenal's, which are higher? Higher prices would generate more income and provide you with the extra money for better players.'

Wale countered by saying: 'If we do that the fans will stop coming.' I felt depressed by this negative attitude, but tried to encourage him by saying that I had an idea for a shirt sponsor. He seemed interested in that, and we had a drink together, but the overall impression he left me with was that he was a very cold fish. Although I wrote to him the very next day, he merely passed the letter on to Mike Lewis, then the Commercial Manager, and about a week later Lewis did ring me. I felt that since I had written to Wale, he should at least have had the courtesy to respond, and passing the buck in this fashion was not going to earn any dividend.

As I left England for France, I went via Frankfurt, where Spurs were playing in the European Cup Winners' Cup quarter-final. I travelled, along with many other supporters, on the official team trip. The night before the game I found Sidney Wale sitting in the hotel lounge talking to Steve Perryman. Perryman had known me by sight for several years from my travels watching the team around the country and in Europe, and he invited me to join them.

It soon became clear that neither man cared for Arthur Richardson. I asked Wale if he would ever consider returning as

Chairman, but he ruled it out – it was very clear that he had been deeply hurt by the board's actions some time previously. He was very concerned over the cost of the West Stand, and it turned into one of those characteristic meetings of football supporters with memories of past matches and players, interspersed with thoughts about the future. The warm friendly atmosphere did much to dissipate the negative image I had formed of Sidney Wale after the question-and-answer session, but even then, until Jones met me I had no thoughts that he might be a player in my plans.

Two weeks later, Paul Wayne returned from lunch to find a message: 'Please call Sidney Wale at home.' His immediate reaction was that someone was pulling his leg. When he rang the number, it was indeed Sidney Wale, who wanted to speak to me as soon as possible. I made the call and he came straight to the point. 'I am prepared to accept your offer of £250 per share for an agreed number. You know that I have 734.' I was dumbstruck. 'Mr Wale,' I replied, 'I don't know where you get that figure of £250 from, but I wouldn't pay that much for such a large number.' 'Then what are you prepared to offer me?' he asked. I made a quick mental calculation and said: 'I am prepared to purchase 600 at £150 per share.' As I said the words, I held my breath, not knowing what his reaction would be. There was a pause and then Sidney Wale said abruptly: 'Let me sleep on it and call me back tomorrow at 4 pm.'

As I put the phone down, I could barely contain my excitement. For the very first time since the match at Leeds, when I had begun to formulate my plans, thoughts of the takeover of Spurs went through my mind. If Wale would agree to sell to me, I would have almost 35 per cent of the club. That, given that Tottenham had so many fragmented small shareholders, would mean control.

That night I hardly slept a wink. Why was Wale selling? Were things worse than I had thought? I had seen the accounts, but they were out of date. Was I biting off more than I could chew? My mind was in a whirl, and it stayed like that for most of the next day, where the clock seemed to be moving much slower than normal. I was trying to keep myself occupied so as not to look at the second hand navigating my watch.

Wale had said 4 pm, but finally at 3.30 pm I couldn't contain myself any more and rang his home number. His wife, Cynthia, answered and gave the impression that my call had been eagerly awaited. Sidney was at the bottom of the garden and she went to fetch him. As I waited, I tried to keep cool and calm, desperate not to sound too anxious to buy. I kept on saying to myself: 'Remember he contacted you first.'

At last he reached the phone. 'I've been thinking about your offer.' He paused, and my immediate fear was that he wouldn't accept. Then he said: 'Don't you think you could improve it a bit?'

'Mr Wale,' I replied, 'if you're prepared to sell 700 shares instead of 600, I might be able to improve my offer a bit, say £170 per share.'

Wale seemed happy at that, but he had one further question, and I held my breath in anticipation. 'If I agree to sell, will you win?'

'With your block of shares, I'm certain that I will,' I replied. That was the final key in the lock, and I began to realise how powerful a motive revenge was. Sidney Wale clearly wanted to pay back those who had dumped him off the board.

A verbal agreement was all very well, but I was extremely keen to have his signature on a contract of sale. I explained to him that I had recently been let down by another shareholder, and whilst I felt sure he was a man of his word, would he be prepared to sign an agreement that very evening? He saw no difficulty in agreeing to this, and it was arranged that Paul Wayne would go to Wale's house at 8 pm in order for him to sign the necessary documents. As soon as I had put down the telephone, I rang Paul in London and he confirmed he would ring me as soon as he got back from the meeting.

If the previous night had been a sleepless one, this evening was to be just as nerve-racking. I was having dinner with some friends, but I just couldn't concentrate on the conversation. I kept looking at my watch and wore such a nervous expression that my friends began to wonder if something was wrong.

Eventually at 9.15 pm I rang Paul Wayne's flat in London, only to find his girlfriend, who said he was expected back at any moment. Half an hour later I broke away from dinner again, but he was still not back and by this time my nerves were jangling. The only person who could appreciate what I was going through was my wife at the time, who had been a Spurs supporter since her father took her to White Hart Lane at the age of five.

At 10.15 pm I again made my excuses and rang Paul. This

time he answered the telephone, and my first words to him were almost a bark. 'Where the hell have you been?'

Paul seemed surprised and replied: 'With Sidney Wale, of course, where else?'

'What have you been doing for two hours?'

'He asked me to have a drink and we got talking,' Paul replied.

'But did he sign the papers?' I persisted.

'Of course. He did that as soon as I arrived.'

As I heard these words, the tension that had been gnawing at me for more than twenty-four hours drained away. I felt a mixture of warmth and gratitude towards Paul for all the time and effort he had spent as Dr Watson. I returned to the table with a spring in my step. I could see my wife looking edgy, and as I sat down I said with slow deliberation: 'You are sworn to absolute secrecy. Tonight is a very special night for me. Tottenham Hotspur has just changed hands.'

Now I had sufficient shares to do what I had in mind, but I was in no particular rush. My plan was not to make any public moves for another twelve or fifteen months. In retrospect, this was an amazing and, for me, quite delicious situation. Spurs had, in effect, changed hands, but the public, and very importantly Fleet Street, did not know anything, and Richardson and his coterie could only guess.

Article 14, instead of keeping me out, was preventing Richardson from knowing what I was up to, and I could sense that the Spurs board were keen to find out. Some of them were very intrigued by what was happening, as I realised in August 1982, in Lausanne, Switzerland, where Spurs were playing in a pre-season match just before the start of the 82/83 season. I was walking alone through the stand and passed what must have been the Directors Room. Douglas Alexiou, Sidney Wale's son-in-law, who had been appointed to the board when Sidney was ousted, saw me and came out. He patted me on the back and said: 'Gently, gently.' Then he just smiled and went back inside. The whole episode made me feel very strange.

I had more direct contact with the Richardsons when, in October, I travelled to London to see Spurs play Bayern Munich in the European Cup Winners' Cup. I was just another season ticket holder in the Centenary Club of the West Stand, waiting for dinner to be served (which as it happens was ninety minutes later, three minutes before the kick-off). However, the Spurs board no longer saw me as just another season ticket holder, and that became evident when Geoffrey Richardson, Arthur's son and the Vice-Chairman, made a bee-line straight for me. Normally a director would visit the members, shake a few hands and utter a few pleasantries. He was quite courteous and kept on giving me knowing looks. It was something of a fencing match, and I could not help contrasting his demeanour from almost a year ago. At that time I had, with a couple of friends, watched a game from the bare concrete of the unfinished upper tier of the West Stand. The contractors had given us passes to gain access, but we were interrupted by Geoffrey, who wanted to know what we were doing there. He demanded to see the passes which I showed him.

By the time of the Bayern Munich match, Geoffrey knew that I was probably in a position to get into the boardroom, and throughout the match he kept up those significant looks. What he was trying to convey, I do not know, but I could bask in the knowledge that nobody outside a closely knit and intimate circle knew the true state of affairs.

This was soon to change. Four weeks after the Bayern Munich game the veil was removed. On Friday, 19 November, the *Daily Express* ran an article by David Miller under the heading 'Spurs in Takeover Shock'. The article stated:

A sensational takeover bid for FA Cup holders Tottenham Hotspur is likely to be made at next month's annual meeting of shareholders. Following recent transfers of certain of the club's shares it is now thought that a move is being made from outside the existing board to oust the present regime, headed by Arthur Richardson. Confirmation of this strong possibility was given last night in a speech by Dr Brian Curtin, the Spurs physician, addressing the annual dinner of Saracens Rugby Union Club in London.

Dr Curtin, always an outspoken member of the Spurs staff, suggested in his speech to an astonished gathering of rugby players that:
1.   The figures of the club's balance sheet to be published next week revealed an alarming situation.
2.   There was the danger that Spurs could face the same cash flow problems arising out of their new stand, as Chelsea experienced in the mid-seventies.

3. The original estimates on the new main stand had been grossly exceeded.
4. Problems were accentuated by the meanness of directors.
5. Tottenham's position as one of the richest surviving clubs in England was seriously threatened.
6. A takeover bid seemed almost certain.

I was then in Las Vegas, having gone to see Frank Sinatra in concert. At about 5.30 in the morning I awoke to notice the message light on the hotel telephone flashing. The operator said that my wife had left a message to ring Peter Leaver, one of my confidants about the Spurs affair, in London as soon as possible. My immediate reaction was that a problem had arisen. Peter confirmed my worst fears and read me the *Express* article. Relieved to hear that my name had not been mentioned, I told him to do nothing and that I would be returning on the next flight to Los Angeles. I flew to Los Angeles at 8 am, furiously working out my options. This was not how I had planned it in my mind. My hand was about to be forced approximately twelve months before I wanted to move. It seemed now that I had no option other than to bring forward my plans.

When I arrived back in Beverly Hills, I contacted Peter Leaver again and it was agreed that nothing would be said publicly. As long as nobody knew about me the pressure was on the Spurs board and not myself. Peter was friendly with Douglas Alexiou, and I suggested he get in touch with him and arrange an early meeting with the Spurs board. Spurs were at home the following day to West Ham, and the Saturday morning newspapers were predictably full of stories following up the *Daily Express* exclusive. However, there was not much they could follow as, like me, the Spurs board were keeping mum. But Keith Burkinshaw did say something which, on reflection, brings a wry smile to me now: 'This club has simply become too big for one man to worry about everything . . . if I allowed myself to become concerned about the financial position, I would be in the nut house within a month.'

Peter had arranged a meeting between himself and the directors to take place immediately after the match. We agreed that he would put forward a proposal, on my behalf, that would include issuing the 3,108 shares withdrawn in 1905. My outline proposal also included the appointment of someone of my choice to the board. The price for the shares would be in the region of

£200 each, which would have the immediate effect of injecting around £600,000 directly into the company. Arthur Richardson maintained that there was no problem, although he appeared interested in a cash injection. The idea of issuing shares was not very appealing to him, but some form of interest-free loan was.

It was decided that a further meeting would take place within a couple of days when both parties had had time to consider their positions. The question of how many shares I had acquired was raised, but no clues were given to the directors. It was clear that they were very short of money, and agreed that any discussions would be carried out in confidence.

The following day, James Mossop of the *Sunday Express* was the first journalist to mention my name. I don't know to this day who gave it to him, despite having asked him several years later. I certainly have a very good idea who it was, but the suspicion has never been confirmed. It was my first experience of the rule that 'there are no secrets in football.'

The board had promised Fleet Street a statement which appeared in all the newspapers on the morning: 'Despite rumours to the contrary, Spurs are not in difficulties. An offer has been made to put additional finance into the Club and the Board of Directors are to consider the possibility.' The accounts were due to be published within a few days, and this was clearly a holding statement. By this time phone calls were arriving at all times of the night – 10 am in London is 2 am in Los Angeles – and life was suddenly becoming very hectic.

That weekend several conversations took place between Jonathan Metliss and Richardson, and it was agreed that a written proposal be put forward on my behalf. The board would then consider this at a meeting they had arranged for the Monday evening at Richardson's home in Whetstone, north London. The written proposal was a confirmation of the one outlined on Saturday, with one further condition, that Arthur Richardson would resign as Chairman and director of the company, with effect from the next Annual General Meeting due to be held on 16 December 1982. I wanted his place as Chairman to be taken by Douglas Alexiou.

The board rejected the proposal concerning the issue of shares in the sum of £600,000. They were still seeking some form of interest-free loan in the sum of £750,000, but in addition would give serious consideration to my proposal surrounding a

Rights issue. However, they were beginning gradually to impart certain information to Peter and Jonathan which enabled me to understand in more detail some of the difficulties they were encountering. A sum of £750,000, it seemed, had been locked into an account in Jersey, with the interest going to Ossie Ardiles and Ricky Villa as an agreed part of their employment. The board had been advised that if this money was put into a Trust outside the UK and, as importantly, the original sum was not borrowed, then the interest could be received tax-free by the two players, who were not domiciled in the UK. The main problem was that Tottenham *had* borrowed the money. Not only was this contrary to professional advice, it also meant that the benefit to be received by the players could not now be tax-free.

It was becoming increasingly clear that Arthur Richardson was prepared to fight and believed that there was no reason to discuss any offers prior to the forthcoming AGM. He felt that the bank were happy with the current position and that there were no problems with the club. He could count on his son, Geoffrey, and another director, Ken Kennard. But I was not without support on the board. The remaining two directors, Frank Sinclair, who had only been on the board a relatively short time, and Douglas Alexiou, had been quite sympathetic. I still preferred to have an amicable settlement, but made it clear that if this proved to be impossible, then I would not hesitate to vote against the directors standing for re-election at the AGM. This would have meant their removal.

On Wednesday, 24 November, I put forward a revised proposal. This included an interest-free loan from me of £700,000, repayable no later than 31 July 1985, and which I insisted had to be guaranteed by an acceptable UK bank or insurance company. Furthermore, I offered to underwrite a Rights issue to shareholders to be effected prior to 25 March 1983 in the sum of £600,000.

That same evening I received a phone call which was to prove seminal. The caller was Paul Bobroff and he rang me at my hotel in Los Angeles. I knew that his company had an executive box at Tottenham and a few Centenary Club memberships. I had previously met him in his box at the ground for ten minutes or so, at the request of his partner, Geoffrey Springer, whom I had known for many years. We had bumped into each other again that summer in Monte Carlo, where his parents were living. From his conversation, he was clearly of a similar mind as to what was going on at the club, although he didn't appear to be doing anything about it, just voicing the usual football fan moans. I gave him no clues whatsoever as to what I was doing, and the conversation was not particularly lengthy.

My first impression had been that Bobroff was nowhere near as fanatical a supporter as myself, and over the years I had never seen him at any match away from home. He had been relatively successful building up his property company, Markheath Securities, and floating it on the stock market, but there was something cold about his personality. He never seemed to be able to look you in the eye, and I was not sure of his true interest and motives.

Now he came straight to the point, asking if it was true that I was having discussions with the board, as reported in the newspapers. I asked what his interest was, and he replied that he was in a position to buy the holding of the Bearman Estate, who owned in the region of 13 per cent of the company's shares and were the second largest shareholder behind myself, with 693 shares. This was a bit of a surprise, as I had been led to believe that the Estate would not sell. Discreet discussions had been taking place with one of the family members, and they had given the clear impression that although they were not sellers, I could firmly rely on their support.

Bobroff wanted to know whether, if he were to proceed with the purchase, he could join in with my current negotiations. I asked him at what price he had agreed to buy, and he said it was in the region of £300 per share. I told him he was paying too much, but that if he wanted to be involved he should proceed, perhaps at a lower price, and should contact me again once the purchase had been effected. He rang back a day later, on 25 November, to say that he had bought the shares, and could he now be included in the discussions. He asked that his wife should never be told the amount of his investment, as she would think he was crazy spending that amount of money on a football club. I found this request a little bemusing.

Indeed, within a few days of Bobroff buying his shares, he rang me and asked if I wanted to buy them from him at the same price he had paid, plus a seat on the board when it was reconstituted. I declined his offer to sell, but have rued the decision ever since. I have now learnt to my cost that partnerships involving owner-ship of a football club can never work, especially when people are thrown together. There has to be a benevolent dictatorship, where the club comes before anyone or anything. Egos must not exist, and the only issue that is of paramount importance is what is in the best interests of the club. Nothing else. Anyone buying a football club should do it alone, so long as they are the right type of person, totally dedicated and caring for the club, and have the ambition to do it their way in the best interests of the club. A partnership means that everything is done by compromise. Perhaps the other person will not care as much, have the same dreams and ideals, have the same standards, or the same aims. But these reflections came much later. At that stage we had effectively been thrown into bed together.

The situation had its drawbacks. I was not living in England, and it was important for someone in London, with a knowledge of the stock market, to oversee the financial position during the coming months. I had never been keen on going into this alone, and at the time it seemed like a comfort. In hindsight, it was one of the biggest mistakes of my life. Many of the wrong decisions that were taken in the years that followed would never have occurred had I remained independent.

As a result of Bobroff's purchase we now controlled 50 per cent of the company's shares and were in an unassailable position. The big question was, how to reach an agreement with the board without doing any harm to the club. The Richardsons were not going to go without a fight, and whilst I was prepared for this in private, I was not going to allow this clash to be made public and end up in an undignified squabble.

Arthur Richardson contacted me the day after the latest proposal had been received and said that he was in a position to offer me a seat on the board if I would support him in having Douglas Alexiou removed. I told him that I had no intention of backing such a move and I would be putting forward a final proposal, to which I expected an immediate response from the board. The following day, Spurs published their trading figures for the previous season 81/82, and all the newspaper headlines were full of £52,000 missing from the Ticket Office (there was no question of any fraud) and non-payment of VAT since 1 July, of £67,000. 'Someone forgot to enclose the cheque' was the response from the club. The tabloids began reporting that the players and staff had been handed invoices for thousands of pounds of White Hart Lane tickets, and also for the Cup Final replay the previous May. This was confirmed by the club, which pointed out that it was an internal matter and a case of maladministration.

When quizzed about the takeover, Arthur Richardson merely stated: 'If there was an offer of any injection of money, we wouldn't be doing our duty unless we examined it thoroughly.' By the weekend, the Press were beginning to report the fact that 'a takeover group' controlled an unbeatable 50 per cent of the shares, and were predicting a showdown at the forthcoming AGM.

Amid all this Press speculation, no one had yet realised that Sidney Wale had sold the vast majority of his holding to me. In fact, when one journalist tracked him down, his quote gave nothing away: 'I am making no comment whatsoever about any situation relating to Tottenham at this moment.'

Still the Richardsons would not give up. My revised proposal of 24 November had not even been formally decided upon by the board, and in the absence of a decision, the only alternative left was to call for an Extraordinary General Meeting to have them removed. Paul Bobroff was convinced he could persuade them to retire gracefully. He had a meeting with them, but to no avail. They were determined to hang on at all costs.

Finally, on Wednesday, 1 December, as Spurs were playing at home to Luton Town in the Milk Cup, a notice was formally served on the directors that an EGM was being called by a number of shareholders to remove Arthur Richardson, Geoffrey Richardson, and Ken Kennard from the board of directors. It was proposed by the Bearman Estate, with a further letter signed by Sidney Wale confirming his support for the proposal. With the two single largest shareholders in the company against them, the Richardsons finally realised that the game was up.

The following morning all three resigned. Spurs had always been a club where the idea of a takeover was completely out of the question; the directors had always been seen as holding an impregnable position. We wanted a smooth succession. Arthur and Geoffrey Richardson were made life Vice-Presidents of the club, and Ken Kennard was afforded the normal privileges of an ex-director, which included two seats in the Directors Box at White Hart Lane. Douglas Alexiou took on the role of Chairman, whilst Frank Sinclair became Vice-Chairman. Peter Leaver and Paul Bobroff were appointed directors. The board immediately resolved to recognise and register the shareholdings of Paul Bobroff and myself, and undertook to have the offending Article 14 removed as soon as was constitutionally possible. But I declined an invitation to join the board, due to my business commitments in France.

Everything had happened so quickly that I found it difficult to take it all in. Tottenham had always been my greatest passion: from the days of standing on the terraces as a young boy, to the time I got my first season ticket in the East Stand in Block D, Row D, Seat 117. I can still remember the excitement of eventually acquiring a seat in the old West Stand, which in those days was virtually impossible. Now I was the major shareholder.

It was a situation I could barely have imagined when my Uncle Gerry, my mother's brother, took me to see Tottenham on 6 September 1952. This was just after Tottenham, managed by Arthur Rowe, had won the League for the first time with the famous push-and-run side. On that day Spurs beat Cardiff City by 2-1. Uncle Gerry had a season ticket, and so did a friend of his, but with his friend on holiday I borrowed that ticket and after that was a regular visitor to White Hart Lane. It was the old East Stand camaraderie and atmosphere that gave me a love for the game and for White Hart Lane that has never left me.

If Uncle Gerry hadn't taken me that day I'm not sure whether I would have become a Spurs fan. My father, Morris, had no interest in the game and had never seen a live match, and in my school, St Marylebone Grammar, the only two sports we played were cricket and rugby. I was reasonably good at both, a wicket-keeper/batsman in cricket and their scrum-half and then a fly-half in rugby, once breaking my collar-bone, but there were no opportunities to play football except at weekends. How ironic that many years later the same school was to produce one of the greatest of modern English players, John Barnes, as John himself would remind me when I met him at a dinner many years later.

If you were interested in football at our school you tended to support either Chelsea or Queen's Park Rangers, and looking back I can think of little Raymond Davies, who was a fanatical Chelsea supporter, whose great hero was Terry Venables. Once I had fallen in love with Spurs there was no question of my looking at any other club, but I did like Chelsea, particularly the young diamonds of Tommy Docherty, consisting of Venables and Bonetti and other players who I first watched when they were in the Second Division and who always played very attractive and very entertaining football.

If football is my first love then property is my second. When I left school I became an estate agent, and then a few years later joined my parents in their curtain business in Hendon. My father, who had had a men's hairdressing business in Poplar, was now suffering from bad eyesight and had joined my mother Rose in the curtain business. After a few years I went back into the property business, and received my big break following the property crash of 1973. This is when I teamed up with a very close friend of mine, Paul Norman, to form a joint company with European Ferries, who ran the Townsend Thoresen Cross-Channel Ferries, with the opportunity of developing office buildings in London and the South-East. It was this that brought me in touch with Keith Wickenden, the Chairman of European Ferries, who was the great mentor of my business life. An MP, he was on the board of Brighton & Hove Albion, and a very close friend of Mike Bamber, the former Chairman. Keith had the ability to pick out people; he picked me out and provided me with opportunities which were the making of my business career.

Just before I bought into Spurs, Keith Wickenden decided to expand into Europe, and both Paul and I moved to Monte Carlo to set up operations there. It was as I was settling in at Monte Carlo that the events I have just described took place. Within less than a year, Keith was to die in a plane crash, flying a Spitfire he was lovingly restoring. He crashed as he was trying to land the aircraft at Shoreham Airport in Sussex. I heard the news whilst I was in New Orleans, and it was one of the saddest moments of my life. I will never forget the openings he made for me, for they were the opportunities of a lifetime. Indeed had Keith been alive my involvement with Spurs might have taken a different route.

However, at the moment of the takeover I still did not think of exercising control over the club. I knew there was a lot of hard work and decision-making ahead. What I didn't know – and it is one of the greatest drawbacks of being the Chairman of a major club – is that you never have time to sit back and enjoy the privilege. There are always countless problems that need resolving, and you are trying to plan ahead for the longer term, whereas supporters are normally only interested in the last result.

In the hectic days leading up to our takeover I was still in America, and I heard the news of the Richardsons' fall while I was in Orlando, Florida, visiting the newly opened Disneyland. Looking back now, I can see it was an appropriate place to hear that I had at last become an owner of the club I had always loved. It would be many years before I realised what a world of fantasy and wonder I was entering. So great was the fantasy, that even to this day I do not know exactly how much it cost me to buy into Spurs. I have never sat down and added it up. In any case, what is the price of a dream? It is only now, as I write this, that I realise how much I was deluding myself. Dreams can turn into nightmares, and just as Disneyland in Orlando leads to the bleakest of car parks, so the fantasy world of football can dump you into cold reality with the most frightful of bumps. But that was long, long into the future.

3 | THE MISSING PEN

'I never heard of a fan complaining about the share price. All they complain about is the football results, even if we win 5-0.'
— Paul Bobroff.

Football supporters are a superstitious, credulous lot. I am no exception. I had been brought up to believe that there was a special pen kept at White Hart Lane. That pen was only brought out when Tottenham Hotspur signed a new player. The manager would then hand the pen to the player, who would use it to initial the contract.

So, soon after I took over at Tottenham, my first desire was to see this pen. It was a few days after Christmas 1982. I was in the offices of Peter Day, the Club Secretary. Already some of the scales had begun to fall from my eyes. I had been brought up to believe that Tottenham were the great aristocrats of North London. Whatever Tottenham wanted, Tottenham got. If there was a player to be signed then whatever his price, Tottenham would be one of the clubs leading the chase for his signature. I could still remember the thrill that I experienced when I heard that Jimmy Greaves, who had gone from Chelsea to play in Italy but could not settle there, was to be brought back to London by Tottenham Hotspur. But as I looked round Peter Day's office I felt this was not super, Slick Spurs, but more like something from Charles Dickens's *Hard Times*. Tottenham High Road, at the best of times, is hardly the most prepossessing of places, and the White Hart Lane offices did not seem to have had a lick of paint since the stadium was built. There were even holes in the lino on Day's floor. Never mind, I thought. At least Peter Day would have the magic pen.

'Peter, I wonder if I could have a look at that special pen which is used when you sign new players,' I said.

Peter Day looked at me as if I was slightly barmy, and then he laughed. 'What special pen?'

'You know, the pen that is used to sign new players' contracts.'

'There is no such pen.'

I cannot explain how shattered I felt. The non-existence of the pen, as such, didn't mean very much, but it seemed to symbolise the club I had bought. This was 1982. The World Cup had just taken place in Spain, with the matches played in wonderfully constructed, modern stadiums conjuring up an atmosphere of fiesta and entertainment. Here I was at White Hart Lane, where before every home match the announcer, Willy Morgan, never failed to say: 'Welcome to White Hart Lane, the world-famous home of the Spurs.' But far from looking a modern stadium fit to compare with the best in the world, Tottenham gave the appearance of being a run-down family business still imprisoned in its Victorian surroundings and shaped by Victorian attitudes.

I had been made vividly aware of this when I arrived for my first post-takeover visit, just before lunchtime, for a match due to kick off at 7.45. The first thing that struck me was the long queue outside the ticket office. It was only about midday then, and the ticket office was in any case not due to open until 2 pm. When I asked one of the queuing fans what they were doing, they replied that it was quite normal for a home match. Now I could have understood that if it had been an important Derby match against Arsenal, or one of the other big clubs. But this was a home match against Brighton, recently promoted to the First Division, and the stadium would never be full for that occasion – no more than 23,994 were attracted. There were plenty of tickets available, and I thought it was a bit of a nonsense that fans had to queue up so early when we could easily have arranged to book tickets for them which they could then collect just prior to the kick-off.

I arranged for someone to take the names and telephone numbers of all those waiting, in order that the Ticket Office Manager could ring them as soon as he arrived. At about 12.30 Peter Barnes arrived. He had recently joined the club from Leyton Orient as Assistant Secretary, but was acting as Ticket Office Manager – the previous one having suffered a nervous breakdown. Peter explained that the ticket office staff were not due in until 2 pm, owing to the Christmas holidays, but he accepted my suggestion to open up the office there and then, and together with a friend we undertook to serve at the ticket office window until the staff turned up. Peter must have been taken aback by this, but I must say I thoroughly enjoyed the experience. It made me realise quite how antiquated and archaic the system was.

At that time all the tickets were pre-printed by an outside firm, and that morning as I and my friend sold tickets it quickly became clear to me that if we did not computerise the system we would only prolong the problems the club had been suffering. I had heard stories of how club officials wandering into the ticket office would find the floor strewn with cash and ticket stubs. Money had been found stuffed down the back of filing cabinets, and there had been hundreds of duplicated season tickets when the new West Stand had opened. (There was no question of foul play, of course.)

I couldn't understand why, in this age of the credit card, Tottenham hadn't installed a system whereby the fans could just ring up and buy a ticket on the telephone using a credit card number, much the same way as a theatregoer or opera-lover might buy a ticket. To be fair to Tottenham, no other football club acknowledged the existence of the credit card, but I could quickly see that such innovations were necessary and long overdue.

A few weeks later Peter Day recruited Chris Belt to take over as the Ticket Office Manager, and he proved to be the ideal person to engineer the necessary changes. Chris had worked at Chelsea, and before that at Wembley, and in no time at all he brought an efficiency and a sense of purpose to the ticket office which it had never had before. The accountants Peat, Marwick, Mitchell were called in as consultants to advise us on how best we could computerise the ticket office, and after a lot of consultation it was decided to go with Synchro Systems as having the best technology to suit our needs. It helped us considerably that Chris had had previous experience of working computers, and within a few months we had a system installed that worked very well.

One of the things that had always appalled me about football clubs was the way they treated their season ticket holders. I was well aware that in the late Fifties and early Sixties it was extremely difficult to buy a season ticket for Tottenham, and there was much talk and speculation amongst the supporters about the length of the waiting list. The club would ask people to write in and put their names down, and if at some time a vacancy became available they would be offered a ticket. It was almost as bad as trying to become a member of the MCC.

I myself had experienced this when, some years after applying, suddenly one Saturday morning I received a letter offering me two season tickets. I could never understand why Tottenham, or for that matter any football club, made it so difficult for their supporters to see matches on a regular basis, and one of the first things I wanted to see was the season ticket waiting list. Chris produced around six box-files with letters dating back as far as five years, and I suggested to him that we work out how many season tickets could be made available and start offering them to the letter-writers. Within a few weeks we had sold £150,000 worth of season tickets – this for the second half of the season only. Chris always laughed about this, and said he wouldn't have believed it if he hadn't seen it. Unusually for football, Chris Belt always looked at any change as a positive move, and for me he is the best ticket office manager in football.

During the following summer I took Peter Day and Mike Lewis, the Commercial Manager, for a short trip to America to see if we could learn from the Americans some of the techniques they used to market the game. The trip worked well, but it also provided me with an early lesson about football. Although both Peter and Mike found America interesting, they came back thinking there wasn't anything they could learn from there. I, in contrast, having lived abroad, have always felt that there is bound to be something you can learn from other people, even when it comes to a game you think is your very own preserve.

One of the things I had learned in my business experience and my travels was the use of consultants who are specialists in their field. An approach was made to Saatchi & Saatchi, then riding high as the best marketing men in the country – their famous, or infamous, poster 'Labour Isn't Working' was said to have been instrumental in electing Mrs Thatcher to power – as to how we could better market Spurs. Alex Fynn was a shrewd marketing and advertising man who also had a keen awareness and enthusiasm for the game. It was an ideal combination and I was very interested to hear his views.

Alex suggested we consider television advertising, although

he made it quite plain that selling a football team to the public was not like selling baked beans. Anyway, while marketing a football club could improve its supporters' awareness, it could only work if you had a winning team. And nobody can guarantee success on the field.

However, we decided to follow his advice with a campaign centred upon a fictitious character called Mrs Ridlington. The team was to pretend that Mrs Ridlington and her family were part of the Spurs team, and the punchline came when, to a chorus of 'Join the team', some of the players, together with members of Mrs Ridlington's family and other characters including Peter Cook, an ardent Spurs supporter, were seen coming out of the White Hart Lane tunnel, led by Mrs Ridlington herself. The commercials were shown for the first time just before the first home match of the 83/84 season. This was against Coventry City, not normally the greatest of draws. But the advert had said: 'Come and join the 35,000,' and for that match I was really surprised that 35,500 turned up, showing what modern marketing could achieve.

Yet even as these modest reforms were taking place I was becoming aware that we were disturbing some very ancient cobwebs – particularly cobwebs of the mind. Football, said Pelé, is the beautiful game, and this beauty arouses intense romanticism. Nowhere is this more evident than in the sports pages of the newspapers. Journalists like to portray themselves as a hard-drinking, hard-living, cynical mob, but in my experience some of them are the greatest romantics you can find. Certainly the football journalist is. Although by the time I took over at Spurs it was more than twenty years since the maximum wage had been abolished, and the image of the football player carrying his boots and travelling on the same bus as the supporters to the match in which he was playing (which I had seen many times) was part of a myth, football writers, or some of them, still hankered after a bygone past. Their mental clock seemed to have stopped in the late Forties, when English football enjoyed one of its great boom periods, with almost every match attracting enormous crowds and all willing to watch the match in great discomfort in stadiums that provided few or no amenities. I knew – and so did many of those writers, I suspect – that those days would not come back, but their writing still continued to be shaped by this misguided romanticism.

Yet, as they proceeded to label us at Spurs as nouveaux

riches, computer whiz-kids, and would-be role models seeking to revolutionise the game (none of which we wanted to be or do), I could not help reflecting that professional journalism was also about to undergo some of the greatest changes ever seen. In my time at Spurs I was to see the clichéd image of the reporter in the fawn mac with the Dudley reporter's notebook tucked inside it replaced by the figure of the man with the lap-top computer and a modem to attach it to his telephone. Press boxes at the football grounds no longer reverberated to the clackety-clack sounds of portable typewriters, nor did you hear too many voices dictating copy over crackly telephone lines. Instead, copy was silently written on to portable PCs and then transferred electronically to the newspaper offices. But even as the reporters themselves struggled and accepted these changes in technology, they looked with a baleful eye at some of the modest changes I made as if to suggest we were out to destroy the foundations of the game.

I knew that we had to make changes in order to rescue the foundations of Spurs. Not only was the club in a sorry state – in a wander through the West Stand I found long side areas that had been left unfinished, and in an unused office numerous Spurs trophies and cups stuffed into a cubby-hole – but the club was in a financial mess. At the time of the takeover there was some trepidation about the financial state of the company, and it transpired that we had inherited the biggest debt in football: over £5.5 million.

The first thing we had to do was to turn this round. The debt was running at a level that made it almost impossible to buy new players. We could only fund our first purchase, Alan Brazil from Ipswich in March 1983, on the back of personal guarantees to the bank, offered by Paul Bobroff and myself, pledging repayment within a few months, once the season ticket renewal money started to arrive in the summer. If the money was not repaid within the timescale, the bank would have turned to us for the repayment personally.

Football, of course, always needs large amounts of money. But where could we get £5 million? The answer, when it came, was blindingly simple. Why not float Tottenham Hotspur on the Stock Exchange? I had never understood why football clubs had never been listed on the stock market. The Exchange had every type of company from ball-bearing manufacturers to insurance, and the leisure sector was a particular favourite for investors. At that time in the early Eighties the financial markets were quite buoyant, the stock market was in the middle of its bull phase, and there seemed to be a lot of new money in the City. I believed that some of it must be prepared to come into football. I could see why football clubs did not consider the option. They were mostly run by conservatives, with a small 'c', self-made businessmen who saw these clubs as part of their family heirlooms and personal fiefdoms, with shares handed down from father to son. A public listing would mean loss of control and far more public accountability, and they could not face that. But I did not see my holding of Spurs in that light, and in any case our problems there were so horrendous that something dramatic had to be done.

At this stage the structure of the Spurs board was rather curious. My business commitments with European Ferries still kept me in France, and although I was the largest shareholder, I was not on the board. Paul Bobroff, the next major investor, was on the board, but he was not the Chairman. That post belonged to Douglas Alexiou. Although I did not know Douglas very well at that stage – I was to get to know him intimately over the years – his relationship with Sidney meant that he had a deep feel for the traditions of the club, and this to me was very important. It was not an easy task for Douglas. Chairmen of football clubs are normally the largest shareholders as well, but with me, the major shareholder, outside the board he may have felt that his public position was slightly undermined. However that was not so. He assured me that if I ever wanted to become Chairman he would happily stand aside, but at this stage I had no thoughts of an active involvement, which would have meant living in London, and I was quite happy for Douglas to represent the club.

If I had one criticism of Douglas it was that he seemed to make himself far too easily available to the Press, probably because he is such an accommodating man. The chairmen I had admired from afar were those at Liverpool and Arsenal, whose names were hardly known to the public and whose printed comments were very few and far between. Douglas in contrast was quite keen to issue the sort of statements that easily convert into headlines. So, for instance, one of his first utterances was that: 'Spurs must win the League. We are looking to emulate Liverpool.' This got right up Keith Burkinshaw's nose, and he complained to me that it was putting added pressure on him. I believed in the maxim 'Don't talk about it, do it!' Later Douglas spoke about the club's commercial ambitions saying: 'Sponsorship of Spurs is worth £1 million,' words that would prove a hostage to fortune.

It was clear from the beginning that if we floated, much of the preparatory work would be done by Paul Bobroff. He ran a public company, and he seemed more familiar with the ways of a listed company. He recommended Shepperds & Chase, the firm that had been responsible for the flotation of his own company some years previously. On my next visit to London I met their representative, John Sachs. He came across as very enthusiastic and confident, and I was quite taken with him. He was in favour of a full listing rather than one on the secondary market (the Unlisted Securities Market), and after lunch we walked to the corner of Gresham Street still debating the various advantages between the two. Finally I turned and told him: 'I have one final, simple question. If we go for a full listing, will we raise the money that we need?'

'Yes,' he said.

'Are you sure?' I asked again.

'Positive,' he said. It was decided there and then that this was the route we would take.

The path from this conversation to finality was to prove a long and very time-consuming one, with many pitfalls and miles of red tape. I had very little experience of the minefield, and Bobroff was very helpful with his experience and expertise to help make the whole flotation work.

One of the problems we had was that football regulations restricted the amount of dividend that could be paid to shareholders. Clearly any such decision would fall foul of the Stock Exchange, so we had to come up with a new idea. The answer was to have not one Tottenham Hotspur but two. First a holding company, Tottenham Hotspur plc, was formed to acquire the shares of the football club. It was this company that would be listed on the Stock Exchange and which would have a subsidiary called Tottenham Hotspur Football Club. The club would remain in essence more or less as it had been formed. The idea for a two-tier club structure was not totally unique, but it did make me very nervous, and I kept on having nightmares thinking the football authorities would find some rule or regulation that would make this impossible.

Instead, it was the Stock Exchange that provided a small barrier. We asked them for permission to give shareholders benefits along the line of discounted season tickets, in the way that Sketchleys give discounts on dry cleaning, or European Ferries give a reduction on cross-Channel trips, but they refused. Nevertheless, the essence of the plan went ahead. Just before the flotation we had a Rights issue of £1.1 million, which was fully underwritten by Bobroff and myself. The flotation was meant to raise a further £3.8 million, which would give us the £5 million that we wanted.

As with all such flotations the issue had to be underwritten, meaning that if too few investors subscribed for the shares, there were financial institutions that would buy the shares so that the club were guaranteed the money. John Sachs found the financial institutions, so that whatever happened with the public, Tottenham wouldn't lose out.

Meanwhile, Bobroff recruited Derek Peter as Finance Director to the company. Peter had been with Peat, Marwick, Mitchell, who had recently become our auditors, and he appeared to be just the bright, alert, experienced man we needed while we were selling ourselves to the City. The City always likes to feel that companies are in good professional hands, and Derek and Paul Bobroff had the job of handling the City bosses day to day. I kept out of the details, while Derek reported to Bobroff, who also handled Barclays Bank and oversaw all the financial particulars.

Now all this was meant to be highly confidential until we were ready to release the details, but as I was soon to discover, in the City as much as in football, there are no secrets. I happened to be in Paris during the summer of 1983, and suddenly on the BBC World Service I heard that Spurs were planning a flotation. I immediately made phone calls to Bobroff, Peter, John Sachs and the others, and it transpired that there had been a leak in the City. Some time later much would be written about the fact that football and the City did not go together, but in at least one respect the two were well matched: in neither could you keep any secrets, and there was always the danger of leaks.

The share issue was publicly launched on Sunday, 2 October 1983, when ITV showed Spurs playing Nottingham Forest as the first ever live League game. The prospectus giving details was wrapped around the match programme that afternoon, with the official launch the next morning, when the issue got fully under way.

In pure financial terms it was a success. The shares were over-subscribed three and a half times, and the £5 million we were seeking was in the bank, much to the delight of Barclays! But although the shares, which were sold at £1 each, started trading at £1.08, a number of professionals who expected a quick killing sold immediately, and forced the price down to around 90p. Three and a half years would go by before the shares rose above the issue price.

Our success drew plenty of interest. A short time after the flotation I had dinner with some of the Manchester United directors, who spent the whole time saying that they were giving some thought to following suit, but were concerned about the payment of dividends. It is interesting to note that, not long ago, they finally came round to taking the same route. A number of enquiries did come in from other football clubs in Europe, including Bayern Munich and Paris St Germain.

The flotation was also followed by us acquiring a shirt sponsor. Mike Lewis had been trying to get one for some time, and I couldn't understand the delay. In November 1983 we played Bayern Munich in the UEFA Cup, and Mike asked his newly appointed assistant, Mike Rollo, to try and find a sponsor for the return game at White Hart Lane. He eventually agreed terms with Holsten Breweries, and they were so happy with their involvement that Rollo persuaded them to have their names on our team shirts for the remainder of the season, with an agreement for two more years. Holsten's name first appeared on Spurs shirts in a live BBC televised League game at Old Trafford, just before Christmas, and they have supported the club ever since. It has proved one of the ideal partnerships in football, and Holsten's profile became so high that when, some years later, the Football League Marketing Department carried out a survey on club sponsorship, more than 90 per cent of those questioned recognised Holsten as the Tottenham sponsor.

But the flotation had contained a germ of an idea which was to create many future problems. The financial advisers had insisted that in order to attract investors, the offer document should state that Tottenham would become 'a broadly based leisure company'. I could see future problems in such a commitment, but Bobroff made it clear that if the company wanted to take advantage of the money on offer, certain concessions had to be made. The City, he said, were not handing us £3.8 million without expecting any sort of return. What they wanted us to do was diversify and make larger profits, to enable them to have larger dividend cheques.

To my mind, a football club is a little like a property company: it is the assets that should be increasing in value each year, rather than the dividend pay-out. Football and its related activities were areas where I saw the real potential and long-term benefits for the club. I had got involved with Tottenham because I foresaw financial problems, and all I ever wanted was to play a part in solving them. My interest and passion had always been the team and the club. My business background was entirely related to property, and I did not want to start going off into areas where we had no knowledge, no experience, and furthermore that we could not control.

The flotation was meant to free the business from debt, and to strengthen the football club by providing money to construct the sort of team that the fans wanted to see. But while the flotation had been a success, I was soon made aware that it had its drawbacks as well. In the prospectus we had given a profit forecast of £900,000 for the year, and Bobroff began to get very nervous that we were not going to meet this. His solution was to have a dramatic impact on both the football club and the players.

I came back one evening to my flat in France to find a message on my answerphone machine from Steve Perryman, asking me to ring him urgently. When I returned his call, he wanted to know why the players' share of the television income had been omitted from their bonus payments. (Historically, the players were given a bonus for European matches, which included a percentage of television revenue.) He was taken aback when I told him that I knew nothing about it and could only assume there had been an oversight. If it is a contractual responsibility, I said, the club will meet it in full. He was adamant that the payment had been left out on purpose, as he had checked with the club that day. Perryman and Tony Galvin were the players' representatives in the event of internal disputes, and Perryman made it clear that he was speaking on behalf of all the players affected.

I immediately spoke with Paul Bobroff, and he confirmed that he had instructed the Accounts Department not to make the payment, as he was very nervous that, the way things stood at that point, the projected forecast would not be met. I pointed out to him that the one thing he couldn't do was meddle with the players' contractual entitlements. He countered by saying that if I read the bonus schedule carefully, it could be argued that the players were not entitled to a share of the television income.

It turned out that the payments were a matter of custom and practice, continued over many years. In the previous rounds of the UEFA Cup up to that point, they had received a share.

I spoke again to Steve Perryman and reiterated that this action had been taken without my knowledge, but assured him that they would receive whatever they were entitled to in due course. We arranged to meet the next time I was in London, and in the meantime, the matter would be looked into. No settlement had been reached by the time of the UEFA Cup Final, although at our meeting in London I explained to Perryman privately what the problem was and told him that if the club refused to pay, I personally would underwrite their entitlement, as I felt it was properly due. In the end the players did receive their full entitlement that summer, on the condition that the bonus agreement, which had been running for some twenty years and was ambiguous in its wording, would be replaced by a new one which everyone could understand.

The negotiations for the new bonus agreement were attended by Paul Bobroff and myself on behalf of the club, Steve Perryman and Tony Galvin representing the players, and Gordon Taylor, the Secretary of the Players Union. I spoke to Taylor beforehand and said that I wanted no further confrontation. This was the first time that I really got to know Gordon Taylor, and I found his manner and way of negotiation extremely helpful. He had the ability to see the problem from both sides of the table, and I gained great faith and trust in him.

After a lot of toing and froing, and about five hours of discussions, we finally reached agreement on a new bonus structure, which encompassed all matches played by all teams in the club. To avoid any future need to renegotiate, it was agreed at the time that the new schedule would be annually increased in line with inflation. It ended with handshakes all round, and the players seemed genuinely pleased that a satisfactory outcome had been achieved. But further problems did arise. Prior to the start of any season, all players must sign the club's bonus schedule and lodge it with the Football League, otherwise they are ineligible to play in matches. Unfortunately, having finally agreed the new schedule, the players refused to sign it. Bobroff and Frank Sinclair had a heated meeting at the club's training ground, where apparently Steve Perryman became quite offensive to Paul Bobroff.

Bobroff rang me in France in a panic, telling me that I must get over to England immediately to sort out the problem, which was getting out of hand. I pointed out to him that we had an agreement and I expected the players to honour it. I said I would make a call to Gordon Taylor to explain the latest predicament. Gordon reassured me that the deal had been agreed and he would get the players to sign. He promised to travel to London from the PFA's headquarters in Manchester to meet the players. The next day Taylor's intervention worked and the players signed. The agreement was still in force in 1991.

So it had ended well. The players had received their bonuses and Bobroff had avoided acute embarrassment by meeting the profit forecast. But had it really ended well? Those early months of the flotation provided a foretaste of what was to come later. Bobroff as Chairman of the holding company and responsible for the activities of the plc had clearly found his niche at Tottenham. He was the money-man, happy in a world of finance and figures, and he quite revelled in it. But I couldn't work out why he had got involved in the football club in the first place. He clearly did not have my feel for football, or my love for Spurs, and I was slowly beginning to believe that Bobroff's number one love was Paul Bobroff.

Soon I was to have an insight into his thinking that would make me realise how differently Bobroff and I approached our involvement with Tottenham. We were standing at the top of the steps in the Directors Box at White Hart Lane, a couple of hours or so before the beginning of a match. The stadium, as usual at that time, was completely empty. Suddenly Bobroff turned to me, gestured to the vast, immaculate-looking empty stadium, and said: 'Isn't it a nice feeling to know you own all this?' That gave me a real jolt. It turned my stomach to think that anybody involved with football could feel that way. As far as I am concerned, no one owns a football club apart from its supporters. The directors are merely trustees and guardians of the club. We may own shares, but the spirit of the club belongs to the fans. Directors come and go, but the fans and club go on for ever.

In midsummer 1984 I took over as Chairman of the football club. I was still living in Monaco, but now I had more time available to become involved. Almost the first task was to address a large gathering of Fleet Street's soccer reporters for the launch of the Rothman's Football Yearbook, which coincidentally was being held at White Hart Lane. Douglas had been supposed to speak, but felt it would be more appropriate if I did.

I had never made a public speech in my life, and the thought of doing so in front of perhaps the most battle-hardened and cynical of journalistic assemblies was a daunting prospect. It took me three weeks of sleepless nights to write the speech. I could have done what US Presidents and even Lady Thatcher do, and hired a speech-writer, but I wanted this to be my own effort. As a passionate football supporter I had developed a lot of ideas about the game, and this was my first opportunity to share them with the soccer opinion-formers. A friend of mine told me: 'Irving, just before you speak, gulp some brandy and then knock them out.'

I did just that, and within a few minutes, from the corner of my eye, I noticed a very strange thing happening. Steve Curry, the large, rumbustious chief soccer correspondent of the *Daily Express*, and widely regarded by the Fleet Street soccer writers as the leader of their tribe, was frantically searching for a pen and notebook. He had clearly decided that my speech was worth recording. Journalists, as I was to discover, rarely allow anything to pierce their cynicism, but at the end of the speech they rose and gave me a standing ovation, which completely took me aback. At the rear of the room, Alan Parry, then of the BBC, turned to Peter Day and said: 'That was very impressive. Who wrote it for him?' 'You must be joking,' said Day. 'He's been writing it for three weeks and driven us mad in the process.' Later on, the journalists asked for copies of my speech, as they were anxious not to misquote me. I had to print quite a number. I also learned that Tom Clarke, then Sports Editor of the *Daily Mail*, was so impressed with this speech that he asked Jeff Powell to write an article based on it. Shackleton's comment that directors know nothing about football was clearly not true.

It is almost a decade since I made that speech, but many of the themes that I struck then remain valid. The need for football to change, and for the government to reduce the incredible amount of money siphoned off from football. The need to sell the game. At Tottenham, as I've said, we were already involved with Saatchi & Saatchi in trying to sell football, and it was clear that we could not do that the way you sell a can of beans. Baked beans are of a consistent value, football is not. One week a game may have you at the edge of your seat for ninety minutes; the next it may send you to sleep.

What I was concerned about was the fact that in the previous 1983/84 season, Liverpool had been outstanding: they won the Milk Cup, as the League Cup was then called, in March – defeating Tottenham in the process – and then went on to win the League Championship and the European Cup. Yet that season saw their home gates actually drop from an average of 34,000 to 31,000. If the most successful club in the country couldn't keep up with home gates, then who could? I felt, I told the assembled journalists, that we should learn from Europe, particularly France, which had just won the European Championship in wonderful style, although the number of matches the French played was not all that different from our own heavily congested League.

It was this reference to the French that was to produce a curious postscript. Peter Shreeve had just taken over as Manager. That afternoon he came to see me and said: 'Sorry to bother you. I just wanted to know what you said about the French team in your speech.' As I looked a little bemused he continued: 'You know, er, about how they play.' 'You mean *joie de vivre*, Peter?' 'That's the word. What does it mean?' I explained that it was a Gallic expression that stood for gay abandon, and Peter nodded his head, obviously taking it in.

Steve Perryman, then the club captain, had already accused me of suffering from Europeanitis. Peter, whose background should have made him very insular, was one of the few to appreciate why I held European soccer in such high regard.

4

THE DREAM-MAKERS

'The trouble with Irving is that you've got to know the Spurs Double team to get on with him. In fact, I understand that is almost the first thing he has asked his wives and girlfriends.'
– Jeff Randall, City Editor, *Sunday Times*.

The French writer, Stendhal, had two great passions in his life: eating spinach and reading Saint-Simon. I have had, with respect to my wives and children, only one great passion: Tottenham Hotspur. The Spurs Double team does mean a lot to me – as it does to any Spurs fan who was privileged to watch it – but to name all of them is not the ultimate test of friendship with me. It was love of players such as those, and above all the style they played, that made me and will keep me a Spurs fan to my dying day. They were the dream-makers of my youth.

Like all Spurs supporters I can spot a Spurs player a mile away. There is a certain elegance, style and quality about them that lift them apart from the run-of-the-mill player that you see at most other clubs. It is like class and true grace: something you cannot put into words, but the moment you see it you know what it is. Long before I became involved with Spurs I had come to recognise such players: Greaves, Blanchflower, John White, Gilzean, Mackay and many others. I could write a whole book about these players and the memories they hold for me. If I did, Gilzean and Greaves would have a special section devoted to them. They were the G-men, with Gilzean probably the player I truly cherished and loved. But during the decade when I was running the club there were four players who to me epitomised what playing for Tottenham was all about. They were, not necessarily in order of merit, Ardiles, Hoddle,

Waddle and Gascoigne. Of these I would say Gascoigne was undoubtedly unique. I may be a bit biased in this – after all, I signed him from Newcastle – but even if I had just been an ordinary supporter at that time, the quality of Gascoigne would still have shone through. Just as Calais was said to be inscribed on Queen Mary's heart, so Gascoigne is imprinted on mine, but for very different reasons.

On the very day that he agreed to join us I turned to Mel Stein and Len Lazarus, his advisers, and said that I felt we were signing, potentially, one of the best players in the world. What made him special was that he was a wonderful combination of several of my favourite Spurs players. He had something of the Dave Mackay about him, even down to the barrel chest, and yet like Waddle he struck me as an old-fashioned player who might not have been out of place in Arthur Rowe's push-and-run team that came up from the Second Division and immediately won the League Championship in 1950/51. This may sound strange given that Gascoigne is now considered the epitome of media hype. But that relates to Gazza, the person who was created after the 1990 World Cup, not Gascoigne the player.

Gianni Agnelli has said that Paul Gascoigne is 'a dog of war with the face of a child'. To me, Gascoigne suggests a parallel with Marilyn Monroe. Just as Monroe had the body of a woman and the heart of a child, so Gascoigne has the body of a very well developed man with the instincts of a teenager who can never stop playing pranks. Bobby Robson, the then England manager, called him 'daft as a brush', and Gazza responded by turning up for the next England practice match with a brush tucked under his shirt. Some time later, when there was a great deal of Press speculation about his contract, he turned up at the training ground with a £50 note sellotaped to his forehead and trained the whole morning in that manner. That summed him up. He was a man who could never stay still and could only keep his restless mind active by indulging in the most outrageous and silly antics.

So if the team coach got stuck in traffic and Gascoigne had finished reading his *Beano*, he would go round the coach aggravating and annoying everybody. Alan Harris once said that if Gascoigne hadn't been such a talented player, he'd have run him out of Tottenham so fast his feet wouldn't have touched the ground. But even Harris, while describing him as a pest, couldn't help liking him and thought that he had some of the mental make-up of John Burridge, who was very short and tried to extend his goalkeeper's reach by hanging for hours from his landing. What singled out Gascoigne was that he carried on such childlike activities all the time. Bored by standing in the Tottenham reception, he would superglue all the phones together, or when he was staying at the Swallow Hotel in Hertfordshire – while he looked for a house in London – he let off the fire extinguisher at 3 am. Not all his pranks were quite so innocent. He enjoyed shooting, and tried to get a licence to obtain a gun by getting Alan Harris to sign a form. When Harris questioned it, Gascoigne pretended I had approved the idea. When Harris said that he would check with me, Gascoigne, realising the game was up, immediately withdrew the application.

At least one of his pranks nearly led to disaster, and Gascoigne might have never become Gazza but for a stroke of fortune. In the old east stand we had an area called the Crow's Nest where the Press box of the Fifties and Sixties had been located. This had long since been condemned and sealed off, and nobody went there except the pigeons whose droppings would occasionally cover the seats beneath, leading to loud complaints from season ticket holders. Soon after Gascoigne arrived at Spurs the groundsman started noticing dead pigeons on the pitch, but before we could call in Hercule Poirot, the mystery was solved by Gascoigne himself, albeit unwittingly.

It seemed that, somehow, he had been climbing into the Crow's Nest and picking off the pigeons with his air-gun. He might have got away with it, but as luck would have it, one afternoon, as he was trying to shift to a better position, his foot landed on one of the weaker floorboards and he went right through. I shudder to imagine what might have happened, but luckily for him and for us he landed on a seat nearly ten or fifteen feet below. Apart from bruising on his arm there was no serious injury. After this his air-gun was taken away and he was banned, but when I recovered from the shock of thinking what might have been, I could not help laughing. He'd showed the childlike quality of the man. Gascoigne was twenty-one going on eleven.

Perhaps this was best summed up for me when I later learned that like so many children he was terrified of the dark. He would often share a room at away matches with Waddle, who would get up in the middle of the night to find that Gascoigne had left the lights on because he couldn't sleep in the dark. Waddle somehow coped with this, but he was tempted to show Gascoigne the red card when he got up one day to make a cup of tea and found bubbles coming out of the kettle's spout. It seemed Gascoigne had mixed shampoo in the water.

Monroe's beauty combined with her childlike qualities made every man want to possess her. Gascoigne's ability on the field combined with his tomfoolery made us fantasise that we could play like him. To an extent all football players generate such dreams. They give us a vicarious thrill, and when I was a young boy still dreaming of playing for Tottenham, I would go home after a match rehearsing the moves my heroes had made as if by doing so I could recreate the same magic. It is only when you see the truly great players that you realise that such magic cannot be easily reproduced. Genius may be 90 per cent perspiration, but the hallmark of a great player is that he makes it appear as if it is 90 per cent inspiration. The difficult is made to look ridiculously simple, the impossible quite mundane. It is only when we ordinary mortals try and copy them that we realise how devilishly difficult it is.

For those who don't care about football or sports, grown men watching twenty-two other grown men kick a ball may seem daft. If I have spent most of my life watching it with pleasure it is because football has the ability to lift you to another sphere, and recreate the uncomplicated world of childhood we all would like to re-enter.

The other striking quality that great players have is their self-belief. Ardiles had it, so did Hoddle and, of course, so does Gascoigne. Ardiles was already one of the stars of Tottenham when I took over the club. Like all Spurs fans I had been thrilled when in a brilliant, audacious move, Tottenham, just promoted from the Second Division, had signed him and Villa after the 78 World Cup. To me he seemed handcrafted for Spurs, with an air of self-belief that was marvellously uplifting.

I came across it, soon after I took over Spurs, when I got involved in the negotiations to bring him back to White Hart Lane. The Falklands War, which had started as Tottenham were on their way to make their second successive appearance at Wembley, had forced him into exile on a year's loan to Paris St Germain. But by the winter of 1982 it was clear that he was not happy in Paris and wanted to come back to London. I, along with Keith Burkinshaw, then Tottenham's manager, flew to Paris to arrange for his return, and I was struck by his inner self-belief. I had met him before when I was a star-struck fan and he was a great player. Now we met as equals, and it was at this meeting that my relationship with players changed. I no longer experienced that sense of wonder and awe that I had felt before.

After we had quickly and successfully concluded the negotiations with Paris St Germain, Ardiles drove us back to the airport and kept reassuring Keith that the moment he was back in Tottenham's colours, the team's fortunes would pick up. In a lesser player this might have appeared irritating bombast. In the case of Ardiles it only illustrated why he was an exceptional player.

Of course, Ardiles was different, and not merely because he was Argentinian. Generally European and foreign players have higher educational standards than English players, but even by this criterion Ardiles was special, having qualified as a lawyer in his native Argentina. This gave everything he said a certain weight and gravitas which no English player could match. But what made him special was that he had the ability to blend in with another culture and another style of playing while retaining his own distinctive personality – both on and off the field. I cannot imagine any English player travelling to Buenos Aires and making such an impact. Even before I had arrived in the Tottenham boardroom this had made him a hero amongst the supporters and a mentor for some of the players. Tottenham's song during its 1981 Cup winning run was centred upon Ardiles, and when I met him I could easily see why he had made such an impression.

Ardiles managed to strike up a rapport with almost everyone at Tottenham, even Steve Archibald, and that is saying something. It's not for nothing that the Scots are known for being dour, but even by this standard Archibald could be extremely taciturn. However, Ardiles managed to communicate with him, and this always seemed to me to be a testimony to his exceptional character. Not everyone at Spurs always appreciated him. Both Burkinshaw and his successor Peter Shreeve did, but I had to fight hard to keep him at Spurs when David Pleat arrived. Pleat, for all his reputation as a connoisseur of good football, wanted to release Ardiles. True, by then he was not quite the player he had been before the Falklands War. Indeed he was, to an extent, the football casualty of that war. After his return from Paris to Spurs he was often dogged by injury, fracturing his shin not once but twice, and by the time Pleat arrived he had rarely completed a full season, having played only forty games in four seasons between 82/83 and 85/86.

But at the end of the 86/87 season David was to thank me for preventing him from letting Ardiles go. In that season Ardiles had once again demonstrated his class and his greatness as a player. If Hoddle was the stoker in the engine room of Pleat's almost revolutionary five-man midfield, then Ardiles was his most able first mate. Long before the end of the season David had begun to purr with pleasure in the way these two combined to produce some of the most thrilling moments of that beautiful, but in the end, sad season.

The only man at Tottenham that Ardiles didn't strike a chord with was Terry Venables. I could never quite get to the bottom of this. Certainly they couldn't have been more dissimilar. Terry from Dagenham and Ardiles from Buenos Aires were not only geographically but culturally worlds apart. Nothing could have seemed more strange to Ardiles than leading the karaoke as Terry, I am told, now does at one of his clubs in London; similarly the measured, thoughtful utterances bred in the middle-class suburbs of Buenos Aires must have seemed a world removed from the Essex boy who saw the ready smile and the quick riposte as his way up the greasy ladder.

Later, and particularly during my final year at Tottenham, it became fashionable to speculate that if Terry took over the club he would appoint Ardiles as manager. It always amused me to read such speculation, because I knew that they were like chalk and cheese, and it seemed to me that Terry could not wait to get rid of Ardiles almost as soon as he became Manager. He did not play him in the notorious Port Vale match that saw one of our worst Cup defeats, and towards the end of the season when Blackburn, pushing for promotion to the First Division, came for him he was quick to offload him. It is ironic that Ardiles, probably the best passer of the ball English football has seen in the last twenty years, should have played his last match for Tottenham at Wimbledon, where they only pass the ball when handing it to the referee before the start of the match. But then life is full of such ironies.

Ardiles' and Gascoigne's presence at White Hart Lane was in the great tradition of Tottenham buying talent rather than making it. This had been the case with much of the Double side, and of course with players like Gilzean, Greaves, Chivers,

Peters and many others. It was this that had given Tottenham the reputation as big spenders, in contrast with Arsenal, who were more inclined to parade home-grown talent. This was even more evident during my time at Spurs. George Graham's great successes at Highbury were built on the back of a remarkable array of young players who knew nothing else but Arsenal: Davis, Rocastle, Thomas, O'Leary, Adams, Merson, and now Kevin Campbell and David Hillier.

The Highbury youth system goes back to the Bertie Mee/Don Howe era when Arsenal produced their own Double side, and is based on the club's philosophy of producing clones of the senior side. I don't mean this unkindly, but Arsenal, dating back to Herbert Chapman in the Thirties, whose success made the club, have always believed in a system. To a Spurs fan such methods are anathema, as is Arsenal's play in general, but I must say that in recent years they have worked. The young player joining Arsenal is allotted a role within the Highbury system and groomed for a place in the first team. Every club produces a type of player that expresses its personality, and there is a definite Arsenal type where brawn seems to be more prominent than brain, and method and application more valued than skill.

It is not that we at Spurs did not attract young talent. There was plenty of it, but somehow – and this went way back before my time – we never seemed to keep hold of them. Des Walker, Kerry Dixon and Graeme Souness were all youth players at Tottenham who did not make the grade and had to go elsewhere to show their true worth. Steve Sedgley was another such player, although he doesn't fall into the great bracket.

Of course it is not easy to judge young talent. In the old days at Spurs the decision as to whether professional terms should be offered to young players was decided by a committee of three: Keith Burkinshaw, Bill Nicholson and Peter Shreeve. Shreeve, for instance, was keen to keep Kerry Dixon but was outvoted by Nicholson and Burkinshaw. In my experience Peter was probably the best picker of young talent that I know. It was Keith who persuaded Ian Walker, then a schoolboy goalkeeper, to sign for Spurs amid very stiff opposition from other clubs. The moment he did Peter rang me and said that he had signed the next Peter Shilton. (I believe Peter may well be right. The only doubt I have about Walker is his height.)

But if you win with one young player, there are others who

never make it. David Cliss was hailed at Chelsea as the new Jimmy Greaves. In the Sixties Tottenham had a player called Shoemaker, and the same week that we signed Chris Waddle we also signed Sean Murray from the same part of the world as Waddle. Every major club in the country was chasing him, and he'd been invited to spend a week at several clubs including Manchester United and Arsenal.

Peter got young Sean to spend a week at Tottenham, and for one five-a-side game he put Sean into Glenn Hoddle's team, with Steve Perryman in the opposition team. Before they kicked off knowing winks were exchanged between the players, and Steve allowed Sean to go past him at first, in order to give him a bit of confidence. But Sean put the ball through Steve's legs, a beautiful little nutmeg, and Steve got very angry about it, thinking Sean was taking the mickey. At the end of the game several of our first-team players were convinced that Sean would be the next great talent. But he never made it, and eventually Terry Venables sold him to Portsmouth for £100,000.

The one young player I regret Spurs missing out on is Bradley Allen, Clive's younger brother. I had seen him play in a youngsters game at the training ground, and although only thirteen, he seemed to have all the tricks of Clive plus the added benefit of pace. With Les having played for Spurs, in the Double team, and David Pleat talking to him I was convinced we were going to sign Bradley, but just as everything seemed in order I found that he had gone to Queen's Park Rangers, where he was Jim Gregory's last signing for the club. I made my displeasure known to David in no uncertain terms, saying that we might end up having to pay a large transfer fee for him in the future, but he just shrugged it off.

It was poor Clive who felt the backlash from the Tottenham players, and for a few days he was sent to Coventry, with none of the first-team players talking to him. Clive kept protesting that he had nothing to do with it and it was all his father Les's doing. Much later, when I mentioned this to Jim Gregory, he made a joke of it saying: 'How dare you try and sign one of the Allen family. Don't you know that I have a contract on each and every one of them?'

In order to judge talent, you also need an expert scouting system. At Tottenham, alas, we do not have one. So we missed a few who went on to win England caps after being rejected by Tottenham. Stuart Pearce, the England captain and Nottingham

Forest defender, had been playing at Wealdstone, across North London, when we sent our chief scout Ted Buxton to watch him. The word came back he was not good enough. The fee then would have been around £40,000. Coventry came in and paid it. Within twelve months Brian Clough had cleverly gambled on him and paid £375,000. He has proved to be an outstanding investment.

Ted Buxton was guilty of another error in judgement when he was sent to watch a young striker playing at Hibs called Gordon Durie. Chelsea and Tottenham were both interested at around £350,000. Ted told us he was not strong enough or good enough for the First Division. Chelsea signed him, and in the summer of 1991 he went to Tottenham for £2.2 million. It was another example of the inefficiency of our scouting network.

David Pleat rejected Ian Wright and Andy Gray when Crystal Palace, then in the Second Division, offered us the pair for £150,000 each. Wright later went to Arsenal for £2.5 million and Gray joined Tottenham in the summer of 1992 for £750,000. But the miss that really upset me was when Manchester United moved in to sign Lee Sharpe from Torquay for £60,000 in the summer of 1989. We had taken a full back from Torquay a year earlier for a week's trial. Cyril Knowles managed Torquay, and when I saw that they had sold Sharpe to United I asked Terry Venables if we had ever been offered him, or if any of our scouts had watched him. The answer was no. The signing intrigued me and I asked Terry to find out why Sharpe had not been recommended to us.

Bill Nicholson contacted Cyril Knowles, and he told us that he had been upset at the way that we had treated Torquay over the transfer of King. He had been recommended to us by Knowles when Pleat was manager. Pleat gave King, then rated at £100,000, a seven-day trial and rejected him. King eventually played First Division football with Sheffield Wednesday. Knowles felt hurt by the way we had treated him. So when Manchester United came in, Knowles decided to sell. Sharpe helped United win the European Cup Winners' Cup in 1991, and was the Professional Footballers' Association Young Player of the Year in the same season. He was probably their best signing for five years.

Contrary to popular belief, money can buy success. Liverpool is the outstanding example of that fact, and until the 91/92 season one could hardly name a single player of any note that Liverpool had produced from its youth system. But a home-grown player is an obvious advantage. It means a big saving on the transfer market, and I was never able to work out why the coaches at Tottenham could not produce more of them. The most striking example was the comparison of the two Pauls: Paul Merson and Paul Moran. They emerged at about the same time but while Merson, working his way through the youth set up at Highbury, has flowered so well that he has played for England, Moran – despite much promise – has never even secured a regular first-team place at White Hart Lane.

Critics have suggested that this may be because Spurs look for individuality rather than consider a player as a piece to complete a pre-determined jigsaw. Spurs coaches always seem to be looking to produce another Glen Hoddle. Clearly it is much easier to clone players for a system such as Arsenal's rather than produce a whole race of Glenn Hoddles. Hoddle, of course, was the one great Tottenham player to emerge from the youth team.

I remember being told about Glenn when he was still in the Tottenham youth team by a friend who knew Alan Curbishley's brother well. Curbishley, who was in the West Ham junior team, told my friend that Tottenham had the best young player he had ever seen. The friend excitedly passed on the information to me. 'If this lad gets to the first team,' he said, 'then Spurs will have one of the great players.'

Hoddle was only sixteen at the time, but already other players were beginning to notice the talent that was to blossom at White Hart Lane for the next thirteen years. I shall always cherish the fact that I saw his full début. It was against Stoke City at the Victoria Ground on 21 February 1976. I was just an ordinary supporter who followed the club all over the country at that time, but I recognised something special in Hoddle. He scored a wonderful goal that afternoon. He beat Shilton, then the best goalkeeper in the country, all ends up with a left-foot shot to score his first of many goals for Tottenham. Over the years Hoddle was to epitomise everything that Spurs stood for and embody the principles of Tottenham's footballing tradition.

By the time I took over at Spurs, Hoddle had already played for England and become the darling, not only at Spurs, where he was given that rarely bestowed accolade 'King of White Hart Lane', but with a wider group of fans who saw him as the great white hope of English football. That he did not fulfil those expectations is now well known, and Ron Greenwood, who initially picked him for England and then discarded him despite a wonderful début against Bulgaria, has a lot to answer for. England team managers always seem to distrust natural talent. Alf Ramsey will never be forgiven by Spurs fans for dropping Jimmy Greaves during the final stages of the 1966 World Cup. England went on to win the Cup, but Greenwood, who could have built his team around Hoddle, treated him as a luxury, and in the process achieved little.

However, what shook me when I took over at Spurs was to discover that Keith Burkinshaw had doubts about Hoddle. Hoddle himself believes that Keith was really a follower of the long-ball game, who was always chiding him for his low work-rate and unwillingness to come back to defend. Four years before our takeover Keith and Glenn had had a public row, with Keith dropping Glenn from the side and Glenn rowing with him on the team coach and asking for a transfer. After the story leaked in the Press, Keith accused him of being a spoilt child.

However, by 1982 I thought all this was history, only to discover that Keith still felt that Hoddle was a bit of a 'Glenda', the unkind nickname given to him by northern critics and fans who saw him as a southern softie. Keith's own Yorkshire origins may have contributed to this distrust, and every now and again he would come to the boardroom and have a moan about Hoddle: 'We'll never win the League with Glenn in the side.' The logic of this was very suspect, since a good team cannot be made better by dropping a great player. But what annoyed me was that Keith never came up with an alternative. He did not suggest a player who could replace Hoddle and win us the elusive League title. Keith just seemed to be hoping that Hoddle would go away, preferably abroad, as he himself wanted to do.

Glenn could have moved to Cologne when he was twenty-one. He agreed terms, and then at the last moment decided, wisely, that it was not the right move. But he lived in the hope that one day his fairy princess from the Continent would come, and this led to a strange contractual situation. Throughout the Burkinshaw era the longest contract he would sign at White Hart Lane was for two years. More often than not he was on a one-year deal. Each April and May there would be masses of newspaper talk of Hoddle moving but no firm enquiries, so another one-year contract would be signed. I was unhappy about this, but it was not until after Burkinshaw had left that I could do anything, and then it provided a wonderful insight into how insecure a player, even a great player like Hoddle, can feel.

In August 1984 we were in Nice on a pre-season tour in the first year of Peter Shreeve's management. We had Mario Kempes, the Argentine World Cup star, on loan at the time, and had arranged the match to look at him. Unfortunately, after about only twenty-five minutes Glenn damaged his Achilles tendon. He was carried off on a stretcher and it was soon clear that his ankle would have to go into plaster. Glenn was going to be out of action for almost half a season. I suddenly recognised my chance.

Players are fatalistic. When they get injured they all wonder if they will ever play again. In those times of doubt they all look for some security. I thought the best way to give Glenn that hope was to offer him a four-year contract. We held some preliminary talks and then, with the first team playing another pre-season match at Brentford, I felt that I could conclude a deal.

The talks began around lunchtime, and it was not until five or ten minutes before kick-off that I managed to force my way into the Griffin Park directors' box. Peter Shreeve was already sitting there watching the pre-match routines. 'How did it go?' he asked. I turned to him: 'Glenn Hoddle will be a Tottenham player for the next four years.' Hoddle was now a Spurs player until the end of the 87/88 season, when he could go for a fee of £400,000. This is something he had insisted on, and I was happy with that. Peter's face lit up. He was a great admirer of Hoddle, having worked with him since he appeared in the youth team, and they were kindred footballing spirits, with a passion for pure football and an abhorrence of the long-ball game.

What was really memorable about that agreement was that Glenn signed a blank contract. This showed the bond of trust between the club and the player. Hoddle knew that whatever was agreed would be fully honoured. His dreams of playing abroad did not die, but apart from one cursory enquiry from Ajax, then managed by Cruyff – who shared an agent with Hoddle – there was never a whisper. I was able to persuade him to disregard the Ajax interest, predicting that a much bigger Italian or Spanish club would one day come for him. In the end I couldn't keep Hoddle, although I could hardly have imagined that he would sign for my alternative home-town club – Monaco.

If retaining Hoddle in the mid-Eighties had provided me with a glimpse of the fears and prejudices of a player, then his eventual departure for the Continent, or 'frogland' as the *Sun* calls it, was an illustration of the complicated world of player transfer – something that people outside football have difficulty in understanding. Buying or selling players is not like buying a can of beans or even a property: apart from a player's emotions and feelings, it often involves the whims and the prejudices of the men who run the clubs.

Paris St Germain was the first club to show its hand. They had been watching Hoddle for some time, and they came to see him at White Hart Lane in the penultimate match of the 1986/87 season against Oxford. Spurs won 3-1, but what is more, Hoddle, as a gift to all his fans, scored a breathtaking goal. I can still picture it. He picked up the ball on the halfway line, knocked it between two defenders, drew the goalkeeper, waltzed round him, and stroked the ball calmly into the net. As it happened, that turned out to be his last goal for Spurs, but what a perfect way to end a glittering career. Afterwards, sitting in one of the seats in the stands, he was interviewed by Brian Moore and Glenn spoke about his plans to play abroad.

The contingent from Paris St Germain were very impressed. This included the same Francis Borelli whom I had dealt with over the re-signing of Ossie Ardiles, and their Vice-Chairman and coach Gerald Houllier, now national team manager. After the match, accompanied by David Pleat, we arranged to meet at a restaurant in London's West End to discuss the details. Little did I know that we were about to see the start of a French farce that would test the ingenuity even of Peter Sellers's Inspector Clouseau.

The farce began, as farces always do, in a simple enough way. Paris St Germain wanted to know the price for Hoddle. After the finish he had provided against Oxford I felt confident at asking for £1 million. The Parisian contingent ate their dinner, talked pleasantly and left without giving a definite answer. For several days we heard nothing. Then the phone rang and the Paris President said the club was serious about Hoddle and that they wanted to come to London to discuss it further.

In flew their Vice-President, Charles Talar, along with Houllier. I told them again our asking price was £1 million. They again said they were interested but made no serious offer. It was now that what should have been a simple negotiation was acquiring the element of a charade. Paris St Germain began sending us a flood of telexes. Some would contain an offer, then this would be countermanded by other telexes denying that any offer had been made, and offering totally different figures. Eventually, I tired of this nonsense and flew to Paris to see the club's officials. I had had a telex which said that they were prepared to start talking at £600,000. But when the talks began it appeared that they were not prepared to pay more than £500,000. Producing their own telexes I said: 'Read them. These are your own telexes and they clearly indicate you are prepared to pay at least £600,000.'

It was clear that we would not get near £1 million and I informed the Paris officials that we were prepared to accept £750,000. I shall never forget their reaction. They went white. In the end I was convinced that Paris St Germain was just playing games and, probably, did not even have the money to make the deal. What really annoyed me was that Borelli kept telling me what a great player Hoddle was, but could not even find £600,000 to buy him.

However, the farce ended not in tears but in smiles. This is because while Paris St Germain were messing us about, Monaco came up with the goods. The day after the talks broke down with Paris St Germain, I met Jean-Louis Campora, the Monaco President, at the Beach Plaza Hotel in Monte Carlo. The setting matched the mood of the discussions. It was nine in the morning, the sun was already high over the Mediterranean and the water looked invitingly blue. Jean-Louis asked: 'How much do you want for Hoddle?'

'We price him at £750,000.'

As I spoke these words Jean-Louis fell silent, and I could hear the waters lapping the beach. But the silence did not last for more than thirty seconds. Then he said: 'OK.' We shook hands and Hoddle was on his way to Monaco. I just could not believe the difference in the attitude of these two French clubs when it came to buying players. Certainly Paris St Germain could outmatch the most perfidious Albion.

I have said that great players always know what they want, both on the field and off it. And while Richard Gough had not yet proved himself to be a great player in the same bracket as Ardiles or Hoddle, his self-belief was the first thing that struck me. If his signing for Tottenham in the summer of 1986 was a major coup both for me and David Pleat, it also brought home to me the complex world of English soccer transfers, involving as it does chairmen, the role of the Press, and also that most pernicious unseen power: the wife.

Gough was not Pleat's first choice. It was only when Terry Butcher slipped away to Glasgow Rangers from Ipswich that I could persuade David to look at him. He was then at Dundee United, and I had been told that he was unhappy and might be available for around £600,000. I immediately rang Alex Ferguson, then still managing Aberdeen, to ask his advice. Ferguson had no doubts. 'Richard is the biggest winner in football. If you can sign him do not hesitate – you will not regret it.' I gave David the go-ahead to negotiate with Jim McLean, the Dundee United Manager, and we settled on a fee of £650,000. The United board ratified this on a Thursday evening, and it was agreed that Gough would play his last game for them at Ibrox on the Saturday and then fly the next morning to London and tie the knot with Tottenham.

It was at this stage that the first of the outside influences that affect English soccer transfers began to manifest itself. You may not always believe all that you read in the newspapers, but their back pages, particularly that of the tabloids, can make or mar a transfer. On the Saturday evening, having blissfully spent the day thinking that Gough would at last solve the hole in Tottenham's defence that had existed since the departure of Mike England, I was jolted to receive a call from David.

'Do you know what's happened?' he asked.

'No,' I replied.

'Ken Bates has jumped in with an offer of £750,000 for Richard Gough, and when he comes to London he's going to see Chelsea first. You must speak to the Dundee United Chairman to save the deal.'

It seemed what had happened was that on Friday the *Daily Record* had broken the news of Gough's impending departure to Tottenham. On Saturday, the *Daily Mirror* had picked up the story from its sister paper in Scotland, and it was this item that had sparked Bates's interest. He was offering cash plus Doug Rougvie, which Dundee thought came to £750,000.

I could have insisted on our legal rights. The law in Scotland is different to that in England: there an agreement between two parties is binding and the words 'subject to contract' mean nothing. Our offer on Gough was only subject to agreeing personal terms with him and his passing a medical, but I knew that the law could not help me here. I initially appealed to the Dundee United Chairman's sense of professionalism – he was an accountant – and then realised that it was a question of money. Before we came in he had received an offer of £800,000 from Rangers, but did not want to sell to a rival. I offered him

£750,000, with the extra £100,000 to be paid in two years' time.

He agreed, but still insisted that Gough would first see Chelsea. This was too much for me. I knew first come first serve is an important principle as much in the supermarket as in buying players, and I got the Chairman to agree that when Gough emerged from the plane at London the first person he would see would be David Pleat.

This is just what happened, and David took him to an hotel in Hertfordshire, where I joined them. The first thing that struck me was Richard's firm handshake. A player being transferred can often be like a virginal bride on her wedding night, shy and unsure. Instead, Richard knew exactly what he wanted and quickly spelt out his terms, which after a little bit of haggling – they were on the high side – we agreed. I have always believed that players should be given an incentive, and his five-year contract had a review after two years. I was sure we had signed a future Spurs captain, and whispered as much to David as we left for lunch.

I was even more convinced of this with Richard's first act on becoming a Spurs player. He turned to me and said: 'Do you mind if I make a call to Chelsea? I owe that to Ken Bates to tell him that I have signed for Spurs and won't be meeting him.'

I still remember the conversation vividly.

'Mr Bates? Richard Gough here.'

'Hello Richard, how are you?'

'Fine Mr Bates. I'm ringing to tell you that I have signed for Spurs, I won't be seeing you today. Thank you for your interest.'

'You f****** Scottish c***,' Bates replied, in a voice that we could all hear. 'I have wasted my Sunday morning. Sunday is a family day for me you f*****, I've got better things to do now, now f*** off.'

Blaster Bates at his best!

Gough's arrival at White Hart Lane provided me another little peep into managers' psychology. He was Pleat's first major signing, and when we opened the season, with a 3-0 victory at Aston Villa and Clive Allen scoring a hat trick, the Press, naturally, wanted to talk to David about Clive Allen. But he only had words for Gough, comparing him to David Mackay. Allen had come to Spurs under Pleat's predecessor, and managers, as I was to learn, always like to talk about the players they have bought rather than the team they have inherited. Gough himself was rather amused by how easy the opening game had been, and afterwards asked me: 'Is it this easy every week?' I assured him it was not, but the tougher it got the better he got, and long before the end of the season I had begun to share some of David's feeling that we might have discovered another Scot in the mould of Mackay.

However, it was not to be. Gough lasted just one season at White Hart Lane, his departure almost coinciding with David's, but for very different reasons. It was this that brought home to me the influence of football wives, an influence that cost us a potentially great player. Even before coming to London, Richard had a turbulent marriage. London worsened it. His wife never settled and eventually moved back to Scotland, taking their young son with her. Throughout the autumn of 1987 I tried to persuade him not to follow her back north of the border, and suggested all sorts of ideas, including spending alternate weekends in Scotland and London. But Richard had made up his mind to go, and launched what was the most remarkable guerrilla campaign I have ever seen in football. It seemed from his actions that if we didn't let him go he would make life impossible for the team: the great leader was threatening to become the great wrecker. In September, we played Manchester United at Old Trafford, losing by a penalty. A mistimed tackle by Ardiles had led to the penalty, and back in the dressing room, Richard threatened to virtually demolish it. He began screaming and shouting at the other players and in particular Ardiles. His language that day could not have been bettered by Ken Bates at his Sunday best, and he never played for Tottenham again.

By this time Glasgow Rangers had made an offer for him, and I knew we could not hold on to Richard. Even then I tried to make it as difficult as possible for Rangers to buy him, and when David Holmes, their then Chairman, asked me a price I said: '£1.5 million.' This was unheard-of then, and both Holmes and later Souness thought I was being crazy in asking such a stupid price. However, within days of the first enquiry they came up with the money, and a little over a year after I had shaken his hand in the Hertfordshire hotel he was back in his native Scotland.

Two years later, when we played Rangers in a friendly at Ibrox, I once again shook hands with Richard. His marriage had ended and his career both for Rangers and for Scotland had been dogged by injury. He said: 'I made a mistake when I came back to Scotland. I should have stuck it out at Tottenham, you were right.' His words did little to cheer me up, although they rekindled some hopes that we might sign him again. We spoke once or twice after that, and Terry even spoke to Souness, but nothing came of it. A man made for Tottenham had been lost because of women problems.

Gough's was not the only case where wives either wrecked our plans or caused complications. Paul Allen's wife, Dominique, nearly threw a spanner in the works when we were trying to sign Paul from West Ham. In 1980, at the age of seventeen, he had become the youngest player to play in a Cup Final for West Ham, but in 1985, just as we were signing Chris Waddle, he was out of contract. Bill Nicholson was very impressed with him and felt that he could become the next Steve Perryman for Tottenham. We thought we had all the aces in trying to persuade Paul to come to us. He was being advised by his Uncle Denis, who was an old friend of Peter Shreeve.

This is where Dominique came into the picture. She was expecting their first child, and encouraged him to listen to all offers, particularly from Liverpool, who were very keen to get him as well. Eventually we persuaded him to sign, and for a fee of £400,000 set by the tribunal he proved an excellent buy. I was delighted when in 1989, a year before his contract finished, Paul decided to turn down a move to Millwall. Terry had accepted an offer of £700,000 from them, and despite the fact that they dangled before Paul substantial increases in salary, he decided to stay at Tottenham and fight his way back into the first team.

Two years before Gough signed I had tried to bring Maxime Bossis, who became part of Platini's wonderful European Championship-winning side, to Spurs. He was then out of contract at Nantes and I flew there to meet him. He seemed very keen, we could meet his personal terms, and soon afterwards he and his wife came to London to look around the town and Tottenham. It was then I realised that whatever Bossis might propose, his wife decided. She was a formidable woman, in the way some French women can be, and raised a number of doubts about the education of her children, the language problems and housing in London. The moment they left I knew Bossis would not be back, and soon he signed for the now defunct Racing Club of Paris.

Another woman, this time a Belgian lady, came close to wrecking our plans for getting Nico Claesen. David and I had spotted him during the 1986 World Cup in Mexico. He had been particularly brilliant when Belgium beat the Soviet Union 4-3 in what I thought was one of the best matches of the World Cup. David, who was in Mexico as a television expert, rang me in the morning after the match and I asked him what he thought of Claesen. David shared my enthusiasm for the player and had already asked a Dutch journalist friend of his to find out more details. In September, his club, Standard Liège, who had pressing financial problems, appeared interested in offers, and David quickly arranged a meeting in Brussels to discuss matters with the player's adviser and the Liège general manager. Everything went smoothly, but then we discovered a problem. Claesen's wife Dominique, the daughter of a wealthy Belgian builder, was well settled in her native country and not too keen to move. I invited both of them to London and arranged for an estate agent to show her the area where most of the Tottenham players lived and give her some feel of what family life she might expect.

But if she was impressed she kept this to herself, and when she returned to the ground she told Nico that they could come to no decision until she had returned to Belgium and discussed it with her parents. By this time we had agreed almost everything else with Nico, and he was quite keen to sign for Spurs there and then. But Dominique would not budge and the couple started arguing. Claesen's manager then made a disparaging remark about her in English, and to our amazement she answered back in English. We had been told she didn't speak a word. It seemed her reluctance to let Nico sign on that day stemmed from a short spell he had with Stuttgart, when he had been unhappy and she had ended up hating the city.

Dominique won out that day, and Nico and she went back to Belgium without agreeing anything, but clearly, in this case, our powers of persuasion worked. Within a few days Nico was back in London signing up as a Tottenham player. I don't know whether David was thinking of Dominique when he referred to the purchase of Nico as a bit like buying an expensive fur coat for your wife and not knowing how good it was until she put it on, but as it happened Dominique settled in very well, and was well liked by the other players' wives. Nico as a player was just as great a favourite with the supporters, and I enjoyed his play immensely. But he never got the opportunities his talents deserved, and as David played a five-man midfield with a lone striker up front in Clive Allen, he often found himself playing out of position.

David's departure decreased Nico's chances of playing even more. He didn't seem to fit in with Terry Venables's plans, and it became clear that it was only a question of time before he was sold. Souness was interested in him, and when Terry told him he could go for £600,000 this did not seem to bother Souness. But nothing came of it, and I wonder if it was because Claesen was a Catholic. At that stage Rangers had never signed a Catholic player, and when Souness did sign Mo Johnston he was later to admit that he had to make sure that the first Catholic player was the right one. I do not know what Dominique would have made of Glasgow and its environs. Eventually the couple returned home when we accepted an offer of £475,000 for Nico from Royal Antwerp.

Of course, wives are not the only ones who can make or mar a transfer: so can dogs. In 1984 I was convinced that I had secured Morton Olsen for Tottenham. He was an integral part of the successful Anderlecht side whom we had beaten in the 1984 UEFA Cup Final, and the central element of the rise of the Danish team to European soccer supremacy in the early Eighties. Although he was thirty-six he was still supremely fit, and when Peter Shreeve and I met him in Copenhagen he was quite keen to come to White Hart Lane. His only condition was that his dog must come with him. However, despite our best efforts we could not get the Customs to agree not to put Olsen's dog in quarantine for at least six months, and Olsen decided that if his dog was not immediately welcome then he would not come.

I am inclined to think that even more than women and dogs, the big problem in signing players is the tribunal. This comes into play when a player is out of contract but the club he wants to leave cannot agree a fee with the club he wants to go to. I was to become quite a dab hand at the tribunal, and my most memorable experience of it came when we signed Chris Waddle. His arrival at Spurs showed the number of influences that can be at work during a transfer. Chris had been unhappy at Newcastle for some time, both because of the low wages he was paid and the strange managerial quirks of Jack Charlton. He was coming to the end of his contract, and had heard that both Chelsea and Spurs were interested in him. He had met Glenn playing for England, and Glenn had glowed about

Tottenham, telling him that if he should ever decide to come south, Tottenham would be the club for him.

As the transfer deadline approached, I was so keen to sign Waddle that for almost three weeks I rarely left my house, spending endless hours on the telephone to Stan Seymour, the then Newcastle Chairman. At one stage we even had a plane ready to fly him to London, but in the end, Seymour would not agree and wanted to wait out the season. Had Chris joined us before the end of the 84/85 season, when with ten of our last seventeen games at home we were ideally placed to win the League, things might have been different. He became a free agent on 14 May, and we moved for him just a few days before that. As luck would have it, Spurs were playing at Newcastle, and with the air full of Waddle moving to Spurs, one of the first incidents in the match led to Miller sending him sprawling with a mighty kick. As Waddle dusted himself he said: 'Here, steady. I shall be signing for you in a few days.'

Soon he was in London, and everything went smoothly except for a slight scare raised by the doctor, whose examination discovered a back injury – something to do with his disc, which explains why he has that stoop. It seems even Waddle did not know about this, but fortunately we were able to get an insurance without any exclusion clauses.

I knew the big problem would be the fee. Newcastle and ourselves could not agree, and Waddle, Peter Shreeve, Peter Day and I took the train to Preston North End, where the tribunal were to meet to decide. Newcastle were looking for £750,000; we felt anything under £600,000 would be a bonus. It was on the train that I began to discover that there was more to Waddle than his public image of a shy, taciturn north-easterner. As I normally do on such occasions, I decided to have a football quiz. Peter Day moaned, but to my delight Waddle, who had hardly spoken a word until that stage, perked up and proved to be a good and enthusiastic player.

It proved a happy augury for the tribunal. Newcastle had brought a strong contingent led by Gordon McKeag to argue their case, but these can be delicate affairs. I kept our case simple and spoke for only a minute. Chris explained he wanted to move because he felt it would further his England career and prospects for European honours. McKeag, a solicitor, took fifty-five minutes to argue the Newcastle case. I can still remember how, as the sunlight streamed into the room, most of us –

including the tribunal – started to nod off during his monologue. His verbosity, in my view, cannot have done him any good. The tribunal fixed the fee at £590,000. It would be invidious and untrue to suggest that they must have docked £10,000 because of the time McKeagh took but I couldn't help joking to my team that this might be so. I was delighted, although Newcastle showed themselves to be rather poor losers and left without even wishing Chris good luck.

Detractors of Spurs often talk of the club just buying players, as if the player who arrived at White Hart Lane is a finished product. This is rarely the case. Gascoigne became Gazza two years after he had been at Spurs, and while Waddle was already a fine player when we bought him, I like to think that we had our part in making him a better player, certainly a more round-ed personality. Glenn, whose influence had helped steer Chris in our direction, brought Waddle out of his shell. The two of them ended up making records together, and it was interesting to watch how Waddle grew in his time at White Hart Lane. So much so that four years later he had little hesitation in making the move to Marseille – another world, another culture, and very removed from Newcastle, let alone Tow Law and the sausage factory that he had worked in.

If Waddle's and later Gascoigne's arrival from Newcastle showed that the clubs of the north-east have to contend with their richer, more successful southern rivals, then we at Spurs also had to watch out for others seeking to poach our players. The most daring such attempt on a man widely seen as symbolic of modern Spurs was that by Liverpool on Gary Mabbutt. In some ways this was almost a re-run of the Waddle affair, except we were now at the receiving end. In 1987 Mabbutt had reached the end of his contract and Liverpool were very keen to buy him. So keen indeed that a few weeks after the Cup Final, Kenny Dalglish arrived in London and parked himself outside Mabbutt's home, trying to lure him north. Dalglish saw Mabbutt as a player round whom he could build another Liverpool team.

Mabbutt was then injured, and as I have said, injuries can play havoc with a player's mental condition. Pleat was able to persuade him that his future lay with Spurs, and with Gough's departure he became the captain, a position that further an-chored him to the club. Indeed, even as Dalglish waited in the car, Mabbutt signed for us and then explained to Dalglish why he couldn't join Liverpool.

I could understand why Liverpool would want to sign Mabbutt. They have always looked for players around whom the whole team if not the whole club can be organised. Some years before this, Peter Robinson, their Chief Executive, had pointed to another Spurs player whom he had seen as the sort of person you could build a football club around. That player was Steve Perryman.

Steve, of course, was the club captain when I arrived at Tottenham. Although the captain in football does not mean the same thing as a cricket captain who combines the role of manager, selector and sometimes chairman, it is a position of great symbolic importance in the game. I had no quarrels with Steve as Tottenham's captain. In successive seasons, 1981 and 1982, he held aloft the FA Cup and was the sort of player who could personify the club.

His problem was that he was, at times, a bit too abrasive. There was a great deal of the barrack-room lawyer in him and he often tried to be advocate, judge and jury on behalf of the players. However, irritating as this was, perhaps the most disappointing thing about him was his insularity. Despite the tremendous European experience he had with Tottenham, his attitude gave me the impression that he felt that the ideas of Europeans had to be automatically resisted on all counts. It was this that made him say to me: 'The trouble with you is that you suffer from Europeanitis.' He did not like my references to how the Europeans organised the game, or their very different training methods.

But it had always struck me as absurd that in England the players only train in the morning. I believe this has led to the men-only mates culture that is such a curse of professional English soccer. A few hours' training in the morning, then the player is down in the boozer with his mates drinking his life away. A Continental club would never tolerate the amount of beer drinking English footballers are allowed to indulge in, and I was always struck by the sight of the Monaco players who would eat their post-match meals in a restaurant I frequented. There would be some wine, but generally the drinks would be non-alcoholic, with no sign of beer. The English beer habit arises from an innate belief that football is still a boys' game where a little kick-about in the park is all you need to do well.

Such a culture creates a lot of problems, and we at Tottenham were not exempt from players who could not control their drinking and whose behaviour led them to trouble and reflected on the club. A classic case of this was Jimmy Greaves. George Best has also suffered from it, and in recent years, Arsenal's Paul Merson nearly allowed drink to ruin a promising career. English managers like to talk about their professional approach to the game, but it is surprising how few of them manage to instil even a modicum of professional behaviour in their players. As I write, Terry Venables has had to issue guidelines on discipline, drinking and other matters, which suggests that Spurs players may be very far from the professionals they should be.

I cannot blame the players for this. Soon after I took over at Tottenham I went on a tour of Israel with the team. What struck me then was their enthusiasm for the game and their desire to learn and improve. I think the problem lies with the training system in England, and the fact that the coaches have now devised lifestyles around the fact that many only have to work for their club for half the day. At Tottenham, Ray Clemence and, of course, Terry Venables had outside business interests which took up much of their time during the afternoons.

On the Continent, in contrast, football is seen as a professional game where the player is as much a professional dedicated to his craft as a stonemason or any other person practising a physical activity. The players not only train in the morning, when it is mainly physical training and five-a-side games and other team pursuits, but they are back on the training ground in the afternoons trying to sharpen their individual ball skills. They realise that for all his physical fitness and endurance, a footballer is nothing if he cannot make the ball do his bidding. And you can only do that if you have practised and trained with a ball for long enough to be able to master the basic skills of control, passing and shooting.

I was horrified to discover that not even at Tottenham did the players spend much time with the ball, let alone try and improve their skills on it. When Peter Shreeve took over as Manager I did try and get them to change the routine and take in the best of the Continental methods. Peter, a keen student of the game, and one of the few English managers to go to the 1984 European Championships, was eager. But the players were not, and I was left with some comical ruins. At my suggestion, a wooden cut-out representing a wall of defenders was erected at Tottenham's training ground for players to practise perfecting free kicks. I had seen Platini and Zico use such cut-outs to great effect, and in this case it was clearly better to have wooden dummies than real defenders acting as dummies. I'd been surprised and not a little saddened to see that not even the best of English players could bend the ball round or over a wall at pace. Not even Hoddle could do it, and I've only seen Gascoigne emulating the Continentals in this respect. But on the first day somebody knocked the head off one of the wooden dummies and my little European experiment came to an end.

This desire to inculcate some of the best European techniques made me keen to bring European players to White Hart Lane and with a bit of luck Platini, Boniek, Gullit, and even Maradona might have played for Spurs. In January 1985 I received a call saying that both Platini and Boniek were ready to leave Juventus at the end of their contracts and come to England. Peter and I flew to Turin and we took Boniek out to dinner. But while he claimed he was interested in Spurs he was really also talking to Roma, and later that spring he did join that club.

Platini might have come to White Hart Lane but for Heysel. He had been in the Juventus side in that ghastly European Cup Final, and even scored the winner from the penalty. However, I hoped to persuade him to reconsider and in October 1985, learning that France were playing at home, I went to the team's headquarters just outside Paris. We spoke for an hour and a half, and it was clear that the horror of Heysel was still with him. It caused him nightmares, and he felt he just could not face playing in England. Also there was a relentless pressure being exerted by Gianni Agnelli, the Juventus owner, who kept warning him that England with the number of games and style of play would be too much like a hard slog. Platini would have been out of contract, and had he agreed would have cost no more than £800,000. What a bargain! Eventually he signed again for Juventus, although when that contract finished he did express an interest in coming to Spurs. But by then his personal terms, half a million pounds net a year, for two years, were more than we could afford.

Ruud Gullit and Maradona also proved a bit beyond what we could afford at Spurs. Gullit was then playing for Feyenoord, and they wanted only £250,000 for him, but he wanted the sort of salary that would have wrecked our wages structure, and we just couldn't do that. Instead he went to PSV Eindhoven.

I might have been tempted to break the bank in order to get Maradona to Spurs, and there was just a glimmer of hope when in 1986 he came to White Hart Lane to play in a testimonial for Ardiles. Ardiles had been an idol of Maradona and become something of a footballing father-figure, and just before the match Ossie told me that Maradona would like to meet me. We met for breakfast at 7.15 the next morning at the Portman Hotel. He had two more years of his contract at Napoli, and I suggested that when he came to the end of it we could sign him. He would then be available for the UEFA fee, and we could have arranged a sponsorship to pay him the million that he probably would have wanted. But signing Maradona was never going to be a straightforward transaction, and at the meeting I glimpsed some of the forces at work on him. Maradona, as he has proved, is turbulent enough, and in the end his presence at Napoli proved too combustible. Maybe he was using me as a bait to get better terms elsewhere. Within a year he had signed for Napoli, earning a lot more money, but in the end found he couldn't cope with the pressures, some of them self-generated.

It is ironic to think that back in 1978 when Burkinshaw signed Ardiles and Villa, Maradona very nearly came to England. That signing was done through Harry Haslam, then Manager of Sheffield United. He had been contacted by Rattin, the notorious Argentinian captain sent off at Wembley during the 1966 World Cup Finals. While Haslam was in Argentina Rattin took him to see a seventeen-year-old player who was available for £400,000. Haslam was keen but the Sheffield directors were not. That player, of course, was Maradona.

Just as no man is a hero to his valet, so I suppose no Chairman can be expected to be a hero to his players. In my more than forty years' association with Tottenham, both as supporter and then as Chairman, I saw the relationship between players and chairmen change dramatically. The old regime at Spurs saw the players as commodities, treating them in a very distant and formal fashion. Paul Bobroff may have preferred to carry on that approach, and curiously Terry Venables always spoke of players as 'stock'. He always wanted to have sufficient stock, as if he was a stallholder selling ladies' underwear in Petticoat Lane. It made me bristle every time he used that word. My age – I was only thirty-six when I became Chairman of the football club – let alone my inclinations and nature meant that I saw players as fellow workers, if not friends united in a common cause.

I must say my enthusiasm was at times misunderstood, and has continued to be misrepresented. I may like telling stories and testing people on abstruse football facts, but I don't remember taking Maurice Keston up to the Crow's Nest, nor did I damage my Achilles tendon playing at the training ground. If truth be told, I did it playing for the staff team at that wonderfully evocative venue of mighty European matches, Brisbane Road, home of Leyton Orient.

But the fact that my enthusiasm became the source of improbable stories about my association with players reveals how stuffy and old-fashioned the football world was when I took over at Tottenham, and to a certain extent still is. English football is a young man's game ruled by old men, a sort of sporting version of China, where you have to be at least eighty to be Chairman. That was almost the norm at Spurs before I arrived, and after a generation of the Richardsons and the Wales – 'Mr Richardson and Mr Wale to you, young man' – the idea of a Chairman who was not all that much older than the players and a good deal younger than the coaching staff came as a shock.

Even in the liberated Eighties the idea of a Chairman in football kit seemed outrageous, albeit that I was playing in a friendly kick-about with the staff. Some of the Tottenham staff never got over this, and on one occasion when I was playing at White Hart Lane and a ball was passed in my direction I heard Doug Livermore shout, 'Chairman's ball', in a tone that caused the whole team and me to collapse with laughter.

When I took over as Chairman my mission was to bridge the gap between the playing and coaching staff and the directors, to break a barrier that had grown up and seemed even more impregnable than the Berlin Wall. It was this that led me to start the annual Christmas lunch, when the directors acted as waiters and served all the players and the coaching staff. I cannot say that this was a very original idea. I borrowed it from Douglas Alexiou's father, who did the same in his restaurant in Chelsea, but it worked very well and even Bobroff, who made the most unlikely waiter, began to enjoy it. One man who didn't was Terry Venables, and in his first season as Manager he tried hard to persuade me to cancel it, but I resisted, and in the end Terry accepted that it was not such a bad idea after all.

You could say that there was an element of gimmickry in this, but ever since I became Chairman I had been concerned that the gap between players and supporters was growing. This has been the curse of the modern game. When I first went to White Hart Lane as a boy, players were very close to the supporters. They not only sprang from the same working-class communities but their lifestyles were very similar. I can remember players arriving at the ground having travelled on the same bus or train as the vast majority of the supporters. By the time my car left the gates of White Hart Lane for the last time, players' lifestyle had moved so far away from the fans that not only did they drive in cars that most supporters could only fantasise about, they were even flashier than the cars the directors had – and remember that journalists always wrote about the White Hart Lane car park as if it was the Bond Street of directors' car parks. The end of the maximum wage had meant that players could earn real money, and in the decade that I was at Tottenham, some of the players did earn very considerable sums.

During this time the standard of living had gone up considerably, and the supporters whose money helped pay for the players were themselves earning a lot more than the ones who watched the Double team. But the gap had grown wider, and the game as such was driven by the need to find more money in order to satisfy players' and managers' needs.

I was made vividly aware of this when, in my last season at White Hart Lane, we signed Justin Edinburgh from Southend. As signings go, this hardly matched the glamour ones that we have discussed. Also it followed the by now standard contract whereby Southend was due more money if Justin played a certain number of games: a further £50,000 after he had appeared in twenty-five League games or more. But what made it unusual was that the then Southend Manager, David Webb, had an agreement with his Chairman for a percentage of the money paid to Southend when the appearance clause came into effect. During the negotiations Webb wanted the contract to say twenty-five League and Cup games, which would have meant we would pay the money earlier. In the end we settled for twenty-five League games, and as it happens, with a sense of timing that I still find astonishing, Terry Venables chose him to play in our last match of the 1990/91 season against Manchester United, two days after we had won the Cup, and triggered the £50,000 payment that season instead of the next. I hope David Webb got his cut.

5 | THE MODERN WITCH-DOCTORS

'I did a two-year course in finance. It was a course that lasted one week one year and one week the next.'

– Keith Burkinshaw.

In Terry Venables's view, the most important relationship in a football club is between the Chairman and the Manager. He made the comment just as I was about to sign him. Then I disagreed, now I am inclined to think he may be right. For they are the modern witch-doctors of the game.

To be fair, I never really experienced any serious problems with managers, as we were always straightforward with each other, understanding one another's views and always aiming for the same thing – what was best for Tottenham Hotspur. At least, that is what I believed, although there were instances when managers did what was right for them rather than the club. If I joined the club thinking that both the managers and I had a common goal, I left it aware of how selfish some can be.

Terry had, at that time, just finished working under a completely different system in Spain, where the Manager was really the coach, and all the truly important decisions relating to recruitment of players, finalising of contracts and all other incidental tasks, were dealt with by the General Manager and the board of the club. In contrast, in England the managers seek complete power to run the club.

Keith Burkinshaw, the first Manager I was involved with, wanted to be in on every aspect of the club, many of which had absolutely nothing to do with the football side. Indeed he claimed a universal authority which was vividly illustrated early in 1983 when he came to visit me, with his wife, in the South of France. At the end of several days discussing how we could take Spurs forward, the question of finance came up. He explained that earlier in his career he had taken a two-year course in finance, and was fully capable of handling this side of the club. I couldn't work out how this was possible, bearing in mind that he had been a player, and immediately upon retirement had turned to coaching. How could he have found two full years to devote to the course?

His reply was classic: 'It was a course that lasted one week one year and one week the next.' As he said so he guffawed loudly, clearly relishing the joke. I have replayed those words often, and it has made me realise that there is something called truth, and then there is managers' truth or soccer-speak. They have a way with words which, whilst they may not be untrue, do not quite mean what we all think they mean.

Maybe this springs from the fact that football management is a paranoid profession. George Graham said when he signed as the Manager of Arsenal: 'The only thing on this contract which I don't know is the date I will get the sack.' Tommy Docherty's joke, 'I don't want directors behind me, I want them in front of me to see what they are doing', is well known and explains some of this feeling of insecurity. Their constant fear of the sack, the incessant Press conjecture, together with their own fickleness and that of the crowd, feeds this paranoia. After all, which other profession or business is judged so publicly every seven days or less? Certainly no widget manufacturer could live with such scrutiny.

This explains why managers' behaviour can be so different to most other mortals'. Normally, after a match the team Manager will join the directors and guests for a drink. But many is the time when he hasn't appeared, perhaps unable to face people when everyone is disappointed. I have always found managers at their most humble when things aren't going as well as expected, and it is at these times that it is vital to keep their spirits up and not let everything get on top of them. Losing becomes as much a habit as winning, and managers can start to lose their self-confidence very quickly. I have never put pressure on any Manager during a string of bad results, and always worked hard to put them in a positive frame of mind.

I pride myself on always having been straightforward with all employees, especially managers. There were many times when the crowd were unhappy and results disappointing, and even times when we were sitting at the bottom of Division One. It is at these times, more than any other, that managers need support and confidence from the Chairman and the directors, so that their own self-confidence is not dented even further, which would probably worsen the results.

Even the most confident of managers can become paranoid, as I was to realise just before an important Littlewoods Cup replay at Blackburn in 1988. Terry Venables was looking to replace Bobby Mimms just six months after buying him from Everton, and had a tape of the Norway v. France match in which Erik Thorstvedt kept goal. Terry was keen that I should see it. I explained that if he felt Erik was the man he wanted and the price and terms were acceptable, my seeing the tape was irrelevant as I would back his judgement. But Terry was insistent, and we arranged to meet at my house at 6.30 pm on the night before the Blackburn match.

I arrived about ten minutes late due to heavy traffic to find that Terry had already been waiting thirty minutes. This was unheard of, as he was often late for meetings, so my curiosity was aroused. We talked for about an hour and a half, during which Erik did not really come up in the conversation, but Terry was clearly edgy. Eventually I asked what was wrong, and he said he had received information from a reliable source that I had been in discussion with Steve Coppell at Crystal Palace and that he would be appointed as his replacement within a few days. I explained that no talks whatsoever had taken place, and that he should know me better than to listen to tittle-tattle. Unfortunately, there are a large number of people close to football clubs who seem to delight in other people's misfortunes, and this was obviously yet another case of mischief-making.

I was more than a little surprised to find Terry so nervous, as he always appears to the outside world as a super-confident person. But here he was, clearly stripped of his self-confidence, and very edgy. I felt that he just needed an arm around his shoulder and a lift to know that the people near him were fully supportive. Eventually he left at 8.30 pm to drive up to Blackburn, leaving the tape of Erik, which I must admit I haven't watched to this day. The replay at Ewood Park was won in extra time by a marvellous solo goal from Paul Stewart, the results improved, and so did Terry's confidence.

On the other hand, when the team is doing really well, the Press is good, and the crowd is on their side, managers can be impossible. They become difficult to talk to and start believing their own publicity; real know-alls, arrogant even. They think they have cracked the secret of winning all the time, when as we all know there just isn't one. All the other chairmen I have discussed this with have had similar experiences. It all comes back to the old adage of humility in victory and grace in defeat. The first rule of football management is never believe your own publicity – no matter how good or how bad. Managers in the flush of victory tend to forget all that.

It is then that managers display their most deep-seated and disagreeable trait. This is their belief that unless you have played football professionally, you know nothing about the game – you just don't understand it. This charge is made against nearly all directors and certainly all of the spectators. Their phraseology of calling supporters 'punters', which I personally find deeply offensive, is a clue. They try to create a certain mystique which suggests that only they comprehend the game. Even simple questions can be answered with a combination of arrogance and bluster, so much so that this simple game that has been played for more than a century and is watched by more people on the planet than any other is made to appear more complicated than chess.

The most difficult job in football management must belong to the England Manager, at present Graham Taylor. Like all his predecessors, going back to Alf Ramsey, Taylor appears beleaguered. In some ways his career as England Manager has paralleled that of the man he succeeded. Just as Bobby Robson had a horrendous European Championships in 1988, and faced two years of vitriol from the media, so Graham Taylor, after having qualified for the European Championships, found that England's lack of success made him the target of some remarkable abuse, particularly in the *Sun*, which began to characterise him and the England team as turnips and reported the defeat against Sweden as: Sweden 2, Turnips 1. Graham has been deeply hurt by this criticism, but he is a strong enough individual to recover. Who knows, like Bobby Robson in the 1990 World Cup, he may after all prove a success in 1994.

I hope he does, although I must say I was surprised that when he was appointed as England Manager the short list did not include Terry Venables. Soon after it became known that

Bobby Robson would not be carrying on but would be joining PSV Eindhoven, I got a call, fairly early one morning, from Doug Ellis. Had I received a letter from the FA concerning Terry Venables? I hadn't, and although I scanned the post carefully for the next few days there was no such communication. Later I learned that Terry was not on the list. Apart from Graham Taylor, then Manager of Aston Villa, it included Howard Kendall, then of Manchester City, and Joe Royle of Oldham. In order to avoid Terry's blushes I kept fobbing off journalists who rang me to find out whether he was on the short list. In particular Joe Lovejoy of the *Independent* was ringing me almost every day for confirmation that Terry was in the frame. I don't know what went against Terry – perhaps the sharp tongue and mercurial personality.

While Graham Taylor didn't quite have Terry's credentials – he had played most of his football in the lower leagues and was not quite as prominent a personality – there was no mistaking his ambition. In the summer of 1986, when Arsenal were looking for a replacement for Don Howe, there was some talk that they might turn to Graham Taylor. In the end they chose George Graham. There was no disguising Graham Taylor's disappointment that he hadn't got the Arsenal call. He certainly saw his move to Aston Villa, after managing Watford, as a move upwards and outwards. Not that he enjoyed the best of relationships with Doug Ellis. Despite the fact that in his first season he saved Aston Villa from relegation, and in his second challenged Liverpool for the title, the electricity between the two men was very evident – and never static. By this time I would often bump into Graham, particularly at international matches at Wembley, and it would be a feature of such meetings to hear him gripe and moan about Doug Ellis. What he resented was that Doug not only wanted to be Chairman but Manager as well.

What I liked about Graham was that he was so approachable and open and, unlike other managers of my acquaintance, never afraid to tell a story against himself. While many managers like to portray themselves as omnipotent, particularly when it comes to selecting players, Graham readily admitted to me that the best players he ever selected were due to his wife and not him. Once, when he was managing Watford, he took her up to a match in Scotland to see a defender. When he asked his wife what she thought about it she said: 'I hope it's the centre-forward you are looking to buy.' The centre-forward was Mo Johnston, and Taylor took her advice and brought him to Watford. It was the start of a remarkable career for one of Scotland's most high-profile strikers.

However, I suspect that the media criticism, and particularly the turnip twaddle, may be having an affect on Graham Taylor. The son of a journalist, aware of the media, he began his campaign promising to be open and approachable. Instead he has lately given signs of going into his shell, which would be a bad thing for him and for the England team. I wonder if he did think of quitting after the European Championships. One thing is for sure, the tabloids are turning it into the job that no one will want, rather than the position that everyone craves, as the pinnacle of the profession. It is interesting to note how differently these things are arranged on the Continent, particularly in France. There, after France's equally poor performances in the European Championships, Michel Platini resigned from his post as team Manager. This despite the fact that an opinion poll by a national sports magazine found that the overwhelming majority of the public wanted him to stay, and that Platini still comes high on the roll-call of France's all-time greatest players.

Platini just felt that it was a question of honour. English managers don't tend to see their jobs that way. Ever since Alf Ramsey, with the exception of Ron Greenwood, they have been pushed out of their jobs by circumstances rather than departing voluntarily. Perhaps that is not surprising: after all, English managers at club level do not go voluntarily either. Indeed, they invest their sacking with an air of tragedy, as if to suggest that to ask an unsuccessful Manager to leave is to offend the laws of nature. Why this should be so I have never quite understood. Football is different to any other business, but like all other businesses it has successes and failures. Somebody has to pay the price of failure. Since managers of English football teams invariably claim all the glory when their teams are successful, why should they not pay some of the price when their teams fail? Are they, somehow, immune to the general law of life in business? It certainly appears so, given the way that managers bleat their hardships to the Press and the role of those romantic, albeit misguided, journalists who play up their bleatings.

One man who was an exception to this was Bill Nicholson. In 1974, when he felt he could no longer command the support of the players or the board, he resigned. Bill was pushed, and the real dishonour was that the then Tottenham board allowed him to leave White Hart Lane and work at Upton Park for eighteen months. This for a man who was really responsible for the glory glory days of Tottenham, and for making the club great in the Fifties and Sixties – the greatest manager Spurs ever had. When I took over at Spurs I was determined that we should utilise the expertise and the experience that Bill had.

Yet it was not that easy to make the Tottenham managers appreciate Bill Nicholson. Just as one of Howard Wilkinson's first actions in taking over Leeds United was to remove a photograph of Don Revie and his team from the foyer, to banish the ghost of Revie's winning sides of the Sixties and Seventies, the Tottenham managers that I worked with in the Eighties were always trying to pull down Bill Nicholson. They knew they could not hope to match his Double achievement, or to supplant him in the memory of the Tottenham fans. They would often niggle and moan about what Bill did.

By the time I arrived at Spurs, Bill was in charge of the scouting system, and nobody was more critical of his scouting abilities than Keith Burkinshaw, the then Tottenham manager. Keith felt that Bill never seemed to like modern players: none of them seemed good enough to be signed for Spurs. Yet, ironically, it was Bill who signed one of the best players Tottenham was to have in the Eighties: Gary Mabbutt. One day Bill received a phone call from Peter Anderson, then Manager of Millwall, asking him what he thought of Gary Mabbutt. Bill thought he was worth around £250,000, and that he was an outstanding prospect. Anderson told him that he had just put the phone down to Bobby Gould, then Manager of Bristol Rovers, who wanted to sell Mabbutt at around £105,000. Millwall couldn't afford the fee, and Bill urged Keith to sign Mabbutt. Fortunately for Spurs Keith took the advice, and despite Mabbutt's diabetes, something that had put off other clubs, he became a Spurs player and has proved an outstanding talent.

The only Tottenham Manager during my time who shared my admiration for Bill Nicholson was David Pleat. Like me, David would often sit in Bill's office and ask his opinion on team matters and listen to his views. One of my lasting regrets is that I never managed to give Bill Nicholson the sort of father-figure role that Bob Paisley acquired at Liverpool. Who knows, had David Pleat remained at Spurs, that relationship might have developed, making a lasting bridge between the Tottenham of the Sixties and the Tottenham of the modern era.

In my time at Tottenham I dealt with four managers, and

with all of them I insisted on an understanding that as long as we were surrounded by just four walls, each of us could, without taking it personally, speak our own minds, honestly and openly. I could never accept disloyalty or dishonesty from a Manager – if they wanted my backing, they knew what was required in return. Sometimes, though, it became a one-way thing where they seemed to be doing all the taking and everyone else was doing the giving.

Keith was a straightforward, but difficult Yorkshireman, yet one with whom I got on extremely well – contrary to the usual public misconception. His wife once told me that if he didn't want to listen to anyone, he used to light his pipe and go off into his own world, where he became oblivious to everything being said to him.

I had first met Keith just before the Cup Final of 1981, when a friend had invited him to be guest speaker at a Rotary lunch he had organised. The friend knew I was Spurs mad, and invited me along. We had to pick Keith up at the team's training ground at Cheshunt, where they were having their Press Open Day for interviews and a photocall. Keith followed us to the venue at Potters Bar and we chatted briefly before we sat down to lunch. He struck me as a warm character, and not at all as he came across on television – rather dour and humourless. Many supporters by then had forgotten the quite vociferous campaign of 'the Burk must go'. It is amazing what a good Cup run can do for the supporters.

Like most managers on occasions like these, Keith much preferred to answer questions than make speeches. He dealt very ably with his audience, and then offered me a lift back to my car. What an opportunity for a supporter, to be alone with the Spurs Manager, to put all the questions you always wanted to ask, particularly the ones the Press did not. The one that still sticks in my mind was: 'Who was the player you most regret not signing?' Instant answer – Alan Hansen. He saw him play in midfield. Liverpool later switched him into the back four, where he was outstanding. 'I wasn't sure at the time,' said Keith a trifle sorrowfully. Little did I realise as Keith drove me back through North London, the many times I would hear those same words from him and other managers, regretting not signing someone who subsequently became very successful.

Signing players is always a bit of a hit-or-miss adventure. I was always fascinated how Liverpool hardly ever got it wrong, whilst other clubs had a mixture of successes and failures. Spurs were no different. Crooks and Archibald hit it off immediately in 1980, after we had suffered a number of Keith's signings he wished he hadn't made – and we did too. So when I asked him if he was sure they would work as a pair when he signed them, he just shrugged his shoulders, saying: 'They were good players, but it was a bit of a gamble.'

I rained questions on Keith and he didn't duck any. In fact I think he quite enjoyed it. My final impression as he dropped me off was that I liked him, and I felt confident that we were going to win the Cup. This we duly did. So Keith, after five years, was a winner – and a popular one too.

I remember talking to Sidney Wale, who had appointed him as Manager, about Keith's relationship with the old board. I was intrigued by how the then board felt when Spurs suffered relegation from the First Division in Keith's first season. Sidney said that at the first board meeting following relegation he had heard mutterings of a lack of confidence in the Manager, but he had made it perfectly clear that he would hear nothing of the sort. It was the directors who had appointed him, and they should either stand by their decision, or resign. There were no resignations.

I began to establish a working relationship with Keith during Christmas of 1982, when the return of Ossie Ardiles to White Hart Lane was agreed. It was on the flight back to London that Keith and I began to discuss football matters. I persuaded him to arrange a testimonial for Bill Nicholson – this took place at the start of the following season – and then we talked about a subject close to the heart of every football supporter: the buying of new players. I explained to Keith that it was my intention to try and buy only top-quality players. He agreed. I eagerly turned to him and asked: 'Who do you have on your shopping list in order to improve the side?' The answer devastated me. He replied: 'No one.' I just could not believe this. The newspapers were always linking Spurs to big-money transfers, and here was the Manager saying he had no thoughts specifically of buying anyone. Were Tottenham that good that they didn't need improving? True, they had won the FA Cup for the last two years, but they had also been eliminated from Europe, and that before the quarter-finals. I did not press the matter then, but it was a few months later that I saw how managers can change their tune.

By this time autumn had turned into winter, and it was

a bleak winter for Tottenham. We had been knocked out of the FA Cup by Everton in the fifth round, and the team was drifting in the League. At the end of February, Keith informed the directors: 'If Irving Scholar wants to help, let him give me £750,000 to buy Alan Brazil from Ipswich.' I rang up Keith and asked him how long Brazil had been available. I was told he had been on the market for quite a few months, but without any bids. It was clear the transfer market was not what it had been, recession having finally hit the dream world of football. The ridiculous prices paid only a few months previously, when ordinary players were changing hands at over £1 million, had now become more sensible, and the highest players' transfers were going at between £300,000 and £400,000.

So I suggested to Keith he offer £300,000 to Ipswich. They had recently carried out a rebuilding programme, and it was common knowledge in football that they needed cash. Keith could not believe that the player would be available for that sort of sum, and he told me: 'They have been in football a long time.' I ignored this and pointed out to him that if there had been no bids the player was obviously overpriced. However if we did not want to pursue it on a sensible basis then we should forget it for the time being. As it happened, Peter Shreeve was friendly with Bobby Ferguson, the then Ipswich Manager, and a few weeks later Keith rang to say that a bid in the region of £400,000 might secure Brazil. Interestingly, neither he nor I mentioned the earlier conversation.

As in all such situations, we were competing for Brazil with another club: Manchester United. Indeed, after Brazil had played a match on Saturday, and just as he was getting off the coach, he was told to go home and wait for a call as terms had been agreed for his transfer to another club. Brazil was sure this was Manchester United, so when he picked up the phone he expected to hear the voice of Ron Atkinson, then the Manager of Manchester United. Imagine his surprise to hear the very Yorkshire accent of Keith Burkinshaw arranging a meeting the following morning. On the Sunday Keith and Brazil met, personal terms were quickly agreed, a medical arranged for the next day, and Brazil became a Tottenham player.

The only slight hiccup came with the bank. The horrendous financial problems we had inherited from the Richardson regime were still being sorted out, and the bank would only finance the purchase on the condition that both Bobroff and myself give personal guarantees that the money would be repaid that summer. This meant that if the company did not fulfil its obligations we would be personally responsible to the bank for the transfer fee. This was the first time in the history of Tottenham that directors had to give such an undertaking – something more in common with Third and Fourth Division clubs. It indicated what an Augean stables we had to clean up before we got it right.

Brazil's signing in March of that year (1983) had an immediate effect. With twelve League matches left, we won nine, drew two and lost one. One of the victories came in the final match, when we beat Stoke City 4-1 and finished fourth – the highest ever First Division position under Keith's management. It also meant we had qualified for Europe, which for me was the important thing.

Perhaps the victory that gave me the greatest pleasure was over Arsenal at Easter. Back in 1978 Arsenal had come to Tottenham, scored a goal in the first thirty seconds, and beaten us 5-0 at home. To lose at home is one thing, to lose to Arsenal by any score is a numbing experience for any Spurs supporter, but to lose by that margin to Arsenal makes you feel suicidal. Revenge is sweet. This time we reversed the score line, with two goals in the first fifteen minutes followed by an incredible right-footed volley from just outside the penalty area by Mark Falco. Brazil scored his first goal for Spurs in the second half.

In the close season we signed Danny Thomas from Coventry and Gary Stevens from Brighton, quick footballing defenders who would be priceless against intelligent racy European forwards. But while these signings were to be applauded, the Terry Gibson saga made me realise that managers are not quite as clever as they think they are.

I never liked players reaching the end of their contracts, and much prefer to negotiate renewals well in advance, but Keith had allowed Terry Gibson's contract to end, and he was negotiating new terms. I kept on asking him whether the matter had been settled, and it seemed the only sticking-point was that Terry was seeking two years, whilst Keith was only prepared to offer twelve months. I explained to Keith that I didn't see the point in arguing, and in fact it was in our favour to agree to the two years, as under the one-year agreement he would only have to sit down with him again at the end of the season. The salary was not in dispute.

Terry Gibson was an extremely quick, powerful forward,

who had come into the team on an irregular basis, never letting the side down and always popping up to score important goals. He was a player who I personally enjoyed watching, as he was exciting and always gave 100 per cent in every match he played. I tried hard to persuade Keith to sign Terry on a new two-year contract by reminding him of something he told me a couple of months previously. Several first-team players had been injured and Terry had done extremely well as a replacement. But now that they were fit Keith called Terry into his office to explain that, unfortunately, he was going to have to give him the number 12 shirt as he was looking for experience in the side. Terry replied: 'Mr Burkinshaw, please understand it's an honour for me to wear the number 12 shirt of Tottenham Hotspur.' I don't think Keith had ever received such a reply from any player when dropping him.

I said surely he should be looking to sign players with such commitment, not giving them the opportunity of leaving. Keith felt a little embarrassed as I recounted the story, but he just did not seem to understand that not only was Terry a Spurs man through and through (as a junior he had turned down Anderlecht of Belgium, preferring to sign for Tottenham), but all he wanted was a little security.

However, as I was discovering, when dealing with players' contracts Keith had a habit of digging holes for himself, which he found difficult to get out of without losing face. So whilst I thought I had persuaded him to get Terry Gibson signed up, a few weeks later Keith told me he had received an offer of £70,000 from Bobby Gould, then Manager of Coventry, which he had accepted. He had spent around £1 million since the New Year, and I think he was trying to show that he could sell players as well as buy them. From a financial point of view the sale made no significant difference in the overall scheme of things at the time. However, I think Keith came to regret it later on, as Terry became quite a hot property during his spell with Coventry.

Terry's sale angered the fans, and I was made aware of this when the team travelled to Liverpool for a League game by train. I had been quite keen to get the team to travel by train as they used to do in the old days. Since then, nearly all away travel was either by coach or by plane. That journey to Liverpool came soon after the Gibson sale, and Keith felt the backlash of it. We were all sitting in the restaurant car when a crowd of supporters walked through. I was perturbed by the hostile reaction and comments directed at Keith. There could be no doubt that he had made an unpopular decision. Keith took the criticism out by deciding against train travel, and the Spurs team never travelled by rail again.

The Gibson sale had also shown a side of Keith's character which was not very attractive. The 83/84 season was barely two matches old when he faced a much more serious problem. It had begun poorly. We had been tipped as Championship contenders, but we lost away to Ipswich on a boiling hot summer's day 1-3, and then we played Coventry at home on the Monday evening. A television campaign featuring Mrs Ridlington and her family had attracted a crowd of 35,000, but we could only draw 1-1. However it was events off the field that were to prove more dramatic. Truly, that evening proved the turning-point in Keith's career. During the second half, Steve Archibald, never Keith's favourite person, came out of a melee in the six-yard box limping and signalling to the bench to be substituted. Keith apparently told him to carry on and run it off, but Archie thought he had injured himself, and in the end forced Keith to take him off, much to Keith's annoyance.

At the Press conference after the match, Keith let rip and called Archie a 'cheat', protesting he wasn't injured enough to come off. Fleet Street loves a bit of controversy, and the headlines screamed out the following morning. Archie turned up for training on the Wednesday, showing no signs of injury, but refused to speak a single word to Keith, which amused the other players no end.

A few days later Keith rang me, and I could feel the concern in his voice as he asked me how to handle what was proving to be a very delicate situation. Players are always testing managers to see if they can get one over on them, and Keith was being tested to the limit. I asked him how he would have felt if any player had publicly called him the same thing, and he admitted he wouldn't have liked it. I reminded him about privacy and discussions in confidence surrounded by four walls, but attacking a player publicly gained nothing. I suggested that he try to act normally, and asked if he had thought of apologising. What a question to ask a stubborn Yorkshireman who had never apologised for anything in his life. 'How about transferring him?' said Keith. I told him that this would not be in the club's interest, as we needed to keep all our good players, especially after only two League games. My advice again was to act naturally and apologise, or ignore it.

This started a battle of wills of gargantuan proportions. Archie had a reputation for being difficult and for being a bit of a loner, but I had always found him to be a very likeable fellow. Ossie and Chris Hughton were his great friends, but others like Steve Perryman and Ray Clemence couldn't stand him – they thought he was aloof. I think he was just a little different and a private person.

Time went on, and Archie had effectively sent Keith to Coventry. This had a devastating effect on Keith, who began to get very edgy and started to imagine that his authority was being usurped and undermined, that people were talking behind his back. There is no question the players were beginning to lose respect, as Archie was getting the upper hand, culminating in a game at Watford, where we were losing 1-0. Archie had been on the bench, but within a few minutes of coming on he had equalised with a terrific strike from twenty yards into the top right-hand corner, and at the final whistle we had won 3-2. Touché!

Keith's problems were escalating. Archie was the hero, and still he wouldn't talk to Keith. He was back in the team and then proceeded to score in each of the next six matches, all of which the team won, and by March, the continual strain was taking its toll. Keith by now had accepted my suggestion that when it came to negotiating the players' contracts Tottenham would follow the example of Liverpool and negotiations would be handled by the Club Secretary on the direct instructions of the Manager and board. He was not overjoyed, but he agreed. Bill Nicholson had often said it was very difficult for a Manager to get a player to give him everything when the Manager was not submitting fully to the player's financial demands. It seemed obvious to me that it would help a Manager manage a player if there was a buffer between the two when it came to contracts.

This agreement was secured during our UEFA Cup match in Austria, and it was on this trip that I became very concerned about the effects the Archie saga was having on Keith. He looked extremely pale and had clearly lost weight. He looked so dreadful that I feared he was facing a possible breakdown. Indeed, just before boarding the coach for training during this trip, and while Peter Shreeve was taking the orders for the players' lunches, Keith suddenly started shouting and demanding to know why nobody had consulted him about this. Shreeve as Assistant Manager taking orders for lunch was doing something very normal, but Keith's reaction showed that the stresses were getting to him.

After we came back from the match, I discussed the toll that the previous months' pressure was having on Keith with Douglas Alexiou and Paul Bobroff, and they decided to see him. The moment Keith received their summons he rang to enquire why they wanted to see him. I explained that they were concerned about him and his health, and as we talked it quickly became clear that Keith was very unhappy with the situation. The press-ure had begun to tell, it was affecting everything he was doing, and Keith finally said that under the circumstances he did not want to continue after the end of the season. We agreed that an announcement would be made at that time and not before. I was very keen that Keith should part on good terms, and in view of everything that he had achieved, I proposed a testimonial to be played at the end of the season from which he could expect to receive around £100,000 tax-free, in addition to being paid for the remaining year of his contract. Keith thought this was more than fair.

The decision seemed to lift a large weight from his shoulders. His general disposition improved enormously. But, as I was to realise so often in football, nothing could be kept a secret. Within a short time Peter Blackman of the *Evening Standard* ran an exclusive story about Keith's impending departure. I knew Blackman was a particularly close friend of Keith's, and when I asked Keith he confessed he had leaked it, despite the fact that he had given me his word that nothing would be said until the end of the season. I think there was more to this than a simple leak. Now that he was feeling a lot more relaxed he was probably having second thoughts, and the leaking of the story may have been aimed at generating popular support in an effort to put pressure on the directors to persuade him to stay.

But this wasn't easy. The fact was that Keith had fallen out with Paul Bobroff in a very serious way. During the previous fifteen months Keith had attended a number of board meetings where he had dealt with Bobroff. I was not present, as I was not yet a director. Bobroff had an unfortunate attitude towards man-agers, which was never to change. The way he behaved towards them made me think that he saw them as merely employees of the company, who should do exactly what they were told and never ask questions. Keith naturally resented that view, and it led to violent clashes. Douglas Alexiou related one incident to me. After a discussion between Bobroff and Keith, Bobroff left the board meeting. As he did so Keith banged his fist on the table and said angrily: 'I'm going to squash that little man.' The feeling was mutual.

On the last day of the season we played Manchester United at home and Keith said that Ron Atkinson, their Manager, was prepared to buy either Steve Archibald or Alan Brazil for £350,000. Keith recommended we accept the offer for Archibald, but I felt it was grossly underrating him and turned it down.

The season ended in the most dramatic way. Spurs beat Anderlecht to win the UEFA Cup on a penalty shoot-out. After the final whistle Steve Archibald spoke to Keith for the first time in months. As it happened Archibald would soon follow Keith out of Spurs. The match was overlaid with emotions, and the Press built up a romantic saga, seeing Keith as the rejected hero hounded by a heartless Spurs board. They made much of Keith's departure despite winning a Cup, quite ignoring the fact that it was he who had initiated the moves for his departure and made working relationships with the board difficult. I didn't mind that so much as Keith's comments as he left, words which were hung around the neck of the board like an albatross. He is supposed to have said, metaphorically waving his hands in the direction of the Board Room: 'There used to be a football club over there.' This was a gross distortion of our actions at Tottenham. The changes we had initiated had to be made, and if Keith had examined the issues rationally and properly he would have agreed with them. But then in his state of mind reason and logic was probably not easy.

So who could replace Keith? I had been talking to Alex Ferguson, then managing Aberdeen. These conversations had reached the point of agreeing personal terms, and we shook hands on a deal. However, he had second thoughts about the matter and decided not to accept my offer.

Ferguson would have been a good choice. He had managed to break the Glasgow monopoly of Rangers and Celtic and had considerable European experience, having won the Cup Winners' Cup by beating Real Madrid in the Final a short time previously. The way his teams played was also very important: whilst they were winning, they were also entertaining – a vital prerequisite for any Spurs side. He was very intense and totally dedicated, something I found very appealing. He also had the reputation of being a strict disciplinarian; it was a good combination for any Manager. Unfortunately for Spurs, he had a father-son relationship with the Aberdeen Chairman, and I think, on reflection, he felt he would be letting him down if he left. We remained good friends afterwards and he kept in touch concerning the Scottish scene. I am delighted that he has done well at Manchester United, after a difficult start and a rather stormy relationship with their supporters.

There was no one else outstanding available in England at the time, and Ferguson's change of mind made me think of Europe. By far the best Continental coach was the Swede, Sven Goran Eriksson, who at the time was at Benfica. He was fluent in English and keen to come to England. But he had given his word to the Roma President that he would accept their offer. He told me if that didn't transpire he would be in touch.

Continuity is important in a football club – just look at Liverpool. Their teams never seem to go through large upheavals, just gradual natural change and progress, and it is similar when it comes to managerial changes. Everyone has a role to play, and the heir-apparent always seems to be ready to step into the breach. The nearest we had to that was Peter Shreeve. He had joined Tottenham eight years previously, starting with the youth team and producing a number of players who had graduated to the first team. From there he progressed to Reserve Team Manager, and in 1980 to Assistant Manager. As soon as he assumed this position, the team's quality of performance seemed to improve, together with results. Throughout this period he had success and played a fundamental part in Keith Burkinshaw's most successful time at the club.

With no one else available Shreeve was a natural choice, although my deepest concern was how he would adapt from being a number two to a number one. There is a big difference between being a coach and a manager. The coach basically carries out the instructions of his Manager, who effectively has the final word on all team selections, style and tactical play, purchase and sale of players, and carries overall responsibility for all teams in the club. He is the person that the public identifies with, whilst the coach has a much lower profile, but can have a tremendous influence on first-team matters. The Manager is the leader, and may sometimes give the impression of being a little aloof. The coach is more in the background, and invariably much closer to the players, working with them every day. There are very few people who have the ability to perform both tasks well, although I have always felt that coaches are frustrated managers and vice versa. I remember Peter Shreeve telling me that on many occasions he disagreed with Keith's team selection, only to lie awake at night after a victory puzzling how Keith had got it right.

Peter was appointed in midsummer. He quickly made it clear he wanted to concentrate on the team and didn't want to be bogged down with negotiating players' contracts, but would give his advice on how highly he rated each player in his plans. He was a Spurs man and understood the inner workings of the club. Most important, he believed wholeheartedly in the traditions concerning style of play, entertainment and the type of players Spurs supporters had come to expect to see. Unlike Keith, Peter wanted Glenn Hoddle to stay, and meant to build his team around him. I remember him saying one day how he was going to get the full potential out of Glenn, as he believed he was probably the most gifted individual he had ever worked with.

Pre-season 1984/85 took us to Norway and Sweden, and the team spirit and camaraderie were exceptional. Everybody enjoyed each other's company and the team seemed confident. There was a lot of fun on the coach, and Mike Varney, the physiotherapist, was organising quizzes and games to keep everyone entertained and occupied. The mood of the team gave me a lot of optimism and I felt confident that a good season lay ahead. Steve Perryman, who had been another of Keith's critics – 'a lucky man' he called him – had nothing but good things to say about Peter's early transition. This was another good sign.

The close season had also seen us solve some of the problems Keith's management had caused. Steve Archibald moved to Barcelona, followed by Alan Brazil to Manchester United. Clive Allen joined us from QPR and John Chiedozie from Notts County, and after Mike Varney had recommended David Leworthy, we signed him from Fareham Town for £5,000.

Clive Allen's purchase was a neat partnership between Peter Shreeve and myself. Given that Allen was eventually sold to a French club, it began appropriately enough in a restaurant in the South of France. It was there that I saw Jim Gregory and thought I would ask what terms he was looking for for Clive. Jim is famous in football for his line that: 'Everything is for sale, it's just a question of price.' He mentioned that he was looking for £750,000. When I replied I was interested only in Clive, not in his entire club, he smiled – but that was the beginning of the deal. Three weeks later I went to his offices just by the A3 near Roehampton to finalise it. As I arrived I saw him sitting behind a huge desk and I noticed that he was only visible from his shoulders up, suggesting that he was hunched down below the desk or was holding something below it. It was some time before I found out what he was holding.

We discussed the Clive Allen price again and Jim said: 'I gave you a price a few weeks ago. £750,000. You thought I was pissed. I wasn't.' Over the next hour and a half, Jim maintained this sort of curious sitting position as we haggled about the price. Finally we agreed at £725,000. I felt, given the state of the market, that Clive Allen was probably worth between £600,000 and £650,000, but I agreed. Alan Mullery, the QPR manager at the time, thought we had more money than sense, but in retrospect it was a great buy.

As I got up to shake Jim's hand on the deal I noticed that he was now only visible from the chin up, and seemed to be leaning even lower under the table. Just as I extended my hand I heard a sudden pop, and Jim emerged from behind the table holding a bottle of champagne in his hand and two glasses. What had happened was that he had been, throughout our conversation, holding the bottle under the table, and the moment he heard me say Yes he produced it to celebrate. It neatly illustrated Jim's philosophy that everything is for sale. Years later I was to be told a story about him and David Dein travelling to a meeting of League clubs in Birmingham. Jim, who was in the motor trade, turned up in a Rolls Royce at David's house to give him a lift. He said that he was feeling a little tired, and would David mind driving? Halfway to Birmingham David remarked what a nice car it was, and Jim immediately countered: 'It's yours, if you want to buy it.'

Terry Venables considers Jim Gregory his mentor, and I am convinced that Terry's business philosophy has been much influenced by Jim: everything is for sale, it's a question of price. Curiously, Jim himself seems to think that Terry has a problem with the friends he keeps. Back in 1984, when Keith Burkinshaw left and Terry Venables was being linked with the job at Spurs, Jim Gregory rang me up one day and said: 'The trouble is it's the people Terry runs with. He's all right himself.'

The changes seemed all for the good as we started our League campaign at Everton, the FA Cup holders. They paraded the trophy about half an hour before kick-off, and within fifteen minutes we were one down from a penalty. But we then proceeded to take them apart, finally winning 4-1 and hitting the woodwork. Peter sat in the stand for most of the match, and ten minutes from time left to sit on the bench, saying: 'I am going to enjoy this one,' as he fully deserved to do. Alas, it proved a pyrrhic victory, for Everton were to become a thorn in our side during Peter's reign, and that season they denied us the Championship. Perhaps that defeat had a galvanising effect on them in the months to come.

Our early season form was inconsistent, but we weren't losing too often. Whilst we were winning at Norwich, the game just before Christmas, Everton lost 4-3 at home to Chelsea, which put us top of the table. We were going well in Europe and had reached the quarter-finals of the UEFA Cup, where we were due to meet Real Madrid in March. Peter's team was performing particularly well away from home, but the big test was the game at Highbury on New Year's Day. Nearly 50,000 turned up to see us go a goal down just before half-time, but Mark Falco and Garth Crooks scored the goals to give us victory in the second half. What a start to the New Year.

I vividly remember the noise from the street whilst we were in the Arsenal boardroom, with thousands of Spurs supporters chanting and simply refusing to go home. The curtains were drawn, but I had to look out and see the joy on their faces. A few fans who had been looking up noticed me, and I gave them the 'thumbs-up'. I'm sure they didn't understand that I felt the same as them and really wanted to join in the celebrations. It always means so much to beat Arsenal. It is much more than just three points, it is a case of pride and achievement. This rivalry will never die, and that is why a game between the two sides is always a high or low point in a season. If you win, you can hold your head high; if you lose, you are dreading meeting the next Arsenal supporter. The rapport between the clubs is very good, but at that time Arsenal were going through a sticky patch. Terry Neill had been replaced as Manager by Don Howe, and it would be eighteen months before George Graham took over.

But while Peter was doing a good job, these were early days, and I was aware that the move from being number two to number one is a much larger one than most people realise. You are now giving the orders rather than merely acting on them. It is your decision whom you buy and sell, whom you promote from the reserve and youth teams, and whom you employ or dismiss on the coaching and scouting side. On top of all this, you are supposed to be at the beck and call of the Press twenty-four hours per day. Peter was always very open and honest with them, and there are always some that take advantage of that privilege.

Early success for a Manager can be dangerous. They sometimes end up believing their own publicity and feel they have discovered the secret of success. It is very important to keep their feet on the ground and – just in case they are getting carried away – to keep reminding them that nothing has been achieved yet and there is a long way to go. It is also very easy to get carried away in their wake, something I had to guard against. This meant that in a way you never quite get the opportunity to enjoy the high points which should be the object of the exercise. Football *is* a sport, it is entertainment and should be enjoyed by everyone who watches it. This particularly applies to supporters, but although I was the most fervent of Spurs supporters, my position meant that there were many times that I could not enjoy a match in the way I had done before being involved. I just could not allow myself to get carried away.

Soon both Peter and myself were to be reminded of what the wise man had said just as I was buying Spurs: 'Football will lift you into the clouds one minute and kick you up the backside the next.' That moment came in the UEFA Cup quarter-finals when we played Real Madrid. Before the game I went to see Peter Shreeve and told him how much the board appreciated the good job he was doing and that I wanted to reward him with a new improved two-year contract, which he was very pleased with.

We had done this despite the fact that Spurs, who are really a Cup side, had lost 1-0 at Anfield in the fourth round of the FA Cup. (It might have been different had we had an early penalty when Steve Perryman was tripped in the area with the score at 0-0.) We had also gone out to Sunderland 2-1 in a quarter-final League Cup replay at home, missing a late penalty. But for the first time in many years, since the days of Bill Nicholson, Spurs were mounting a real challenge for the Championship, which we had not won since the Double in 1960/61, and the board and I felt that Peter, in his first season, had done a good job.

The Real Madrid game was to prove how much more needed to be done. We lost 1-0, which does not sound too bad, but this meant that the proud Spurs record of never having been beaten at home in a European match – one that went back forty-two home games, all the way to Gornik Zabrze in 1961 – was at last broken. But more than the result, it was the gap in class the match exposed. I remember going back to my hotel in London after the first leg feeling very depressed, a mood caused by the realisation that we were far behind them in technique and natural ability. In a way I felt we had been outclassed. In England we held our own. It had taken a top Continental side to expose our weaknesses. Whilst the Press thought we were unlucky to lose, I felt I had seen some of the writing on the wall. In hindsight, that evening was the beginning of the end of Peter's reign as Manager.

When the draw had first been made, Terry Venables, who was at Barcelona at the time, said that Real wouldn't score against us. I don't know if this was adding a little bit of needle against their fiercest rivals, but he was right in so far as the only goal of the tie was an own goal. The second leg in Spain took place a fortnight later in front of 95,000 spectators, and our performance was completely different from the first leg. We had our chances, and the referee disallowed what I believed was a perfectly good headed goal by Mark Falco. To this day, I still don't know why it wasn't given. No Madrid player appealed, and afterwards their directors admitted that they couldn't understand the referee's decision. Steve Perryman had been sent off towards the end, which completed a miserable tie for him. He had been the unlucky player who, in the first leg, scored the only goal of the tie when the ball hit him on the knee and bounced into his own net.

The next few weeks were to see us suffer from a Real hangover as our title dreams disintegrated. On paper it should have been in our grasp. By the time we played Manchester United on 12 March, we had fifteen League games to play, ten at home and five away. We did have some bad luck. Gary Stevens, who had been converted to midfield and was probably our most consistent and best player that season, suffered a very serious knee injury against Manchester United and was ruled out until the following October, having been ever present until then. That game was one of six home games lost out of the ten. The following Saturday, the team picked itself up and scored a timely and historical victory at Anfield. The most widely known statistic in football was that Spurs had not won at Liverpool since 1912, the year the *Titanic* had gone down. The Liverpool directors took the 1-0 defeat well, and sent champagne into the Spurs players' dressing room. Liverpool have a reputation of being bad losers, but I never ever saw that. We had beaten them earlier in the season 1-0 at home in the League, and 1-0 in the League Cup, and each time they had accepted defeat with good grace.

After the League Cup win I was walking to the Directors Room with John Smith, the Liverpool Chairman. Peter Robinson, the Club Secretary and Chief Executive, was a step behind when the Chairman called to him to say: 'Peter, Irving has just offered me two bob for Michael Robinson and I am seriously considering it.' Michael Robinson had played that evening but never kicked a ball for the Liverpool first team again.

The season finished with us in third place in the First Division. Having chased Everton for much of the time, we had seen the Championship slip away with a defeat by Everton at home, when 48,108 crammed into White Hart Lane to see the explosive evening game that ended our hopes. That's your lot Spurs, screamed the *Sun* headline the next day, and for once they got it right. We could blame no one but ourselves. We had the chances but spurned them. One curious feature of Peter's first season was that while we did well away from home, we just could not win at White Hart Lane. Had we won our home matches the title would have been ours. However, we had qualified for Europe for the fifth consecutive year, a club record.

Playing in Europe is essential for a club like Tottenham. Apart from the vast financial rewards, it is for me the real test, the barometer to measure your real standing. The supporters love it, as do the players, and European nights at Tottenham are something really special. For the public it is an opportunity to assess where English football stands in international terms and to compare the technique and skill of top Continental players against our own. From a personal point of view, there is simply nothing else to match it. Unfortunately within a few weeks the Heysel tragedy took place, and like all English clubs we were not to resume playing in Europe for six long years.

We did play an Italian team, Udinese, a little over forty-eight hours after Heysel, but this was a friendly in Australia where we were on tour at that time. Realising this could turn out to be a bit of a diplomatic incident, we arranged to offer a bouquet of flowers to each of the Italian players before the kick-off. Peter spoke to the players before the match, and told them to turn the other cheek if they were fouled and ignore it. They followed his instructions, despite some extreme provocation from the Udinese players, and the match passed without incident. Except for one moment which had their President's son haring down to the bench. Their top player Massimo Mauro was due to sign for Juventus on their return to Italy for a fee of around £4,000,000, and he was rolling around on the pitch with a turned ankle. It proved not to be serious, but the official had a somewhat pasty look on his face for some time after.

I went into the dressing room after the game and thanked the players for their good behaviour. The only one who could not understand was Paul Miller. He started moaning that if that was what football was about he wanted no part of it. He just couldn't grasp the gravity of the situation. However later that evening back at the hotel, Paul Miller came up to me and apologised for his outburst, saying that he hadn't appreciated the position. I think Peter, who was visibly annoyed with Miller, had a word with him, and I was proud of how Tottenham had behaved in a difficult and potentially explosive situation.

The close season saw us sign Chris Waddle and Paul Allen, both of whom scored in our opening 4-0 victory over Watford. But this proved a false dawn. The 1985/86 season was one of bitter disappointment. It was the year of the Broadwater Farm riots in Tottenham, and while this had no impact on us, except for a match being postponed, the gloom that hung over the area appeared to have been transmitted to the team. By November the Press were already calling for Peter's head, and by the New Year, which saw us lose three home matches on the trot to Nottingham Forest, Manchester City and then Coventry, quite the most dispiriting defeat, some supporters were demonstrating at the ground after matches. Jokes abounded about Peter, who had been a part-time taxi-driver before he came to football management. Few were funny, most of them cruel, and this was not helped by front-page reports in the tabloids of misbehaviour while the team was in Jersey.

None of this dimmed my personal liking for Peter. I found him very dedicated and hard-working; he believed totally in the high ideals of Tottenham Hotspur and the way football should be played. He was good-humoured, never tried to make excuses, and unlike many managers I found him to be the straightest man in football. But by the end of 1985/86, when we finished tenth, with some humiliating home defeats including one by Everton in the FA Cup, something had to give. Football is an unforgiving world and Peter had to go.

Even then I found it a very difficult task to call him in after the season had finished and tell him that the board had decided to terminate his contract as Manager. He arrived at my office at Tottenham at 10.30 am one morning, looking a little pale, as I think he knew the reason for the meeting. However, Peter is a very positive person: he reads a lot about positive thinking and was probably trying to dismiss all negative thoughts from his mind. As I broke the news to him I could see the disappointment etched on his face, and there was merit in his argument that this was his first bad season at the club.

I spent two hours trying to explain the reasons for our decision. I had warned him earlier in the season that it had reached me that the players were very unhappy with his assistant, John Pratt, and that he should think about replacing him. Peter felt loyal towards him, insisted he was doing a good job and said the rumours were ill-founded. I tried to persuade Peter to stay at the club in a coaching capacity, but he felt that having been a 'number one' he could not do so. I was very disappointed at his reluctance to stay, as it is very hard to find first-class people, and Peter was certainly that. He had recruited a number of very competent staff members, most of whom are still there today. The only easy part of the meeting was the financial settlement, which we reached there and then.

Peter was also unlucky in that 1985/86 was in any case one of the most depressing of seasons. The deaths at Bradford and Heysel cast a pall over football from which the season never could recover. Some of the scars inflicted were permanent. Others were minor by comparison, but still damaging. The sentence of banishment from Europe began the long exile of the domestic game from European cup football. This had disastrous consequences whose effects are still being felt and will be felt for years to come. I can understand why the FA had to withdraw English clubs from Europe following Heysel; I was less than happy about the way they arrived at the decision. They took it unilaterally without consulting the clubs. We suddenly awoke to find that we were not playing in Europe. Of course we had to do something following Heysel. Nothing could atone for what happened there.

In many ways the FA's unilateral and arbitrary decision, however right in hindsight, skewed the post-Heysel debate about English football and crowd control. There was a constant battle with government ministers, in particular the need to teach Mrs Thatcher that government fiats to introduce identity cards were not the answer to football hooliganism. It took us almost the rest of the Eighties to get it right, and in the process we had to struggle through stupid government panaceas, temporarily encouraged by an extremely short-sighted away-fan ban by Luton. Mrs Thatcher threatened to be one of the most destructive influences on football, and David Evans was not far behind. I'm not sure who was the worst.

Amidst all this chaos and confusion, the big questions that Heysel, Bradford and later Hillsborough raised were obscured. How can football clubs manage big crowds? What is the response of clubs, some of whose supporters, or people who claim to be supporters, run riot? Should the clubs and the game as a whole be penalised due to the conduct of a few fans? After the Battle of Britain, Winston Churchill said: 'Never has so much been owed to so few,' immortalising the bravery of the British pilots in their epic fight against the German Luftwaffe which saved this country from conquest. After Heysel, I am inclined to think that never have so many been brought to ruin by so few.

I don't think anybody connected with football will ever forget Hillsborough. Like the assassination of President Kennedy, most of us can remember where they were when we heard the appalling news. I was at Wimbledon, watching Spurs play in a First Division match, when after about twenty minutes Derek Peter's father came up to me, tapped me on the shoulder, and said there had been a big problem at the FA Cup semi-final between Nottingham Forest and Liverpool. A few days before this, the news had finally come that English clubs were to be invited back into European competition for the 1990/91 season. My immediate reaction, without knowing any details, was that there must have been an outbreak of hooliganism, and I wondered what effect this would have on the clubs' return to Europe. It was only at half-time, when I went inside and saw the television, that I realised the full extent of the tragedy, and the scenes from Hillsborough made me think that it could happen anywhere and could well have involved us. The first action I took on the following Monday morning was to have Tottenham's fences dismantled.

Whoever chose Lord Justice Taylor to chair the inquiry into Hillsborough had a moment of inspiration. When he came to White Hart Lane for a match, along with Colin Moynihan, then Minister for Sport, I was immediately impressed with him and the way he tackled his brief. It was at this meeting that I made an impression on Lord Justice Taylor with my point about reducing the football pool levy and the fact that the government was taking a lot out of the game – something like £250 million per year in addition to VAT and various other forms of taxation. Could not the government, I suggested to him, arrange some form of grant on a £-for-£ basis so that the clubs could have some help in rebuilding stands and improving their grounds? Lord Justice Taylor clearly listened to what I was saying, and I remember going to Wembley a few months after his report was published and bumping into him. 'Well,' he said, 'we managed to get the recommendation through about the football pools levy, didn't we?' I agreed, and congratulated him on his recommendations. It was good to meet somebody in authority who listened to the people who were involved in the game.

Lord Justice Taylor's report called for all-seater stadiums for football clubs, a decision I endorsed, and which I saw as bringing us more in line with Europe, a concept foremost in our minds when we were doing our own reconstruction at Tottenham. Lord Justice Taylor, a devoted Newcastle fan, knew his football, understood the problems, and came up with exactly the right recommendations to ensure safety.

However, the path to Taylor's heaven was paved with some very bad ideas, and I was to spend much of the latter half of the Eighties fighting three of them: the ridiculous away-fan ban by Luton, and Mrs Thatcher's fiats to prohibit alcohol at football grounds and to impose the ID scheme.

I do not disagree that there is a link between hooliganism and drinking, but you cannot get drunk because there isn't enough time. Most people, in my experience, found drunk at a football match come to the ground already pretty tanked up. Furthermore, a lot more drinking takes place at other sporting events than at football. You only have to go to the Varsity match at Twickenham to realise that. Indeed, after one Varsity match the Metropolitan Police set up a breathalyser unit to check drivers as they were leaving the Twickenham car park. The difference between rugby and football is that the Oxbridge crowd that go to Twickenham drive there with their car boots packed to the gunnels with bottles of wine, while the football supporter saunters to the ground holding a can of beer.

There is a class factor here, and while Mrs Thatcher spoke eloquently against the class system in this country, her decision to ban alcohol from football grounds reflected a dreadful class prejudice.

After a great struggle, and with a lot of help from Tom Pendry, a Labour MP who is Chairman of the all-party committee on football, we did manage to modify the alcohol ban, but in the process we perpetuated a haves versus have-nots distinction in football which I greatly regret. The original ban meant that nobody in football, anywhere in the ground, could consume alcohol. This even applied to our executive boxes, where there had never, ever, been a single incident of hooliganism. Like all football clubs we were deluged with letters complaining about the ban, and wondering whether we might continue using the boxes, which had become a popular entertaining area for a lot of businesses. When the ban was relaxed, supporters in the executive boxes could have alcohol before the match began, but at 3 o'clock liquor had to be removed. Also, they could not drink in sight of the pitch. This is how the situation stands today. The effect of this is to keep the crowds in the pubs until about fifteen minutes before the kick-off. At Tottenham we found that 60 per cent of the spectators would enter during the last twenty minutes or so.

Even worse than the alcohol ban was Mrs Thatcher's obsession with the ID scheme. Like the Poll Tax, this will always be remembered as one of Mrs Thatcher's follies. She just got it into her head that a compulsory national membership scheme would solve all of football's problems. In the years between 1985 and 1988 there was no other issue which raised quite as much emotion in football, and no issue on which I felt more strongly. I felt right from the beginning that this was a ruinous scheme, and as I said in my speech to a group of peers in the House of Lords on 24 January 1989, it was a ridiculously dangerous solution to the problem of hooliganism. Of the people who attend a football match, 99.99 per cent are perfectly law-abiding citizens. It is just the 0.01 per cent that is loutish and causes hooliganism. Introducing an ID scheme for all football supporters was worse than using a sledgehammer to crack a nut.

In the 1987/88 season over 600,000 people attended matches at Tottenham and only seventy-three were arrested both inside and outside the ground, a figure which included touts selling tickets at black-market prices. Nobody in his senses would suggest legislation for such a small minority, and I could cite to the Lords the support of leading national newspapers and of *The Police*, the official magazine of the Police Federation, which had condemned the national membership scheme as an extraordinary mish-mash of good intentions and half-baked nostrums whose results would be disastrous.

By the time Mrs Thatcher started pushing for the ID scheme the government already had powers to exercise control over football crowds and kerb hooliganism. They had the exclusion order which gave them the right to ban people from being anywhere near a football match, let alone inside a football ground. These exclusion orders were very rarely employed, and I had many complaints from the police at the time that they were not being enforced even when the police made recommendations for such an order to be granted. The machinery for crowd control was there. ID cards were completely unnecessary. It is typical of the sad, chaotic football history of the late Eighties that it required the tragedy of Hillsborough and the loss of ninety-six lives finally to convince Mrs Thatcher that the ID scheme was a non-starter. Why do we British always have to wait for tragedies before we realise the follies of our ways?

It was during the debates on the ID scheme that I got to know Colin Moynihan, Minister of Sport, or to give his more appropriate name the Miniature of Sport – a reference to his diminutive stature. Moynihan had drawn the wild card from Mrs Thatcher as the minister responsible for implementing the ID scheme. I met him on numerous occasions trying to persuade him to change his mind. Moynihan always came across as a real politician, never shy to give an interview, never at a loss for words, and always eager to lecture football on how it should put its house in order. He was forever stressing to me that football clubs had to make themselves commercially viable and it was not for the government to foot the bill. He never seemed to take on board the argument that through the football pools the Exchequer raised around £250 million a year and that a reduction in the football levy would go some way in helping football clubs construct their grounds and stadiums. The loss of income, as a result of people staying away from football if the ID scheme came in, made no impression on him whatsoever.

Despite our differences, I enjoyed meeting Moynihan – pleasure increased by the fact that he was invariably accompanied by Peter Lee, his private secretary, who has since joined the Football Trust as their Secretary. Peter, a Spurs supporter, could not have provided a greater contrast to Moynihan. He is an engaging character, always with a smile on his face, and always wanting to help. Moynihan, in contrast, was like a little jack-in-the-box, although on one occasion I did manage to pierce his ministerial façade. This was when we met at Selhurst Park, where Charlton were playing Spurs. Moynihan, as a Charlton supporter, was showing his loyalty. I managed to collar him for a private chat for about half an hour. At this time the government was about to push through Parliament an enabling bill on football which would have allowed them to introduce ID cards. (An enabling bill is, in effect, a blank piece of paper on which a government can write the rules later.) As I put my anti-ID cards arguments, Moynihan kept on presenting the same ministerial front, but finally, prodded beyond endurance, he cracked. Suddenly he said: 'You've got to understand, Irving! I see your points but my career is on the line here!' Almost as soon as he said that, he regretted it and tried to back-track, but the damage had been done. It was probably the most honest answer I have ever got from a politician, and it made me realise that the real driving force behind the ID scheme was Mrs Thatcher.

Mrs Thatcher's views were considerably shaped by David Evans, then Chairman of Luton Town. He created the biggest division I have ever seen in football when he brought in the home-fans-only rule, much to the chagrin of supporters and clubs. This was Evans's response to the dreadful riot by Millwall fans during their Cup match against Luton in March 1985. The match was being televised by the BBC, and dreadful scenes of Millwall fans invading the pitch and fighting with the police were shown to an astonished nation, and round the world. I saw it televised in America and Australia. There is some merit in the argument that away fans have contributed to football hooliganism. In the Fifties, when I first started watching Spurs, the lack of adequate transport – motorways didn't come into being until the late Fifties – meant that fans rarely travelled away from home to see their team. Indeed, the tradition was that fans would go every Saturday to their home ground, either to watch the first team or the reserve team. Tottenham's reserve team games at White Hart Lane, or for that matter Arsenal's at Highbury, attracted crowds that would be the envy of Wimbledon today. The arrival of the motorways changed all that and brought us the travelling fans.

Despite this, I thought David Evans's away-fans ban was misguided, and my thoughts were confirmed when he stood up at the Conservative Party conference and waxed eloquent on how he was helping law and order by banning away fans at Luton Town. It was that speech which removed the scales from the eyes of the Press, who turned against his campaign and eventually helped kill it. By then David Evans had, in my view, done immense damage to Luton, converting a well-liked, homespun club into an ogre. Luton has never really recovered from that.

I believe there was much greater merit in our own membership scheme. By encouraging our supporters to become members of the club, we both gave them priority for tickets, and reduced prices. We used the scheme very successfully to distribute FA Cup final tickets in 1987 – always a protracted and contentious business for most clubs. But although it was successful, I could not see how we could make the scheme compulsory. To say that somebody must be a member of a football club in order to watch football is both wrong and completely unconstitutional. To me it is a denial of basic freedom, and I could never understand how Mrs Thatcher, who could speak so eloquently about all sorts of freedoms, could not understand that point.

To an extent the debate about football hooliganism confused cause and effect. Just as in the Sixties the low productivity of the English worker and the constant tendency to strike created the image of the English disease, so in the Eighties it became very fashionable for everybody, be it in government or in the media, to talk about football hooliganism as the new English disease. I do not deny that football hooliganism was a plague for English clubs. All the same, it was not merely English clubs who suffered. Indeed, as was to become evident by the middle of the decade, some of the Continental clubs had just as great a problem. Two years before Heysel banned English clubs from Europe for six years, Spurs had had a glimpse of that when we played Feyenoord in the UEFA Cup. Then we were fined for a crowd disturbance but, as we explained at the subsequent hearing in Switzerland, prior to the trouble the chants from the Feyenoord end were 'Ajax!' and it was this rivalry between two Dutch teams which caused the crowd disturbance, and not the Tottenham supporters. We did get the fine slightly reduced, but it made me aware that when there was trouble in Europe it was not often easy to find out who was responsible, unless matters were very clear-cut as they were at Heysel.

It took Continental clubs a long time to realise the need to segregate fans. At some clubs they still do not appreciate it, and some months before Heysel this caused us a tremendous problem when we played Bruges in a UEFA Cup tie. As always when playing in Europe, some days before the match Peter Day flew over to Bruges to check on the arrangements for tickets, hotels and train facilities. Much to his surprise he found that Bruges – contrary to UEFA regulations – had made no attempt to segregate the Spurs fans, and he rang me in some panic from Belgium.

I made tremendous attempts to persuade the club to segregate the fans, but finding them totally unresponsive, I decided to take a bold initiative. I called a Press conference at White Hart Lane and told the assembled journalists that we badly needed their help to try and persuade Spurs fans not to travel for the match. I pointed out that with Bruges unable or unwilling to segregate the fans there was grave danger of crowd trouble, and this could lead to UEFA banning an English club. My fear was that this was what UEFA were seeking to do, as an example. The only trouble they seemed to be getting came from English teams. To their eternal credit the journalists made much of my message, and instead of the thousands that normally would have gone, only around 120 travelled to Bruges. Given that Bruges is closer to London than Manchester, that was quite something. In the end, on the day of the match, Bruges relented and allocated a small area which was segregated for Spurs fans, but by then I was so incensed by their behaviour and lack of co-operation that for the first time ever I insisted our directors boycott the dinner the night before the match.

I thought the way around the away support would be to show the match live, on closed-circuit television, at White Hart Lane, but here again Bruges would not budge. They refused to be realistic about the rights fee, demanding £30,000, when the BBC had made it clear to me that if they were to buy it for highlights and broadcast it nationally it would only have been worth £10,000. Try as I might I could not persuade Bruges to change their minds.

Fearful that we might face a serious crowd problem, I flew to UEFA headquarters in Berne and had a meeting with their

The Orphaned Day. Mabbutt holds up the FA Cup.

The year ends in '1' and Spurs have set a new record:
8 times FA Cup winners.

The Glory Game that inspired me - Spurs' Double team of 1960/61:
Brown, Baker, Henry, Blanchflower, Norman, Mackay, Jones,
White, Smith, Allen, Dyson.

Paul Bobroff

Keith Burkinshaw, Sidney Wale and myself
en route to a match in Israel. December 1982.

The day Paul Gascoigne signed for Spurs. May 1988.

Glenn Hoddle on the day he signed for Monaco. 1987.

Chris Waddle and Gary Mabbutt receiving Spurs Members Player of the Year Awards

Chris Hughton, Garth Crooks, Steve Perryman
and Ray Clemence en route to Israel. December 1982.

John Motson and Chris Waddle when Chris won the
Spurs Player of the Year Award in 1988.

Diego Maradona, the night he
played for Spurs. 1968.

The G-Men: Jimmy Greaves and Alan Gilzean with
Dave Mackay in the background - my real heroes.

Bruges 1984 - with
Martin Chivers (centre)
and Douglas Alexiou.

With Ossie Ardiles
at a football dinner in 1988.

The team that agreed the revolutionary Ten-Point Plan. *Back row left to right* Bill Fox (Blackburn), Lawrie McMenemy (Sunderland), Martin Edwards (Man Utd), Martin Lange (Brentford), Irving Scholar (Tottenham). *Front row left to right* Reg Driver (Aldershot), Philip Carter (Everton), Gordon Taylor (PFA), Ron Noades (Crystal Palace).

Giles during the 1985 TV blackout.

General Secretary, Hans Bangerter, to explain the problems and talk about my misgivings. The meeting proved very fruitful. UEFA said they fully understood our concern and agreed not to hold us responsible should there be a crowd problem. It is one of the iron rules of European competition that the club is held responsible for its supporters, and should there have been any problem it would have been the club that was censured, fined or even banned. With Bruges so bloody-minded, and pirate tour operators threatening to run coach trips to the game, I feared the worst. As it happened, things passed without any incident: our fans were magnificent, and to cap it all we knocked Bruges out.

If that was an example of the strain of playing in Europe, it was more often a pleasure than a pain – and always provided a new, fresh experience. There was the inside of new stadiums to be seen, new people to be met, and a whole new type of game on the park. I particularly liked the pre-match dinners, which are a ritual of European competitions, and developed a little party piece which not only worked very well but for me summed up the European experience. A pre-match dinner or lunch inevitably meant a speech, and I would write out my speech in English but then have it translated by the interpreter into the language of the country we were visiting. I would then write it down phonetically, carefully noting down the interpreter's pronunciation, and would read this phonetic address in the native tongue of the interpreter. It always went down well, and the hosts were impressed that the traditionally insular English could take so much trouble to speak in their own tongue.

One of my great regrets is that during my time at Spurs there were only two European seasons for the club. As we have seen, the post-Heysel situation meant that Spurs took no part in the 1985/86 UEFA campaign, and by the time they returned to Europe in 1991/92, I had gone. So that last 1984/85 season in Europe has a special memory for me, like the sepia-coloured prints that our grandparents used to have.

In those bleak years following Heysel, as we struggled to get English football right – a struggle as much inside football as with forces outside it – I would often look back on the memories of Europe and think of what might have been. Like, for instance, going to play Bohemians in Prague and being taken to an old castle in the centre of the city with an atmosphere like something out of the film *The Third Man*, only with Frankenstein's laboratory inside it. An enormous cobblestone courtyard led to a dungeon lit by candles, in whose centre stood a table, and on it a local drink with dry ice giving off steaming vapours. At any moment I expected Mr Hyde to emerge, but the only one who did was a member of the Bohemians club, who turned out to be a Spurs fanatic with an almost encyclopaedic memory of the team of the Sixties.

Europe provided many such memories, and it was always interesting and uplifting to meet officials of these clubs who were not only great admirers of English football but were also very knowledgeable. The Spurs side of the Sixties would often be in vogue, and as I swapped stories with them I could not help thinking that not too many English officials would have such knowledge, let alone interest, in European clubs.

One of the consequences of the exile was that not only did our playing standards degenerate from being deprived of contact with the best in Europe, but we were also squeezed out of the decision-making process which was changing European football. It was during the Eighties that Bernard Tapie would emerge in France, owning Marseille. In Italy, since his purchase of AC Milan in the mid-Eighties, Silvio Berlusconi has dominated the scene as no other owner before him, not even the great Gianni Agnelli.

Berlusconi's emergence in Italy opened a further divide between the Italian and the English game. It had always intrigued me that people such as Lord Hanson and Lord Weinstock, great industrialists, had never become involved in what is after all our national game. Yet in Italy the biggest industrialists of them all, like Agnelli (involved with Juventus), and now Berlusconi with his vast media empire, seemed very keen to promote the great national game. It is interesting to speculate what Hanson, who comes from Bradford, could have done for Bradford City. But in England they are drawn to other sports such as horse-racing and polo. Working-class football is left to the more working-class owners. The absence of this divide explains a lot about the Italian game. Football is not seen as a male pursuit; it is not unknown for a man to take his wife or girlfriend on a date to a football game, and there the whole experience of watching a game is part of a live Italian event, a celebration.

It is Berlusconi, who owns a number of television stations in Italy and Europe, who has been the driving force behind the European super-league, but while the idea is attractive I doubt that it will ever come about. It would mean too many top teams opting out of various leagues, and would completely destroy the idea of domestic league soccer. What may happen is that it could emerge as a TV extravaganza in tandem with UEFA and the European Cups. What has happened is that the lure of television has changed the format of the European Cup. After a preliminary round of matches it has now turned into a mini-league from which two winners emerge who compete in the Final. I cannot say I am much taken by this format, as the European Cup has lost a little of its glitter by not having a normal two-legged semi-final. Much of the drama that these semi-finals produced has gone, and I would prefer a formula which produced four semi-finalists then followed by the final. However, this format brings in money, and I can well see it being extended to the Cup Winners' Cup and the UEFA Cup.

Money and television is driving these changes forward, and the change came about when Real Madrid were drawn to play Napoli a few years ago in the first round. While both clubs took record amounts at the box office, and Napoli that evening took £2.2 million for one game – to put it in perspective, Spurs record gate receipts are probably in the region of £300–400,000 – they both complained vociferously that in the very first round the match was bound to eliminate one of the top sides in the competition, and in so doing it defeated the object of real European competition.

During the long night of exile for English clubs from Europe, Scottish clubs continued to participate. But, sad to say, they did not make the most of their chance. Although Celtic had been the first British club to win the European Cup, Scotland's record in the mid to late Eighties in European competitions was very poor. This is particularly so in the case of Rangers, Scotland's premier club, who have made a virtual monopoly of the Scottish League during this period, but made no impression whatsoever on the European Cup. I think one of the problems faced by Scottish clubs, in particular Rangers and Celtic, is that they go into Europe without facing any real test in their own league. It is one thing beating the Falkirks and Kilmarnocks by a hatful of goals, quite another to face the likes of AC Milan and Bayern Munich. Tottenham, Arsenal, Liverpool, Everton and Manchester United face much tougher opposition in their own league, and are better able to prepare themselves for the very different world of European soccer.

Ironically, Rangers' lack of success in Europe has come at a time when they have been the pathfinders in British football. No British club has been through as many dramatic changes as Rangers did in the Eighties. While these changes have made a deep impact on Scotland, and also on England, reversing an almost century-old tradition of Scottish players invariably drifting to England, Europe has proved beyond them. Scottish parochialism may be one of the reasons for this, and I understand Graeme Souness felt this very keenly, which also explains why he moved with such great alacrity to Liverpool when the opportunity presented itself in 1991.

I followed these changes at Rangers with great interest. They had been my favourite Scottish team ever since I can remember. When I first went to Ibrox, one Sunday afternoon in April 1986, to watch Spurs play in a testimonial match, I was struck both by the imposing surroundings – the first thing that hits you at the entrance is a large painting on the wall of an ancient Glasgow Rangers player, hung at the top of a huge wooden staircase, and its trophy room is clearly designed for a club that expects to win a lot – and by the fact that it was a club with a glorious past and a very sleepy present. It had just been taken over by the Lawrence Group in Glasgow, and within a few days of the match David Holmes was to take over as chairman, but it was still managed on the field by Jock Wallace, who had also managed clubs in England and maddened journalists with his almost impenetrable Glaswegian accent. Indeed, after one interview Jimmy Greaves had joked: 'Now can we have the interpreter on, please.'

That day, Rangers looked a very poor side, Spurs with mainly a reserves side won 2-0, and on the way back I remarked to Peter Shreeve how subdued Wallace looked. He must have known what was coming, for within a few days he was sacked as Manager and replaced by Graeme Souness. It proved to be a bold, imaginative choice, although I wonder if Souness would have gone to Rangers had we been able to find a place for him at Spurs. As a young professional he had been on Spurs' books in the early Seventies, before being transferred by Bill Nicholson to Middlesbrough for just £30,000. That had been the springboard of his success, as he moved from there to Liverpool and eventually to Sampdoria. It was as he was nearing the end of his Sampdoria career that I heard from an intermediary that he was looking for a job as a player/coach and wondered if we would be interested in employing him. We couldn't, and a few days later Holmes snapped him up, beginning the biggest turnaround in British football since the war.

I could sense some of these changes when a year after this I was back in Glasgow to see the old firm derby between Rangers and Celtic. Before the match I was invited to have lunch with Lawrence Marlborough, a Scot living in America, and the new owner of Rangers. He came over as a Harvard Business School type, and made it clear that he saw Glasgow Rangers as another investment on which he expected to make an annual profit. What made me smile, albeit inwardly, was that not only did Marlborough seem not to realise that football was not like any other investment, but that match itself illustrated the parochial, partisan spirits that animate Scottish football. The noise in the derby match was many millions times more than in any derby match between Tottenham and Arsenal – you could not hear the person sitting next to you – yet in the Rangers boardroom the Rangers and Celtic directors hardly spoke to each other.

I had entered the boardroom babbling away in my normal fashion, only to find that when I stopped talking there was a deadly hush in the room. Nobody was speaking to each other. On one side of the room were the Rangers directors, all dressed in navy blue suits with light blue shirts and Rangers club ties, and on the other side of the table the Celtic directors, with their green jackets, white shirts and club ties. Unlike English clubs, where the bitterest rivalries are forgotten in friendly chat, not one Rangers director was speaking to a Celtic director. I am not normally shocked into silence, but the sight of these two sets of grown men glowering at each other across a table filled with sandwiches and other eatables did shock me.

I also got the impression that day that Lawrence Marlborough would not hold on to the investment very long, and sure enough he sold to David Murray, who besides being a very good friend of Graeme Souness is a man of great strength of character. Although he lost both legs in a car accident when, I believe, he was in his late teens or early twenties, he understood the sport of football and how to manage it, striking up a very successful partnership indeed with Souness. I got to know David very well, liked him, and liked his forthright stance and ability to take tough decisions. When Graeme Souness made it clear that he wanted to leave Rangers to go to Liverpool, and although the season was not yet over, he took the view that if he wanted to go he should go now.

Murray, like Souness, was frustrated by the internal politics of the Scottish League. He would often come up to me with proposals in order to break out of what he saw as the laager mentality of the Scots. After the World Cup in 1990 I went to see Spurs play a pre-season match against Heart of Midlothian in Edinburgh, but when I got to my seat I was surprised to see David Murray and Graeme Souness sitting behind me. They explained that they had only come to the match to take me out for dinner afterwards. We went to an Italian restaurant in Edinburgh and David Murray poured his heart out. He really wanted Rangers to form part of a British super-league involving the big clubs in England.

The idea was attractive, but I had to explain to him, as I have done every time the question is raised, that if this was to take place then FIFA would immediately question the right of Great Britain to have four national teams, England, Scotland, Wales and Northern Ireland, and demand that they all be merged into a single Great British team. This was an historic right won by the home countries because of their pioneering role in foot-ball, but it is not possible to have four representations in world soccer and yet at the same time have just one domestic national league. That would be a case of having your cake and eating it too. In time it may come, but I cannot see it happening soon or easily.

Of course, it is impossible to predict changes in football. I could not have anticipated when I took over at Spurs in 1982 that by 1992 we would have had a Premier League in England with the Football League torn asunder. Many reasons contributed to the change, and it is time to pause and look at why and how football changed in this country.

6 | THE FATAL ATTRACTION

Scholar to Greg Dyke: 'What I want to know is, is there a cartel between the BBC and ITV?'

Greg Dyke: 'Yes, there has been a cartel in existence.'

Although Saatchi's had been involved in our Mrs Ridlington TV and radio commercial, these had been done when I was an absentee landlord, and I had never met Alex Fynn before. Just a few days before I made my Rothman's speech, in August 1984, I went to see him at Saatchi & Saatchi's offices in Charlotte Street, and it was a meeting that both of us had good reason to recall. Alex keeps telling me that he will never forget the sight of me hobbling into his office.

A couple of months earlier, at that most fashionable centre of world football, Brisbane Road, Leyton Orient, I had damaged my Achilles tendon playing for the Spurs staff. This was the match Ossie Ardiles was going to use as a warm-up, trying to get fit for the UEFA Cup Final. But as I turned to get a through ball I snapped my Achilles tendon; it felt as if someone had kicked me in the back of my leg. As I fell to the ground the nearest person to me was Tommy Taylor, the ex-West Ham centre-half, and I just looked up at him and said: 'What on earth did you do that for?' He replied: 'I didn't touch you!' I knew there and then the injury I had suffered. I was very fortunate in that Mike Varney, the club physio, was also playing, and was standing only about ten yards away from me at the time. Next day I went into hospital, where it was operated on by the specialist, John Browett, who was later to operate on Glenn Hoddle, Danny Thomas and Paul Gascoigne.

It was some weeks after this, and having cheered Spurs to the UEFA Cup on a highly emotional night at White Hart Lane, that I went to see Alex. I wanted to find out more about television and football, a subject that had already begun to fascinate me. As long as I can remember I have been fascinated by football on television. Football and TV have a habit of appearing like oil and water. The question that I debated was – Is television good for football? Is football good for television? I had no doubts that the answers were Yes to both questions. Promotion on television of football creates more interest in the national game, and certainly football was good for television because it is the only major sport that can command audiences of 10 million plus.

I agree with Brian Glanville that there can be no substitute for actually going to the ground. However much television improves its technology, however many cameras they employ, whatever gimmick they use – though some, like the use by Sky of my old mate Bob 'the Cat' Bevan, suggest that in some cases television may be going backwards and trying to recycle music hall routines – nothing can match actually being present in a stadium. For a start you appreciate the full dimensions of the game, even if you do miss the action replay, and you just cannot experience the same thrill or sensations in your living room. If there was a choice I would always vote for the former.

Indeed, producers of televised football are all too aware that they need an audience, and a good audience, to come to watch what they want to televise. Modern sports television is all about showing events, and you cannot have an event if it is watched by two old men and a dog. This explains why until the beginning of the 1992/93 season Wimbledon had never had a League match televised live to the nation. With home support of 3,000, not all the ingenuity of a good producer can conjure up the necessary atmosphere. For television there is nothing worse than showing a stand full of empty plastic seats: with hardly anybody there, the viewer is half-expecting a duff game.

It was at that meeting in 1984 that I began to appreciate the role of television and football. I had never met Alex before, but I found what he said fascinating, particularly his theory of TV as an event, which holds that television can show a live sport provided it is a sufficiently compelling event or can be made such. The theory has a role for both small and big clubs, but the role for the big clubs is at the top of the pile in a smaller First Division. At this meeting Alex did most of the talking, which those who know me will know is a major surprise! But I listened carefully and wanted to explore this vital area. Even then I had begun to realise that while many people talked about football and television and everybody had a theory, few bothered to study it or gather any reliable facts.

In those days football was busy experimenting with the concept of live televised matches. Today such matches are here to stay, and we all have to accept that more people will see football on the little box than actually go to a match. Even those who do not like television and hate televised football accept that. Alan Hardaker may turn in his grave, but football has to live with live television. The only questions now are how many games, how much money, and on which channel.

Yet when I saw Alex, it seemed very doubtful that football would accept the 'experiment' of live television; indeed, soon after this, as we shall see, football nearly tore itself apart as a result of trying to live with the new developments. Nearly all the changes we have seen since have been the result of television's impact on football. If Greg Dyke, head of London Weekend Television, can now claim to be the Godfather of the Premier League, then some feel that Sam Chisholm of Sky may well prove to be its gravedigger. Television now talks megabucks, yet the problem for football has always been to get a right price for its product from television. The vicious battle going on in the Premier League is about the share of this loadsamoney that clubs believe they can get: all a far cry from that day in 1964 when the Football League reached agreement with the BBC to televise a new highlights programme on a Saturday evening called 'Match of the Day'.

After I got involved with the television negotiations I got Lee Walker at the commercial offices of the League to show me the file which contained details of the contract signed between the BBC and Alan Hardaker, then the Secretary of the Football League. Although Lee took the file out of a modern filing cabinet, the material inside it spoke of another time, long gone. It staggered me to realise that under that deal, done in 1964, each individual club got just £50 a year, with television paying £5,000 for the entire season, and the money divided equally between the ninety-two clubs.

If the League was wary of football, then television did not know how the product would be received, and the programme was first shown on BBC2. It is curious to note how the second channel always uses football to try and experiment – a tradition that has been continued with Channel 4's showing of Italian football. I wonder what might have happened, back in 1956, had the League gone through with Associated Television's proposal to show live the second half of a game every Saturday evening at 6.15. ATV were then offering £50,000, and would be responsible for compensation should the clubs suffer any loss in gate revenue 'for any reason whatsoever'. But only one match was shown and the idea ran into the sands – a pity. It would have enabled the League to discover once and for all whether or not this was likely to affect attendances. Just as the Sunday live match has altered the geography of our football schedule – much to the disgust of my journalistic friends who write for the Sunday papers – so I am sure a live second-half match shown late on Saturday night would have had an impact.

By 1982, as I became the largest shareholder at Spurs, the live argument had been revived, with the television authorities keen to have as 'an experiment' ten live League matches in addition to a diet of recorded highlights. The television bosses, particularly the ITV ones, had been looking across the Atlantic, and there television had discovered that live sport could be an event, something that the highlights could never be. With highlights most people knew the results before they started, whereas the unpredictability of a live event was something that even an audience at home, maybe thousands of miles from where the event was taking place, could actually participate in.

I had no part to play in these negotiations, although, as I have said, we were chosen for the very first live match shown on ITV, in October 1983, when Nottingham Forest visited White Hart Lane. One of the great fears before the match was that a live match would turn the viewers at home off football. Recorded highlights were supposed to remove the dull bits, only represent the entertaining moments; with a live match the gold and the dross would be there. Would the viewers accept the dross as they waited for the odd nugget? Some newspapers carried two reports: in addition to the normal football report on the match, one correspondent sat at home and watched it on television. I recall one report which said little about the match or television but described how the writer had to show a red card to his four-year-old in the middle of a tense moment.

I was personally very nervous about live television, because I felt sure that it was going to have a marked effect on gates. Why should people pay substantial amounts of money and endure the hassles that going to a match entails, when they could sit in the comfort of their own armchair at home and watch the match effectively for free, as they had already paid their licence fee? My concerns turned out to be ill-founded, as our gate that day was just over 30,000. The BBC and ITV had decided to share the ten live matches equally, and as it happened we were also chosen for the very first BBC match when we played Manchester United at Old Trafford a couple of months later.

Football's relationship with television is like the lady from Riga who stepped on the back of the tiger, hoping to have a nice ride. She ended up inside, and television is always threatening to do the same to football. As so often happens in television, what starts out as an experiment quickly ends up becoming the norm. ITV were ecstatic about the experiment but were no longer satisfied with just ten live League games. They wanted to increase to sixteen, plus the 'option' to screen regional live matches. Twelve months before the 'experimental' contract expired, the Football League Television Negotiation Committee, headed by Sir Arthur South, was in deep discussions with both BBC and ITV to renew it.

My concern was that as long as television operated a cartel, football could not make the companies compete against each other. The League asked for clubs to express their views in writing about the live experiment. On 31 January 1985 I wrote to Jack Dunnett, then President of the Football League:

> In order for football to gain most from television it is funda-mental that the Clubs in the first instance decide how much television they are prepared to sell and in which format. It is for the members to decide whether they have a preference for selling certain live matches which I would sincerely hope would be kept to a minimum thereafter. The two networks should then be invited to tender, quite separately. Initially, the edited highlights package, which could be extended in screening time, to 90 minutes instead of the customary 60 minutes, would be bid for. Following the outcome of this first stage, the live football package, if this is what the members wanted, should be quite separately tendered, making it clear to the television companies that only one company would be screening highlights and possibly the same or other would be screening live.

It is quite probable that your negotiating committee will say that these proposals are unworkable, but until they attempt to force the television companies to negotiate separately, there is no definitive answer. What has disappointed me most in the past is that television always seems to be dictating to football what it wants rather than football offering television what it is prepared to allow. I have noticed quite recently that following the athletics television tender, ice hockey has now followed the same successful route, and I am interested to know why football should be very different. When there is no competition there is no need for the television companies to pay the true market value, as there is no alternative. It is like an auction with only one buyer in the room and no reserve price.

It is fundamental for the long-term well-being of our national sport that we are strong enough not to allow television to force the game into further demise.

Neither the Television Committee nor the Management Committee appeared to take much heed of this, but it prepared the ground for what League historians now call the St Valentine's Day Massacre of 1985 at the Great Western Hotel in Paddington. At this historic venue of many a Football League meeting, history was truly made. It was a seminal moment in the long history of the somewhat stormy marriage between football and television.

Gathered together in that room – standing room only – were the great, the good and the noisy of football, both Ken Bates and Robert Maxwell. Dunnett was presenting an ITV and BBC proposal offering £3.8 million in the first year for a four-year deal. Year 2 was to be plus 6 per cent; Year 3 plus 6 per cent; and Year 4 plus 8 per cent. This was for nineteen live matches which included sixteen League games and two League Cup semi-finals, plus the League Cup Final and with an option for regional live games. It was soon very clear that the clubs had a lot of misgiving about the deal, particularly the option of live regional matches. This could mean as many as seventy to eighty live matches a season. We could have ended up with live matches in Yorkshire, Central, Granada and all the other regions, with thirteen live games on any one Sunday afternoon. Yet the clubs did not want to budge from ten live games all season. Tempers ran very high, and I realised how emotive the subject was and the growing feeling, echoing my own, that while we ran football it was television that was dictating the shape and nature of the game.

I made no bones about my opposition to the deal, but the man who took the headlines was Robert Maxwell. It was the first time that I had ever seen him in person at a meeting, and his powerful, persuasive manner dominated the proceedings. He summed up the contract in a very simple way. He called it bad, mad and sad. Brought down to this simplistic level he managed to take the clubs along with him, and by the end of the meeting they were eating out of his hand. His clinching argument was that the clubs were grossly underselling football, and in his opinion television should be paying £10 million a year – a figure that sounded fantastic then, but seems, if anything, a great understatement now. Given this piece of information it was hardly likely that they were going to accept the current offer.

The meeting voted on a number of resolutions:

1   Do the clubs accept the TV Committee's proposals as a package?
    No.
2   Do the clubs accept the present proposals for two years?
    No.
3   Do the clubs accept the present proposals eliminating regional live football on television?
    No.
4   Do the clubs prefer to retain the current package of ten live Canon League matches plus a recorded package of a minimum of 76 Canon League matches, minimum transmission time of fifteen minutes each match on both channels?
    This resolution was accepted. Clubs felt that the principles that applied at present should remain.
5   Do the clubs wish to have a television contract for:
    (a) two years (b) four years (c) four years with a two-year break clause at the League's option?
    The two-year option was carried unanimously.
6   Do the clubs accept a Milk Cup package of rounds 2–5 recorded (including re-plays), plus 2 live semi-finals (Wednesday), plus live final?
    This resolution was carried.

The other point he made which struck a chord with me was that the only way to get the best deal from television was to break the cartel of BBC and ITV and make them bid separately for televised football. Eventually it was decided that the Television

Committee would be mandated to reopen discussions with BBC and ITV. Robert Maxwell, Ken Bates and I were co-opted into the Committee, and the bottom line was that no more than ten live League games a year should be sold.

What concerned me was that nobody knew how much televised football was worth. When you want to sell something, you should have some idea of what price it is worth. Yet when I asked my fellow Committee members this question, I was met with blank stares. I suggested we should go to a professional, independent expert to advise us in television terms what our product was worth, and once again I approached Saatchi & Saatchi.

The result was a paper by Saatchi & Saatchi called *Football and Television: Its Influence on Programme Costs and Advertisement Revenue*, in which it analysed the approximate hours of football transmissions between August 1983 and May 1984. On ITV there had been 42 hrs 5 mins; on BBC 44 hrs 50 mins, making 86 hrs 55 mins of transmission at an average cost of £29,000 per hour to transmit. According to Saatchi & Saatchi ITV earned an extra £6 million in advertising revenue gross through football transmissions in which air time was sold of 7 mins or more per hour. ITV took in an estimated £17.7 million advertisement revenue, gross, in football transmissions but would only take in £11.7 million without. For the first time we could price our own product.

This was the first time I had been invited to the inner sanctum of the football world, and I was fascinated by the people I was meeting. Maxwell was, obviously, the biggest personality. For some reason I would always arrive late at these meetings, invariably held at the Great Western Hotel. As I tapped on the door and walked in, Maxwell would look up and indicate a vacant seat next to him – there always seemed to be one vacant. He would then whisper out of the side of his mouth: 'What are the various points we want to make today?' I would scribble down a few notes, three or four headings. He would take one glance at these, ask the Committee if he could speak first, and then speak for thirty to forty minutes, non-stop, covering every single detailed point, all based on jottings on a scrap of paper. When he had finished he would gather his things together, saying he was terribly sorry, he had to dash off to another meeting, 'but Irving will pick up any other loose points that need to come up.' I suppose he intimidated the Committee by his very physical presence, but he was also well liked, and there was a certain charm which combined with his aggressive, gruff manner to make him very formidable indeed. He thought nothing of picking up the telephone and speaking to someone very high up at the IBA, which was the overseeing watchdog of commercial television, to try and pull strings. This never failed to make a big impression.

Apart from Maxwell, the one other character you could not miss was Ken Bates. I nicknamed him 'The Bearded Barbarian', a remark he took quite well, probably revelled in, and he and I got on extremely well together. His bark is certainly worse than his bite and, as I was to learn over the years, his title of 'Blaster Bates' is certainly deserved. Although he was aggressive he always came across as a very clear-thinking man, and his determination can hardly be doubted given the way he has pursued the purchase of Stamford Bridge.

The only thing is, he made a dreadful mistake back in 1982 when he could have purchased it. Indeed it was in connection with Stamford Bridge that I had first met Bates, even before I was involved with Spurs. I was the first person to tell him the ground was for sale. This was in September 1982, when I went to lunch at a restaurant in the West End and was waiting at the bar for my guest. There was no mistaking the white hair and white beard, and I approached Ken and said that I was a very keen football fan and in the property business, and wondered if he was aware that SB Property Company was trying to sell Stamford Bridge. He wanted to know who I was and where I got my information from. I explained that the property business was a very small one and such information got around. It was clear from his response that he was completely unaware of what was going on behind the scenes. I gave him my telephone number and said if he wanted to contact me for any further information, he should do so, but he never called.

Some months later, after I had become involved with Tottenham, Bates did express his appreciation and said he was working on it. But the unfortunate mistake he made was not to buy Stamford Bridge from SB Property Company then. Controlled by the Mears family who built Stamford Bridge back in 1905, they wanted £1 million but would have sold it to Chelsea, the club they were associated with, for £800,000. Dear old Ken in his inimitable fashion offered them £600,000, and they subsequently sold it to Marler Estates for around £1.2 million.

It was an opportunity missed for Ken, and one I'm sure he has lived to regret. It is only as I write this that he has been able to buy the ground from Cabra, after a long involved struggle, and paying many millions more than he would have done in 1982.

Years later, after I got to know Ken, Stanley Tollman, his South African partner who lives in New York, told me: 'One of the reasons he likes you so much, Irving, is that you don't take him too seriously.' I explained that it wasn't a question of not taking him seriously, but taking some of the things he says in the way they are given, with a pinch of salt. I discovered this almost as soon as we started working on the Television Committee. He would come to the meetings with some very good ideas for football, but for every seven or eight ideas, only one or two at the outside were feasible in my view.

Maxwell, when he was present at the meetings, tended to dominate them, but he did not often attend – which in some ways was just as well for Sir Arthur South, our Chairman. He was then Chairman of Norwich, although not for long. There were people plotting to get rid of him, as I was soon to discover – the plotters wanted me as a consultant! Sir Arthur was a product of the old Labour Party, busy in local Norfolk life, Chairman of the Regional Health Authority and, shall we say, a nice old buffoon. I do mean this well. But it was clear that many of the technicalities of the negotiations passed him by. Also he was, at times, so inclined to find a solution that he would try and circumvent our mandate.

At one particular meeting, when we realised we were covering the same ground again and again, Sir Arthur tried to break ranks by saying: 'What would you pay us for twelve live League games?' I asked at that moment for the TV companies to leave the room for a short recess. Then, with only the football people present, I took Sir Arthur to task: we had no authority whatsoever to seek or even attempt to seek any offers over and above ten live games. I thought that Arthur South would explode, but he took the criticism on board, accepted it, and duly called the television companies back. After that I had no problems with Sir Arthur.

I heard about the plot against him some time in 1985, when I was introduced to Robert Chase by a mutual friend who said that Chase wanted to meet me privately to enquire how I had taken control of Tottenham. I went to his house in Norwich on the morning of a match where we were due to play. Chase turned out to be a large man who told me he was somewhat addicted to Coca-Cola, drinking something like fifteen bottles a day, and finally gave it up to lose weight. He explained that he and a friend, Jimmy Jones, had bought a large block of Norwich City shares and wanted to know the best way to remove Sir Arthur South. It seemed South had a very small holding indeed. I explained that if he had the shares, all he had to do was call an Extraordinary General Meeting of the company and remove him, but he seemed very loath to take that step, pointing out: 'People in Norfolk don't deal with things that way.' I then said that the only other way would be to do it by agreement, which is what he did some six months later.

The takeover proved traumatic, particularly when supporters got incensed about the sacking of Ken Brown as Manager. It got so bad that one day when Chase was out in his Rolls Royce, somebody dropped a milk crate from a bridge which went clean through the windscreen and nearly killed him. Apparently for some time afterwards he had a bodyguard with him at all times.

For various reasons Norwich became something of an alternative Spurs down the M11, and we did a lot of deals. But I did not always take to Chase's negotiating style. His attitude was always sell for a high price and buy for a low price. Our paths crossed in 1990 when he signed John Polston from Spurs at the end of his contract. The tribunal set the figure at £300,000, which we felt was far too low, but as Chase had been through the exercise on numerous occasions, he had by then got it off pat and knew exactly how to play it in order to get the best possible price. If you look at Norwich City's record at purchasing players, there don't seem to be too many bought by way of agreement between clubs. The majority of their signings have come via the tribunal. They have never been slow to cash in on highly valued players. Looking back, for all the Old Boy air of Sir Arthur I would rather deal with him than Chase, particularly when it came to selling a player.

Graham Kelly, then Secretary of the League, was also Secretary of the Committee. He didn't have much to say, and came across as competent, with a keen sense of humour, and willing to seek a solution. He had in some way the making of a typical bureaucrat, and this was revealed to me some years later when I became an FA councillor and Kelly had become Secretary of the FA. I was curious to find what were the terms of the television contract between the BBC, BSB and the FA, but I could not get a copy. I finally asked Bert Millichip, President of the FA, if it was true that the television contract, as described in a national newspaper, was a secret document. He replied: 'No, of course not.'

'Well then, can I have a copy?'

'No.'

'Then it is a secret document.'

After that I wrote to Kelly several times trying to get a copy of the document, but failed so thoroughly that Kelly even stopped replying to my letters. Eventually, I got my own copy. What the Football Association hadn't realised was that it was a public document, registered at the Office of Fair Trading. When my term expired and I stood again, I found myself in a duel with Reg Burr, Chairman of Millwall. He won the second tie-break, and Kelly informed me of this in a cold, formal, precise letter with not a word of thanks for my three years of service. I just felt it summed up the man.

I was also introduced to a very different kind of administrator while on the Committee. Early on it was broken into several subcommittees, and the one that I was appointed to contained Peter Robinson, Chief Executive of Liverpool. Jack Dunnett had told me that he was a person of great technical knowledge, and I quickly realised how shrewd he was and how well he understood the practical problems of television and football. Peter had over the years worked well with the BBC; he was a football figure television respected, and it was a joy to work with him.

Over the years I got to know him very well and began to be impressed with his immense all-round ability. Now I feel I know him so well that I can accurately diagnose that a particular football initiative has Robinson's signature tune. Shankly, Paisley, Fagan and all the Boot Room boys have taken the credit for the amazing success machine Liverpool have built in the last thirty years, but in my book nobody merits more congratulations for Liverpool's success than Peter. I believe much of the credit for their having just gone on winning goes to him – the calm way he runs the club, the shrewd way he orchestrates the whole thing, particularly the media. Indeed Robinson, who has very good contacts with the journalists who cover soccer on Merseyside, is by far the best source of stories on Everton.

In the gossipy world of football he knows how to keep secrets and who to trust – as was illustrated just before he appointed Dalglish. Round about late February/early March of 1985, Peter and I, after a tiring meeting in London, decided to stop off for a drink and a snack in the West End. Peter suddenly looked me in the eye and said: 'Can I ask you something in confidence?' I nodded and he asked: 'What do you think of Kenny Dalglish?'

'A great player,' I replied. 'You've told me on many occasions that he is probably the best player to wear a Liverpool shirt since the war. Why do you ask?'

'No, no,' he replied. 'Do you think he'll make a good player/manager?'

At that time there was no such thing as a player/manager in the First Division, and normally you had to go down to the Third or Fourth Divisions to find players in the twilight of their career combining the roles. Peter started to explain that Joe Fagan was going to stand down at the end of the season and that the board were thinking of promoting Kenny Dalglish. I said to him that if he was a good communicator with his players and he was confident of his coaching abilities, although it was risky, I was sure it would work out.

About two months later, on the day of the ill-fated European Cup Final at the Heysel Stadium in Belgium, Joe Fagan announced his retirement before the match and broke the news that Kenny Dalglish was to be appointed as his replacement.

In the intervening months between my conversation and the announcements, there had been no Press leaks. John Smith was Chairman at the time, and was later knighted for his services to sport. He was also Chairman of the Sports Council and on the Committee of the All England Club at Wimbledon. Together, John Smith and Peter Robinson made an unlikely but by far the best double act in football I had ever seen. They were the cleverest, shrewdest pair imaginable.

What is amazing about Peter is that for all the power and influence he exercises, he is quite the most unassuming man I know. He knows who he is, and does not need to flaunt his authority. I was made aware of this during the 1986 FA Cup Final at Wembley when Liverpool followed Spurs and Arsenal and did the Double. I had arranged to have my son photographed with the Liverpool team, something they did very graciously, and it was intriguing to learn that Peter had travelled down to London in a minibus with his friends. At Wembley he sat with them towards the back of the Stand, and I was amused to think that the man who ran Liverpool should be happy with such anonymity on a day that meant so much for the club. If only the hordes of Liverpool supporters around had realised who he was, they would have been a little taken aback, I'm sure. What a contrast to the squabbling to sit in the Royal Box at Tottenham during the 1991 Cup Final – and this by people who had not been two minutes at the club. But for all his love and devotion to Liverpool, Peter's greatest love is cricket, and I am sure he would happily run Lancashire cricket if he got the call.

Being on the committee meant that this was also the first time I met the two television negotiators, John Bromley from ITV and Jonathan Martin from the BBC. They were very contrasting personalities. Bromley – an ex-journalist and the man who took Michael Grade under his wing when Grade was a novice on the *Mirror* – is an urbane, bright man, always good-humoured and immensely liked both in football and television. With him, more progress was made at the bar after meetings than behind the closed doors. Occasionally he would bring Ronald Allison along. A former Buckingham Palace Press Aide, his smooth exterior concealed a very tough, unrelenting approach. I had encountered him some months previously when I had discussions concerning the sale of rights of a Spurs UEFA Cup tie. I thought the match against Real Madrid, involving a British club, would be a good product, but was amazed to find that all he was interested in offering was £45,000 for the match. He could not understand why I sniffed at such an offer.

Unlike League and FA Cup matches, where the television rights are supposed to be owned by the competition organiser, the home clubs own their rights when it comes to European competition. Over the last few years, owing to deregulation and the breaking of monopolies, these have become extremely valuable.

Jonathan Martin could not have been more different from his opposite numbers at ITV: humourless, sour-faced, and a man who always preferred the scowl to the smile. His nickname was the Little Colonel. Unlike Bromley he seemed a very institutional man, although the two of them did represent a Laurel and Hardy double-act, with Martin the straight man and Bromley a bit of a comedian. Watching them operate I sometimes felt that they were on the same side, holding hands under the table: Martin pleading poverty on behalf of the BBC, and Bromley, albeit with a smile, nodding to this same Dickensian tale. ITV always seemed to be hiding behind the BBC arguments of poverty and taking advantage of them. It was clear they could offer a lot more money than was being put on the table, but it suited them to take advantage of the BBC's position. BBC had then begun to suffer in the ratings war and they did not want to be caught out. They didn't want ITV to go for live football without doing the same. Instead of the BBC being the great sports innovators, they were giving the impression of being merely the imitators.

What upset me particularly was that Martin was always talking down football and in particular 'Match of the Day', which the BBC had slowly strangled to death by switching its regular slot. Having spent years building up 'Match of the Day' into a national institution, Martin and his friends were now undermining it. It was easily done. For years we had grown used to watching highlights of two top matches on Saturday evening, with all the interviews, starting at 10 pm. It came just after the News and was followed by the late movie, to round off Saturday evening. But suddenly the BBC started playing with the times. It would be 10 pm one week, 10.20 pm the next, 10.55 pm the one after; then 11.15, 11.35, all sorts of random times. In television terms this is equivalent to murder. Let us say 'Coronation Street', instead of going out at 7.30 pm every week as it does, goes out one week at 7.30 pm, then 7.45 pm, then 7.15 pm, then 8.30 pm. It wouldn't take much to start disfiguring the ratings, because television is a creature of habit. People switch on the television at a particular time each week and expect to see a programme they have previously seen. Nothing is more frustrating to the viewer than to switch on his television set expecting to see his programme, and find its start time has been altered.

Cliff Morgan's presence by the side of Martin did lighten the mood at times. I could see that as a great sportsman who cared deeply about sports, he was embarrassed that this type of charade was going on, and that the national sport was being squeezed to sell its products at whatever price was on offer with no regard to value.

When our Committee started its work both Martin and Bromley were more than a little put out at having to start all over again. They knew their deal with the previous Committee was subject to club approval, but they had assumed it would go through on the nod. Now here they were discussing with another Committee, and one that contained Maxwell. Robert Maxwell seemed to be the *bête noire* as far as the television companies were concerned. At one stage both BBC and ITV refused to attend meetings with him on the Committee. For them he was too fierce an opponent, with his considerable publishing and television interests.

On one point we quickly reached agreement. Regional live games were quickly buried. Bromley and Martin recognised that they could not budge the clubs on this, and soon it was very clear that the sticking-point was the ten live games. We could not depart from our mandate; television, its appetite whetted, wanted more; and for much of the meetings we circled around this – Martin and Bromley pushing for more, while we resisted. We wanted the guarantee of recorded highlights, but the television companies refused to give any. Impasse.

Having been elected on to the TV Negotiating Committee in February, we sought no further contact with the TV networks for a couple of months, on the grounds that we were seeking advice from Saatchi & Saatchi and looking into the question of preparing ourselves fully to go back to them with packages to tender. Two months later, on 1 May 1985, two virtually identical letters were received by Graham Kelly, with identical phrases written on exactly the same day. Whoever said there wasn't a cartel at the time only had to look at these letters to realise that it was still flourishing in the depths of Broadcasting House and South Bank Television Centre.

In fact ITV in their proposal actually suggested that: 'An ITV/BBC rota should operate on the 32 weekends of the Football League season. Each organisation should have the right to League football on sixteen weekends.' One of the disappointing things was that both ITV and BBC were talking about the 'option to televise recorded highlights'. They weren't even going to guarantee that 'Match of the Day' was going to be shown at all.

On the Television Sub-Committee our task was to prepare for the first time a schedule of what football wanted to sell to television, rather than to wait and see what television wanted to buy. Peter Robinson, Lee Walker and I spent a Sunday in May having a brain-storming session at the Great Western Hotel and finally came out with three packages which were approved by the Committee and sent to ITV and BBC. The idea was to break the cartel and get the best deal for football.

Package one was for ten live League matches plus recorded highlights on the other twenty-one weekends. Package two was for thirty-one weekends of recorded highlights plus the Milk Cup, with two semi-final legs appearing live. Both of the offers were for two years, and we were prepared to consider a third proposal for all or part of the packages. In other words, if someone wanted to buy exclusivity, they could.

A deadline of around two weeks was set for the tender. There were no raised eyebrows or surprises when ITV and BBC sent in letters almost simultaneously to the Committee stating that they had no intention of bidding but were interested in taking the discussions further. The letters were virtually identical, and it was clear that this was a cartel. They refused to be separated – or at least not then.

By the middle of the summer of 1985 it was becoming more and more difficult to get ITV and BBC to alter their stance at all. Both of them were making it clear to us that they were not fussed whether they got football on television or not. They told us that we had become less and less attractive to them and that they had hardened their attitude against football. There was by now real danger that the new season could start with blank screens.

At one meeting at the beginning of September, in the White Hart Lane boardroom, I did make an attempt to break the cartel, but this was like trying to find a player with a forty-yard pass through the eye of a needle: the idea was good but it could just not be executed. At that particular moment, Jonathan Martin, the BBC negotiator, left the room for a few minutes. In frustration I turned to John Bromley and said to him, in front of all the Committee members: 'Why don't you stop messing around and make a bid to buy the ten live games on an exclusive basis? That way you don't have to share five with the BBC.' He looked at me, smiled, and did not say anything. Phil Carter interjected to point out that I had no authority to make such a proposal. I am not making a proposal, I replied, merely seeking it. A few minutes later Martin re-entered the room and Bromley, laughingly, said he'd just been offered the exclusive. It was then absolutely clear to all of us that we were not going to break the cartel between them, and they were just trying to wear us down to a point where we would give in out of sheer frustration to their requests.

By then we were three weeks into the season, and the discussions were reaching the point of a possible one-season bridging deal. The television companies were seeking fourteen live League games whilst we were mandated only to offer ten. Ken Bates pointed out that over 70 per cent of what they were looking for was better than nothing, but this was met with a blank stare. The other big problem was that neither of the television companies was at all prepared to guarantee recorded highlights.

Our difficulty had always been that we were dealing with people who were not genuine decision-makers. It seemed that our opposite numbers, John Bromley and Jonathan Martin, were acting on instructions from above and had a set agenda that they were glued to. We were always trying to get to the real decision-makers, the people above who might see our arguments and reach some form of agreement. It was to be several years before we managed to achieve this aim.

It is possible that in the summer of 1985 we might have got a deal, but then fate dealt football a very bad hand. A series of disasters took place which brought the game into disrepute, to use the phrase so loved by the FA. The Bradford fire killed fifty-six people. Earlier there had been an appalling riot by Millwall fans at Luton. A fan died at Birmingham when a wall collapsed. Finally and terribly came the Heysel tragedy, which caused the deaths of thirty-nine Juventus fans.

About this time I became aware that if the matches were going to be blacked out by the BBC and ITV, suddenly football was going to go the way of other British industries which spent years building up a big export market then found that they were not making the products that the rest of the world wanted and were overtaken by foreign competition. The Football League has a programme which is sold throughout the world on a weekly basis. At that time it was a highlights programme hosted by Brian Moore, called Big League Soccer. In addition to that there were numerous matches beamed out live to Scandinavia, whose own season finished early due to the bad winters. These were very valuable to the clubs that appeared, due to the perimeter boards which were sold to Scandinavian advertising. At the time there was no commercial television in those countries.

I remember asking Lee Walker what would happen to these matches. Suddenly the penny dropped that they wouldn't be shown and there would be a huge outcry from the clubs. In addition the German Bundes League and the Italian First Division were trying very hard to get into these markets, and it would be disastrous if after all the years of promotion and support from Scandinavia these markets should be lost. Also the football pools in Scandinavia are very lucrative to the pools companies in England, and form quite a large income.

Lee and I eventually got the television committee to agree

to us meeting Thames TV, who were distributing the highlights programme to fifty-three countries. As a means of protection, Thames Television International agreed a deal with the Football League by which they would commission and send out cameras to League grounds throughout the season in the event of there being no football on television. This proved to be very important, for soon our worst fears were realised and the season began with no football on television, for the first time since 'Match of the Day' had started in 1964. It was a curious situation: English football was being televised all around the globe, except in England.

This was also the season when Frank McAvennie came down from Scotland to play for West Ham and score a hatful of goals, and I had an idea of producing what was really the very first football video, showing highlights of all the matches that had been recorded and beamed overseas so far that season. I got Maxwell to underwrite the cost and it was heavily advertised in his newspaper under the title 'Soccer '85', which sold extremely well.

Yet all this did not solve the problem of soccer on television. We knew that both BBC and ITV were quite happy not to show any soccer. 1986 would be World Cup year. BBC were planning to show some fifty hours of World Cup football – almost as much football as they had shown in the previous 1984/85 season.

We did try to break the cosy cartel by going to the Football Association, who agreed not to conclude any TV deal until the Football League had concluded their negotiations. This worried the BBC, and Martin expressed concern at possibly having to face a cartel against his own cartel. We also wrote to the Office of Fair Trading, but they showed no enthusiasm for stepping in and finding out.

By late October, no further progress had been made, and Jonathan Martin was offended at a letter sent by the Football League criticising both BBC and ITV for the fact that 'a will does not exist on the part of television' to conclude negotiations. He rejected the suggestion that negotiations had irretrievably broken down and insisted that as far as the broadcasters were concerned, they would be willing to continue negotiations for as long as was necessary. I was a little miffed at this, as the broadcasters had promised, following a meeting some six weeks before, to confirm to the League the value of live and recorded football, but had failed to do so.

The BBC began to reveal their hand more openly than before. They said that they were prepared to consider a deal for the balance of the season, and willing to accept six live League games to be shared between them, starting in the New Year.

The joint Press statement given by Graham Kelly read: 'Sufficient progress has been made to justify a further meeting in the near future.' Nobody on the League side felt that confident.

The final meeting took place on 1 November at the Holiday Inn at Heathrow. If the previous February had been the St Valentine's Day massacre, this was Black Friday. For nearly four hours we argued back and forth, endlessly repeating the arguments that had been going round in circles for months. The one thing that the television companies refused to do was to price the package that they wanted to buy. On our side everybody was completely fed up with the entrenched position of both ITV and BBC. Every time something was put to the cartel, Jonathan Martin said that he had to leave the room and get clearance from Michael Grade. It was obvious to us that Martin was merely acting as a puppet for the Controller of BBC-1, the same gentleman who had attempted, in 1979, to hijack 'Match of the Day' for ITV.

Not surprisingly, the meeting broke up round about three in the afternoon, amidst scenes of acrimony. Ken Bates lost his cool and said he was going home to dig his garden. He accused Martin and Bromley of being merely the 'office boys'. The words were actually uttered by Bob Daniel of Plymouth Argyll, who hardly said anything at these meetings, but were quickly appropriated by Ken Bates and caused quite a few laughs at BBC Television Centre. But that was how Martin & Co appeared to us and Ken Bates had actually got it right.

About ten days later the First and Second Division clubs met at the Cumberland Hotel in London and were brought up to date concerning the irretrievable breakdown of the negotiations. Some clubs, incensed by the television companies' attitude, advocated blacking out the World Cup due to be held in Mexico the following summer. But this was futile anger, as until BBC and ITV could be prised apart they remained the one and only piper, who would always call the tune.

However, the television negotiations had caused a great deal of tension within the League, as can be seen from the fact that on 18 October 1985 Graham Kelly wrote to Jack Dunnett, his own boss, expressing fears that the Management Committee was planning to take over the negotiations:

The Television Committee are seeking your unconditional assurance, on behalf of the Management Committee, that the Management Committee are not contemplating such action as stated in my first paragraph, until such time as the Television Committee have completely exhausted their negotiations with the Television Authorities, and the conclusions are placed before all the Clubs. This assurance is required before the next meeting which is to be held on Wednesday 23rd October.

This threat from the Management Committee was easily seen off, for television was now the catalyst for wider changes within the League, changes that were eventually to lead to the break-up of the oldest Football League in the world and the formation of the Premier League. As I write, the birth pangs of the Premier League have been accompanied by controversy and dissent, but the first step for this was made in the summer of 1985.

For some time now I had been concerned about the structure of the League and the way it operated. Much of the money that football earned came from the First Division, and a handful of First Division clubs at that. We at Spurs, Arsenal, Liverpool, Manchester United and Everton were the game's big attractions. It was our drawing power that also brought in television. One particular Saturday in 1985, for instance, the attendances at Highbury, Anfield and Old Trafford had amounted to 118,074 people – 10,000 more than all the other First Division games put together. But when it came to making decisions it was the League's tail, the Third and Fourth Division clubs, that seemed to be wagging the dog.

Many of the bigger clubs shared my unhappiness about the rule that changes could only be implemented by a three-quarters majority – it left us in hock to the Third and Fourth Divisions. We wanted it down to two-thirds, and it seemed quite absurd that the League's Management Committee were nearly always composed of Second, Third and Fourth Division clubs – in 1984/85 only one representative of the so-called Big Five, John Smith of Liverpool, was on that Committee. Above all the television money that we brought in had to be shared equally. It was very clear that television only really wanted the big clubs. Halifax got the same money as Manchester United. Was television interested in showing Halifax matches? Of course not. And then there was the question of the 4 per cent of our gate receipts which had to be paid to the

League pool but which amounted to a subsidy of the smaller clubs.

When I had met Alex, back in 1984, he had outlined proposals for the reorganisation of the League which I found very interesting. Liverpool v. Everton was a television event, he said, but not Liverpool v. Charlton Athletic. What we needed was a First or Premier Division of between ten and eighteen clubs, then a Second Division with a Third and Fourth regionalised. The apex of this structure would be the England team, and the whole thing would take into account the fact that football was one product and that spectators were encouraged to come to League matches if England performed well. A year before this Sir Norman Chester, presenting his second report on football, called for something quite similar: a Football League reduced to sixty-four fulltime professional clubs with the remainder linking up with the Gola League to form a separate, intermediate League. The idea was not to kill off the smaller clubs but to provide them with an atmosphere in which they could grow and flourish.

In the summer of 1985, as the television screens blacked out football and the tragedies at Bradford and Heysel darkened the mood for the game, I became more than ever convinced that we had to do something to break out of the straitjacket we were in. I found ready support for my ideas from Philip Carter and Martin Edwards. Carter had been involved in restructuring the League for some years now, and in 1984 he had actually stood against Jack Dunnett, losing by 35 votes to 17. He had a lot of time to devote to football, having retired as managing director of Littlewoods in 1983, and although he had a reputation for being a cold fish I found him a quiet, nice likeable man – always ready to seek a compromise. Although it was under his chairmanship that Everton was to find success, I never gained the impression that he was a football fanatic or had an intuitive knowledge or feeling for football. What he was good at was seeing issues clearly, delegating, and being very straightforward in his dealings.

My other great ally was Martin Edwards of Manchester United. If Carter was the generation before me, Edwards was my generation. I had got on very well with him both from the first moment I saw him, when both Spurs and Manchester United were invited to a close-season tournament in Swaziland. Unlike me, Martin had inherited his involvement from his father Louis, and by the time I met him he had been on the board of Manchester United for almost thirteen years, having got on in 1970.

Martin was very proud of Manchester United and he couldn't abide any situation where it appeared in any way inferior to any other club. I was made vividly aware of this on the Swaziland trip, when we decided to have a staff match between the two clubs. Peter Shreeve had organised it brilliantly, we were kitted out in the first-team strip, and Manchester United took the field wearing T-shirts and swimming costumes. Martin was most upset. He immediately had the first-team kit brought out, saying he was not going to be outdone by Tottenham. Shreeve had clearly prepared us well, because we won the match by eight goals to four, with me getting three goals. This despite the fact that in the very first minute I was felled by a rabbit punch in the back of my neck by Ron Atkinson, then Manchester United's Manager, who was doing his imitation of Maradona in mid-field. Atkinson apologised, saying he thought I was Keith Burkinshaw, who was the butt of all the Tottenham players watching the match. Every time Burkinshaw, playing in defence, kicked the ball long the players hooted and screamed 'Watford', because this is what he did in training when the Spurs players used the long ball.

Over the years I was to get to know Martin very well. Whenever Manchester United played in London he would come and stay with me, and could never work out why he was never liked by the supporters at Old Trafford. He was often the butt of very cruel jokes there, and I really felt for him the night we played Manchester United in a League Cup match at Old Trafford in 1989. Despite losing Terry Fenwick when he broke his leg, we won 3–0, in one of our best displays of the season, and as I was leaving my seat I saw Martin sitting on the other side of the gangway with two very furious supporters trying to get over the barrier to attack him. They were spotted by the stewards in time, and Martin managed to get away to safety, but it showed the feeling generated.

Often Martin dreads going out on the pitch to make any presentation, because all he gets is abuse from everyone. I do not know why this should be so, because he has made the club both successful and financially secure. The ground development programme is nearly complete and will make it the finest League ground in England. His lack of rapport with the crowd makes plain why at the beginning of the 1989/90 season he decided to sell out to Michael Knighton. Before this he had had discussions with Robert Maxwell, and would have sold to him had he offered the right price.

When Martin rang me to tell me about Michael Knighton I quickly sensed that there was something wrong. Michael Knighton was supposed to be in the property business, but I had never heard his name, and the property business is a little too small for mysterious strangers with lots of money to appear. I remember asking Martin whether he had proved that the money was available. Martin seemed to get a bit nervous about this and quickly ended the conversation. As it later turned out, Michael Knighton did not have the money and the deal didn't go through. Martin ended up looking rather foolish, increasing his alienation from the Old Trafford public. He later told me that he knew he had made a mistake on the afternoon of the day after the deal was announced. This was on the first day of the season, with Manchester United entertaining Arsenal, the League champions. At 2.30 pm Martin looked down and saw somebody emerging from the tunnel and going on to the pitch. At first he thought it was a player, then suddenly realised it was Michael Knighton, who was just about to do his ball-juggling act. It was some months before the mistake was unravelled, but I think that Martin has learnt from it.

All this, of course, was well into the future. In 1985 I was concerned with producing a more equitable structure for the Football League without unravelling it.

On the morning of Sunday 29 September, Spurs, Arsenal, Manchester United, Liverpool and Everton met, together with a number of other clubs including Newcastle and Southampton, in Birmingham. We thought the best way forward would be if we invited other clubs to join us in a completely new super-league which would be free from the control of the Football League and able to negotiate its own lucrative television and sponsorship deal and dictate its own policy. Two days later Jeff Powell in the *Daily Mail* revealed our discussions.

However, I was willing to defend what we had proposed – the only Chairman among the big clubs to do so – and felt very strongly that we should not be portrayed as men of greed. It was an act of self-preservation. It was not as if football clubs were doing well: very many were virtually insolvent and two, Wolverhampton Wanderers and Swansea City, were in imminent danger of going out of business altogether. The season had also started bleakly, what with lack of television and the fall-out from Bradford and Heysel, and our gates at Spurs were to be down 24 per cent. I told the Press: 'If we continue without modification to design and to promote the best in entertainment, standards and facilities, then the future outlook for our sport will continue to decline.'

I was supported in these views by Sir Norman Chester, who said: 'A break-away would be good for the game.' Our proposals were to release a torrent of discussion which provided me quite an insight into the way football politics worked and convinced me that change in football was always difficult and never quicker than the pace set by the slowest member. Although the romantics in the Press, unable to see that change was necessary (and all this at a time when First Division attendances had fallen by 350,000 the previous season), attacked our plans, the lower division clubs began to see that they could not push against the tide. How could anybody justify that Bury received exactly the same money as Manchester United, £25,000, although Bury had not appeared once in television during the previous contract and Manchester United appeared eighteen times?

I was all for the romanticism of the little clubs, romanticism that is part of the FA Cup, where any club – even a non-League side – can win the Cup. Indeed, the proud boast of any Spurs supporter is that Spurs are the first and the only non-League club to win the FA Cup. But in the 1980s one could not deny that the big clubs were not like the small clubs. As I went round the football grounds and met the directors in the boardroom and the people who ran the game, I would come across problems at Arsenal, Manchester United, Liverpool, Everton which were very similar to the ones we faced at Spurs. But as I went down the Division there was very little in common either in the day-to-day running of the club or future dreams. Big clubs had a tradition and a consistency which the others did not have. Even some of the bigger clubs such as Newcastle and Sunderland couldn't match the Big Five. They are, of course, part of the great history of English soccer, and the North-East remains a vibrant, enthusiastic source of support for the game. But unlike the Big Five, Newcastle and Sunderland have spent long periods in the Second Division. Manchester United did go down to the Second Division, but only for a season, just as Spurs did in 1977.

The tragedy of smaller clubs trying to become like the big ones was vividly illustrated by Swansea, who came up to the First Division under John Toshack, for a time even led the First Division, but in the process accumulated such large debts and unsustainable players' contracts that they slid back to where they had risen from, except that this time they were left with large debts. Some of the smaller clubs appreciated this very well indeed. I remember going to see Wales play Uruguay at Wrexham, and the Wrexham board pointedly telling me that they did not want to be like Swansea and rise above their station. They knew their potential, they knew their capacity, and they knew that if they rose above their level, supporters' expectations would be far higher. The additional money which they couldn't afford would have to be spent. What it would provide is a few moments' thrill, only for reality to hit them with a bump, as it has done to Swansea.

True, Wimbledon, who were to be promoted to the First Division in that 1985/86 season, have since proved that dreams can be realised in the Football League. They only joined the League in 1977, and their first crowd was 3,300, but by 1988 they had won the FA Cup. Wimbledon is an exception that proves the rule. In any case the club now survives by selling players. Indeed, in the late summer of 1988 I may have played a part in helping Sam Hammam, Wimbledon's owner, to make up his mind whether he should sell Dave Beasant and Andy Thorne to Newcastle. I was coming back from a League dinner and Sam gave me a lift back home. On the way he mentioned that he had received offers for these two players, hoped to get £1 million for Beasant, and explained that Wimbledon survived by selling players. He couldn't make up his mind whether he should break up his Cup Final team. I thought £1 million was a good offer: Beasant was no longer a youngster, and Wimbledon had already achieved the impossible dream by winning the Cup. We spoke for nearly an hour and a half parked outside my house. Sam gave no indication what he would do, but I noticed a few days later that Beasant and Thorne were on their way to Newcastle.

What I could not make Sam understand was that there could be no equality between Wimbledon and Spurs or Manchester United or Arsenal or any of the big clubs. Wimbledon did not have the League tradition, and their long-ball style of play made them very unattractive to watch. Their home gates are rarely more than three or four thousand. Whenever we went down to play them we often took three or four times the home support. Wimbledon's turnover of £1 million is quite dwarfed by Manchester United's £20 million or Arsenal's £16 million, yet Sam wanted to be an equal partner with the big clubs. He has since pushed this argument in the Premier League, but this has only confirmed the feelings of the big clubs that Sam is out to get their money. As David Dein, Vice-Chairman of Arsenal, would often say, 'Sam, will you get your hands out of our pocket!'

Sam Hammam hadn't yet become a player in the politics of football, but a former owner of Wimbledon was quite prominent and would play a big part. He was Ron Noades, who represents a certain kind of migratory Chairman. Having been a keen Derby fan he had owned the then Southern League club Southall, and had bought Wimbledon for £2,872 in 1976 before selling it to Hammam and buying Crystal Palace. By the time I met him he had begun to turn the situation round at Palace, which was nearly £2 million in debt when he bought it, and his dream was – is – to create a South London club which could match Spurs or Arsenal. Over the years he has tried several times to merge with Wimbledon, and their present ground-sharing might well be a prelude to a proper marriage.

Ron felt that there was tremendous potential in that part of London, but like Bates and many other smaller club Chairmen he saw potential in terms of having more gates which would generate more income through the turnstiles. What he found difficult to accept was that however many games a club played there was a limit to how much income this could bring. To generate the sort of income we needed required partnership with television and the promotion of what Alex Fynn had called an 'event'. Ron Noades was once described by David Lacey, perhaps our finest football writer, in the *Guardian*, as the League Management Committee's Chiang Kai-shek, who almost every day would hatch a bright new scheme in his fertile mind. Chiang Kai-shek of course was defeated by Mao and exiled to Taiwan, pining for mainland China. I don't know if Ron's ownership of Crystal Palace can be seen as an exile – after all he graduated through Southall and Wimbledon – but, like Chiang he does pine for a larger stage, except that he hopes to make his Taiwan as powerful as the mainland clubs of North London or the North of England.

With Ron as the spokesman for the Second Division, our plans to change the League structure became a battle between the First and the Second. On 12 November 1985 the First and Second Division Chairmen met at the Mount Royal Hotel in London. We wanted to reduce the First Division, with a 70–30 split of the sponsorship money and two votes for each First Division club. We knew we had to woo the Second Division, for its votes would be crucial to get any proposal through the League. We were prepared to offer three up and down from the Second to the First Division. But Ron, leading the Second Division, was not mollified. He had some ideas of his own, which included a sponsorship money split of 55–45, one vote each for First Division clubs, and maintaining the sizes of the First and Second Division at twenty-two clubs each. It was clear we could not agree, but on one point there was agreement: we could no longer allow the Third and Fourth Division clubs to dictate our agenda. The First Division had nominated Martin Edwards, Philip Carter and myself to form a committee to negotiate with the Second, Third and Fourth Divisions to see if a compromise within the League structure could be found.

The day after the Mount Royal deadlock, Gordon Taylor, Secretary of the PFA, intervened and tried to play the role of mediator. Having so often been at loggerheads with the League, the PFA now wanted to save it, and while he was in favour of some change he did not want to make its scope too broad.

In this ever-changing situation the Scots had also entered the argument. Although the Scots had formed their own Premier League some time before this, their two leading clubs, Rangers and Celtic, were quite unhappy with the sort of competition the Scottish Premier Division offered. They told us they were ready to leave the Scottish League and form a British League for which there would be a British Cup with such exciting prospects as Spurs v. Rangers, or Arsenal v. Celtic. I went with Philip Carter and Martin Edwards to meet the Scots, and it turned out that apart from Rangers and Celtic, four other leading Scottish clubs would be prepared to leave their League. The First Division clubs met again at Villa Park on 28 November, when opinion was hardening. If Ron and his friends were not willing to meet us halfway, we might just have to chart our own course. We were still prepared to compromise, but the lower division clubs had to show some give. Four days after Gordon Taylor held a meeting of his Footballers Association, and the players gave him the right to call a strike if there was a break-away. Taylor was now busy formulating his own plan, whose chief purpose was to prevent the First Division from holding overriding authority in the League.

All these discussions came together at the Post House at Heathrow on 18 December. I, along with Philip and Martin

Edwards, represented the so-called break-away clubs; Ron, Laurie McMenemy of Sunderland and Bill Fox represented the Second Division; while the associate members had Reg Driver from Aldershot, Martin Lange from Brentford and Ian Jones from Doncaster Rovers. Gordon Taylor was cast in the role of the UN Secretary General and mediated between the various groups.

After six hours of talks, a lot of give and take on all sides, innumerable cups of coffee, and almost two discarded packets of cigarettes on my part, we finally reached what has been known as the Heathrow Agreement – an appropriate word, because during the talks there was always the fear that one of the groups would just fly out. It was always referred to in football circles as the ten-point plan. In the end it seemed we had reached a fine old British compromise, in the classical muddling way. There was still some muddy water to wade through, but that winter evening it did look as if we had got somewhere. It was agreed that the First Division would be cut to twenty clubs, while the Second would be increased to twenty-four. The changes would be phased in over two years, and the system of promotion and relegation play-offs introduced. This idea had come from Martin Lange, who wanted to compensate the Third and Fourth Divisions for their losses in revenue, and it was similar to what the American Leagues used. Ron Noades found it so attractive that he immediately appropriated it, and in a curious way it helped bridge the divide between the various divisions.

The three-quarters majority for change was reduced to two-thirds, the First Division would have two votes each, and would receive 50 per cent of all moneys earned from television and sponsorship. The Second Division would receive 25 per cent and the Third and Fourth Divisions would share the other 25 per cent. Also the 4 per cent League levy would be cut to 3 per cent and the constitution of the Management Committee would be so changed that the First Division clubs were guaranteed four representatives, the Second Division three and the Associate Members one. As in any such compromise there were parts of the agreement I did not like, but I thought we could live with it. What was extraordinary was that our conclusion had been reached without any member of the Management Committee present. Gordon Taylor may have felt that we had preserved the League, but in effect the meeting had demonstrated that the present structure of the League just did not work.

We also agreed that there should be automatic relegation for the club finishing last in the Fourth Division, which would be replaced by the club finishing first in the Gola League, the premier part-time competition and later to become the GM Vauxhall Conference.

The ten-point plan worked so successfully that League gates rose afterwards for an unprecedented six years in a row from 1986/87 to 1991/92. In addition, the reduction of the First Division to twenty clubs helped the national team to such an extent that England had its most successful World Cup campaign in 1990 since the trophy had been won back in 1966.

The irrelevance of the Management Committee was emphasised even more two days after the Heathrow meeting when Philip Carter stitched together a television deal with Bromley for the remainder of the season. Philip Carter at this stage had not been elected to any League position, although, at the previous League AGM, Maxwell in his usual fashion had suggested that Carter replace Arthur South as Chairman of the Television Negotiating Committee. At that stage Carter himself pledged his support to Arthur South, and Maxwell resigned from the Television Committee. In the few short months since then everything had changed. We all knew how badly we were suffering from the television black-out, and Carter's deal was no more than a salvage operation. It provided us a measly £1.5 million for the remaining half of the season.

Given that the infamous St Valentine's Day Massacre had meant the League clubs turning down £3.8 million for the whole season because of the potential overkill of live matches, it was only too obvious that now they were giving in to television. This was underlined when the following July we signed a two-year extension for £3.1 million per season. What was worse, Carter conceded free access to any League game for edited highlights, while the TV companies gave us no guarantee that they would show recorded football on a regular basis. They continued destroying the recorded product, with the result that we in England were the only European country to have this incredible, and dangerous, imbalance between live and recorded football – something that the Continental Europeans or even the Scots would not accept. I was well aware that in France if people wanted to watch a live League match they had to pay for it on a subscription channel.

To say I was less than gruntled with the television deal would be an understatement. But I sympathised with Philip. He had a wretched hand to play with and he had done the best he could. It just wasn't good enough. It made me realise even more that football could not break out of the thrall of television until or unless we broke the cartel between BBC and ITV. We had to part the waters. To some extent, as we shall see, we did. Curiously enough, the parting was linked to the efforts to restructure the League.

Philip did not find it that easy to sell the ten-point plan to the First Division clubs, some of whom were unhappy that we had to compromise so much with the Second. These points were made particularly forcefully by two directors: David Dein, Vice-Chairman of Arsenal, and Doug Ellis of Aston Villa. I was to get to know them very well, and although both men came to occupy positions of great influence with their clubs, just about the time I was taking over at Tottenham, the contrast between them could not be greater.

As I was soon to appreciate, it was not for nothing that Ellis was known as 'Deadly Doug'. During the decade that I ran Tottenham I was involved in a great many transfer negotiations about buying and selling players, but I never had as much trouble with any other club Chairman as in the case of two transfers that I attempted with Doug – a purchase and a sale. One painful lesson came when David Pleat wanted to purchase Steve Hodge from him. I didn't want to pay more than £600,000, but Doug kept on asking for £650,000. He explained to me that he had a problem with the bank at the time and would much prefer the transfer fee to be £650,000. I was prepared to go along with it provided there was an understanding between us that he would reloan a sufficient amount, interest-free, which would then give us the opportunity of saving £50,000 in interest charges for the year. That would neatly bridge the gap between what I was prepared to pay and what he wanted.

But when we met on the Sunday morning at a hotel in the Midlands he produced a letter from his pocket. I read it with absolute incredulity. It was a plea to me not to ask for the loan of the money. In my business dealings, when I made an agreement, whether it was written or not, it was meant to last. I explained all this to Doug, but it clearly made no impression, and so in the end we went through with the Hodge deal but without Doug making the loan. At that time I thought he was getting his own back on us because, as he never ceased to moan, he felt that he had had an agreement with the sports kit manufacturers Hummel, but they had backed out of it and signed with us. But I was to have one further deal with Doug, when the sale of Vinny Samways came up, and I have since heard of many transfer deals involving Doug – not least the one with Liverpool and Dean Saunders – that make me realise that my experience was not unique.

David Dein had bought into Arsenal the year after I bought into Spurs. In view of what football clubs can be worth, particularly Arsenal, it is astonishing to think that back in 1983 David paid a mere £300,000 for his Arsenal shares and for a seat on the board. This caused quite a stir at the time, given that Arsenal had become identified with the City, having been run by Denis Hill-Wood and then his son Peter, who was an Old Etonian and a prominent City merchant banker with Hambros. The Hill-Woods had always run Arsenal on a very low-key basis, often allowing the public face of Arsenal to be presented by their Managing Director. For much of the Fifties this had been Bob Wall, who had been known as 'Mr Arsenal', and he was succeeded by Ken Fryer who, in many ways, is as important to Arsenal as Peter Robinson is to Liverpool.

Although I found Peter Hill-Wood immensely charming, with a wonderful sense of humour, I always felt that he was a bit out of place in the world of football. His upper-class background might have been well suited for the MCC Committee Room, but it did not always gel with the directors' boxes of football clubs, where most of the men are either working-class made good or aspiring middle-class. Peter has always been keen on Arsenal's aristocratic stature, and in the Arsenal directors' box is a stickler for ties and jackets. I remember one instance when one particular person didn't conform and Peter provided a glimpse of his character which was very revealing. This was just after a match we had played at Highbury in 1986 when Don Howe, who was Manager of Arsenal then, came to the boardroom, still in his track suit, and started complaining to Peter about something that he hadn't been told about. Howe got little out of Peter and finally left, at which point Peter turned to me and said: 'Bloody managers! They are all the damned same! They need a good spanking at times. They seem to forget who is the employer and who is the employee.' Within a few weeks, Don Howe, who had already fallen out with the North Bank, was on his way out and George Graham was signed from Millwall.

In many ways my buying into Spurs encouraged David Dein to look at Arsenal. A close study of the Arsenal accounts revealed that 15 per cent of the shares were unissued. He contacted Peter Hill-Wood and, as David himself confirmed to me later, arrived at Hill-Wood's City offices at Hambros Bank with a banker's draft for £300,000 thrust into his pocket. Hill-Wood immediately took a shine to him, impressed both with his knowledge of Arsenal and his tremendous enthusiasm for the club, and agreed to present his proposals to the board. A few days later he met the board and the deal was done. Hill-Wood was amazed that David wanted to invest in Arsenal. As he would later say, this was 'dead money', but then David, like me, had seen it not as an investment on which he hoped to get a return, but as backing the great love of his life with money. Within four months David was Vice-Chairman of Arsenal, and since then he has become the largest shareholder.

While his love for Arsenal almost matches mine for Spurs, I have always felt that David possibly was a little out of place at Highbury. There can be no doubting his aggressiveness, his youth and his ideas. He has been responsible for a lot of Arsenal's commercial innovations, and many of them have proved very successful. He has a schoolboy enthusiasm for the game and is never afraid to put his head above the parapet and be shot at. This has led to him making some enemies in football, where change is always resisted and the innovator always suspect. What I think has held David back is that he has never established a rapport with the Press. When you want to be a mover and shaker in an industry, you've also got to establish an identity with the media, and there David is seen as a man who is difficult to talk to and almost impossible to relate to. This is a pity, because David has some very good ideas and there can be no doubt that his heart is in the right place. His overriding concern is the good of Arsenal, and he has the best interest of English football at heart.

Where I have always disagreed with David is about paid owners. He is now a paid director at Arsenal, working there virtually seven days a week, and I have always felt that football does not go with paid owners. I feel this way as much about David Dein as about Terry Venables or, for that matter, any other owner.

Going back to the winter of 1985, both David Dein and Doug Ellis were unhappy with the ten-point plan and with the television deal that Carter had done. They felt that Carter was weak, and had too readily compromised with television and given away too much to the Second Division. As if this was not bad enough, the Management Committee, instead of presenting the Heathrow formula directly to the League clubs, decided to have their own say on two key points in that agreement: the change in the voting system and the restructuring of the Management Committee. Their point was that if the First Division was patient then by 1987, after retirement and other such vacancies, it could end up with nine out of the ten places on the Committee. We met at Villa Park on 17 February and unanimously rejected the Management Committee's proposal: 22–0. As the saying goes, the Management Committee were lucky to get nil. With the agreement also under attack from Third and Fourth Division clubs, the proposed Extraordinary General Meeting due to be held on 4 March was postponed and a new date fixed for 28 April.

There was certainly a head of steam building up in the First Division for a break-away, and this was confirmed when we met again at Villa Park on 24 March. All the twenty-two clubs agreed that if our ten-point package based on the Heathrow Agreement did not get the necessary three-quarters majority, then we would walk out of the League.

The League EGM was held at the Cumberland Hotel on Monday 28 April, and was one of the most extraordinary I have ever been to. We seemed to take over the entire hotel, and almost every meeting room in the hotel, with the various divisions meeting in separate rooms. The sticking-point was the number of votes that First Division clubs should have. The lower divisions did not want to give us two votes. Eventually the clubs accepted a compromise suggested by Jimmy Hill, then a director of Charlton Athletic – about to win promotion to the First Division – who came up with the idea of one and a half votes. It happened less than an hour before the Extraordinary General Meeting was to start.

We had given all our proxy votes to Philip Carter, which was unprecedented but perfectly legal, and meant that the meeting went through quite smoothly. The ten-point plan, with Hill's amendment, was accepted by 43–10. The old Management Committee had to go, and when postal elections were held only one member – Jack Dunnett – survived. But even he could not hold on to the presidency, and in a moment of that tumultuous year that set a precedent, he became the first League President to be voted out of office. Philip Carter defeated him by 37½–26½.

One item in the ten-point package was the question of compensation. It was agreed that 10 per cent of the total television fee would be put aside for compensating those clubs showing live games but suffering a reduced gate. This worked very well until the Football League's Annual General Meeting of 1988. Then Coventry City put forward a rule change which effectively abolished compensation. Their argument was that clubs appearing on television were benefiting by way of perimeter board advertising and also by television exposure for their shirt sponsor. I, along with other First Division clubs, argued strongly against this change, but Coventry City's amendment was accepted. That was the catalyst for the television revolution, and in many ways for the Premier League. Perhaps it might have come in any case, but Coventry lit the fuse. By removing one point of the carefully worked out ten-point plan, they had unravelled the whole deal. Like a house of cards when one card is withdrawn, the whole pack fell. The fallen Humpty-Dumpty of football and television could never be put together again.

In early January of 1988, Spurs, Arsenal, Liverpool, Everton and Manchester United were all contacted by the Football League Commercial Department, headed by Trevor Phillips, and invited to a dinner at a hotel in St James's. We didn't know why we were meeting, but sometime during the dinner Trevor Phillips explained that the reason for calling us together was to get our views on a potential approach the Football League had received from British Satellite Broadcasting (BSB). Phillips gave what amounted to a sales patter, and it was clear that he and Lee Walker were very keen on pursuing this as an alternative to the cartel of the BBC and ITV.

In principle I was delighted that, at last, there was going to be some form of competition. But we all had grave reservations about a satellite broadcasting channel that had not yet put its satellites into orbit. We made our position perfectly clear, voicing concern that the national sport could be relegated to the role of a fringe one where we were likely to be watched by the sort of audiences who watch the Epilogue on BBC1. Neither Trevor Phillips nor Lee Walker enjoyed our response, and I remember watching them both walk up St James's Place with their tails between their legs.

Obviously they were thinking in terms of the cash benefit, whilst we were thinking of both the exposure and the cash. I further explained to them that there was no question that satellite and cable television would definitely have a part to play in the future, but it was a very risky move to sell exclusivity to them at this early stage. My suggestion was that they should try to get terrestrial television to sign up for another three or four years, and following that it would be possible to look at a mixture of terrestrial, cable and/or satellite in the future.

On the Management Committee at that time were Ken Bates and Ron Noades, both of whom were particularly keen on the BSB approach, and whilst we were unaware of the type of figures that BSB were prepared to pay, it was clear that they were going to be substantial. Bates and Noades were also committed to the idea put forward by BSB for forming a joint company, and they were pushing this very hard. Eventually, in early May 1988, the Management Committee went public on their having received a formal approach and an offer from BSB, and a presentation took place at the Royal Lancaster Hotel.

That presentation certainly suggested twenty-first century television: there were video displays, laser lights, and the right kind of hype both from Trevor Phillips for the League and Peter Bell for BSB. I emerged from the meeting convinced that the day would arrive when satellite and cable were definitely going to play a part in football. However, I did not believe that 1988 was the time. It was far too early. In addition, BSB were looking for a ten-year contract, and I argued long and hard that this contract was a grave mistake that might kill off football as a major sport on television. Football just could not take the risk of selling its product for a term as long as that without terrestrial television.

What I was praying for was that ITV would make a play for the Rights. Peter Hill-Wood, the Chairman of Arsenal, through Hambros Bank, had looked into the financing consortium for BSB and told the clubs that he was less than happy with the financial figures that BSB were putting forward. He felt it was extremely risky from a commercial point of view, and very much doubted their ability to perform. BSB tried to counter these arguments by saying that they would submit a bank guarantee on an annual basis, so that if everything went wrong, the Football League would have at least a year's Rights fees covered.

One obstacle in the path of BSB was a rule change we had put through back in 1985, when the regulations were altered to include a new one stating that any contract with satellite and/or cable television had to be approved by the clubs in a general meeting. This meant that the Management Committee could not agree and sign a deal, as Dunnett had done with the football pools companies, and commit the whole Football League for something like twelve or thirteen years, without reference to the clubs. In hindsight this was a very important and material new regulation. Had we not insisted on its adoption, in 1988 the Management Committee – who with the exception of Carter and Dein were all unanimously in favour of the BSB approach – could have entered into a contract and announced it to the clubs as a fait accompli.

My personal belief is that had they had the power they would probably have done that, as they were so keen on the new agreement. Trevor Phillips, who had come from Beecham and not been that long with the Football League, saw this as his great moment, in much the same way as in 1992 Rick Parry, Chief Executive of the Premier League, saw the Sky deal. The only plus side of the BSB deal was that it gave us a chance to break the cartel and get genuine competition. Ever since the 1985 negotiations and the unfair way the broadcasters had dealt with us, which had hurt me very deeply, I had been determined that if I did anything at all in football, I was going to break the cartel.

After 1985 I had pursued various avenues in that campaign. In the late 1980s I had contacted Lord Young of Graffham, who was then the Chairman of the Department of Trade and Industry. Margaret Thatcher had once said of him: 'Everyone brings me problems, David brings me solutions,' and I had known him for many years. In the 1970s he had been head of a property company in London specialising in building industrial estates, and I knew he was reasonably keen on football, having been to Queen's Park Rangers with him once or twice. I arranged a meeting at the DTI, seeking his advice on how it might be possible to break the cartel, and explaining to him the reluctance of the Office of Fair Trading to become involved in any dispute.

He made it clear that his solution would be to try and promote some form of competition by finding a cable or satellite company that was prepared to bid. He asked me whether I knew Michael Green of Carlton Communications. I had known him since the age of seven, when we used to sit next to each other in Sunday morning Hebrew classes. At that time Carlton Communications was certainly not the major player in television terms that they have since become. In any case, no change had emerged by the time that BSB bid.

It was clear that the general feeling of a large number of clubs, and the consensus on the Management Committee, was for BSB. But the five clubs who had attended the dinner at St James's had not altered their opinion, only hardened it. Different sections of the Football League have different requirements. We, as one of the major clubs, were looking for a mixture of exposure and the right cash deal. Other clubs felt differently. Exposure meant very little to them, as they weren't shown on television in any event, so it was a question of how much were they going to get out of it.

The negotiations went on, and Phillips was mandated to take them to the point of presenting an agreed contract with BSB to all the ninety-two clubs. Then came the League AGM, the acceptance of the Coventry compensation amendment, and a phone call from Greg Dyke. At no time during all previous negotiations had we ever managed to contrive a face-to-face discussion with anyone high enough in television to be described as an executive, a decision-maker. They were always professional negotiators, and whilst they were negotiating with football, they would also at the same time be negotiating with a multitude of other sports: cricket, athletics, golf, boxing. Here at last was a real high-flyer. The difference was immediately apparent: ask him a question – he'd give you an answer. There was no question of referring back to numerous committees.

Following Greg Dyke's call, we arranged to meet him at the Belfry, a restaurant in Knightsbridge, on the evening of 16 June 1988 – a date I have particular cause to remember, as we shall see. Before we met Dyke and his team we arranged to have dinner, and here the Big Five were well represented. Apart from myself there was Ken Fryer, Peter Hill-Wood, David Dein, Sir John Smith, then Chairman of Liverpool, Peter Robinson, Martin Edwards and Philip Carter, who brought along Jim Greenwood, Secretary of Everton, as well. A private room with glass doors overlooking the remainder of the restaurant had been booked. Then just as we were finishing dinner I saw a shortish, bearded man in his mid-forties coming in our direction at the head of a large working group. Greg Dyke was that man. He had brought with him John Bromley and a number of financial people – quite the largest delegation from ITV I have ever seen. Immediately they sat down they started rubbishing BSB. We were treated to a detailed voyage around the mystery financial position of the company.

After about twenty minutes of such anti-BSB rhetoric by the ITV financial crew, I tried to bring it down to basics, asking Greg a direct question: 'Are you attempting to negotiate an exclusive deal with us or not?'

'Yes,' he said.

I was immediately impressed with his direct, forthright manner. He seemed likeable and prepared to give straight answers to straight questions. I must say the 1985 television negotiations with BBC and ITV had bruised me. I could never forget the way they always ganged up against us, and ever since then one question had kept nagging me: was there a cartel? As I talked to Greg and listened to him I felt that here at last was a television man who might give me the answer I had longed for. So I asked: 'What I want to know is, is there a cartel between the BBC and ITV?'

No sooner had I asked the question than I could feel the disapproval of my football colleagues. By then most of them knew me, knew my penchant for expressing my views clearly, directly and at some length. The moment I asked my question, I could sense what they were thinking: 'There goes Irving again, asking the most indelicate questions.' They almost seemed to hold their breath as they waited for a response from Dyke, and before he could speak John Bromley, for so long part of the cosy cartel, tried to break in and give a fuzzy answer. Greg Dyke stopped him with a motion of his hand and said: 'No, I've been asked a fair question, I'm going to give a straight answer. Yes, there has been a cartel in existence.'

If there are seminal moments that change everything, then this certainly was one of them. What we had long suspected was now confirmed. The ice had been broken and the cold war that existed between football and television suddenly began to thaw. For the first time that I could remember there was a warmth from football towards television, and the feeling that we had finally come across a man who told us the truth.

I decided to make the most of the new situation by suggesting to Dyke that he make us an offer. He and Bromley excused themselves from the table and conferred for about ten minutes or so, then they returned and Dyke said that ITV would be prepared to make an offer, only not to the whole League but to a select list of clubs. He wanted to buy the exclusive rights to put television cameras in our grounds.

This was an interesting approach, because Regulation 18 of the Football League stopped any club selling its rights to

matches under the jurisdiction of the Football League and the
FA to any third party. They had to be sold by the governing
bodies. (By way of an historical understanding between the
Football Association and the Football League, the clubs retained
their own rights when it came to European matches.) Greg Dyke
was prepared to pay each of the five clubs £750,000. In addition
he was prepared to offer a further £2 million in total to another
five clubs to be chosen in due course. The money surprised us,
bearing in mind the 1985 discussions when TV wouldn't price the
contract at all. Now here was somebody prepared to give a verbal
offer at the first time of asking. Compared with the £50,000 that
each First Division club was then getting, this was like manna
from heaven. The gods of ITV had spoken.

That was the beginning of a marriage out of which the
major clubs would father the Premier League. Many bones
of contention were brought up that evening, now that we had
actually managed to get to somebody who would give us direct
answers. For example, a couple of years previously I had seen in
Italy what are known as 'Revolving Boards': premier advertising
boards that actually change adverts, perhaps with three adverts
on one particular board instead of a fixed, flat painted board. I
had commissioned a couple of these for Tottenham, and whilst
we could use them for non-televised games, the question was,
would we be allowed to use them for a live game? Jeff Foulser
of ITV came to Tottenham to transmit a Spurs League game
live on Sunday, and he warned me in no uncertain terms that
if they were turned on, 'we turn off'. I raised this problem with
Greg Dyke, and he said that, although he didn't know too
much about them, as far as he was concerned he didn't have
objections. Some time later we got a call from ITV to say that
the revolving boards were OK, and if we wanted to use them,
they were happy for us to do so.

By now, David Dein and I were in constant contact with
Greg Dyke, working on a plan to get ITV to increase their
offer of £750,000. Soon after, at a meeting at David Dein's
office in Pall Mall, Dyke was joined by the equally powerful
David Elstein, the Managing Director of Thames TV, who was
very keen on securing several of the live mid-week matches.
Elstein was a tall, dark-haired, rather debonair-looking individual who presented a complete contrast to Greg Dyke. Much to
my delight he turned out to be a Spurs supporter. After much
bargaining David Dein and I persuaded them to up their offer

from £750,000 to £1 million each for the five clubs. A few weeks later we had a second meeting in a conference room at a hotel near Manchester Airport, where the Big Five were joined by the other five: Aston Villa, Newcastle United, West Ham, Sheffield Wednesday and Nottingham Forest. The Big Five had become the Big Ten.

We now had two conflicting groups: the League Management Committee negotiating with BSB and ten First Division clubs negotiating with ITV. Here it is worth bearing in mind that ITV is made up of fifteen regions, and what they wanted was a geographical spread to satisfy all of the network: London Weekend with Greg Dyke and Thames with David Elstein were quite happy with Arsenal, Tottenham and then West Ham; Tyne Tees were with Newcastle United; Yorkshire Television with Sheffield Wednesday; Central with Nottingham Forest and Aston Villa. The size of the network contributed to the size of the fee, with London Weekend and Thames the largest, Central second, etc. The negotiations definitely led to a lot of friction, and I think Coventry were arranging meetings for the other ten First Division clubs, for which they had their own nickname of 'The Unwashed Ten'. It was clear that an atmosphere was generated through the Press, and the feeling was one of a great split in football, exacerbated by the fact that BSB had not only made public their offer, but had increased it.

On 23 June 1988, Greg Dyke wrote to me inviting me formally to put to my board an offer to buy the exclusive rights to televise from our grounds all matches in any domestic football competition, with the possible exception of the FA Cup. He proposed:

1   A four-year agreement starting 1988/89.
2   In the first year we would receive £1 million for exclusive rights.
3   ITV would guarantee to broadcast a minimum of one live game per season. In addition ITV would pay £50,000 for each live game transmitted as compensation for loss of income. ITV would only buy the British broadcasting rights, so the clubs would retain the overseas rights. But ITV wanted the first option to negotiate television rights should the club appear in any European Cup tournament.

This was conditional upon the Big Five all accepting the terms offered, or the offer would be withdrawn.

ITV wanted to broadcast no more than twenty live matches in a season. A maximum of six would be played and broadcast mid-week, and in the final year of the contract ITV would have the first option to negotiate for the four years beyond 1991/92 and a right to match the best bid. They also had a separate budget of up to £2 million for the FA Cup and England internationals that they wanted us to help them to negotiate.

When the Big Ten met in Manchester on 6 July 1988 there were loud moans and groans about the payment of £1 million to only five clubs. As a compromise we, the Big Five, agreed to accept £600,000, but ITV guaranteed to televise a minimum of two live home games per season from each of the Big Five clubs, with the right to a maximum of three live home games from any single ground. In addition to the £600,000, ITV offered to pay a match fee of £150,000 per game – £50,000 to the away club and £100,000 to the home club. They were also offering to do recorded programmes.

On 11 July the Big Ten wrote to the Football League saying that they did not wish to participate in the proposed arrangements with BSB. The next day we were given notice that Lovell White & Durrant, a firm of City solicitors, had been instructed on behalf of the Football League to obtain an interlocutory injunction from Mr Justice Peter Gibson in the Chancery Division of the High Court that very afternoon against Philip Carter, David Dein, Arsenal Football Club, Everton Football Club, Liverpool Football Club, Manchester United Football Club and Tottenham Hotspur plc. The order was 'that the defendants be restrained until after the 19th July, or until further order, in the meantime not to enter into or further negotiate without the consent of the Management Committee any agreement for the televising of football matches in which members of the Football League take part during the 1988/9 season in breach of their agreement with the League'.

Curiously, the order named Tottenham Hotspur plc, who were not in fact members of the Football League. It was the club that was, and when we complained about this the judge said that the costs concerning Tottenham Hotspur should be paid for by the Football League.

Inevitably, a lot was written about the narrow self-interest that the so-called Big Five followed. Everybody jumped on to this bandwagon. But the charge was false. We as the bigger clubs were the most attractive thing on television: we drew the money, and we felt we had the right to a fair share. We also felt that ITV had the facilities to provide the best showcase for football, as opposed to a channel, BSB, which had not yet come on stream and which was also going to be available only by satellite to a very small audience. With hindsight I have no doubt that the Big Five clubs were proved right. BSB got hugely into debt, and had to merge with its great rival Sky. I remember talking to Lee Walker about this and asking: 'Lee, what would have happened to the League and to football if we were still connected with BSB?' Lee, a large florid man who likes his long liquid lunches, went absolutely red and could not say another word for a few minutes.

By now we were saying quite openly that we refused to go along with the BSB deal and that we would be prepared to break away from the Football League if necessary. This did cause great public disquiet, but only because the Big Ten clubs failed to present their proper story to the public. The version that did get into circulation was that in seeking to break away from the Football League we would ban promotion and relegation to this super-league. That was never, ever, contemplated. If you don't have promotion and relegation, if you don't have dreams, you really kill football. Any form of break-away was supposed to be on the pattern we now have in the Premier League. The one thing we were seeking was autonomy.

The First Division had always wanted to run its own affairs without having to worry about the other divisions. I have always felt the Football League was a Tower of Babel. You had ninety-two clubs speaking something like twenty different languages – one for the Big Five, another language for another five, and so on.

In the meantime, when it became clear that ITV were prepared to bid alone, the BBC were so completely shaken that they now tried to disown the cartel whose existence they had never acknowledged in the first place.

On 12 July 1988 a meeting was held at Old Trafford between the Big Ten and Gordon Taylor. Taylor's efforts did not endear him to certain members of the Management Committee, although I felt no resentment towards him and always thought he would make the best Chief Executive of the Football League. (In 1985 I had discussions with Gordon about a possible break-away. I had suggested he should become the Chief Executive, and he showed great interest in this, admitting that football needed to change.) That proved to be a long meeting, on a very hot day at Old Trafford. It lasted well over eight hours, and it was there that a compromise began to be hammered out.

We recognised at the meeting that there was opposition to the Big Ten breaking away. Worried supporters had written shoals of letters, and we decided that Philip Carter should put out a statement confirming that it was not our intention to break away, but that nothing could convince us that the BSB deal was better. The difficulty we faced was that BSB's was the only offer on the table that covered all the clubs. ITV's offer was only tabled to each of the ten clubs. And it was on that day that Greg Dyke realised that the only way to conclude a deal was to put forward a formal proposal to all the ninety-two clubs. Now he had to meet the Football League.

On the plane home from Manchester I had a long talk with Greg Dyke, and suggested that I should try to arrange a meeting between him and Lee Walker. Most of the clubs had already agreed in principle to the Football League's proposal to enter into an agreement with BSB, and by the end of June Heads of Agreement had been drawn up but not signed between the Football League, the Football Association and BSB to form the joint company. A document had also been drafted confirming that the ten clubs did not wish to participate in the BSB agreement but intended to make independent arrangements with alternative broadcasters.

As soon as I came home that evening I telephoned Lee Walker to ask if he was free next morning for a meeting with Greg Dyke. Lee, in contrast to Trevor Phillips, was a man most of the big clubs got on well with – he was very close to Peter Robinson. He was delighted, and arranged to meet Greg Dyke at 8 am. It was at this meeting that Dyke confirmed that ITV were ready to make an offer in the region of £11 million for an exclusive package of eighteen live League games, two live Littlewood Cup semi-finals on a Sunday, and the Littlewoods Cup Final. David Elstein insisted that some of the live games should appear mid-week, and it was envisaged that between fourteen and sixteen would take place on a Sunday, with between two and four mid-week.

An Extraordinary General Meeting was arranged for 8 August, where the clubs would vote on the deal. On 2 August I received a letter from BSB confirming what we already knew, that BSB had withdrawn its offer. The letter also disclosed for the first time that the BSB initiative had started in the Management Committee:

'You will be aware that BSB was approached by members of the Management Committee last summer to see if BSB could help break the stranglehold the BBC and ITV had on the televising of the game and create a fair market price for football.' On the same day Jonathan Martin sent a letter to Graham Kelly saying that he was withdrawing his offer, although BBC still remained interested in the televising of Football League matches.

Clearly the pressure had told on BSB. They might have had the support of the Second, Third and Fourth Division clubs, but they knew they could not get all of the First. When they realised the game was up they decided on a flanking strategy and opened secret negotiations with the FA and the BBC about the FA Cup and international matches. The deal they eventually got was actually quite an attractive package. The FA Cup is the most romantic football tournament in the world, and the FA, fed up with the League, also threw in the right to televise foreign League football – mainly Scottish, but other European countries as well. The FA had never allowed this, and it marked a new and very interesting trend.

The real power that the League had over the clubs was that they could refuse to register a player's contract. Although a player was contracted to a club, the contract was registered with the League and was binding. If the clubs broke away, those contracts would effectively be terminated, and without players you do not have a team. Ken Fryer, who had an eye for such legal matters, examined the players' contracts closely, and one year he worded the new contracts so that there was an additional clause stating that the agreement between the club and the player would be for whichever League Arsenal were playing in. But the League spotted this and removed it.

I had always felt, both in 1985 and in 1988, that if we were going to have a break-away then the only way to do it was with the support of the Football Association. If the players' contracts were registered with the Football League, and the League itself was licensed by the FA, then without the permission of the FA the League could not run its fixtures. This country is unique in having two separate organisations for football. The Football Association is responsible for the game all over the country, right from the grass-roots amateur club to the top professional league. But while in other countries such an umbrella organisation also runs the professional league, football has developed differently here, with a separate League for the professional clubs. The relationship between the League and the FA had often been stormy, and there was a lot of envy and bickering between the two – mostly private but occasionally in public. If we were to break from the League it made sense to talk to the FA and see what they had to offer.

Back in 1985, I had spoken briefly with Ted Croker, then Secretary of the FA, who made it clear that the Football Association would be very supportive should the break-away ever occur. He felt it was in the best long-term interest of football in England: it would benefit the national team and prevent the constant squabble as football spoke with two voices not one, something the politicians had complained about for many years.

However for the moment this remained in the background, and politicians who were in the League began to lose their cool. It was round about this time I remember going to meet Jack Dunnett at his flat in Whitehall. Since 1985, when the television negotiations had brought me in contact with him, I had admired his shrewdness, the calm way in which he dealt with matters, and his not inconsiderable charm. I was particularly taken by his precise manner. If a Management Committee meeting was to finish at 12.30, then you could bet your house on the fact that Jack would bring the meeting to a close by 12.29. But on this occasion, with the newspapers full of a super-league and a break-away from the concept of the ninety-two clubs, Jack lost his cool and screamed at me: 'If you want to go, then clear off! We don't need you. Stop talking about it. We'll manage to survive!' It was only after he stopped shouting that he realised that I had prodded him so much that I'd actually got him to do something he never did, which was show his true inner feelings. Once he realised he had gone too far he did calm down, and it was clear that the pressure was telling on him.

BSB's withdrawal left only ITV, and a compromise fell into place when Gordon Taylor agreed to take a cut in the percentage paid to the players' union. The deal was finally agreed at a meeting on 8 August when the entire Football League gathered at the Cumberland Hotel, the First Division locked in one large conference room, the Second in another, and the Third and Fourth in yet another. What was surprising and encouraging was that the First Division unanimously agreed a formula whereby they would get 75 per cent of the television moneys, any club whose home match was shown live on TV would receive an appearance fee of £145,000, the away team getting £45,000, and any team appearing in the semi-final of the Littlewood Cup, which would be shown live on television, would receive £100,000, with a base sum of £200,000 to be received by all the twenty First Division clubs.

When Ian Stott, Chairman of Oldham (then in the Second Division) and a member of the Management Committee, came into our room I think he was surprised and dismayed to find the unanimity among the First Division clubs. It was this that was the key to the deal, because the Second knew they could no longer hold out for anything better. Ken Bates, whose club Chelsea was then in the Second Division and who was seeking to lead their fight, got so disgusted that he stormed out of the Second Division meeting fifteen minutes before the end.

When the EGM approved the deal that afternoon, all of us could take satisfaction – we had after all achieved a contract worth four times the previous one. But one man I expected to be whooping for joy showed signs of relief rather than exultation. That was Greg Dyke. There had been rumours before this that he had put his head on the block and gone out on a limb in order to get exclusive coverage of football. That, perhaps, explained why his face had a look of relief rather than the joy of glorious victory. As he went out of the room he turned to me and said: 'Thanks. I don't forget my friends.'

So an ITV deal of £11 million a year over four years was accepted. 'Match of the Day', which had started it all in 1964, was dead. 'The Match' had arrived.

ITV could not have chosen the year of their exclusive coverage more brilliantly. The 1988/89 season ended with just the sort of event that television craves for. The Cup Final had been played, Liverpool had won it, but the League's destiny had not yet been decided. Arsenal still had to play Liverpool at Anfield. This match was originally scheduled for Saturday 22 April. It was moved to the Friday after the Cup Final. Liverpool had only to draw to do the Double for the second time. Arsenal had to win by two clear goals. In the last minute of the match Michael Thomas scored the second goal to give Arsenal the Championship. I felt sick. It was an event made for television. David Lacey had written: 'The most powerful man in English football is Greg Dyke . . . who has both become Paymaster and Ring Master.' That final shoot-out at Anfield showed that Greg was indeed a superb master at orchestrating events.

I remain convinced that the exclusive ITV deal of 1988 was a good one for football and television. It did not flood the screens with live football, the fee was index-linked to the Retail Price Index, and the League was free to sell its overseas programmes, as ITV were only buying the UK Rights.

However, within months of the 1988 deal it was clear that the compromise worked out proved only as durable as a manager's reputation. At the Annual General Meeting of the League in 1989, Ken Bates put forward a rule change which effectively challenged the agreement reached the previous August about the allocation of the television money. I instructed a firm of solicitors to write to all the clubs to remind them that they couldn't possibly vote in favour of this, as they were subject to the 1988 agreement and so would be putting themselves in breach of contract.

Ken Bates was also sent a solicitor's letter saying that he was proposing to induce a breach of contract. Bates was very upset by this. In typical fashion he replied: 'May I make it quite clear that I regard the contents and the timing of your letter as absolutely outrageous.' Then, in full sight of the Press at the AGM, and just before he withdrew his proposed rule change, he proceeded to rip up the letter. I was particularly amused by this because he had just won a libel case against a national newspaper for damages of £75,000. But if this was the sort of Bates performance that we in football were familiar with, it also showed the hostility and the resistance to change within the League.

However, if Bates was unsuccessful with his rule change, another of his moves was overwhelmingly approved, and dug further into the crumbling foundations of the League. This was his infamous proposal to increase the First Division back to twenty-two clubs, after the ten-point plan had reduced it to twenty. The only three clubs that voted against were Arsenal, Manchester United and Tottenham, and in fact we were prepared to go as far as to eighteen. The crazy thing about this is that we three probably stood to gain as much as anyone from a rise to twenty-two clubs. The only way the other clubs can sell themselves to the public is by having more and more matches. The bigger clubs are in a different position: they value themselves more highly, their commercial spin-offs are far greater, and their pursuit of excellence creates a better product. They do not make the false equation, more matches = more money. I felt very unhappy about the change – it had dealt another blow against the ten-point plan.

At that Annual General Meeting, the Management Committee, again led by Jack Dunnett (who had replaced Philip Carter), had also put forward a new rule which effectively meant that any club leaving the Football League had to give at least three years' notice. The clubs accepted it, and its object was to stop any group of clubs from forming their own League elsewhere and leaving the others on their own. Yet if there was a single certainty in this shifting situation, it was that things could not stay as they were.

David Dein too felt very strongly that something had to be done, and within a few months of this he contacted me. He was convinced that despite the new television contracts and the money provided to the First Division, the League structure had to change. We needed a new system, one that would benefit not merely the big clubs, but the game itself and the national team. I agreed with that, but warned him that if we were not going to have the same old music again, to the same old tired routine, we could not merely talk about break-aways. That was hot air.

Our previous attempted break-aways could be brushed off as the work of greedy chairmen of the big clubs. This came under the auspices of the FA blueprint for football, presented by the FA Secretary. Ted Croker had been replaced by Graham Kelly, who had moved from the League headquarters at Lytham St Annes to the FA's at Lancaster Gate. At Lytham he had barely managed any sort of Press coverage, and if he did it was always negative. But when he presented the blueprint for football suddenly Fleet Street began to look at him through different eyes. Here he was speaking about the future of the game, and of the England team, and arguing the need for a small Premier League at the top that would help the national game.

The Press may be interested in change in football, but they rarely have any ideas about what the changes should be. Kelly's blueprint met with their complete approval, and they supported it from day one. This I believe had a profound effect on its success and implementation. Past attempts at break-aways had resulted in the big clubs being portrayed as villains. This time we were part of the process of making the national team better. It is ironic that when the FA invited Kelly to be Croker's successor there were not many members of the League Management Committee who shed tears. Indeed, many of them were astounded that the FA should approach him. They didn't see his departure as a great loss, but I believe he has blossomed in his new role, and that while he may still be a bureaucrat he is beginning to acquire some of the authority of a mandarin.

If the FA blessed the Premier League, then its birth can be traced to the night in early November 1990 when we were invited by the dignitaries of ITV, especially Greg Dyke and Trevor East, to a dinner in the dining room of London Weekend Television. It was here overlooking the Thames that the first discussions took place concerning a possible Premier League. That night we agreed to authorise Noel White, Chairman of Liverpool at the time, and David Dein to go and talk to Bert Millichip and Graham Kelly of the Football Association and see whether or not they would sanction and approve a break-away from the Football League.

That is when the seeds for the Premier League were sown. Afterwards numerous meetings took place with Michael Crystal QC and Mark Phillips, his junior, dealing with some of the leading legal questions, including the substance and validity of the three-year notice rule. Kelly brought in Rick Parry, who had no background in football and was formerly with Ernst & Young, a firm of chartered accountants. Throughout the spring of 1991 Parry went round the big clubs discussing ideas for the Premier League, and on 8 April 1991, Kelly presented the proposals to the Council. They came as a shock to the Football League, and were met with predictable hostility by people like Sam Hammam, who, at one meeting, denounced them as a search for loot.

But amid all that humming and hawing, the creation of the Premier League was also helped by the fact that the League itself had completely lost control of its own affairs. By this time Jack Dunnett had been replaced as Chairman by Bill Fox of Blackburn Rovers. When the various candidates who wanted to stand for this office made their speeches to the clubs, Bill Fox announced: 'If you vote for me I will have Gordon Taylor in as my Chief Executive.' This really swayed me, and I voted in his favour. After he had won by a slim margin, he rang me one evening to ask if it was true that the only reason I had voted for him was because of Gordon Taylor. He was taken aback when I told him that it was, because he found himself in an embarrassing position. Apparently he had agreed a deal with Gordon Taylor, and also discussed a contract, but he couldn't carry his Management Committee, which asked Taylor to apply for the job along with others. When Taylor refused to do this,

Fox really should have stood down, because he did come in on the clear mandate that if he was elected, Gordon Taylor would be the Chief Executive.

So within weeks of his election Bill Fox lost the platform on which he had stood. He never recovered from that, and neither did the League. It is interesting to think that had Bill Fox been Chairman of the League with Blackburn as it is in 1992, financed by Jack Walker's millions, the situation might have been very different. Blackburn then was a lowly Second Division club, pining for the First and far from certain of getting there.

But while the Premier League has come, I believe it has within it the seeds of its own destruction. A twenty-two-club Premier League is a nonsense. A compromise on the eighteen-club ideal set out in the FA blueprint was a mistake, and I do not think that the clubs will find it easy to come down to eighteen. It is sad to say that Liverpool and Everton voted in favour of twenty-two clubs. I could never convince Peter Robinson of the logic of a smaller First Division. And with a twenty-two-club Premier League, what we have is the same situation of haves and have-nots that characterised the Football League. Except there we had ten haves and eighty-two have-nots, whereas now we have between six and eight haves and fourteen have-nots.

The central argument in the Premier League, as it was with the Football League, is the share-out of money. I felt that the bigger clubs deserved more money because they had earned it, but this did not mean that I wanted to cut out the smaller clubs completely. What I was seeking to do was to develop something more like the Continental style of relationship between the bigger and smaller clubs. Italy, France and Spain have no dearth of big clubs. Indeed their big clubs – Barcelona, Real Madrid, Juventus, AC Milan, Inter Milan – dwarf even the biggest of ours. But what they have is a much more co-operative arrangement. A club in the lower division has a fraternal relationship with the bigger clubs, which may park one of their players for a year or two with their smaller brethren if circumstances so dictate.

In Britain envy, which has been a feature of our politics and economics for so long, also bedevils football. Smaller clubs are jealous of the big ones and aspire to the same status. It is pure English romanticism to believe that a team that plays on Hackney Marshes can win the FA Cup. It is lunacy to believe that a team that plays on Hackney Marshes can one day rival

Manchester United or Arsenal. That way you breed dissatisfaction, distrust and eventually despair. I fear that fate awaits the Premier League, where the Bateses and Noadeses of this world have already made it clear that what they want is centralised commercial negotiations, with everything shared out equally. They have got everything to gain and absolutely nothing to lose, because they are not giving anything up.

If you have a centralised sponsorship you centralise everything, and it is the major clubs that are going to lose. Here we go back to what David Dein kept on saying to Sam Hammam: 'Keep your hands out of our pockets.' I always argued long and hard in football about trying to make the cake larger, not dividing the slices into thinner and thinner portions. If you make the cake larger – improve your product, improve the income, make it more attractive – then more money comes in, and there will be more to share out. Is it right that clubs which have spent a fortune in building themselves up and improving themselves, and others which have invested very little, should all take equal shares from their anything but equal contributions?

Ken Bates, of course, is still sore that back in 1988 we overturned the BSB deal and went for ITV instead. Yet today there would be no Premier League but for the ITV deal. Recall that the BSB deal was for ten years, and think what would have happened when BSB merged with Sky. The same thing that happened with its contract with the Football Association: it would have been passed sideways to Sky. By 1992, when the Premier League was formed, there would have been another six years of the deal to run. The last figure BSB offered the League was in the region of £8–9 million. Index-linked, this would now be worth something like £12 million. Yet the Premier League's contract with Sky gives it a basic television fee of £40 million a year, and over five years, after overseas rights, advertising and sponsorship are thrown in, it is worth £304 million. Based on the 1988 BSB deal, the Premier League would have been lucky to get something like £70 million to £80 million. So our decision to go with ITV in 1988 means that the Premier League today is £200 million better off. And there are some clubs that still say we did badly in 1988 – clubs that are benefiting in the Premier League from the ITV deal!

There is not much that shocks me in football, but I was shocked to read about the way the Premier League clubs came to their decision in favour of Sky. That Rick Parry, negotiating the deal for the Premier League clubs, should have tipped off one of the bidders, Sky, about the offer made by another bidder, ITV, is quite amazing. Certainly it would not be allowed in any properly run business. But then I understand that at the crucial meeting at the Royal Lancaster Hotel, the clubs did not even have copies of the Sky offer, and had to take the figures down in longhand as Parry read them – an equally astonishing way to handle the largest-ever sporting deal in British history. What saddens me is that the man who has lost out in all this is the very man who encouraged the clubs that formed the Premier League to try and reach an agreement with the Football Association, and who was even ready to sponsor the League – Greg Dyke.

Yet, had even one more club voted against the Sky deal in that meeting in May 1992, then it would not have carried the required two-thirds majority. It was Tottenham's defection from the ranks of the Big Five, led by the arguments of Alan Sugar, that swung the deal. Had I remained at Tottenham I would certainly have voted against it, because it went flatly against two of the very basic and hard-fought principles of the last decade and more: to break the cosy cartel of television, and to guard against the over-exposure of live games on the box. By voting for the Sky deal, the Premier League clubs have re-invented the cartel. Sky has not only the top League matches but also the FA Cup and the England matches, and we are back where we were at the start of the Eighties, or if anything in a still worse position, with one broadcaster in charge of televising the most important and lucrative of football matches. After years of struggle to break the cartel, is this what the clubs really wanted?

How dangerous that bond can be is already becoming evident. Having struggled for most of the Eighties to curb television's voracious appetite for live football games, we are suddenly awash with live football: on Sky, on ITV, where regional First Division games are head to head against the Premier League, and on Channel 4 with live Italian League matches. In television terms the Channel 4 deal is undoubtedly the steal of the season, but can football cope with so many live games? Remember that whereas until the 1991/92 season there were only eighteen live League games, now there are sixty on Sky alone, not counting the games on ITV and Channel 4. Such abundance can only pall.

Once that happens, and the TV moguls find that football no longer attracts audiences, then the answer, particularly from ITV, would be to put a blockbuster film or a major event against football. Back in the early Eighties, when ITV, as a fall-out from Michael Grade's 'Snatch of the Day', got the right to show recorded highlights on Saturdays, Bill Cotton Jnr, who was running the BBC, retaliated by putting a big film against it. The big film always won, and that was one of the nails in the coffin of recorded football. I fear that the Sky deal and the glut it is leading to may well be the death of live football.

Nor do I understand this wild enthusiasm for Sky as opposed to ITV. The fact is that ITV were offering to show thirty live matches and Sky, for not much more money, are showing sixty. That amounts to paying half the price per match, so how can it be counted a better contract? The winners from this deal appear to be the BBC, who not only have recreated their 'Match of the Day' but also updated and modernised it, showing all the goals on a Saturday. This, along with the mid-week sports programme showing highlights of Sky's Sunday and Monday live matches, means that not too many people will be tempted to buy a Sky dish in order to watch live football.

If my experience is anything to go by, then sales of Sky dishes have been very slow. At the end of August 1992, just as Sky was moving to a subscription channel for its sports and testing out the decoder cards, I rang to find out when my television was to be unscrambled. The girl who dealt with the enquiry indicated to me that only about 250,000 people had subscribed to the sports channel – and this was a few days before it became a subscription channel. Even if that number has gone up considerably, that is a pretty small audience to watch a live televised match supposedly between two of the best teams in England. I hope for football's sake that it has not made an enormous misjudgement, but I cannot feel very optimistic here. Attendances early in the 1992/93 season have been down, and while the recession – and the quality of football – has certainly played a part, I consider that the television deal is also responsible. I have always believed that football is good for television, and television for football, but only with the right exposure. With Sky it is a case of over-exposure, and we are in danger of picking up a very fuzzy picture. I can only hope that, lured by the instant money Sky was offering, the Premier League clubs have not killed the goose that laid the golden eggs.

7 | TOTTENHAM'S CAMELOT: THE SEASON OF HEART-ACHES

David Dein: **'I cannot believe what a good loser you are.'**

Scholar: **'I have had a lot of practice.'**

After Scholar had sent the crate of champagne from the Tottenham dressing-room to the Arsenal dressing-room, following the traumatic Littlewoods Cup semi-final defeat at White Hart Lane on 4 March 1987.

The 1986/87 season was beautiful and sad. It began with a new Manager, it promised us all three titles – the League, the FA Cup and the Littlewoods Cup – it gave us nothing, and in the end, a few months after the season had ended and a new one begun, we were looking for another Manager. In the season Tottenham played some of the most breathtaking football during my time at Spurs, but in the end all we were left with was the heartache. Yet it had begun all so differently.

The departure of Peter Shreeve at the end of the 1985/86 season meant we were once again looking for a Manager. We quickly decided to approach Luton Town to seek their approval to talk to David Pleat. He had done an outstanding job over a long period on limited resources, and most important of all, his teams always tried to play football the way it should be played – on the ground. The game is called football, not airball or skyball. His teams played 'the Tottenham way'.

I rang David Evans to arrange to see him at his office in Cheapside in the City, later that afternoon. I do not know what he thought when I asked for the meeting, but apparently he was very surprised when I revealed the purpose. However he immediately said it was in order for me to contact David, and rang him in front of me. It transpired later that David had an agreement with Luton that if any approach was made by another club, he would be allowed to talk to the interested party, should he so wish.

I spoke with David later in the evening and arranged to meet him for lunch the following day. I immediately liked his enthusiasm and he confided he had always dreamt of being the Manager of Spurs, as their ideals and his own were the same. Personal terms were quickly agreed, and we shook hands on an agreement. He said he wanted to bring his assistant, Trevor Hartley, from Luton, together with his physiotherapist, John Sheridan. Neither I believe had contracts, and they were free to leave. I explained that Mike Varney had been at the club for many years and that he was doing a good job, and was definitely an asset. He should consider keeping him. But much to my disappointment David decided to sack him. Managers always like to bring their own backroom staff with them. It seems that in the paranoid world they inhabit it brings them added security.

Things had been going smoothly – perhaps a bit too smoothly – and I should have been warned. There was to be a bitter taste to Pleat's signing, and this was provided quite unexpectedly by Evans, who initiated a period of ill-feeling between Luton and Spurs that was to get badly out of hand. When I had approached him about Pleat he had been very amicable. He was, in fact, originally a Spurs supporter and his company had an Executive Box at White Hart Lane. So it came as a complete surprise that within a day or two he was making a lot of noise in the newspapers and on television, saying why it wasn't right for Pleat to leave and that the bigger clubs hire and fire people at will. He made it out as if we were doing something wrong. Actually we had agreed terms with Pleat only after the Luton board had given approval, and in order to get him we had to pay a transfer fee of £100,000 to Luton, with a further £100,000 should we win a major trophy within three years. Pleat was very annoyed when he heard that Luton had demanded a fee for relinquishing his services: to him it seemed ungrateful after all he had done for them over a period of many years, and he didn't want us to pay it.

Evans said nothing publicly about this fee. Just as at our meeting he had been a pleasant Jekyll, now he was a fearsome Hyde, carrying out a violent Press campaign against Pleat's moving to Spurs. Evans was probably huffing and puffing to show his supporters he was doing everything to keep a good man. Sad to say, even after Pleat had become Spurs' Manager

Evans kept up a campaign against us, taking his departure as a personal slight and making ludicrous remarks about how Luton would be a bigger club than Spurs.

I was getting rather fed up with all the backbiting, and when we played against Luton at home in October, I had a quiet word with their Chairman before the game. I pointed out to him that we had done everything above board and that he had said a number of inaccurate things, some of which I felt were libellous. Unless he stopped immediately, I would sue. It was done in a friendly manner, and suffice it to say that David Evans kept quiet about the matter from then on. However, the damage had already been done. Evans's public complaints had stirred up a lot of hostile feeling from his supporters, which became evident in the match at White Hart Lane. There the Luton supporters chanted against Pleat and directed the moronic, racist animal noises made by some crowds at black players every time the ball was touched by Mitchell Thomas, who had been signed from Luton. But worse, much worse, was to come when we played at Kenilworth Road.

This took place on 28 March, almost nine months after we had signed David, and was one of the nastiest atmospheres I had ever witnessed at a football ground. It was clear that their supporters had been well primed for this match ever since the previous summer, when David Evans had added fuel to the Pleat signing by throwing gallons of four-star all over it. As David Pleat took his place in the dug-out, some stupid fellow held up a white placard with the word 'JUDAS' emblazoned in black ink, directly above it. Fleet Street photographers were quick to snap the event, and there were pictures all over the Sunday papers of David with the word Judas above him. A number of genuine Luton supporters nearby did shout at this man to tear it up and sit down, and it was nice to know not everyone had forgotten what David had done for Luton over ten years on limited resources. But the damage had been done.

The atmosphere that day in the ground was extremely intimidating and hostile. I have never experienced anything like it. Abusive chants were directed at David and Tottenham throughout the match, and about two minutes from the end a stockily built lad of around twenty marched past the front of the Directors' Box. He was looking straight ahead of him, chanting what I can only describe as a highly provocative racist anti-semitic song, which I had first heard some years previously at Maine

Road. It went: 'The Jews are on their way to Auschwitz. Hitler's going to gas them again.'

This last episode, with its clear anti-semitic references to Tottenham and David Pleat, was the final straw. The Luton Board did not, of course, have anything to do with the mindless anti-semitism but as the game finished, I went as usual into the Directors' Lounge, where John Smith, Luton's Managing Director at the time, was standing behind the bar. I verbally laid into him and accused his Chairman of being responsible for the bad atmosphere which I felt had been created by his comments of some months earlier. He turned white and babbled a few excuses. David Evans appeared within a minute or two and told me that if I had any complaints I should address them to him, and I did. We had been beaten 3–1 and he accused me of not being able to take defeat. But I pointed out in the strongest possible terms that the result was irrelevant, and explained the reasons for my fury.

I am normally quite a placid person, but the provocation that day made me snap. One or two of the Spurs directors held me by the arm, afraid that I might do something stupid that I would regret. There was absolute silence in that area, where many of the club's guests had, by now, congregated. A few minutes later, I turned to my colleagues and said that I was not prepared to stay any longer in a place where we were clearly not wanted. I grabbed my coat and left, followed by the entire Spurs board. The game had finished no more than four or five minutes previously, and this was to say the least unusual. I have never before, or since, had cross words with anyone after a match, but the provocation that day was beyond endurance.

I struck up an immediate rapport with David. A Press conference had been arranged for the Friday afternoon on the day of his signing, and as I was leading him towards the Press Room, on the first floor of the West Stand, I stopped to ask him the theme of what he was going to say. I pointed out that what the supporters wanted to hear was that he would produce the most entertaining team in the country. He told me that he wanted me to sit back and just enjoy my football. It was music to my ears, and I must say, I did just that.

David turned up with Trevor Hartley and John Sheridan to start work clipboard in hand and with a real spring in his step. I felt confident that we had made the right choice and I liked his approach and enthusiasm. David's biggest hero in football is Brian Clough, and many was the time that he tried to ape him. This became evident the first Saturday of the season. That morning a newspaper article appeared saying that directors were not allowed on the team coach and that David Pleat had put his foot down. I had arranged to travel to Villa Park by car with some friends. On the way someone pointed it out to me, and I was surprised to read it. I asked David where the story had come from and he finally admitted that he had given it to a friendly journalist contact of his. He apologised and said that, obviously, if any director wished to travel with the team, it was perfectly in order.

What he was trying to do, I think, was to establish his authority like Clough. There had been a number of articles previously, when Peter Shreeve was in charge, that suggested he had been a puppet, which was not true. David clearly wanted to start off by asserting he really was in charge, and this was the type of thing that Clough had done at Forest, where apart from the players he only allows the Chairman on board.

David's attempt to ape Clough would in time cause more problems. Just before Christmas, David had received an offer from Glasgow Rangers to buy Graham Roberts, and simultaneously he had been in discussion with Aston Villa to buy Steve Hodge. After our match at Chelsea, the journalists asked him for a comment about Roberts and he replied: 'He's kicked a few down here and I expect he'll kick a few up there.' When I heard it on the radio I rang him to say that I thought his comments were completely unnecessary and were not becoming of a Spurs Manager. I further explained that Graham Roberts had always given 100 per cent for the club, and had been our captain when we won the UEFA Cup in 1984. He was an extremely nice fellow and didn't deserve such a stupid parting remark – if David felt that way, he should keep it to himself.

David apologised and said he didn't really mean it – then why did he say it? He was often guilty of trying to be too clever with some of his remarks to the Press. 'Misquoted', how many times have I heard that word. Much as I like David, I do not like Managers to be too familiar with the Press, and in any case there are far too many big-mouths with nothing of importance to say in the game. You never hear people like Dalglish or Ferguson putting their foot in it. They prefer to let their teams do the talking. I detected this was another instance of David mimicking his hero, but while it may have done for Brian, who has become a character, it didn't quite suit David, who is a very different type of person.

I realised that it was an enormous cultural change for David to move from a team like Luton, without much media attention, to a big club where they can make a big headline out of nothing – although, in this instance, it was far from that. The next time I saw Graham, I apologised to him on behalf of Tottenham and told him that he was, like all ex-players, always very welcome at White Hart Lane. He was appreciative, and said he hadn't taken the remarks seriously. Graham was to remain friendly with some of the players at Spurs, and I am sure he was involved in some way later when Richard Gough returned to Scotland.

The acid test for managers, of course, is the strength of their signings. Clubs cannot afford to keep on making bad signings. It is the Manager's judgement that is examined, and if you think of the really successful clubs – Leeds, Arsenal, Manchester United, and until lately Liverpool – you will notice that their failure rate in the transfer market is a lot less than others'. It always surprises me how many times managers watch players before buying them, yet still end up making mistakes. Every club buys players, right down to the Fourth Division and Vauxhall Conference. It may only cost them £1,000 or £10,000, or it could be up to £2 or £3 million, but a good manager rarely makes mistakes, while bad ones usually do. I have always likened the signing game to a coconut shy at the funfair: the object is to knock the coconut off each time you throw the ball, and a missed one is a wasted one.

David quickly showed his hand in the transfer market. Two players were out of contract, Mark Bowen and Ian Crook. I had told David that if he wanted to keep them, we should get terms settled as soon as possible. Manchester City had approached both of them, but they were not too keen on moving there. David said that he was happy for them to leave, and made it clear, in words I shall never forget, that 'neither of them will come back to embarrass us.' They both signed for Norwich City eventually, and they did come back to embarrass us at times. I think in retrospect David may have thought that he acted too hastily.

That summer of 1986 it was the World Cup in Mexico, and David had a prior commitment to ITV as one of their experts. We arranged to meet at his hotel when I went out there for the second and final phase of the tournament. In a restaurant nearby, he explained that defensively Spurs had always been suspect. His proposed solution was to buy Terry Butcher from Ipswich and Mitchell Thomas from Luton (more fuel for David Evans), to strengthen the team. We had previously agreed that £½ million was his budget for the season and was immediately available, plus any further cash raised from the sale of players.

I asked him what he felt it would cost us to get Butcher, and he was adamant he wouldn't pay anything above £700,000, due to Butcher's age. As far as Thomas was concerned, I pointed out that Peter Shreeve had been talking for some time with Wimbledon and we had first refusal on Nigel Winterburn. The figure was in the region of £200,000, plus a further £100,000 after around thirty first-team matches, and we could sign him immediately if he approved. But it was clear that David had made his mind up on signing Thomas, whose contract had just expired, and that if we couldn't agree terms with Luton, we would have to go to the Transfer Tribunal. Thomas was signed about a week later. David kept on saying that Mitchell was a tremendous prospect, who reminded him very much of Manuel Amoros, the French International left back. I must admit, I never quite understood the similarity.

As for Butcher, I just couldn't believe Ipswich would sell for his valuation. Why not look at Richard Gough, I suggested. However, David wanted to pursue Butcher and felt that the competition for his signature was not that great. Manchester United were very keen on him, but Ron Atkinson had been told that players must be sold before any new signings took place. We knew that the market wasn't that good for players already earning high salaries, so we felt confident that there would not be competition. Finally, at the end of July, David found out that someone had offered £725,000 cash for Butcher, whilst we were offering £700,000 – half down and the balance over the next twelve months, which is the normal trading terms between English clubs.

I eventually spoke to Patrick Cobbold, the Ipswich Chairman, who advised me that he wasn't sure whether Butcher would sign for the other bidder, and if he chose not to go there, he would accept our offer. We were still in the dark who the other buyers were when it emerged it was Glasgow Rangers, who eventually bought him. As fate would have it we were playing them in a pre-season testimonial match at home a few days later. It was after this setback that David decided to change direction and go for Richard Gough.

If Gough proved David's most successful signing, then his most incredible failure, one I never understood, was his unwillingness to sign David Rocastle. David Pleat had joined us just as George Graham was joining Arsenal, and a few days later I received a call saying that Rocastle was out of contract and would quite like to go to Spurs. Apparently George Graham had told the Arsenal players that there would be no new contracts until they had earned them from him. Martin Keown, also out of contract, immediately upped and signed for Aston Villa, and the tribunal valued him at £125,000.

I rang David Pleat and asked: 'What do you think of Rocastle?'

'Wonderful player,' said David, and in his usual manner he enthused about him for a bit.

'You know we can sign him tomorrow. He's out of contract at Arsenal and he is not sure he will fit into George Graham's plans. I've got a number where we can contact him.'

I then gave David the number, but a few days passed and I heard nothing. When I finally tackled him he didn't seem very eager to talk about it, but it was clear he had done nothing to contact Rocastle. When I finally pressed him he said: 'I couldn't do that to George.' Years later I told the story to Terry Venables, who is a great friend of George Graham. I asked Terry whether it would have worried him taking Rocastle away from his friend Graham, and Terry smiled and said: 'No, not in the least, that is football.' David Pleat could at times be too much of a gentleman.

To be fair to David, whilst he was wrong on some purchases he was almost right on Steve Hodge. Initially, I wasn't very keen on the purchase, as David had spent far in excess of the agreed £500,000 and I couldn't see him reducing the difference to the agreed level before the end of the season. Curiously, Paul Bobroff didn't seem too worried and was, in fact, quite keen, completely out of character; so if it was going to improve the team and its chances for success, I certainly wasn't going to complain. Hodge made his debut on Boxing Day and scored twice in a 4-1 win over West Ham.

That victory was one of a series of fine victories both in the League and the Cup, and it came about after David had finally found the right tactical formation. From the beginning he had not been happy with the conventional 4-4-2 formation and was searching for a system to bring out the best in the players. In the process he had dropped Hoddle and caused a bit of a frisson in the team and amongst the supporters. It was when we played at Oxford in late November that David's tactical search was to end. He played a five-man midfield for the first time, with just Clive Allen up front, based on the French national team's tactics that had been very successful in the 1984 European Championship and 1986 World Cup. The players were very keen on it, which is three-quarters of the battle, and it proved to be very attractive to watch for our supporters.

We were two goals up in ten minutes thanks to Clive Allen, and Chris Waddle scored twice in the second half and, but for a coat of paint, would have scored the best hat trick I've ever seen, curling the ball just past the far post. We won 4–2, and the only sad note was that Nico Claesen pulled a hamstring and had to go off and spent the rest of the season in and out of the side. The five-man midfield system was soon winning us a lot of friends, and one national newspaper voted us the most entertaining team in the country, which every Tottenham team should be. It's what the club has always stood for, and I pray will always stand for. David had repaired his relations with Hoddle, and he was running things in midfield. Clive Allen was having his best scoring spell since joining Spurs. Chris Waddle was at last showing the consistent form and talent that I always knew he possessed. They played and looked like a team, something that many previous sides had lacked.

By early February, we had progressed to the fifth round of the FA Cup, where we were drawn at home to Newcastle. We had also reached the semi-final of the Littlewoods Cup against Arsenal and were riding high in the League. We travelled to Highbury for the first leg, and felt confident that if we played the way we were capable of, we could get a result. As it turned out, Clive Allen scored the only goal of the game and we could have done even better with sharper finishing. Newcastle came to Tottenham towards the end of February for the FA Cup-tie, and brought, as always, tremendous travelling support. We beat them by the most slender of margins when the referee awarded us a disputed penalty, which was converted by Clive Allen.

Eight days later we played the second leg against Arsenal at home. At half-time we were leading 1–0, which meant 2–0 on aggregate, and David Dein, the Arsenal Vice-Chairman, came up to me in the Directors' Room and said: 'Irving, I think you're going to Wembley.' I replied: 'I think you might be right.' We seemed to be playing well and looked comfortable, without Arsenal really troubling us. How I was to regret my reply. Never again was I to assume anything in football until the final whistle had been blown.

Arsenal came back to score twice in the second half to tie the scores on aggregate. David Pleat won the toss for choice of venue for the third match on the following Wednesday night. For the third time in the tie, Clive Allen scored to put us ahead in the second half, and again we seemed to be comfortably in control when Arsenal made their substitution, which turned the game. Allinson, who had come on in the previous match, scored the equaliser, and when extra time seemed inevitable, a left-wing cross took a deflection off the heel of Danny Thomas and fell right in the path of Rocastle of all people, who beat Ray Clemence from no more than six yards.

The entire Spurs crowd, myself included, were stunned into absolute silence. After five hours of football we had been behind for less than sixty seconds, and were out of the competition. Arsenal do have a habit of late goals. I shook hands, as always, with their Chairman, Peter Hill-Wood, and wished him luck in the Final. Peter Day asked me what he should do about the champagne we had standing by, and after a moment's hesitation I told him to deliver it to the Arsenal dressing-room. Humility in victory, good grace in defeat, but I can tell you it was hard, and a very bitter pill to swallow.

Our support over the three matches was magnificent. The crowd really got behind the team, and I felt very sad for them. David Dein shook hands and remarked: 'I cannot believe what a good loser you are.' 'I have had lots of practice,' was my response. I didn't know it then, but we were to get our revenge some years later.

Many club chairmen visit the dressing-room before every game to wish the players luck. The number and stature of clubs where this happens staggers me: they include Liverpool, Manchester United, Chelsea, Everton, etc. It is not something I, or anyone previously, approved of or encouraged at Spurs. I have always seen the dressing-room as a private area where the Manager and his staff are preparing the team to give of their best, and in my mind, they do not want anyone else around. I am quite certain that I wouldn't if I were them. But after this defeat I felt I should go to the dressing-room to commiserate. I really felt for David Pleat and his players. In my opinion we had been the better footballing side over the three games, and I did not feel that we deserved such a cruel fate. But football spares no tears for losers.

As I entered the dressing-room, the first thing that struck me was the total silence. You could have heard a pin drop. I walked over to near where David was standing, and he tried to put a brave face on it by shrugging his shoulders and creasing his brow. He had a forlorn expression, as if to say it just wasn't meant to be us. As I glanced around, I saw the tears on some of the players' faces. Others held their heads in their hands. They were visibly, bitterly disappointed, and still no one made a sound. It was a very eerie atmosphere, a little like a funeral – sadness was everywhere. Most of the players still had their full kit on, muddy shirts full of perspiration, which bore witness to the effort they had put in. Those supporters who think that players don't care whether their team wins or loses should have been in the dressing-room that night. They would soon change their opinion.

Then suddenly I became aware of the noise drifting across the corridor. It was coming from the Arsenal dressing-room, where their players were singing: 'Wembley, Wembley.' It brought a very hollow feeling to my stomach and a lump to my throat. I stayed about ten minutes and then monitored that I ought to go back upstairs. As I left I took with me a memory that will stay with me for the rest of my life.

The following Saturday we played Queen's Park Rangers in the League at home, and before the game someone's wife asked me whether many players' careers were cut short by injury. I pointed out that serious knee injuries involving the cruciate ligament were the worst, but thankfully they were very few and far between. After about twenty minutes, Gavin Maguire crashed into Danny Thomas after he had just released the ball, and Thomas looked to be in agony on the ground. As he was being stretchered off, my earlier conversation raced through my head. We had not lost a first-team player for some years, but I had a strange feeling there and then that he wasn't going to make it back. It was a horrendous injury caused by a reckless tackle. Danny was such a nice boy and always had a smile on his face. He was friendly, warm and open, and everyone really felt for him.

Danny's contract was going to expire at the end of that season, and the League regulations state that a club must offer at least what the player is earning during the last year, or he is entitled to a free transfer. I advised Peter Day to offer Danny a £5,000 a year increase, which he greatly appreciated.

Football is such a short career and it can end in an instant. I have never blamed players for trying to do the best for themselves, as no one knows what is lying around the corner. Some time later, I was contacted by Danny's solicitor, who said that he was advising Danny to sue for damages, and asked if the club was prepared to help with the costs, as it could become pretty expensive. I said that I was prepared to fund him, as I was sure Danny would win, which eventually he did, by settling with the insurers at a later date out of court.

It was after Danny's sad injury that the Luton match came, and the taste it left in the mouth could not be removed by all the Listerine in the world. The only consolation was that it was behind us, and it was with some relief I got back to the normal roller-coaster ride that football provides. But not even I could have predicted that following the Luton match, the League game when we played Norwich at home would see the most amazing performance by a striker I think I have ever seen. That season Clive Allen just could not stop scoring goals, but in that match he was having a nightmare. Every time he went to control the ball, on the very wet pitch, somehow it skidded away, or hit him on the knee or thigh; just about everywhere except where he wanted it to. It was becoming an embarrassment, comical even.

Then, with fifteen minutes to go and with the score at 0–0, he got a half-chance in the box and scored. When the game finished, the score was 3–0 and Clive had got another hat trick. Sheffield Wednesday, who were due to play at Southampton, but had the match rained off, stopped off to see the game. At the final whistle their Chairman, Bert McGhee, a real northern gentleman in his sixties, said to me: 'Irving, I have now seen everything.' And he wasn't far wrong. When your luck is in, it's in.

All managers are different in the way they approach their work. David was quite unique. He used to spend a lot of time in the afternoons telephoning other managers for a general chit-chat, and always had his ears open for what was going on elsewhere. He had a lot of friends in football, and was liked because he was open and honest and people trusted him. They did not look upon him as a smart Alec, or a spiv. They knew he was very hard-working and totally dedicated, and they respected him and his opinions. The number of matches he used to see in a season was incredible, and he seemed to know most players both in and out of the League. To be successful in any walk of life, especially football, there are no substitutes for dedication and hard work, and he certainly had both of these characteristics.

David's work on the telephone soon resulted in a remarkable transfer coup. Earlier in the season, he had decided that Mark Falco, who had been with Spurs since he was a schoolboy, didn't quite fit in with his plans, but he could drum up little interest with no firm offers forthcoming. Then one evening David rang me at home to relate a telephone conversation he had had that afternoon with Graham Taylor, then Manager of Watford. He had mentioned to Taylor that Mark Falco was doing very well in the reserves and was worth a first-team place, but the board had asked him to sell a player to raise some money (which was a bit of a white lie). He explained that there were several clubs interested in Falco, and David made out that he was seeking Graham's advice on what he would do in the same situation.

Taylor's interest was aroused, and he then asked if David was serious in releasing Falco, as Watford would be very interested. The conversation ended with a transfer fee agreed, and the deal went through a few days later. David had worked out in his mind that Watford were short of a forward, and did what I still think is one of the best selling jobs I had heard of, bearing in mind they had never even thought of enquiring.

Some managers are a bit like magpies: they like to hoard players, even if they have no chance of making it into the first team. Somehow, they feel more secure with a larger pool of players than is necessary. It can often work out to be counter-productive, as it begins to clog up the system. David was not like that.

It is very important to allow young players to progress, and I have always been very much in favour of developing the club's youth system. If the younger players feel they haven't got a chance of breaking through, it will curb their enthusiasm and stifle their confidence. It also goes a lot deeper: players will choose, as schoolboys, to go to other places, where they feel they will have a real chance to express their talents. Spurs in the Sixties and early Seventies produced very few home-grown players, and most of the teams contained players mainly bought from other clubs.

David, however, was keen on a strong youth policy, as was Peter Shreeve before him. There is a very old saying in football – 'If they're good enough, they're old enough.' It seems ridiculous now that Graeme Souness could never make it into the Spurs first team, and was sold to Middlesbrough for £60,000 after having made only one appearance as a substitute in a European match in Iceland.

David's sale of Falco meant that when we played the semi-final of the FA Cup against Watford we were faced with one of our old players. By this time, in early April, it was clear that David and the team had just got over any disappointment experienced in the Littlewoods Cup semi-final defeat by Arsenal. As it happens we could have met Arsenal in the semi-final, but they were beaten in the quarters by Watford, a superb 3–1 victory. We had reached there by beating Scunthorpe, Crystal Palace, Newcastle and Wimbledon, all at the first attempt with no replays necessary, having scored ten goals and conceded just two, both scored by Scunthorpe in the third round.

Semi-finals are cruel occasions. Lose them and nobody re-members you: win them and the world seems your oyster. This proved to be an occasion where we could claim the oysters. Everything about the match went well. The night before, the team stayed in the Midlands, and I had arranged for the directors and their wives to meet at a country hotel in Worcestershire for dinner the same evening. It was the only time the whole board stayed overnight before a match.

The next day's lunch, laid on by custom by the FA, went even better. After I made a short speech and presented a large silver salver to Elton John, then Chairman of Watford, he responded with a similar gift, saying: 'Unfortunately, my one is not as big as his one.' It quite brought the house down.

The only thing daft about the semi-final was that two clubs from the London area were being made to travel to Birmingham. The thought of using Wembley had not occurred, and due to the volume of traffic on the motorway, with both sets of supporters coming from the same area, the kick-off was delayed. But this apart, the semi-final was a dream, at any rate if you were a Tottenham supporter. Poor Watford just did not have a chance.

Their goalkeeper had sustained an injury before the tie. His place was taken by the son of Eddie Plumley, the club's Man-aging Director and one of the top administrators in the game. He had never played for Watford, and before that was looking after a wine bar. Within minutes of the start he was shipping goals, and there were cruel shouts of Go back to the wine bar. Steve Hodge gave us a very early lead, when young Plumley let a shot slip out of his hands. Ten minutes later Clive Allen had a shot diverted into the net. Remembering the disappointment of the Littlewoods Cup, neither David nor myself moved when the goals were scored, whilst everyone around us was jumping up and down. At that stage, the thought of a possible victory never passed through my mind.

We were playing well, passing the ball and not allowing Watford into the game. John Barnes, in particular, was being kept very quiet. A few minutes before half-time, Paul Allen, who as always had been running as if his very life depended on it, scored to make it 3–0. It was at that point that I turned to David and quietly said: 'I think we are going to Wembley.' He just gave me a little smile.

The second half was more about containment, and with about ten minutes to play, Steve Hodge scored again with a good shot from the edge of the penalty area. Watford scored with a header from a free kick a few moments later, but the game ended with us in the Final. At the whistle, Elton John and his directors wished us all the best at Wembley, and then he asked if he could go into Spurs' dressing-room to wish our players luck for the Final. I took him and our directors, together with a crate of champagne, to see them.

What a difference a good result makes. If the semi-final dressing-room against Arsenal was a morgue, this was a temple of joy. The players were cock-a-hoop, singing and laughing, and generally making a lot of noise. Clive Allen wanted to know if his goal had broken the club's individual scoring record for a season, which had been set by Jimmy Greaves some twenty-odd years previously. It had. Elton was talking to Glenn Hoddle, and privately cursing John Barnes – 'He played like he wants to leave. Well if he does, let him. He's no good to us like that, the quicker he goes the better.'

David was beaming from ear to ear. At long last he had made it. I am sure he spent a second or two that day thinking back to his start in management many years previously at Nuneaton. He had deserved it. We had played well nearly all season and entertained people everywhere we had been. The spirit was good and the supporters, at last, had something to shout about.

My most lasting memory of the day was the drive home to

London. There were thousands of cars draped in blue and white: it was like an Armada sailing back to port. Nobody seemed to be in any rush, and it wouldn't have mattered if the journey home had taken a week. There were cars for as far as the eyes could see down the motorway, and they were filled with happy, smiling faces. I think it was the best journey home from a game since, perhaps, we had got back into the First Division in 1978, or was it when we won the semi-final replay in 1981 at Highbury . . . it didn't really matter.

The next day it was confirmed that Coventry would be our opponents at Wembley on 16 May.

As often happens when teams get to a Cup Final, their League form seems to suffer. Perhaps it has something to do with players not wanting to risk injury, which I can understand, as playing in the biggest showpiece match of any season can be the highlight of most players' careers. Out of our last nine games, we won three, drew two and lost four. At one stage we had a chance of winning the League, but Everton won it, as in 1984/85, and we finished the season in third place. Clearly Cup Final fever was in the air.

The night before the game, the team stayed at Tesco's teaching and training college in Hertfordshire, which had previously been a hotel. The company, whose head office is in Cheshunt and which has long been a Spurs supporter, had offered us the use of it. I went there to meet David for dinner at 8 pm, and while the atmosphere was relaxed, with the players strolling around and generally taking it easy, I could see David was clearly wound up for the game. Cup Final time is always hectic: all the staff at the ground are working flat-out, and there is terrific media build-up. But I was anxious that David remain calm, and I tried to get him to relax over a very enjoyable dinner. This was the first time Spurs had reached Wembley since I had got involved, and I wanted to savour the occasion.

The next day I arrived at Wembley at 10.30 am and wanted to walk up Olympic Way to feel the atmosphere outside the stadium. I looked up at the twin towers with the flags flying. The sky was clear and the mid-morning air was fresh – perfect weather for football. As I was walking across the bridge towards the stadium, a handful of Spurs supporters called out to me: 'Don't worry, today is our day.' I hoped they were right.

We had been sent a programme of events, which is carried out with military precision, right down to: 'the teams will assemble in the tunnel at 2.46 pm and be led on to the field of play at 2.49 pm by Mr R. Bird of the Football Association.' At 12.30 pm I was ushered into the Royal Box ante-room, together with a number of other people. We were positioned in a semicircle, waiting to be presented to the Royal guest, the Duchess of Kent.

The Prime Minister, Margaret Thatcher, was first in line, accompanied by her husband, Denis. The Sports Minister, Dick Tracey, and the Chairman of the Football Association, Bert Millichip, and his wife were also present, as was Brian Wolfson, the Chairman of Wembley plc. The President of Coventry, and his wife, were just before me. John Pointon, the club Chairman, had decided to travel on the team coach and miss the lunch instead. It amused me to see Mrs Thatcher curtsying. I was sure she was more used to being curtsied to, albeit by her ministers.

The Duchess paused for a few words with everyone, and when she reached the Coventry President she began to question him about individual players. I started to get a little nervous, as she obviously had a feeling that Coventry were going to win. She singled out Bennett, the Coventry winger, as the target for most of her questions. He was later to give Mitchell Thomas a very difficult afternoon indeed. When I asked her about her intuition, she gave me a very diplomatic answer, which confirmed her neutrality. She then started to speak to my then girlfriend, about how difficult it must be for someone who she assumed was married to a football nut. They became so engrossed in their conversation that the line broke up and the last few guests were never introduced.

Over lunch I was seated next to the Duchess of Kent and was able to confirm her in-depth knowledge of football. After the lunch was over, I wanted to savour the atmosphere inside the stadium, and Peter Day took myself and the other directors down to the running track. I walked towards the tunnel, where the Spurs supporters were congregated, and saw Ricky Villa, who was giving a television interview at the time. We shook hands and he wished us the best of luck.

As I was just about to return, some Spurs supporters must have noticed us, and started to clap, and as always happens in a football crowd, these things travel like wildfire. The noise got louder and louder as more and more people joined in. I looked up to the supporters and clapped back at them, and got the other directors to do the same. The more we clapped, the louder they did. It was quite an emotional moment. I continued to walk back past the seated section of Spurs fans, giving them the 'thumbs up' as I passed. It was clear to me that they were enjoying themselves.

Back in the Banqueting Hall, I was ushered back into the ante-room, and I eventually got talking to Dick Tracey and Margaret Thatcher about the government's ill-fated proposal for a Football Identity Card Scheme. What quickly struck me was that the Prime Minister was not interested in anyone's opinions, other than her own. She spoke straight through you and seemed totally deaf to anything anyone else was saying. I had never met a person quite like her before or since, and I must say that my impression of her was quite unflattering – in total contrast to the impression left, a few years later, by John Major.

We were shown to our seats in the Royal Box to await the presentation of the teams to the Duchess, and when Spurs were led on to the field by David Pleat, I had a large lump in my throat, as our supporters were making their presence heard, which became larger when the crowd sang the Cup Final anthem, 'Abide With Me'.

The first thing that struck me was that John Sillett, the Coventry Manager, was laughing and seemed very relaxed as he was waving to people in the crowd. On the other hand, David seemed stern-faced and uptight. He appeared very nervous, and I was praying that his obvious mood had not transferred itself to the players.

The game began, and Clive Allen headed his forty-ninth goal of the season after only two minutes. Coventry equalised in less than ten minutes, but we scored again just before half-time, and as we got up at the break, I remember the President of the Football League, Philip Carter, who was also then the Chairman of Everton, saying to me: 'It's going to be your Cup, Irving,' to which I just smiled.

I was so engrossed in the game that it was not until after around thirty-five minutes that someone tapped me on the shoulder to draw my attention to the fact that some of the players had the Holsten logo missing from their shirts. I tried to get someone to find Peter Day at half-time, so that he could contact the dressing-room about the shirts, but he was nowhere to be found.

I later discovered that what had happened was that four sets of shirts had been delivered to the club about three weeks before the Cup Final. There were two sets of long-sleeved and two sets of short-sleeved shirts, but only one set of the long- and short-sleeved shirts had the sponsor's name printed on them. For weeks they lay in Peter Day's office, nobody bothering about them, nobody expecting a problem. The day before the Wembley match, Johnny Wallace, our kit man, who had done this operation often enough in the past, loaded them in the skips for Wembley. Mechanically, almost instinctively, he folded one set of long-sleeved and one set of short-sleeved shirts, but did not check if the sponsor's name was on them. Amazingly, nobody in the dressing-room spotted it, and David Pleat explained to me afterwards that the tension in the room was so great that the sponsor's name and the logo was the last thing on the players' minds.

At the post-match dinner, the Press naturally made much of this blunder, and on the Monday morning I, along with David Pleat, Peter Day and Mike Rollo, met Holsten. Their offices were in Ludgate Circus, and before the meeting I took the Tottenham people to a nearby café to discuss our strategy. We feared the worst, but Alan Bridget, Holsten's Chairman, took a very understanding view and made it clear that there was no question of withdrawing the sponsorship. We offered some compensation for the following season by giving them additional perimeter board advertising facilities, and the meeting ended very well. I did make a point to Alan that as a result of the mistake Holsten had probably received far more publicity than they would otherwise have got, although there was no basis to the suggestion someone floated that the mistake was a deliberate one in order to give Holsten this publicity.

But if relations with Holsten were repaired there were some casualties at Tottenham as a result of this fiasco. Johnny Wallace was relegated to the reserve team, Roy Reyland took over as the first-team kit man, and poor Peter Day lost his job. I was sorry to see him go, and had no hesitation in giving him references later, as I believed that Tottenham had lost a good man.

The protocol in the Royal Box on Cup Final day is that the two competing club chairmen change places at half-time, and in the first half I sat next to the Duchess of Kent, whilst in the second half I sat near Margaret Thatcher. We had a number of chances to increase our lead early in the second half, before Bennett crossed from the right and Keith Houchen headed a spectacular equaliser. The game, to me, was beginning to resemble the 1981 Cup

Final, in that we weren't playing particularly well, although we did get the chance to fight another day. I felt that if there were no more goals, we would win the replay.

At the end of normal time, Mrs Thatcher, who was sitting a few seats away from me, made as if to leave. I turned to her husband, Denis, to say there was extra time, at which she grimaced and started reading through her itinerary for the day, muttering under her breath.

Coventry seemed to get stronger in extra time, and when a deflection off poor Gary Mabbutt spun over and beyond the reach of Ray Clemence, I had my head in my hands. But at the final whistle, I immediately shook hands with John Pointon and congratulated him on Coventry's win. Mrs Thatcher, who had seen this, looked visibly shocked and said to me: 'That was a very brave thing you just did,' to which I retorted: 'Prime Minister, you must understand that we're not all hooligans in football.'

Spurs were presented first, as is customary, and I could see clearly that Richard Gough was crying his eyes out. He hadn't had the best of days, but with a little bit of luck we might have won. I shook hands with each of our players in turn, and they looked very dispirited. Our supporters were, by now, a little subdued, whilst the Coventry fans, who had seemed to get louder and louder as the afternoon progressed, were overjoyed. As Brian Kilcline, the Coventry captain, lifted the Cup I couldn't help thinking we had lost an FA Cup Final for the first time in our history. Before that we had come to seven Cup Finals and won the lot. I returned to the Banqueting Hall and, according to a friend, I looked as white as a sheet. Everybody was very sympathetic, and the neutrals said it was the best Cup Final they had seen in many years.

I got the Spurs directors together, and Peter Day took us across the pitch to the dressing room, which was a morbid place. The stadium was virtually empty. As I crossed the pitch, a couple of Spurs fans were still in their places and shouted out to me: 'Cheer up, it wasn't that bad.' But that was not easy, and the dressing room felt even more miserable than it had the night Arsenal beat us in the semi-finals of the Littlewoods Cup. Ray Clemence kept on repeating: 'That's the second time I've been beaten by a deflection in a Final.' He was referring back to the 1971 Cup Final, when he was in goal for Liverpool and Charlie George scored the winner for Arsenal when the ball took a deflection off Larry Lloyd during extra time. David Pleat looked shot to pieces, and there wasn't very much I could say to make him feel any better. He'd had an extremely successful first season but had nothing to show for it.

At the evening banquet at White Hart Lane, worse was to follow. Richard Gough started to exchange words with David Pleat, and Richard eventually stormed out. Richard was again having problems with his wife, and it was so bad that he didn't invite her to the Cup Final. I left soon after, little realising that just as a season of great promise and great football had ended miserably, so the fracas between Gough and Pleat would be a prelude to the crisis of the following season. Not that I could have anticipated at that time how it would come, and when it did it was totally unexpected.

It blew up one Sunday morning a couple of months later, when David rang me to say that two journalists from the *Sun* had turned up on his doorstep asking him questions. He explained to me that they were about to run a controversial story concerning his private life.

We spoke several times during the course of the day, and I told him to speak to a solicitor as soon as possible. By 10 pm that evening, the newspaper's first edition was already on the street, and I drove to Victoria Station to pick up a copy, which contained no reference to David whatsoever. I telephoned him and told him what I had seen, but he was extremely nervous and kept saying that someone inside the newspaper had seen the article being prepared. I suggested that he came to my flat in London, as I had arranged for him to meet a firm of solicitors the following morning at 8 am.

When he arrived I made a pot of coffee, and we sat talking until the early hours of the morning. I told him that the club would back him financially if the lawyers advised him to sue the newspaper. David spent most of the next day with the solicitors, and it transpired finally that he had been advised that it would be a very difficult case to win should he take legal action. I contacted the other directors to explain the position, and persuaded them to stand behind David.

The articles persisted for a few days, and although his wife and family were magnificent in their support for him, and his many friends rallied round, David became very nervous. Then as the summer turned to autumn and the season began, David must have thought he had seen off his tormentors. But it was not to be.

The new season was well under way and we, without playing particularly well, were winning. By the time Arsenal played us in October we had set up a club record by winning fourteen home League matches in a row. This run dated back nine months to January, when the last visiting team to win a League match at White Hart Lane were our North London rivals. The record had to break some time, but as luck would have it, it broke that day. Despite a goal by Nico Claesen in the first minute, Arsenal won the game 2–1. Within a few days events were to overshadow the result, and the match would become noteworthy for being David Pleat's last game as Manager.

On the following Thursday I received a call at home, just before nine o'clock in the evening, from David. I said I was on the other line, and could I telephone him back in a few minutes. He said it was very urgent, and I immediately thought that he wanted to buy someone to strengthen the team. I finished the other call to discover that David had received another visit from the *Sun*, which had caused him and his family so much grief in the summer. What was worse, they had doorstepped Pleat and pictured him half naked, dripping wet, and looking like a rabbit caught in the headlights.

I told him to contact the solicitors again, and arrange to see them first thing in the morning. Again I offered the club's support should the lawyers advise him to sue. David stayed until late afternoon with the solicitors, who made it clear it would not be advisable to take legal action. An emergency board meeting had been hastily arranged for about 7 pm that evening, which all the directors and David attended. It was clear that, given the publicity, David could not continue. He was the subject of stories in the vicious rumour-mills of football, rival supporters were taunting Spurs fans, and there were whispers that he had lost the confidence of the players. But it was David's decision to go, and as he tendered his resignation we reluctantly accepted. There was a heavy atmosphere in the room, with everyone paying great tribute to what had been achieved in a relatively short period of time. I was particularly upset, as I had believed he was going to be the Spurs Manager for many years to come. I went home and felt completely numb, I was so stunned by the events of the previous twenty-four hours.

Trevor Hartley, David's assistant, took charge of the team for the following day's match at Nottingham Forest, where we lost 3–0. After the game I returned to White Hart Lane, where the

Bruno–Bugner boxing match was taking place. Quite by chance I bumped into one of the top people in the police, and we had a short chat. I was curious to know how the story had reached the *Sun* newspaper. The policeman was quite sure in his own mind that there had been a tip-off from within the police, and he felt that betraying private information like that was utterly wrong. I couldn't agree more. Whatever David had done was his own private affair. Did it have any impact on his ability as a football Manager? But for the *Sun* such considerations did not matter. They were concerned with a story and a headline – hang the consequences.

The shock waves from David's departure were to pursue me for some time, and even now I find it difficult to discuss it. But I knew it was also time to think of the future and try to forget about the past. Curiously, when David's problem first surfaced in the summer I had received a telephone call from a very keen Spurs supporter, who I knew was very friendly with Terry Venables. I had seen them together in Barcelona, and he had also been the guest of one of the Spurs directors at a few matches. He chit-chatted for a couple of minutes, and then he suddenly said: 'I've got Terry's number on holiday, and he would be very interested in hearing from you.' I politely declined the offer.

I never asked Terry if he knew about the calls. By this time I knew that whenever managerial vacancies arise, the person interested never rings, it's always a friend. It is a bit like those friends of Royals and friends of politicians who always advise newspapers about the feelings of the person in the news. One can but speculate who these 'friends' are, and how close they are to the person concerned.

8 | THE MAN WITH THE SILVER TONGUE

'I've come to Spurs to win the First Division, I need it, I desperately want to do it and I know it has to be next season. I'm supposed to have said it will take three years. That's nonsense. A consolidating sixth is no good to me. I must be right at the top with Tottenham.' – Terry Venables after the defeat at Port Vale in the Cup during the 1987/88 season.

Some people are born with a silver spoon in their mouth. Terry Venables was born with a silver tongue. He has the ability to enchant, to sweet-talk most people into most things, and he is a very convincing talker. This is probably one of the clues as to why he is such a good coach and communicator at all levels, especially with players and Press.

I first became aware of this in August 1980, when Terry was in charge of Crystal Palace and Spurs travelled to Selhurst Park for a mid-week match. In that game Vince Hilaire pushed the referee (the first time I'd ever seen it at a professional football match) and was sent off by him. It was Steve Archibald and Garth Crooks's second match for Tottenham. They combined well, as did the rest of the team, and we won 4–3, with Crooks scoring a hat trick and Archibald scoring his first goal for Tottenham. After a result like that, particularly when your favourite team has played really well and won, you look forward to the next day's papers with great anticipation. Imagine my surprise when all I found were Venables's quotes and protestations about how unlucky they were, and had Hilaire not been sent off the result would have been different. At that time I couldn't help feeling he'd been at a different game to me. Now I know that was my first bite from the silver-tongued man.

One thing I don't like, and never have done, is people who

make excuses for losing, especially if the other team played better. You win with humility and lose with good grace. This was
the first example I had ever seen of a highly rated First Division
Manager, supposedly running the team of the Eighties (as Crystal
Palace was classed then), yet instead of actually accepting the
defeat with good grace, offering excuses and moans. It is interesting to note that Terry left for Queen's Park Rangers before the
end of that season. I felt, and still do, that these are unbecoming.
When Alex Ferguson lost the First Division Championship to
Leeds in 1992, he made no excuses and actually questioned his
own judgement. In other words he gave an honest assessment
of what he had failed to achieve. He is an honest man, who is
prepared to look in the mirror and not try and convince you
with soccer-speak how wonderful the Emperor's new clothes
look.

That Venables memory played a great part with me in 1984
when Keith Burkinshaw resigned and the position of Manager
was open. The Press had linked Tottenham very closely with
Terry Venables, who was then at Queen's Park Rangers, not
only as Manager but also as Managing Director. There had been
a lot of stories in the newspapers that Jim Gregory had offered
him the opportunity to purchase the club, in the shape of the
playing staff and football company, whilst Gregory was going
to retain the freehold of the stadium. However, an effective
takeover attempt never materialised, and I received numerous
telephone calls from friends and associates of Terry Venables
suggesting that he would be very interested in the position if it
was offered to him. But we never seriously considered him. He
had always given the impression of being rather easygoing and
jocular, and we were concerned about the discipline – a point
that Terry Venables actually spoke to me about later on, when I
got to know him much better, when he was coach of Barcelona.

Venables got that job through the good offices of his great
friend Jeff Powell, of the *Daily Mail*, who was highly instrumental
in managing to persuade the powers that be at FC Barcelona to
take what was really a very big risk at the time in appointing him
their coach. Once there, his path again crossed mine, for his first
and I believe his only purchase in that first season, when he was
successful in winning the Spanish Championship for Barcelona
for the first time in about ten years, was Steve Archibald.

The Barcelona directors were not keen on Archibald. Their
choice was Hugo Sanchez of Atletico Madrid, the Mexican

International centre forward. Terry mentioned this to me in private and said that whilst he was quite sure Sanchez was a good player, he hadn't seen enough of him to be satisfied that he was going to meet the requirements of the style of play that he was intending to impose on Barcelona. In fact the Vice-Chairman, Juan Gaspar, actually showed me a telex he'd received from Atletico Madrid which contained their offer for the transfer fee, which was absolutely identical to that which had been agreed between the clubs for Steve Archibald.

Terry and I got to know each other quite well when he was in Barcelona, and I warmed to him. He has enormous charm, and a great sense of humour which he uses to great effect in his many dealings with the Press. Our meetings were often the subject of Press speculation, even when it was very innocent. I remember going to see Barcelona play Juventus in the quarter-final of the European Cup in the 1985/86 season, when he arranged for my match tickets. I'd gone there just to see what I considered to be the Clash of the Titans in European competition, but the Press, discovering my presence, saw it as me trying to get Terry Venables to come to Tottenham.

It was on the night of the Bruno–Bugner match that my thoughts again turned to Venables. Denis Roach had been involved in the boxing and had brought Barry Hearn, Terry Lawless and me together, and thereby initiated our agreement to use the stadium. He was a particularly close friend of Terry Venables at the time, and during that evening I quietly asked if he knew where Terry was. His success at Barcelona had faded – he had led them to the European Cup Final but not won it – and after a relatively poor season he had been sacked. He was now, as they say about actors, 'resting'. Roach told me he was 'resting' somewhere in Florida, but if I wanted the telephone number he'd be able to get it for me very shortly. He telephoned me very late that evening, and I rang Terry Venables at about two or three in the morning, London time. It was between 9 and 10 pm in Florida.

I came straight to the point: if he was interested in talking seriously about taking the job at Tottenham then I was prepared to fly out within twenty-four hours to meet with him. I made it absolutely clear that there was no point in me flying thousands of miles if he was just going to listen to what I had to say and politely leave me in limbo. His words were: 'Irving, go and get the ticket to Miami' – words which gave me the confidence that there was a real possibility of our solving our search. It was a difficult time in the season to find a top-class Manager. League rules had stipulated that you could not poach managers from other clubs during the season, and in any event, how many top-class managers are there?

I telephoned back a few minutes later to find that the hotel operator had never heard of Terry Venables. I pointed out that that wasn't possible, I'd only been speaking to him a few minutes before. When I spoke to the Manager of the hotel, he also said that he didn't know who I was talking about but, if I'd like to leave my name and telephone number, if somebody turned up with that name they would call me back. It was quite obvious that Terry Venables did not want to be disturbed by journalists or other people. About five minutes later the telephone rang. It was Terry. I gave him the flight details and he said that he would arrange to pick me up at Miami Airport on the Monday afternoon.

At that time I'd been introduced by Martin Edwards of Manchester United to a man called Peter Owen who was, I believe, number three at British Airways and in charge of all flights worldwide. I spoke to him and said that I wanted to go to Miami on the Monday but I wanted to be able to get to the airport and board the plane without anybody seeing me. There are always certain Press men and photographers around at Heathrow, and I didn't want to be glimpsed by some bright journalist who perhaps might put two and two together. I was met outside of Terminal 4 by a young British Airways stewardess with my ticket; she guided me all the way through the labyrinth of corridors, and eventually we arrived at the aeroplane's door. I had decided as a further precaution, and agreed with Peter Owen, that the ticket should be issued in the name of Mr Arnold, just in case anybody was checking whether I was travelling to see Terry Venables. The precautions were necessary, as the Press had been full of speculation that he was the obvious choice for us.

I arrived at Miami Airport to be greeted by the smiling, tanned face of Terry Venables waiting at the gate. He had arranged for a station wagon to take us back to where he was staying in West Palm Beach. It was the PGA resort hotel, which was run by a friend of his. We sat in the back and Terry immediately showed tremendous enthusiasm and wanted to know exactly what the position was with the club, the team and so forth. That gave me great encouragement.

After about fifteen minutes of chit-chatting in the van, he produced a piece of paper and a pen and marked eleven blank positions representing eleven players on the field. This game, as I like to think of it, is something Venables and I were to play many, many times in the years to come. What he wanted to know was how many of the current team did I believe were capable of being filled in on that piece of paper – players who could win the League Championship. This he said was the ultimate test. 'If you are going to start you must start looking at the very highest point in your quest for achievement.'

'Look,' I replied, 'I think it's best if you actually talk to the coaching staff at Tottenham.'

'No, no, no,' said Terry. 'I want to hear what you think.'

So I filled in a number of blanks, and in all honesty I could only fill in four. Terry looked at my paper and said: 'There are seven blanks on that piece of paper, which means there's quite a large job ahead of whoever took over.'

At this stage I was still not sure whether he would sign, but what encouraged me was that over dinner Terry only wanted to discuss football and not terms. I was fascinated by his stories about Spain, and I warmed to him enormously. I kept on thinking that if I was able to persuade him to join Tottenham it would definitely be a step in a forward direction. The only difficulty I foresaw was that if we were successful the Press obviously were going to signal it as the coming of the Messiah, as he had been very immediately successful in Spain. It was only after lunch the next day – after we had spent many more hours discussing football – that for the very first time we started to discuss contractual terms. He only wanted to sign, if we could agree, for a period of around two years. I felt that was too short a period for a contract, and eventually we settled on three years, although I pointed out that that would have meant it fell in mid-season, which wasn't ideal. Still, that was something we would pick up at a later point.

He made it very clear from the beginning that he was unable, if we were to agree terms, to take over for approximately six weeks. He was thinking of some time in late November, because he had certain commitments. He was taking a breather from football, his daughters were joining him within a few days for a holiday, and he had not anticipated going back into the game until the beginning of the following season. In fact what he wanted to do was to look around Europe and gauge what was going on, and not return to management until the start of the 1988/89 season. I confirmed that if we were able to agree terms this would not present too much of a difficulty, but obviously I wanted him to come back as soon as possible.

After a little toing and froing, which didn't take very long, we agreed personal terms. We stood up, shook hands, had a celebration drink, and decided that we would issue a Press release immediately, pointing out that Terry had agreed to come back to his old club Tottenham as Manager and he would start within six weeks.

Normally when managers are signed there are Press conferences with professional photographers present, but with all this happening across the Atlantic I turned journalist and photographer. We had a new service at Tottenham called Spursline, whereby supporters could telephone in daily and listen to a recorded message giving details of what was actually happening on a day-to-day basis. This meant I had to do an interview with Terry for Spursline, but as I mentioned to him I didn't have a tape machine with me. Perhaps we could go to a local supermarket where we could find one?

Terry thought that I was joking. He had never heard of these telephone systems, which had just come in in England, and he was laughing all the time as we travelled to the local supermarket. Eventually we found one and we bought a tape machine. We sat in his car in the car park of the hotel, and for the first and only time I became the Spursline presenter, interviewing the Spurs Manager-to-be. We did an interview for around ten or fifteen minutes. Terry's humour came out loud and clear, and I tried to ask the questions that I felt all supporters wanted to ask. The interview was broadcast in two parts when I got back, and I believe there were more calls in those two days than on any previous two days.

Terry's signing also made me a Fleet Street photographer. I had taken my camera with me, and I was introduced to Terry's girlfriend, now his wife, Yvette. A charming and very friendly person with a good sense of humour and always with a smile on her face, she took a photograph of us shaking hands in the Florida sunshine. This appeared on the front cover of the Spurs programme the following Saturday in a home match against Wimbledon. My one and only entry into chequebook journalism followed when it was sold to the *Daily Mirror* for several thousand pounds, but I insisted that the fee went to a children's charity.

I returned to England exhausted, having travelled 10,000 miles, but delighted at having achieved what I had set out to do. I was a bit surprised that Terry was actually prepared to commit himself so quickly to a contract, and not only that but to make the fact public. The terms were generous: a three-year contract with a commencing salary in the region of £150,000 p.a., which was to make him, I believe, the highest-paid Manager in the First Division. In addition to that, a signing-on fee of around £50,000 was to be paid. The total deal over three years was probably worth in the region of £550,000–£600,000. Later on I was to suffer numerous references by Terry suggesting that he'd undersold himself at the time, but I couldn't agree with that.

If Terry's signing as Manager was unusual, his arrival at White Hart Lane was even more so. Normally managers take over as soon as they agree, but Terry's inability to come straight away meant Doug Livermore continued to be in charge of the first team, and the team carried on losing. We went out of the Littlewoods Cup the day after I signed Terry, and then, on the Saturday, we lost at home to Wimbledon 3–0. Terry had asked me to telephone him after all the matches just to give a view of how we were doing, and my match report of the Wimbledon game couldn't have filled him with too much joy. I continued to ask who was going to be appointed as his assistant. The name of Dave Sexton had been mentioned. Terry said he was still giving it some thought, and I asked whether he knew Peter Shreeve. He said: 'Not really,' and I suggested that he speak to him, as I felt he would be the ideal Number 2 for Terry. He said he didn't know Peter particularly well but would bear it in mind.

A few weeks later Terry finally confirmed that Alan Harris would be joining him, and that he himself was hopeful of being able to join the club on Monday 23 November, which was approximately two weeks before it was originally anticipated. Terry's first match in charge took place on 28 November – my birthday, and almost twenty years to the day since I had first met Terry as he prepared to play for Spurs in a Cup Winners Cup match in France. We were at home to Liverpool, who at that time were unbeaten in the League and had only conceded eight goals all season.

It was a real baptism of fire. At that stage, in all Terry's years as a manager he had yet to beat Liverpool. Nevertheless, everyone's hopes were high, and a crowd of nearly 47,500 turned up to welcome him home. It was not to be a particularly auspicious first match. Steve Hodge was sent off after about half an hour with the score at nil–nil, but while we managed to hold out until the second half, Liverpool were outright winners by two goals to nil.

Over the previous few weeks between Terry agreeing to come and finally arriving, we had played four League matches, drawing two and losing two but only scoring one goal in the process. After the Liverpool game there was a two-week break, as that was the season when there were twenty-one teams in the First Division and each club had two free Saturdays. This was a timely intervention during which Terry could do what he does best, work on the training field, starting to organise things and bring about his own style, and to get across his ideas to the players.

The following match was at home to Charlton, on a Sunday morning, and again we lost 1–0. Terry was clear that he had a major rebuilding job on his hands, which was consistent with what I had told him in Florida some weeks earlier. I was not against his buying. The problem was that he and I disagreed on the sort of people we should choose. I've always had a theory about new acquisitions. I much prefer to buy players well under the age of thirty, on the basis that it is more likely you are purchasing an 'appreciating asset', rather than someone of say, twenty-seven, twenty-eight, or twenty-nine, who will perhaps enter into a four-year contract which will mean that on expiry they are getting close to the accepted retirement age. I would describe this as a 'depreciating asset', unless you are purchasing a 'special' player at a reasonably good price to begin with – a man like Gary Lineker. To purchase someone of twenty-six or under means your downside if things go wrong is limited. In fact the only player we had purchased outside of this formula was Johnny Metgod, whom David Pleat had signed for £250,000 that previous summer from Nottingham Forest.

Terry had other ideas though. He felt it was important to be able to bring in more mature players, on the assumption that their greater experience would enable them to settle more quickly into the team. The first such player Terry wanted to sign was Terry Fenwick. Terry explained that George Graham was bidding to buy him, but Fenwick preferred to come to Spurs if we should meet his personal terms. Although until that point I had managed to keep the players' salaries at what I considered to be an acceptable level, with this signing we were about to enter a somewhat inflationary period for players' salaries. But despite the fact that Fenwick's terms were a little on the high side, and his age was outside of my adopted formula, it was clear that Terry Venables had made his mind up, so despite my reservations I instructed him to proceed. It amused me to reflect that on the night Richard Gough joined Glasgow Rangers, David Pleat had suggested signing Terry Fenwick as a replacement.

A few days later Terry received good reports on a goalkeeper called Peter Guthrie, who was playing for Weymouth in the Vauxhall Conference League, and the day before our live TV match at Derby County, Terry went to see him play. Newcastle United were also linked with him, and when I saw Terry before the match at the Baseball Ground I asked him what his view was. He said that Guthrie was a very confident goalkeeper, big in stature with a good physique, and had dealt with crosses, normally Spurs goalkeepers' weak point, very comfortably. 'Are you going to sign him?' I asked. 'I'd like to have done, but unfortunately he's agreed to go to Newcastle.' For half a second I felt disappointed, but then his inimitable chuckle, which turned to guffaws of laughter at me for having fallen for his practical joke, confirmed that everything had been agreed and he would be signing within a couple of days.

That afternoon, Terry enjoyed his first success as Manager of Tottenham when we won the match by 2–1. Clive Allen, one of Terry's protégés, scoring the winning goal, and the relief in Terry's voice when he spoke after the match was evident.

Terry was a completely different personality to David Pleat. This had been clear to me at the first Press conference held on the Monday before the Liverpool match, when he was introduced as the Spurs Manager. Terry gave his usual mixture of half-serious and half-joking wisecracks, and the atmosphere was good. It was clear he had a good manner about him and was an extremely good communicator. He was the master of what I believe is called the 'soundbite' – the ability to use a phrase that provides a marvellous quote for the Press. He knew the Press over many, many years and they knew him; some were very close personal friends. He is also the master of soccer-speak, the language of managers.

Terry was later to tell me that the Press in Barcelona could be ruthless. They came from all over the world, and the most interesting questions of all used to come from the Dutch journalists: they were not looking for a quick headline, but asked serious, well thought out technical questions about football. Each country had its hatchet-men, one or two of whom were also present at the inaugural Press conference at Tottenham. Inevitably, the questions raised at the Press conferences focus on the financial terms of the contract, which I always feel very put out about, as it's a private matter between the club and the Manager and nobody else's business. I've often said to journalists, if I asked you that question, I don't think you'd be very forthcoming. Another question is how much will the Manager have available in the transfer market. Again I find that by answering that question all we would be doing is tipping off our rivals as to how active we may be in the market, with the inevitable consequence of pushing prices up.

Our relationship was very good, frank and open, but what surprised me most of all was that he was always asking my opinion on players and team matters, and I always said: 'Look, it's your job, not mine. My opinion doesn't really count.' But he wanted me to feel part of it. There were times when I was brutally frank, and there were one or two occasions when I think he felt a little put out.

Things carried on and, apart from two wins over Christmas, didn't seem to be showing much improvement, although we did have a very good win at Oldham Athletic in the third round of the FA Cup on their plastic pitch. The Oldham Chairman had seemed rather too confident before the match that we were in for a shock, but we had our own two plastic specialists in Terry Venables and Clive Allen, who scored twice, and we were outright winners 4–2 in what was one of the best performances of the whole season.

Terry said he had been reasonably lucky in the FA Cup with QPR and Crystal Palace, and felt it was our best chance to achieve any success that season. In the fourth round we were due to play at Port Vale, and I went up with the team on the Friday afternoon and had dinner with Terry Venables, Alan Harris and the remainder of the coaching staff at the hotel where the team were staying in Stoke. News came that afternoon that Arsenal were about to sign Stoke City's full back Lee Dixon, and I asked Alan Harris what he thought of him and whether or not we should be looking to sign him. But I was told that he wasn't good enough. Dixon, of course, became an integral part of two Arsenal Championship-winning sides and even played for England.

We were all quietly confident about the following day's match. Spurs hadn't lost to a Third Division team in the FA Cup for many years, and it was less than twelve months previously that we had been finalists against Coventry. Early in the game Waddle found himself in the six-yard box with the ball at his feet, but agonisingly rolled the ball past the post. That proved the turning-point. Port Vale scored twice, and although Neil Ruddock coming on as a substitute did score, it was not enough. As it was, it proved to be his last appearance for Spurs before rejoining Millwall at the end of that season.

Terry was visibly shaken after the match, and the Port Vale result had some long-term consequences. Venables now gave the impression of a man in a hurry. This was not an isolated view. It was shared by the *Sun*, which carried an exclusive interview with Venables just after the defeat. The opening line read: 'Terry Venables is a man in a hurry.' It quoted Terry as saying: 'I've come to Spurs to win the First Division, I need it, I desperately want to do it and I know it has to be next season. I'm supposed to have said it will take three years. That's nonsense. A consolidating sixth is no good to me, I must be right at the top with Tottenham.' And looking forward to the next season, he pointed out: 'It will be my team, my system – my fault . . . I have money to spend and I believe I have enough to build a Championship side. When I eventually leave I would like the next man to come in and find the Club in a very healthy state. The Championship would be won, the Squad strong, the kids coming through and everyone at Tottenham happy. I have six months to start the race.' The sub-heading in the *Sun* said it all: 'It will be my fault if we fail to crush the Kop.'

Later on, when the horrendous financial crisis broke, it became commonplace in the Press to say that there was no money made available to Venables to buy players. This was just not so. In his first three months at White Hart Lane, Venables spent £1.5 million. He also pushed up the salary levels of the players so that Fenwick, his first signing, was earning more than Chris Waddle – a development that made me extremely nervous. Indeed as the summer signings came, Venables's moves in the transfer market were considered so reckless that some of the Press described Spurs as throwing money around.

With the results in the League continuing to be disappointing – we only won four League matches, drawing seven and losing seven from 1 January to the end of the season – Terry began to buy. He bought Paul Walsh from Liverpool and Bobby Mimms – yet another goalkeeper – from Everton. Terry had made it clear that he didn't see Tony Parkes as the Spurs goalkeeper. However, Mimms's purchase was interesting in that Terry hadn't actually seen him play recently before he bought him. But he was highly recommended by Dave Sexton, who had been in charge of the England Under-21s. I found it a little strange that a Manager should buy a goalkeeper effectively blind on the recommendation of someone else, but Terry had a great respect for Sexton's opinion and was prepared to rely on his judgement. This can be dangerous, as the man who makes the purchase has to take the responsibility. While Walsh proved a loyal and popular Spurs player, Mimms's arrival gave rise to jokes about the goalkeepers our new Manager was buying; he was one of the many poor purchases Terry made.

In Walsh's case I had seen a newspaper report that Derby County had agreed terms with Liverpool to buy him for £500,000, which didn't seem to them to be an outrageous figure. I rang Terry and asked him what his feelings were about Walsh. He said he liked him as a player and also thought he was good value, and that he wanted to try and sign him. Being on very good terms with Peter Robinson in Liverpool, I rang him, and when he confirmed that £500,000 was the figure, we agreed to pay the same sum. Peter felt that Walsh would much prefer to come back to London rather than the Midlands. Terry tied both of these up while I was away for a short break.

The real start of the Venables spending spree came in the summer when we went for the two Pauls: Gascoigne and Stewart. Just before the Port Vale match I remember leaving the hotel with the team and passing some of our supporters standing in the entrance to the hotel. As we did, quite a few called out: 'Sign Paul Gascoigne. He's the one you need.' What they didn't know was that we had tried to sign him already. I had been approached in the September before, when David Pleat was Manager, and I'd asked him what he knew about Gascoigne and whether he would like to sign him. He appeared to be a bit lukewarm. At one point I had actually agreed personal terms, subject to Newcastle's releasing him at the end of the season. Subsequent events overtook this, and the final terms were substantially higher than those previously negotiated. At that stage Gascoigne was very far from being a 'Gazza', but I was very impressed how perceptive our supporters were.

As I have said before, they can tell a Spurs player a mile away.

The Saturday before we were beaten at Port Vale we had played at St James' Park, Newcastle, on a very heavy pitch. Whilst we had been watching Gascoigne for some time, this was the first chance Terry had of seeing him in the flesh. Terry was very friendly with Jackie Milburn, and his opinion was that Gascoigne was going to become one of the best players in the world. He raved about him to Terry, saying that he should take any chance he got of signing him. At one moment in the first half Gascoigne collected the ball just on the arc of the centre circle in his own half and strode forward. Fenwick went in very forcibly to try and dispossess him, but Gascoigne with just a shrug of the hips shook him off, and Fenwick literally bounced off him.

Newcastle were rebuilding a certain part of the ground at that time, and we were standing in a large Portacabin by the corner flag with the windows slightly steamed up. As Fenwick bounced off Gascoigne, Terry and I looked round at each other. We didn't need to say anything, our eyes did the talking. Terry was astonished at the sheer power and strength of a player who was still only twenty, and I am convinced that at that moment Terry decided that Gascoigne was the signing that we both felt the club badly needed.

A few weeks later I was speaking to Ossie Ardiles. He said he'd heard whispers we were after Gascoigne and he made his own opinion perfectly clear that this was the player we had to buy. With Hoddle gone we badly needed a leader in midfield. However, by this time, the end of the 1987/88 season, there were three clubs all chasing the signature of Paul Gascoigne. Martin Edwards of Manchester United had told me quite openly that his club were going to bid. Liverpool were also interested. Martin said there was no point in each of us bidding the other one up, and why didn't the player decide where he wanted to go? He said he would tell me when Manchester United were going to make their move if we would do the same.

One evening in May, the directors met for dinner with Terry Venables to discuss his requirements for the coming season. He named Gascoigne as his number one priority and explained that he was also looking for a centre forward. Top of the list for that position was Mark Hateley at Monaco, followed by Paul Stewart at Manchester City. Terry had been a great fan of his ever since he had seen him play for Blackpool some years previously when he was in charge at QPR. The directors asked what kind of fee was likely to be involved. I pointed out that I had been in touch with Gordon McKeag of Newcastle. They were seeking £2.5 million for Gascoigne, who would be twenty-one on 27 May 1988. I explained the competition that we were likely to face. My own opinion was that I didn't believe any club would pay above £2 million, and it was agreed that we had the authority to pursue the matter at that level.

We then discussed Mark Hateley, who we both felt was unlikely to leave Monaco, although he was being pursued at the time by Graeme Souness at Glasgow Rangers and there was an outside chance that he might be released. Manchester City were known to be prepared to listen to offers for Paul Stewart. I was on good terms with Peter Swales, their Chairman, and he promised to keep me informed of any developments.

The naïvety of the Spurs board about transfer matters showed up at this dinner when the discussion returned to Paul Gascoigne. Terry and I were talking across the table when Tony Berry turned round and said: 'What are you worried about? You've been allocated the two million to buy the player, why don't you go and do it?' Venables rolled his eyes, and I pointed out to Tony that unfortunately it wasn't quite like going to Tescos and buying a tin of baked beans: you pick it off the shelf, pay for it and walk away. Making the offer which might persuade Newcastle to sell was merely the beginning of the story. After that it's a question of seduction and gentle persuasion and encouragement. Why a player who has the choice of three big clubs should want to join yours as against any of the others is dependent upon the personalities of the people involved.

But while the race for Gascoigne was tight there were other things going for us. I knew Terry had an ability second to none to cajole players into signing. He always looked after them afterwards, and his ex-players have always remained very loyal to him – a highly commendable quality. I also knew Mel Stein and Len Lazarus, Gascoigne's advisers, whom I had come into contact with some years previously when they advised Waddle on his transfer to Spurs. We'd always got on well.

The next morning I telephoned Gordon McKeag and told him that we were tabling an offer of £2 million and were prepared to put 50 per cent down with the balance payable during the course of the next twelve months: standard policy between football clubs. I pointed out to him that this offer was final and would not be increased, as we felt that the price was a very full one for a player only just twenty-one.

Venables was aware of my agreement with Martin Edwards, and I telephoned him, in front of Terry, to say that we had made an offer. But I certainly did not reveal how much we had bid. Newcastle said they would be having a board meeting within a few days and would then contact me further. McKeag asked me to ring at 6 pm the following Thursday. I knew that Liverpool and Manchester United were considering their position very closely. However, by the time of Newcastle's board meeting on Thursday no further offers had been tabled.

Newcastle finally agreed to our fee on the condition that they received 25 per cent of any subsequent resale value over £2 million. I answered that this was not acceptable but we would be prepared to agree to their condition with a base resale figure of £2.5 million and a percentage of 10 per cent, which was finally agreed to. It was only then that we got formal approval from Newcastle to commence discussions with Gascoigne.

Terry had spoken to Chris Waddle, who was in Newcastle at the time. On the Sunday morning Chris took Paul Gascoigne for a drink in a local pub and spent an hour or more trying to persuade him that Tottenham was the club for him. I am quite sure that this did our case no harm whatsoever, as those two were later to become the closest of friends and inseparable.

The following Tuesday I met Gascoigne for the very first time. With Terry on holiday, Alan Harris was to discuss things from the football point of view. I shall never forget my first off-the-field sight of Gascoigne. He was dressed in a slightly old-fashioned way, looking very much like a country boy coming up for his big visit to the Smoke. A little on edge. Mel Stein had told me that his real preference was to go to Liverpool, but they were unable, at that particular moment, to make a proper move for him. Stein even went so far as to say that Gascoigne wanted a condition to be inserted into the contract that if Liverpool came in at any later time we would agree to release him. I was very unhappy about this, and made my feelings clear to Mel Stein.

I understand Gascoigne's reluctance – we had not had a particularly good season, finishing thirteenth in the League and being knocked out of the FA Cup by Port Vale – but I didn't intend us to be a safe parking place for Liverpool. This kind of deal happens very often on the Continent: a smaller team will purchase a foreign player, sometimes with added cash benefits from one of the major clubs, and the major club at some time in the future may sign the player. Michael Laudrup signed for Juventus, then stayed for a couple of years at Lazio before moving back to Juventus, who had originally paid the transfer fee.

This was the very first time I'd ever had to deal with all aspects of a transfer. Normally the Manager will deal with the player's side and often the financial terms, but with Terry on holiday I was having to deal with both sides of the transfer. Finally Mel Stein and Gascoigne left the room, saying they needed ten minutes for discussion. I sat in my office and felt nervous that perhaps they might decide to bide their time and see what other offers were forthcoming. Eventually they both returned to the room. Paul Gascoigne said: 'Mr Scholar, I have changed my mind about the condition I was insisting upon the other day. I don't want any conditions in there concerning Liverpool. I'm a Tottenham Hotspur player and I promise you I will give you everything I have to repay your confidence in me.' He put out his hand and we shook.

I felt potentially we were signing one of the best players in the world. I had no doubt in my mind that he was the best young player that I had seen for many, many years. His strength and power reminded me of Duncan Edwards of Manchester United. As we parted I asked a member of staff to take Gascoigne to the local shop and let him choose whatever fishing rod he wanted. Gascoigne's face lit up like a child presented with a toy.

Their one condition was that they didn't want it announced for another couple of days, which was fine. The delay was due to Gascoigne's contractual commitments with the *Sun*, who wanted to announce his choice of clubs exclusively. I told Gascoigne I would like him to tell Venables of his decision, and I would ring him in the United States, where he was on holiday.

Terry had been patiently waiting by the telephone for an answer, and I said to him that we had a slight problem. He sounded very nervous. I said: 'It's not an easy problem to over-come, but only you can make the final decision as to whether or not you agree to the particular condition he is insisting upon.' Terry said: 'Yes, yes. What is it?' I replied: 'Gascoigne says the only way he will sign is if I play up front with him in the same team.' Terry suddenly realised that his leg was being pulled for a change, and shouted down the telephone: 'Just tell him the deal is off!' and burst out laughing. Terry was absolutely delighted, and it was left that we would meet again on Thursday morning at Mel Stein's office in Park Street, Mayfair, to sign all the final documentation.

The delay in signing did cause complications. We had put up Gascoigne and some friends he had travelled from Newcastle with in a hotel in Hertfordshire. Soon I was getting complaints from the hotel. They'd been letting off fire extinguishers at 2 am, and upsetting other residents in the hotel. I told Mel Stein about the complaints and said I wanted to see Gascoigne's friends before they left. But his friends completely disarmed me. Just after Gascoigne had signed they came to see me. They were lined up like naughty schoolboys waiting for the Headmaster to chastise them. Before I could say anything one of them, with a bowed head, looked up and said: 'Mr Scholar, I want to thank you for the best three days we've ever had in our lives.' With such an apology, how could anyone get annoyed with them?

After the formal signing, I asked Gascoigne where he was going that afternoon. He said he was thinking of going to see Madame Tussaud's. 'Enjoy yourself, but behave,' I said. Little did he know that he himself, in a short period of time, was going to be one of the exhibits.

As I have said, Terry also wanted a striker. He first wanted Mark Hateley, but when that didn't work out I thought he would go for Mark Hughes. I had been told that Barcelona, who had loaned Mark Hughes to Bayern Munich, were definitely going to sell him in the summer. The price they were seeking was £1.5 million, and it seemed he'd had a very rough time in Spain. I assumed that he would be returning to Manchester United, but then I learnt that he had got married at about the same time as his transfer to Spain went through, and his wife was unhappy about returning to Manchester and would prefer to move to London.

Later, Martin Edwards told me that he knew that Mark Hughes's wife didn't fancy the idea of coming back to Manchester where Hughes, before his marriage, had been associated with a drinking school and she felt he might fall back into his old, bad ways. Knowing Hughes's pedigree and his previous success in England I thought that he would have been an instant success at Tottenham. I immediately rang Terry saying: 'I've had a call that Mark Hughes is available for £1.5 million and is keen to come to London. You signed him for

Barcelona, I think you should look at him.' Terry, much to my surprise, replied: 'No, I've no interest in Mark Hughes.' I said: 'Terry, why not? You signed him for Barcelona and I've always thought he was a very good player for the English game. And he's young, only twenty-four, so there is potential there.' Terry came back: 'No, Irving, I'm not interested in Mark Hughes, I wouldn't sign him.'

It was clear that Terry just did not want to know anything about Mark Hughes and preferred to pursue Paul Stewart. He seemed to have a real aversion to re-signing him, and after that, every time his name was mentioned he used to pull some sort of grimace. Even today I can't quite make it out, but after we had signed Lineker I did get a clue. Gary made it clear that he thought Hughes was an extremely difficult player to play with. Gary would often make runs into space expecting Hughes to deliver the ball, but he used to shield it and delay the final pass until it was so late that the good run would have been spotted and covered by a defender. This suggested Hughes was a bit of a selfish player. It is interesting to note that when Manchester United looked certain to lift the Championship in 1991/92, the player who was dropped by Alex Ferguson when they were under pressure was Mark Hughes.

Terry's rejection of Hughes came just as our need for strikers was getting desperate. Clive Allen had gone to the French club Bordeaux, in what was one of the most unusual transfers I ever handled. As the end of the 1987/88 season approached, Clive was reaching the end of his contract, and under the UEFA Tribunal he would have been free to move abroad for a fee in the region of £650,000. The previous season, when he had scored forty-nine goals, there had been no real interest from the Continent, except for a faint enquiry during the summer of 1987 from Torino. This lack of interest in Clive surprised me, and Clive must have given up any hopes of going abroad when I received a telephone call out of the blue from a gentleman called Barin, who wanted to make an appointment to see me the following day. I'd never heard of him, and all he would say was he wanted to fly from Paris to London to discuss something that he felt could be of benefit.

If the call had come from Portsmouth rather than Paris I might have passed it on for someone else, but a call from Paris intrigued me. It turned out that Barin was one of a number of soccer agents operating on the Continent. He was Yugoslav by nationality and worked on behalf of numerous French clubs. Many agents enquire for players in the course of a season, but the majority of cases turn out to be men of straw, just seeking a name which they will then hawk round Europe until they find somebody interested. Barin was different. He proved to be a very serious, straightforward person, I guessed in his late fifties, and as soon as he came into my office he made his purpose clear. He had an interest in Clive Allen. A club in France were willing to offer £800,000 for him – which I have to say I was a little taken aback by. Until then we had had no approaches, he was reaching the end of his contract, and I knew that Terry was thinking about replacing him in any event.

My first question was which club was Barin representing? This is usually the point at which agents display their true colours. Barin disclosed it was Bordeaux, and having lived in France I was very well acquainted with them and the people who wielded the power. He suggested a meeting the following day at the Hilton Hotel, where his client would be present. I said that I would speak to Terry Venables and come back to him with an answer later that evening.

In the morning I met Terry in the foyer of the Hilton, where we were quickly greeted by Barin. He introduced us to Didier Coucou, who I knew was the General Manager of Bordeaux, and apart from Claude Bez, the President, wielded the real power at the club. We went upstairs to the dining room for breakfast.

I had previously discussed with Terry two proposals that we would put to them. Either they could complete the transfer immediately, or they might want to wait until the end of the season. The first basis was to be a single payment of £825,000 now, or £900,000 should they want to complete the purchase in the summer. After a little toing and froing they explained they couldn't take the player at that time but would wait until the end of the season and would be prepared to agree with our proposal of £900,000. Terry and I were a little surprised, to say the least, at how quick and easy it was to reach agreement. Terry had already alerted Clive Allen to the approach, and he had arranged to meet Clive at the hotel, with his adviser Denis Roach, who had a lot of experience of dealing with players moving to the Continent.

We shook hands on the deal, and later that evening over dinner at the White Elephant Restaurant in Curzon Street I presented a contract confirming the terms. The whole negotiation had been conducted with a courtesy and pleasantness often missing in such deals, and I must say I enjoyed dealing with the French.

Paul Stewart's transfer couldn't have been more different. I saw Peter Swales, Chairman of Manchester City, at the Football League AGM in June, and asked him about Stewart. He thought the price was going to be above £1 million. Before that we had believed that we could get Stewart for £900,000, or at least that's what Venables believed. Then I got a call from Swales saying they had two offers: one from Glasgow Rangers and the other from Everton at £1.5 million, which staggered me.

Terry was shocked at how the price had risen, but as there was no chance of Mark Hateley leaving Monaco, we were in a bind and agreed to pay the fee. Again it was to be 50 per cent down and the balance payable over the next twelve months, even though Manchester City had received a cash-on-the-nail offer from Everton.

Venables met with Paul Stewart and very quickly reached an agreement for him to join Spurs, although he would not sigh a contract on the spot. It seemed he had promised his fiancée, who was going to become his wife that weekend, that he would sign nothing until he went back to Manchester and discussed the matter with her. This despite the fact that he had given Terry his word he would sign when they met.

This did worry me a little. He was due to meet Everton the following day and I knew how things could change. However, Stewart was different. His word meant something. He arrived at Goodison Park to find a host of journalists standing outside. When they asked him who he would be signing for, he answered: 'I am signing for Tottenham.' Then he went in to meet Colin Harvey, the Manager, and Jim Greenwood, the Secretary and Chief Executive of Everton. For two hours they tried to persuade him to change his mind. But at the end, when they asked what he was going to do, he said: 'I told you, I'm signing for Spurs.' Their powers of persuasion had failed. Once again Venables's silver tongue had won the day.

Later in the summer Venables paraded Gascoigne and Stewart as his two new signings. He was pictured standing between the two of them, with the caption: 'The Priceless Pauls. Gascoigne and Stewart stand side by side with Manager Terry Venables, the man who has taken the transfer market by storm.'

The signing of Paul Gascoigne for a then record fee of £2 million attracted a bit of criticism. Fleet Street was quick to call Terry 'Mr Moneybags', and for the first time I noticed a defensive reaction as he justified himself. 'I'm not cash crazy,' he told them. 'I haven't been irresponsible with Spurs' money.'

In the *Mail* on 22 July 1988, Neil Harman wrote: 'No one in football has spent as extravagantly as Venables this summer.' Harman went on to mention that Venables had done £6 million worth of business since becoming Manager. In reality he had done £5 million of purchases, but, at this stage in the summer of 1988, Tottenham were seen as a big spender. The very day that Harman wrote in the *Mail*, the *Today* headline was 'Venables Spends Again', and the story linked Tottenham with the chase for David Kelly of Walsall.

I didn't mind that. The money was available and Terry was not slow in spending it. What I was concerned about was his attention-span. He seemed to have a grasshopper mind, never spending too much time dealing with any single item. When I persuaded him to join Tottenham I was clear he was one of the best coaches in Europe. He'd managed to go to Barcelona, purchase one player only, Steve Archibald, and do what no Manager had done for ten years previously, which was lift the Spanish Championship. He'd always struck me as a person most at home on the training field, working with his players. He had a fine reputation, even before he went to Spain, as being one of the leading coaches. I had become used to dealing with David Pleat and Peter Shreeve, both of them very dedicated football managers and coaches whose every minute of the day seemed to be consumed thinking and dealing just with football. Terry wasn't like that.

My first concern was raised the very week he joined us. In another paid *Sun* article he announced that he wanted to buy his own club some time in the future. I felt a little despondent reading this. Our relationship had hardly started. I'd gone to great lengths to secure his services – according to the Press he was the highest-paid manager in the First Division, earning substantially more than David Pleat, his predecessor, in addition to further remuneration by way of bonuses related to results. I had explained to him in Florida that the job was a big one, needing a lot of hard work to improve things, but instead of talking about the job in hand, which hadn't yet been started, he was thinking and talking about a future beyond Tottenham.

This feeling that Terry's attention would always wander was a persistent problem. A few months after he joined there was an article in the newspapers saying that the Welsh national team were considering appointing Terry Venables as their part-time manager – subject, of course, to Tottenham's agreement. I asked him if any approaches had yet been made. He said he'd heard the rumours as well, but had no offers as yet, and what would be my reaction should one be forthcoming? I explained that I felt that the Tottenham job was very much a full-time occupation and that he really didn't have the leisure to think and worry about any other team apart from Tottenham.

We agreed to wait and see whether any official approach was finally made and discuss it again should that be the case. Eventually Alan Evans, Secretary of the Welsh Football Association, wrote to me seeking my approval and cooperation in having discussions with Terry Venables. I was firmly against him taking up even a part-time appointment. Terry seemed quite keen, and said that it would not encroach on his duty to Tottenham, but I insisted that it would be in the club's best interests for him to forget about the Welsh approach and continue with the job in hand, which in fairness to him he took very well and accepted.

Having got to know him over the previous years I knew that Terry was very interested in international football, and I often thought that his real desire was to be Manager of England. But he always seemed to dismiss the notion as not a very realistic one. He did once say to me that the international team that he would like to manage was Brazil, as he felt the natural ability of the players would perhaps benefit from his organisational and coaching abilities. That might well have been a very interesting combination. Tottenham, alas, never seemed to get his full attention. I always had a feeling he had half an eye cocked for events elsewhere.

It is possible that in that first season his mind was not totally engaged on the job. By February 1988 it was clear our season was over. We were out of the Cup competitions and our League form was depressing, in that while our position was well above the relegation zone, very few points separated us from the bottom clubs. We almost began to flirt with the bottom three. But curiously Terry didn't seem to be visibly bothered with our position. He seemed to have decided that we had nothing to play for, but he also appeared confident that we would be secure in the First Division. As I watched him steer the team through in a languorous, almost laid back way, I got the impression that perhaps he hadn't quite got rid of the hangover of Barcelona.

It seemed to me that he still felt hurt and bruised by the way he was rejected by the club, and that his mind was not totally engaged in the job in hand.

What was worrying was that whereas in the previous season David Pleat had entertained the fans and the gates had risen dramatically, the 1987/88 season had seen gates slump. Terry's first game at home to Liverpool had drawn 47,362, but since then, and particularly after the defeat at Port Vale, we had only once managed to draw about 35,000 at home, and that for the visit by Manchester United. Everton, normally an attractive fixture, had drawn an evening crowd of just 18,622. Although Terry had only been there a few months, I was getting the first stirring of a sense that not everybody was happy with Venables. Curiously, I was being identified as his great champion, and this was brought home to me before the Wimbledon match, a bad 3–0 defeat. As I walked through the directors' entrance at Plough Lane, a ten- or eleven-year-old boy looked up at me and said in a rather derisive manner: 'He's the bloke what likes Terry Venables.' Fleet Street's build-up of the arrival of the Messiah had been short-lived, and at times they were getting the knives out for him.

Not that Venables worried much about handling the Press. He knew they craved information, and from the beginning he organised it to suit himself. Very shortly after coming to the club he said that a lot of his time was being taken up by constantly answering the same Press calls. In Barcelona there had been a regular Press conference virtually daily, at which he would answer all the questions anybody put forward. He wanted to do the same in London. I thought it was a very good idea. The Press were invited to the training ground, where Terry would see them all at the same time. If they made the effort, they would get his wisdom, otherwise he would not be taking calls concerning Press matters. Terry had worked out that generally journalists are a lazy bunch and would much rather sit in their offices and pick up the telephone than have to travel halfway across London to attend a daily Press conference. He made them come to him, which they dutifully did to lap up the silver tongue.

That silver tongue did not always work the magic. There were two players Terry missed – and one whose signing would have made him the laughing-stock of the land. Terry was very keen on signing Andy Townsend when his contract expired at Southampton. He had been in touch with Townsend's agent and made it clear that he was very eager to talk terms. This amused me, because I first saw him play for Southampton in the FA Cup semi-final against Liverpool at White Hart Lane in 1986, and I remember Peter Shreeve asking me a few days after the match, who had played well. I said to him that number 10 for Southampton, Townsend, had definitely caught my eye. He seemed on that day to be a non-stop, all-action player covering the whole area of the pitch. Peter said that he had been signed from Weymouth, the same club that Spurs had signed Graham Roberts from in 1980, but Peter didn't seem too impressed with Townsend at the time.

Terry was busy on the particular day that Townsend and his agent travelled to Norwich. He had told his agent not to sign for Norwich but to delay his decision until the next day, when Terry would have had an opportunity of making him an offer and outlining his thoughts to him. But Townsend signed for Norwich that day, and I can say that Terry made the wallpaper peel and the air turn blue when he heard. I don't think I've ever seen him so furious and annoyed. For once he seemed to have been outwitted.

Terry's other great failure was Paul McGrath. There is no doubt he was the centre half Tottenham needed, and Terry believed Manchester United would be prepared to release him. His previous injury record had been very bad and there had been rumours in the newspapers that he was considering retirement. I made it clear to Terry that unless we could get McGrath fully insured, we would not be prepared to support the transfer.

Early in September 1988 Terry asked me to speak to Martin Edwards, the Chairman of Manchester United, and he made it clear that he was prepared to sell McGrath for a fee of £450,000. The basic terms were agreed with Manchester United, and McGrath travelled to London to meet with Terry at his normal venue, the Royal Garden Hotel in Kensington, a stone's throw from where he lived. Everything appeared to go smoothly but the snag proved to be domestic. McGrath's marriage was going through a bit of a bumpy passage – he had been living apart from his wife but she moved back at the same time as the potential transfer to Tottenham came up, and warned him that she would not be prepared to live in London. This brought echoes of what we had encountered for Claesen and Gough. McGrath seemed reasonably interested in coming to Spurs, but his personal terms were high and he also wanted the club to provide him with a house, which was totally against our policy. If we were to do it for one, we would end up having to do it for everybody.

Terry was disappointed the transfer did not look like going through, especially after he had managed to get the offer of a full insurance policy following a medical. This was the only time during my involvement with Terry Venables when we agreed terms to purchase a player but failed to sign him. Terry was particularly upset about this because he was convinced that McGrath was one of the best central defenders in Europe, and I'm quite sure that he would have made a big difference defensively to us over the next few years.

What made the disappointment worse was that during the summer there was a newspaper article suggesting that McGrath had been involved in secret talks with Tottenham before we had spoken to Manchester United. Alex Ferguson was said to be bitterly upset. I was unaware of any talks that took place prior to our agreeing terms with Manchester United, and I think it was just a case of someone making mischief.

At the end of the season Manchester United accepted an offer of £400,000 for McGrath from Aston Villa, which Terry got to know about only when it was announced in the newspapers. Once again Terry was very upset at not being given the opportunity to persuade him to join Spurs instead of Aston Villa, who were never renowned as being big spenders. I found out afterwards that McGrath did not have to move house following that transfer.

But the transfer that did not take place despite Terry pushing for it was the most amazing. This was his attempted signing from Chelsea of Steve Wicks in August 1988. Terry had said to me that he was very keen on signing a central defender and had agreed terms with Chelsea. I was immediately concerned, firstly because of the player's age, thirty-one. It was outside my previously adopted formula, and on top of that I was worried by the number of injuries the player had suffered over the previous two or three years. Terry said: 'There's nothing to worry about. He has fully recovered now, and I tell you Irving, he will be a good acquisition for us. He will be the leader in the team that's so badly needed.' Now he believed that that was what Terry Fenwick was going to be when he signed from Queen's Park Rangers and so I decided to back him.

I could understand why Terry wanted Wicks. He fell into the category of players Terry likes and trusts. He had played under Terry at Crystal Palace and Queen's Park Rangers and was an old protégé whom he knew well and fully understood. But not, it seemed, quite enough. Within a couple of days of my telephone conversation with Terry, he received a call from Steve Wicks saying that he was very flattered and appreciated the opportunity, but didn't want to let him down. Wicks felt that his injuries had got the better of him and immediately announced his retirement. Wicks's announcement greatly annoyed Ken Bates, but the look on Terry's face was classic. It seemed that the supercoach had been completely outfoxed by one of his own players. It suggested to me that even the best managers don't do as much homework as they should before they enter the transfer market.

However, it's Terry's dealing with Neil Ruddock that shows the fickleness of managerial judgements. Ruddock had previously been bought from Millwall, when George Graham was the Manager there, by Peter Shreeve for £50,000. Terry had had one or two run-ins with the player and thought that he was very undisciplined, both on the field and off it. I think Terry had a few problems with him at the training ground, where he had become a disruptive influence. I had my own reservations about him on the field, as I felt his positional sense was not very good, he lacked pace and was possibly a bit naïve. But I was never keen on selling potential talent that could have flowered, and for all I knew he might have matured into a better player as he grew up. However, Terry was absolutely clear in his mind that he wanted to sell him, as he felt he had no future at Tottenham. I agreed, and he was transferred back to Millwall for around £175,000. Because of the conditions attached to the original purchase, this was equivalent to getting £250,000 from anyone else.

Imagine my surprise, a year after I left the club, when I heard that one of the players Terry had signed was Ruddock, at a fee of £750,000. What could have happened in four years for a player with no future at Spurs to become a valued first-team member again? I wonder.

TAKING A STAND

9

'What's the difference between Spurs and
the Star of David?'

'The Star of David has six points.' –

Joke during the 1988/89 season,
when by October Tottenham were
bottom of the League with only five points,
two points having been deducted for
cancellation of the opening home fixture
against Coventry.

One of the biggest problems I faced when I first joined Tottenham
was that despite all the money that had gone into football in the
Fifties and Sixties the directors had done very little to improve
and modernise their grounds. They had the pleasure: we were
left with the pain. The Fifties and Sixties were the time to
modernise. Then, all clubs had to do was open the turnstiles
on a Saturday afternoon and, regular as clockwork, forty or
fifty or sixty thousand people would turn up. Costs were low.
Until 1961 players had a fixed maximum wage of £20 a week,
mortgages were readily available at between 5 and 7 per cent
fixed for twenty-five years, and inflation as we came to know
and dread it in the Seventies did not exist.

To be fair to the old guard at the clubs, the Inland Revenue
did not help matters. This was illustrated in the case between
Burnley and the Inland Revenue. Burnley were replacing their
antiquated accommodation with a new stand, and argued that
as it was merely a replacement they should be afforded full tax
relief. The Inland Revenue would not allow that, and Burnley
lost the court case. The problem was compounded by the heavy
rate of Corporation Tax at the time, in the region of 52 per cent,
which effectively meant that if a club made £1 profit and spent
it on a new stand, they could only do so after paying 52 per cent
in tax, and so had only 48p for the cost of the structure – less
than half. Yet if they had used the same money to go and buy a

footballer they could have full tax relief against the purchase of the player. This made it far more attractive for clubs to go out and spend money in the transfer market than on improving the facilities.

Despite this imbalance, some far-sighted clubs did set about replacing old Victorian grandstands. In particular, Manchester United began their stadium redevelopment in 1964. When the Stretford End is fully complete in the summer of 1993, the whole project will have taken in the region of thirty years from inception to completion. Liverpool also set about modernising their stadium, and began to convert standing areas which ran the length of the pitch into seating. These two clubs were fortunate in that they had, unlike Spurs, a home supporters' end: Liverpool with the Kop and United with the equally famous Stretford End. Sheffield Wednesday, prior to the World Cup in England in 1966, created a 10,000 all-seated cantilevered stand on one side of the ground which cost in the region of £160,000.

Tottenham fell between two stools. They paid taxes to the government rather than bought players. Rodney Marsh had slipped away to Manchester City in the Seventies when Tottenham made a profit of £110,000 but again paid tax instead of buying players – yet little was done to improve the facilities. Tottenham, having won the Double in 1961, the FA Cup in 1962 and the European Cup Winners Cup in 1963, did the first alteration to the ground since the war after that, putting in some seats behind each goal. But these were not new structures, merely the conversion of existing facilities from standing to seating. The North and South Stands had originally been built in the Twenties, the West Stand in 1908 and the East Stand in 1934: they all remained virtually untouched.

As we have seen, it was the board's decision to undertake the first redevelopment in nearly fifty years that had brought me to Tottenham. I was well aware that contemporary football represented a paradox. People lived in modern homes, worked in modern factories and offices, shopped in modern American-style malls with extensive car parking, but come Saturday they had to scramble for parking and were herded into old Victorian facilities that at times had not even had a lick of paint for thirty years or more.

Nevertheless I was very nervous about undertaking major redevelopment. I was well aware of the difficulties such developments had created at other clubs such as Chelsea, Ipswich,

Wolves, Nottingham Forest and Burnley. The big question that haunted me was, how can it be properly financed without affecting the ability of the club to sign players and make improvements on the field? This was the circle most clubs were trying to square, and few succeeded. While certain board members pressed, I remained cool.

However, unbeknown to me, about eighteen months after the takeover Paul Bobroff had lodged an outline planning application to redevelop the East Stand. That something needed to be done could hardly be denied. A steel-framed stand with wooden seats at the upper level and wooden floorboards, it was much the same as the old West Stand. I had often walked round there on a non-match day and was appalled by the facilities. The toilets were damp and very old-fashioned; they seemed never to have been touched since the day they were built. There was a terrible stench from where the police horses were located in their stables at one end of the ground floor of the stand. It smelt more like a show ground than a football ground. It was so dilapidated that Haringey, the local authority, were beginning to look at it much more closely, in the same way as the GLC had previously done in relation to the West Stand. This was a year after the terrible fire at Bradford's Valley Parade when the main stand had burnt to the ground, killing fifty-six people. Bradford made the authorities very conscious of old stands, particularly pre-war ones. A new Green guide had been introduced which gave a whole new range of safety standards that stands had to meet in order to be entitled to their safety certificate.

We realised that major safety work involving several million pounds would have to be undertaken to the East Stand just to acquire the safety certificate. Haringey was also imposing other restrictions. Under the GLC licence, emergency exit time was ten minutes. Haringey was seeking to impose an emergency exit time of 2½ minutes. This would have the effect of reducing the capacity by 75 per cent. Local authorities grant safety certificates based on the amount of time it will take to safely evacuate in an emergency a stand with a given number of exits. Haringey argued that due to the large amount of combustible materials within the stand itself, the emergency exit time must be cut to 2½ minutes. But for a new, normal modern stand, Haringey were recommending something in the region of five minutes.

Bill Jenkins, an architect who had been looking into the general safety of the stadium for some years, was called in to present his views on how best to redevelop the stand to modern safety requirements. He produced a number of plans, and initial talks suggested we were looking at a £12–13 million redevelopment for a new building – way beyond what we could afford: our limit was £4½–5 million. Jenkins then came up with a suggestion of rebuilding within the existing frame of the structure. This would mean effectively renewing everything, but without demolishing the old stand. It also meant that only parts of the stand would need to be closed during the playing season.

The big difficulty we had, along with all other football clubs, was to match capacity and income. When the West Stand was originally conceived, the plans were for a single row of executive boxes – thirty-six boxes. I understand that at a critical point in the construction the architect worked out that they could put in an extra row of boxes at an added cost of a mere £250,000. The directors agreed and it proved to be an extremely beneficial investment, bearing in mind that thirty-six boxes today produce an income in excess of £½ million per season. To meet the minimum safety requirements the local authority were insisting on would cost us about £2 million, yet it would substantially reduce capacity. So we were being asked to spend a substantial sum with no prospect of recovering any of it. Jenkins got round this by producing a scheme for the East Stand which incorporated thirty-six executive boxes, with an actual installation cost of £1.5 million but with a potential income of around £750,000 p.a. This was the one area the club was able to recover a commercial return on its investment.

Eventually the plans were agreed with Haringey and a planning application, supported by the Planning Department of the council, was submitted in January 1987. It had an element of what is called 'planning gain', in that the club would spend £50–60,000 in getting certain things carried out near the ground such as cleaning up on a match day, providing temporary toilet accommodation, etc. There was nothing very unusual in that, as when it comes to planning applications local authorities feel that in order to justify consent there should be some gain for the council.

Later on, much was made of how we started going wrong with the building of the East Stand. But as I saw it we had to go for the reconstruction. This really wasn't a question of us starting something, but of having it forced on us by history,

circumstances and the local authorities. Where we failed initially was in the publicity. If possession is nine points of the law,
then marketing and publicity are the essence of modern life, be
it in politics or sports. In retrospect we just didn't get this right.
Later when the storm was raging, Alex Fynn criticised me for
not handling it better: a lot of agony could have been avoided, he
said, had we employed a PR firm to get our message across. We
eventually did – but by then it was a damage limitation exercise.
The initial storm had already cut down many trees. It began, as
these things often do, with a newspaper story in February 1988.
The *Evening Standard* carried an article saying that Spurs were
proposing to redevelop their East Stand.

This led to an enormous reaction from some supporters who
felt that the club were pushing through a contentious scheme
without consulting them. I must say I was unaware of any other
club ever consulting its supporters prior to putting in a planning
application to improve facilities. Back in 1980, the first we had
heard about the West Stand was well after all decisions had
been taken on its content, design and format. There were no
complaints then. Now, as I was to find out to my cost, supporters had become more militant. There was a feeling that they
were merely being treated as 'turnstile fodder' and that they had
a right to help make the decision. Some fans began accusing us
of only being interested in box-holders and corporate hospitality
followers and not being interested in the ordinary man on the
terrace. The behaviour of Paul Bobroff made me think that these
accusations were not completely unfounded.

The problem of communication wasn't helped by the fact that
there was no real supporters' organisation, as the Spurs Supporters Club was then going through its own traumas. Despite this
we could have done more to reach the supporters. We could
have published full details in the match programme; perhaps
we should have asked for views on what facilities they wanted.
Our failure to communicate meant a mountain was made out of
a molehill, due in no small measure to the perception that we
were trying to railroad this development. We ended up with a
confrontation, and all this for a scheme which I personally had
always feared and was not particularly keen on. I had seen too
many clubs in the past rebuild to their cost.

The bone of contention was the Shelf. This was the upper
standing level of the East Stand, and part of the folklore of
Spurs. It was an area that I knew very well, having stood there

on numerous occasions, the most memorable of which was the
night in 1962 when I was nearly crushed against a safety barrier
whilst Spurs were being crushed on the field by Benfica in the
European Cup semi-final. It was an enormously popular area,
and people who regularly stood there felt it was the best standing
view in England. Nearly all standing areas in English grounds are
behind the goal at one end. This was probably the only standing
view which allowed spectators to stand along the full length of
the pitch and also at an upper level, giving them an extremely
good vantage point.

The redevelopment of the West Stand had seen the accommodation provided by an enclosure in front of it, formerly reserved
for standing season ticket holders, being moved across to the
Shelf. Bearing in mind that Tottenham did not have a Kop End, I
envisaged a White Hart Lane redevelopment which would create
a Kop at the Northern End of the ground, thereby allowing the
East Stand to be converted eventually to an all-seater stand. At
this time Tottenham had around 17,000 seats out of a capacity
of 48,000, which was a very low ratio of seats to standing in
comparison to other major grounds. Although the tragedy of
Hillsborough and Taylor was yet to come, the board was looking
ahead to the need for having more seated accommodation, and
many big games proved the demand was there, where it would
have been possible to sell our seats two and three times over.

But in the welter of emotion now generated, far from getting
any credit for our foresight we were pilloried. As often happens
in such a situation, criticism led to an organised revolt, and some
of the younger supporters got together and created a pressure
group called Left On The Shelf, LOTS. Soon, a meeting was
arranged at Haringey Council between the architect, myself
and a couple of LOTS representatives. Although LOTS had
Rick Mayston as their chief spokesman, who was a die-hard
Spurs supporter, what concerned me was that it appeared to be
led by Craig Brewin, a Leicester City supporter and a member of
Haringey Council, who at the time was also the Secretary of the
Football Supporters Association. This is a group that I believe is
politically motivated, and I've always felt that politics and sport
do not mix under any circumstances.

We tried hard at our meeting to explain why the work had
to be carried out, but nothing we said could mollify them
about the fact that the standing area on the Shelf was to
be replaced by boxes and executive seating. The fact that

standing accommodation was to be retained at the lower level was seen as a sop. We tried to explain that the club was faced with a sizeable investment in taking off the existing roof and replacing it so that everybody would be under cover, whereas at present probably less than 50 per cent were sheltered from the elements. We also pointed out that the vast majority of the work being proposed consisted of safety requirements demanded by the local authority, but their only concern was that the new facilities would encroach on their hallowed Shelf.

A week or so later I agreed to meet with LOTS again at the Spurs Supporters Club building in the High Road. Jenkins was ill unfortunately, and I took along Chris Belt, Peter Barnes and Terry Venables. I found that between eighty and a hundred supporters had turned up. The meeting began ominously. Brewin, a Haringey councillor, began the proceedings poking fun at how the police horses were to be better treated than the supporters, which wasn't true and which I found insulting.

This set the original mood of the meeting, but as time went on and I apologised for not consulting the supporters beforehand, it began to mellow. I think some of the LOTS people were a little surprised when I said I understood their concerns and explained the thinking and the reasoning behind the plans. The mood changed to such an extent that long before the end the supporters started to ask Terry Venables questions as to whether the team was likely to avoid relegation, as our form over the previous couple of months, which included the FA Cup defeat at Port Vale, had drawn us towards the edge of the relegation fight.

The meeting ended with Mayston, who was in the Chair, thanking me for attending and answering all the questions from a somewhat hostile audience. I got the impression that they had begun to understand what we were doing.

The LOTS campaign actually ended in a good old British compromise. I had kept coming up with various ideas as to how we could introduce some form of standing accommodation back on to the Shelf. Then it came to me at one meeting. I stood in one of the mock-up boxes and looked out to see roughly what the head-room was below. It seemed to me that it was possible to get standing back on the Shelf, below the boxes, and I asked Jenkins roughly what capacity we could expect if we did not put seats in there.

Bobroff had altered the design of the boxes, which reduced the headroom below. In spite of this, Jenkins estimated we could accommodate some 3,000 people. This meant that if we were to sell season tickets, at a rough guide price of £120 per season, we would receive nearly as much income as we would from seating. The big problem was persuading Bobroff of this. He was now very heavily involved in the development through his employee Terry Steele, who had been seconded to Tottenham. But I thought I knew how to put it to Bobroff so he would approve. As ever with him, what mattered was the bottom line, so I explained to him that having standing back in the East Stand would not mean any loss of income. Although he had not been very keen on the Shelf campaign, when he saw the figures his eyes lit up. Eventually the board agreed and it was decided that the Shelf would be retained for standing season ticket holders only.

By now, with the help of Saatchi & Saatchi, we had got our PR act together. Interestingly, when we called the Press conference to announce that standing would be back on the Shelf the following season, LOTS had virtually disbanded. The news came as a surprise to them, as they were expecting the club to proceed with the original schemes.

Looking back, there was a lesson to be learnt. If I had been as forceful with Bobroff and the board on other matters as I was on those concerning football and the stand, then perhaps a lot of the trauma could have been avoided. But then general hindsight wins all battles.

However, if LOTS was satisfied, its campaign had an effect on our timing. Already tight, the row made it impossible. The campaign had started as the planning application was due to be heard, and whilst Haringey's Planning Department had recommended the scheme, the councillors became unwilling to approve it, owing to the vociferous supporters who were congregating every time it was due to be heard. What was silly about this was that while the main bone of contention was the inclusion of the boxes, we later learnt that planning permission was not needed to erect them – a view confirmed by a leading barrister and by Haringey themselves. This was on the basis that there was no material change to the appearance of the stand. Both the architect and I doubted this, as we felt it changed the appearance significantly from the original Leitch stand.

So because of the delays it was becoming more and more difficult to meet the timescale of the proposed development.

The playing season at White Hart Lane finished on 4 May, and it became clear that unless we obtained planning permission to erect the new roof over the East Stand within a few days (it was March by now), the work would have to be undertaken out of sequence. Instead of starting at the beginning and going right through to the end, we were going to have to start around a third of the way through, continue with those works, and then come back to the beginning. It would be a little like building a house by putting the roof on first. It would also mean a far more expensive development, and leave us with not enough time to do all we needed to do during the close season.

Our priority was Saturday 27 August, when we had our first home match of the 1988/89 season. I had made it absolutely clear to the contractor that work must be finished before that in order for us to fulfil our fixture obligations. Wimpey Management Construction, who were to do the construction, kept assuring me that they would have the stand ready for the match, so in mid-July I went on holiday confident that everything was all right.

This confidence remained undented even as we entered the final week leading to the start of the season. On Wednesday 24 August I attended a meeting at the ground with the professional advisers. My first question was: 'Will the stadium receive its safety certificate to enable us to stage the match on Saturday?' 'Yes,' came the reply. That same evening all the directors attended the ground, where there was a presentation for the box-holders' Player of the Year. Afterwards they walked round the stand, saw the progress, and once again heard the reassurance from Wimpey that the match would go ahead on the Saturday.

At 4 pm on Friday, after a day spent at the ground, I met with the police and Local Authority Safety Officer, who was responsible for the issue of the safety certificate. Whilst the police were a little concerned, the Safety Officer was in no doubt that Wimpey would have the stand complete and that he would be issuing his certificate the following morning. I eventually left the ground that evening at around 8.45. The stand was filled with workmen clearing the rubble away. They were working overnight as they had done for the previous few weeks. The next day was the start of a new season, always a time of hope and renewal, and I looked forward to driving back to see Paul Gascoigne's début the next day. Little did I know that the evening was to prove the calm before the storm.

On Saturday morning at about 8.30 my telephone rang at home. It was Peter Barnes informing me that the police had objected to the match taking place. The local authority would not be issuing the safety certificate, as some problems had been encountered overnight and the promised work had not been completed. The match could not go on. To say that I was shocked is an understatement. I just couldn't believe that contractors like Wimpey had let us down. We were dealing with an international organisation who had given us their solemn word that the job would be finished over a period of weeks, and here we were unable to stage our first match of the season.

Later I pieced together what had happened between the time I left the ground and the early hours of Saturday morning. The drama had begun some two hours before Peter rang me, at 6.50 that morning. That is when Derek Ryder, the Haringey Safety Officer, had arrived at the ground. The police had been there since 6 am, and they advised him that they felt the match should be postponed. Ryder inspected the East terrace and found there was too much debris to be cleared. Wimpey told him the labourers had got tired and they had not been able to complete the work. Ryder had suggested to the police that the match could go ahead with the East Stand closed to the public, but the police would not agree to this. Apparently they said that they would not police the game if that was the case. It was then that the decision to postpone was taken.

My first concern was for the supporters, and I immediately arranged for the postponement to be announced on radio and television so that they could be saved an unnecessary journey. Soon after, I arrived at the ground, where quite a number of people were milling around, and it was clear that the Press were going to have a field day. Somebody had contacted the Football League and tried to liken it to a case some years previously when Tranmere Rovers failed to fulfil a fixture and were deducted two points. But I didn't believe that the cases were similar, and was reasonably confident that the Football League would understand our predicament.

The management committee of the Football League decided to hold a Commission at the Hilton Hotel in Warwick on Monday 17 October 1988, to consider our failure to fulfil a fixture obligation. The three wise men to decide our fate were Philip Carter (President of the Football League at the time, and Chairman of Everton), Bill Fox (Chairman of Blackburn Rovers) and Ian Stott

(Chairman of Oldham Athletic). I, together with Peter Barnes, represented the club, taking Derek Ryder along as our witness to explain our case.

The League stressed that failure to fulfil a fixture was a very serious matter and the question at issue was whether there was a breach of Regulation No. 24. I felt we had a good case. The Tranmere Rovers decision was no precedent as the circumstances were totally different. The match was all ticket but not all tickets had been sold. Also, the match could have gone ahead with the East Stand closed to the public, but the police had not agreed to this. The Notting Hill Carnival was due to take place the same weekend and there had also been a demonstration on the Broadwater Farm Estate on that very same day. Both must have stretched the police resources, and it was my contention that the police were more than happy to see the match postponed. My defence was both detailed and informed, backed by minutes of a project meeting and memos from Wimpey which provided details of their assurance that everything would be ready for 26 August. Ian Stott asked whether we had considered any alternative arrangements prior to the day of the match, but bearing in mind that we had been led to believe that there was no danger of that, alternative arrangements could hardly be discussed.

Our case received support from Ryder, who explained in graphic detail the events of the Saturday morning that led to postponement, and how it was normal for large events to be inspected shortly before they were due to begin. He cited as an example the recent Docklands concerts by Jean-Michel Jarre.

I had been long enough in football not to be surprised by anything, but I must say I was shocked by the verdict reached by the three wise men. They had all the evidence yet they still felt we were 'unprepared for the eventuality' and had not warned the League or Coventry. The Commission decided that we were fully to blame and deducted two points.

The decision could not have come at a worse time. We had had a dreadful start to the season. By the end of October we were to be bottom of the League, with only five points from nine League games, and the popular joke on the terraces was: What's the difference between Spurs and the Star of David? Answer: The Star of David has six points. Everyone was blaming the cancellation of the first home match as having got us off on the wrong foot, and the Commission's decision meant we had reached a nadir in our fortunes.

Stunned as I was by the verdict, it had the effect of making me determined to reverse it. For me this was now a personal crusade. The team was being punished for something that it had no control over, and I was desperate to overturn that. There was also a silver lining in the decision. Carter had said to me, both in the Commission and in front of the other committee members, that whilst they had every sympathy for us, there was no alternative but to deduct two points, as the rules made such a punishment mandatory. I wasn't sure the wise men had read their own rules correctly, and was prepared to appeal to the Football Association to test it.

As soon as I returned to London I instructed a firm of solicitors. Within a few days a conference was arranged with Michael Crystal QC, who was widely considered quite brilliant in his field and certainly one of the leading legal figures in the country. He wasn't particularly interested in football, although he pointed out that when he was much younger his father had taken him and his brother to watch Leeds United, where he became a regular before moving down to London. I had met him briefly a year or so before, when we were discussing the rules and regulations of the Football League with a view to restructuring and modernising it. Then he had greatly impressed me, and he did so again with his swift and agile mind, which always seemed to grasp quickly the nub of all the arguments.

Much to my delight, Crystal immediately raised the question of whether the deduction of two points was mandatory. He was confident we could fight the decision on this front. The League could be hoist by its own petard. However, it wasn't clear if the Football Association would allow us to have legal representation at an appeal hearing. Normally directors represent clubs, and it was entirely at the discretion of the Chairman of the Commission to agree to Crystal being present. In the days leading up to the hearing Michael kept on saying to me that I might well have to do my own impersonation of Rumpole, something I was dreading. We were so keen to get Michael in at the hearing that it was even suggested we appoint him to the board for one day in order to represent the club as a director. But as it happened the Chairman, R.B. Strachan, a director of York City and a solicitor by profession, accepted that Michael Crystal could represent the club. This proved a godsend.

Immediately the Commission opened, Crystal made his point concerning Regulation 24, arguing very strongly that the way it was worded meant that even if a club was found guilty, the deduction of two points was not mandatory. I could see Bill Fox bristle as Michael spoke. He was representing the League, and had a particular aversion to solicitors dealing with football matters, feeling they should be left to football people. The hearings quickly developed into Michael Crystal v. Bill Fox. One of the members asked Fox whether the Commission had considered an alternative sentence, and he replied in a rather ruffled manner that they had. I protested vigorously and pointed out that Philip Carter had stated to me categorically that the deduction of the two points was mandatory and that the Football League officials had informed Carter and the wise men that there was no alternative but either to deduct us two points or declare us not guilty.

By this stage Crystal was becoming very agitated with Fox. It got so heated that I had to calm Michael Crystal down, as I felt he was getting ready to explode. Yet there was no doubt that Crystal's presence was crucial, and when the Commission came to give their verdict they gave Bill Fox a rather stern dressing-down on not understanding his own rules and regulations. He was told not to waste the Football Association's time in dealing with matters that were quite clear in their interpretation. The FA reinstated our two points but instead decided to fine us £15,000. I joked that at this rate I wouldn't mind getting Tottenham two points every week but the relief was palpable both for me and for Terry Venables, who was in another room awaiting the decision.

But while this had ended well, the trauma of the stand continued to haunt us. The following February Paul Bobroff suggested that one of his employees at Markheath Securities be delegated to oversee the balance of the works outstanding on the East Stand which had stopped the previous August. At the same time he wanted the quantity surveyors replaced, due to the inaccurate advice that they had given us concerning the costings. He got the board to agree that John Lelliott, a major firm of contractors, be asked to complete the scheme. It was estimated at that time by Bobroff and his advisers that the second phase of the scheme would not exceed £400,000, which added to the £2.3 million the first phase had cost, would come to a total cost of around £3 million. Unfortunately, when the stand was completely finished the bill for the second phase itself came to

£5.6 million, and this before professional fees. When £4.1 million becomes £5.6 million then you tend to agree with Denis Healey that all forecasting is rubbish.

As luck would have it, we were constructing the stand at a time in the late Eighties when London was going through a property boom. Inflation in the building industry was running at around 30 per cent p.a., and such was the pace and volume of development that there was a shortage of people in the building trade. Numerous large projects were under way, such as Canary Wharf and Broadgate in the City, with thousands of personnel involved, pushing up the price of construction projects.

This meant we were always struggling against a rise in costs, and I vividly recall a telephone call from Peter Barnes, in late July, whilst I was on holiday, to say that the quantity surveyors were revising their estimate for the total cost of the development from around £5 million to £6.9 million. Such things are part of property development, but we were caught in a squeeze, in that we were building during a development boom, but by the time the reckoning came the boom had turned into one of the worst of property slumps.

What added to our headache, and costs, was that this was not a new construction but a refurbishment of an old one. There was some criticism concerning the large columns supporting the roof of the stand. If we had wanted these removed and replaced by a cantilevered roof it would have cost another £2½ million. We decided not to take this option. This did mean savings, but we also received the brickbats. Sometimes in football you just cannot win.

When the stand was finally complete we received quite a number of letters and, strangely enough, no complaints. The best standing view in football, according to LOTS at the outset, had now become the most comfortable too, where the bar areas had carpeted floors and the proper, decent, modern facilities that supporters deserve.

Some time later, after the publication of the Taylor Report, Jenkins drew up a scheme for the full implementation of its recommendations. Football Trust grants were made available up to a maximum of £2 million. The effect would be to make White Hart Lane an all-seater ground, with each stand fully under cover and the roofs in alignment, at a total gross cost before subsidies of roughly £3.5 million. Jenkins also proposed to extend the West Stand at both the northern and southern ends of the ground.

One trouble with football is that people expect miracles to take place. For instance, after a season that finishes in May they may expect very substantial building projects to be both started and completed in time for the following season beginning in August. The end-of-season break is not particularly long, and the ideal way of carrying out these projects would be to close the stand for a year or more – an upheaval that we were reluctant to inflict on our supporters. The super-optimists also expect such work to be done on the cheap, which is a dangerous delusion. In that sense football supporters are always demanding the circle to be squared. As our East Stand problems showed, that is just not possible.

10

THE STRANGE WORLD
OF FOOTBALL BUSINESS

'Football is business and business is business.'
– Rinus Michels, Manager of the
Dutch football team.

Later, after it had all gone wrong and we were the butt of jokes and cartoons, it became fashionable to say how Spurs had been ruined by sharp-eyed property men who had thought that they could use the same techniques at the Paxton Road end they had used in the West End, only to come a cropper. As we shall see, some of our business diversifications did go wrong, but there was a time, in the mid-Eighties, when not only did we get the business right at Spurs but it was a model of how football clubs could generate more money. In the First Division as it was, and in the Premier League as it is, a top-flight club plays forty-two League games – twenty-one at home. In other words, your supporters come to your home ground twenty-one times for a maximum of three hours each visit. They might come on several more occasions if you have a successful Cup run and if you are drawn at home, but that is your whole opportunity to sell them the club. By any standards it is not a lot of time.

By the time I took over Spurs it was clear that just by opening the turnstiles and letting people in we could not make enough money to run the football side of the business. The famous cockerel worn on the chest of the players had not been guarded by copyright, and neither had any of the club's symbols and badges. We arranged for a firm of copyright lawyers to register everything, and this entailed a redesign for copyright purposes of the badges. I personally didn't like the new badge, as it made the cockerel look more like a hen, and around 1986/87 I redesigned it myself to the logo that is now used. As in designer fashion, the real value is in the name. Until this time, pirate manufacturers could pass off a Spurs product as if it was official, without the club benefiting in any way. The club had granted many licences to third parties, which were not renewed because I felt it was the club that should be profiting directly from its own logos, and the simple logic was to cut out the middle man. Football clubs are notorious for having what I believe is an Aladdin's cave of potential, and then just giving it away for very little reward.

There had to be other spin-off activities built round the football to generate more money. The only question was what form they should take. Kit sponsorship was an obvious one, and even before I arrived Spurs were under contract to Le Coq Sportif, one of the first such tie-ups in this country. They paid £75,000 a year, and it was a very successful contract, largely due to Spurs winning successive FA Cups in the early Eighties.

In the 1984/85 season, the first under my chairmanship of the club, I began hearing noises that Le Coq Sportif were getting disenchanted with football and were about to pull out of the market. However, a number of other manufacturers were keen to take us up, of which Hummel seemed to be the most promising and exciting. They were keen to set up in Britain, and I got Derek Peter and Peter Day to check them out. Soon a meeting was arranged in Munich, where the International Sportswear Fair was taking place, and we agreed that Tottenham would not only wear the Hummel kit but would become the UK distributors for Hummel International. It seemed to fit in well with our corporate remit as a broad-based leisure company and I saw no real problems with it. I felt as long as we kept to a strict, sharp discipline of only buying to match pre-sold orders, the risk was not very great. We were guaranteed to receive £1 million for four seasons commencing 1985/86. Derek Peter appointed Peter Goodwin Managing Director to run the business, and Derek, a chartered accountant and a member of the plc board, was given the task of ensuring that all the financial disciplines were maintained. I was aware that the start-up costs would be quite large, but then in clothing, new brands take some time to get established and there was also enormous competition from Adidas, Umbro, Nike and other leisurewear manufacturers. But the mid-Eighties were a time of boom, a time when companies like Sock Shop and others were coming on the market. Although Hummel was taking slightly longer than I would have liked to get into profit, Derek kept reassuring me that it would turn the corner soon.

The first storm signals about Hummel came early in 1988. A few months previously, in late 1987, I had recruited Edward Freedman to keep a watching brief over Hummel and run the club merchandising, shop and mail order operation. We had also acquired Martex, a women's fashion company, and Edward's domain extended to that. He had twenty years' experience of the business. I was sure we couldn't have made a better choice, and time was to prove me absolutely right. Sometime in March 1988 I received a call from him: there was panic in his voice as he told me something had gone wrong at Hummel, he wanted me to have a look at it immediately. So we went to a warehouse in Ferry Lane where some Hummel stock was kept, and one look made Freedman gasp in disbelief. The state, condition and age of the goods confirmed his worst fears. It seemed that Goodwin had been ordering far more than was prudent, and we had been totally in the dark about it. Even before this I had become concerned about the figures he was showing me: there were puzzling discrepancies when compared with his previous figures. There was never any suggestion of dishonesty, but something had gone wrong. In May 1988, Goodwin was sacked and John Griffin recruited in his place. Edward now took a much more hands-on approach to the business. A complete stop was put on purchases, and he came up with various ideas to reduce stock. This was successful to an extent, but with Hummel we were running against the tide.

While Hummel had, in addition to Spurs, signed up Sunderland, Southampton, Wimbledon, Norwich, Aston Villa and the Welsh international team, their range was mainly football. Adidas, in contrast, covered a whole gamut of sports. Also the sports retail business is still one of the very few real cottage industries, and there are very few major multiple retailers apart from Olympus and Champion Sport. Marketing Hummel meant that we were always dealing with small, single-unit retailers, and getting payment out of them proved a colossal task for our accounts department. In some ways it also showed the problems of a Continental link. Despite all the talk of one Europe and a Common Market, the price that Hummel UK had to pay in order to buy the kit from Denmark made a lot of items too expensive here, and there was a continuing battle between London and Copenhagen.

I have nothing but admiration for the sales team that Ken Grogan ran, a fine bunch of reps who covered the country diligently, but faced with these handicaps they really had an uphill struggle. In the 1988/89 season, with a new Spurs kit and with Gary Lineker having joined the club, we tried to reduce retail margin and concentrate on mail order to the public. It had the advantage of reducing operating costs, and it did work to a certain extent, but by then the whole relationship had soured. Hallbjorn Stenhaag, the man who had signed the original deal with Tottenham, had started having problems with Hummel which led to his departure sometime in mid-1989, and with his departure there were very few people in Denmark that we knew. This had a dramatic effect on our relationship.

By the summer of 1989 it was clear that we were going nowhere with Hummel. Bob Holt, who had joined us in May of that year as Chief Executive, suggested that we should just close down the operation and 'throw away the key'. Eventually that is what we did, but it took another year to do so. It was March 1990 before we could arrange a divorce. The Hummel Chairman and their International Sales Manager arrived in London, and after talks at my offices in the West End it was agreed that Hummel would take back virtually all the stock and reimburse us. I was anticipating that we would get a payment of three-quarters of a million, and I made sure that the contract specifically stated that 'time was of the essence' regarding the payment. This meant that if they didn't pay on the due date, we could sue immediately. As it turned out, Hummel didn't make the agreed payment on time, and Tottenham had to sue. All this rumbled on long after I had left Tottenham, and Edward was eventually successful on the very steps of the High Court in reaching a final agreement that got Tottenham half a million.

On the field Tottenham still wore the Hummel shirt – it was now worth £350,000 a year – but clearly this deal could not carry on. Hummel were very reluctant to continue, and as we still had an enormous amount of stock to shift it was agreed that the one-year contract would be ended with a disengagement fee of £100,000. The search was on for a new shirt sponsor. Adidas, recently taken over by Bernard Tapie, were a non-runner for us at the time, and that is when Umbro came into view. They had made quite an impression with their England replica kit before, during and after the World Cup Final. Sometime in mid-September 1990, Martin Protheroe, one of their

Mike Varney and Peter Barnes flank me after I was injured playing for the Spurs staff team in May 1984.

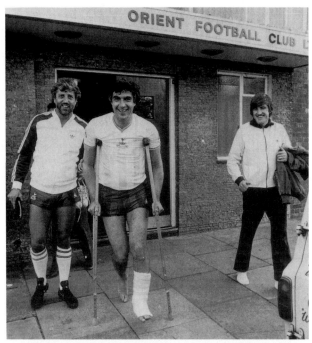

Pitch inspection on the morning of the day we played Bohemians in Prague, Czechoslovakia. *Left to right* Glenn Hoddle, Mark Falco, Graham Roberts, Paul Miller.

Ken Bates and I
celebrate Chelsea's
eightieth birthday,
1986.

David Pleat on the day he
took over as Manager.
May 1986.

Derek Peter, Chris Belt, Marlene and Joe Bugner, Colin Woodridge (Hummel), John Fennelly (Programme Editor), Peter Barnes. Just before the Bugner fight at White Hart Lane, October 1987.

With Elton John (Watford) at Villa Park FA Cup Semi-Final. 1987.

Happy Days. Florida 1987. Terry agrees to join Spurs as Manager.

Barclays announces sponsorship of the Football League.

The morning after the night before . . . Ullyett's view of our problems with the East Stand.

Roy Ullyett's special brand of humour when we were bottom of the table in 1988.

Terry's summer spree as seen by Fleet Street in 1988.

Gary Lineker.

Peter Robinson, unsung hero of Liverpool, and the ever-cheerful Lee Walker of the Football League.

Tony Berry.

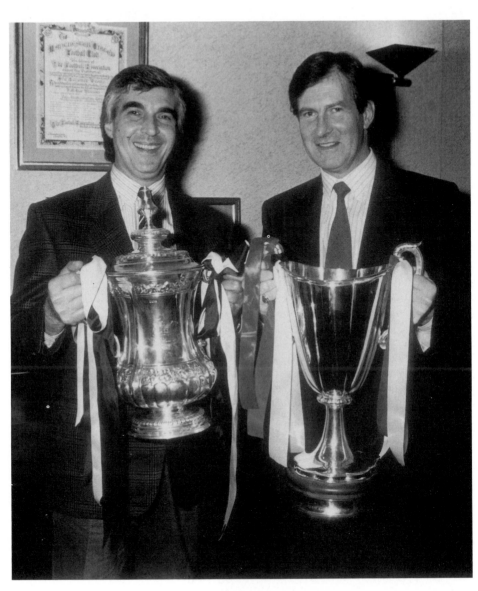

With Martin Edwards. May 1991.

sales representatives, and Peter Kenyon, the Managing Director, came down to London from their headquarters in Cheshire.

By this time our troubles were well known, and I wasn't sure what they would offer. I took soundings from other clubs and found that they were getting between £400,000 and £500,000 a year, and as I went into the meeting with Umbro I thought we would do well to get anything like that. To my great surprise, Kenyon said he had full authority to make a formal offer of £750,000 a year, and that the length of the agreement would be five years. I pride myself on being a good, quick negotiator, and with a little bit of nudging I got them to put forward a four-year offer: £750,000 the first year; £825,000 the second; £925,000 the third, rising to £1 million by the fourth year. £250,000 advance would be paid on the signing of the contract.

In such negotiations I always believe in finding out how far the other side will stretch, and I wondered if I could slightly rearrange the deal with Umbro to make it even better for us. I asked would they be prepared to pay the first two years, making £1,575,000 in advance. Protheroe and Kenyon looked horrified. Clearly they needed to consult with their head office in Cheshire, and we agreed to speak the following day. The next day Kenyon told me he could increase the advance payment, which would amount to £1.1 million. The £750,000 for the following summer would be paid immediately, and in addition they could advance £350,000 of the £825,000 due in the summer of 1993. I could now recommend the offer to the board.

This was to lead to an amusing aside. As I was explaining the deal, Bobroff butted in saying: 'Given the situation we are in, wouldn't it be possible to get them to make some sort of pre-payment?' He nearly fell off his chair when I pointed out that I had indeed arranged that, and there was an audible gasp around the boardroom when I told them how much Umbro had agreed to pay.

I had also secured an additional arrangement for the Spurs shop and mail order outlets to be invoiced at wholesale prices less 15 per cent discount. 1990 was a hellish year for me, but in that hell, the Umbro contract, if not a glimpse of heaven, provided a rare moment of hope. This feeling was considerably strengthened when a few weeks later Edward and I went to Cheshire to look at sample designs for the various new kits. Much to my delight, they had found a shirt that Umbro had supplied to the Spurs team that won the 1962 Cup Final. Could this be, I wondered, an omen for 1991? The four of us sat round a table whilst a sort of fashion show took place, displaying around twenty different designs of kit. I had suggested that we make no comment as each was shown, but instead should note down any particularly appealing features on a pad. Finally we asked for samples to be made up, say of the fabric of number 4, the collar design of number 6, and so on.

I had already told Terry what was going on, and when Protheroe came to White Hart Lane he was very impressed with the designs for the following year. But would the players be prepared to unveil the new kit during the Cup Final? There would be no problems with Hummel, who had already agreed to it. The players were different. Football players are very superstitious. Spurs had got to the Cup Final wearing the Hummel kit. When I raised the matter with Terry he seemed very doubtful that the players would want to change a kit which had proved a lucky omen – but he agreed to consult them, and to my surprise they did decide to unveil the kit at Wembley for the Cup Final. Just as in 1962, Spurs lifted the Cup wearing an Umbro shirt.

The Hummel business deal may have caused us a lot of grief, but I could take satisfaction from the fact that I had left Spurs an alternative shirt manufacturer who was, if anything, even better. In my last season at Spurs the Umbro replica kits outsold virtually every other kit. They outstripped their most optimistic sales estimates, and this during a very deep recession when leisurewear and track suits were taking a hell of a battering. Indeed, it is quite interesting to observe that the replica kit industry appears to have escaped the recession. This may be because it has created a niche which not even this damaging recession can obliterate. When I was a kid and desperately keen to buy a Spurs kit, the best I could do was buy a white T-shirt and go to Elsie's on Tottenham High Road, get a printed cotton badge and get my mother to sew it on. Today, enormous numbers of people turn up at matches wearing their club shirt.

It is fashionable for newspapers to debunk the growth in the replica kit industry. Money-grubbing football clubs, so the allegation goes, change their replica kit every year or so, in order to get more money out of parents with football-mad youngers. My reply to them is: what fashion item has a lifetime of two years? What leisure item would their children get such good wear out of?

If the Umbro deal was good for Spurs, then Umbro themselves were indebted to us for the way we had created a whole new range of club merchandise. When Protheroe and Kenyon signed the deal they admitted it was our success at merchandising Tottenham products that made them expand from replica team strips and track suits to all sorts of other club items. This is one of the innovations of Tottenham that I remain very proud of. During my time at Spurs the shop went through a virtual revolution, and my only regret is that I did not start that revolution earlier. If it did not exactly become Oxford Street, it did acquire a greater gloss and a more inviting façade. When I first joined Spurs the shop was in its pre-revolutionary phase: dark, small, and with no money having been lavished on it and no improvements made since it was first built in the early Seventies. It was run by a manager who had previously played football at amateur and semi-professional level, the range of merchandise hadn't changed for about ten years, and the shop had a turnover of around £350,000 per year.

I didn't really start expanding the shop until 1986. I commissioned a royal blue sweatshirt with a white collar which the team warmed up in before a match at Old Trafford. There were quite a few eyebrows raised at my innovation, and in the first few weeks the sweat shirt didn't sell all that well. Then just before Christmas, sales rocketed. I had clearly unearthed a market, and I was more than ever convinced of this when Spurs got to the FA Cup Final in 1987. I worked with Saatchi & Saatchi to produce a mail order catalogue. This proved to be a big success. After Edward joined Spurs, the mail order catalogue was considerably expanded, and full-time staff appointed. Edward produced a new range of club merchandise at affordable prices, which made our sales soar. Soon, instead of buying through wholesalers we were going directly to manufacturers as far away as Portugal and Hong Kong, and making sure that profits which had been creamed off in the past now went into Spurs and the football club.

As always in Britain, such innovations have a price. We in this country never seem to like change or enterprise, and the fans and supporters often had a go at the mail order catalogues which appeared in our match programmes. Not that this made the programme all advertisements. Far from it. At forty-eight pages we had the largest programme in the League, and the catalogue, in any case, was a separate pullout section. The sales figures proved that the fans did want the products we were marketing, and if I had any doubts I only had to look around the ground, either at White Hart Lane or at away matches, to see a sea of yellow sweatshirts which demonstrated that Edward's ideas were working. His local business knowledge, his retail nous, and his enthusiasm for the club since the Fifties, made him ideal. He knew what the fans wanted and he knew how to reach them.

By the summer of 1991, as I was preparing to leave Spurs, the turnover had risen to £2.5 million a year and the shop had become very profitable indeed. Sad to say, nine months after my departure Edward left to join Manchester United, and their sales have already improved substantially. United's gain may well be Tottenham's loss.

In the mid-Eighties, with the economy booming, there were two other deals which made quite a bit of money for Tottenham. Although they attracted the sort of uninformed criticism that was the bane of my time at Spurs, both proved extremely beneficial for the club. Cheshunt, just off the A10 in Hertfordshire, had been the Spurs' training ground ever since it was purchased in the early Fifties. It consisted of about 10.6 acres of very desirable land, but in the thirty years since it was bought the whole area had changed. Tesco had arrived just around the corner with a very large out-of-town shopping centre. It was very clear that property had increased tremendously in value. Since early 1984 Bobroff had been looking at the development potential, and after consultation with Geoffrey Searle of Denton Hall, someone I had known for many years and an expert on planning matters, it seemed quite clear that if we could obtain permission for residential development it would make sense to sell Cheshunt.

By early 1986 we had received outline planning permission for housing, and estimates suggested that we could sell it in excess of £4 million. I got the board to accept that the best way to sell would be by tender, but instead of using an outside firm of estate agents I proposed to conduct the tender myself and dig into the expertise I had gathered in my youth. I contacted a number of companies who I felt would be interested, but I added a condition that while I wanted the sale to be completed by the summer of 1986, Tottenham would continue to train there until the summer of 1987. Laing Holmes bid £4,900,000, and there was no doubt that the sale made good sense. By going public in 1983 we had wiped out the enormous debts we had inherited, but that had left us with no cash. The sale of Cheshunt wiped out our overdraft and left us in a healthy position.

By handling the deal myself I also saved Spurs something between £70,000 and £100,000 in fees to an outside firm. However, Bobroff's company, which had put in work concerning the planning permission, presented Spurs with a substantial invoice for their work and I could not help thinking that I was one of the few at Spurs prepared to work for nothing. By this time I worked almost seven days a week on Spurs business, dealing not only with football matters but also the various spin-off business activities such as merchandising. Yet I took no money or fee for this, and I recall the shock on Terry Venables's face when he heard that I worked for nothing. He felt it was immoral that somebody in my position should not be paid. But then I did it for the 'glory game' – something that I felt meant nothing to him.

At this time, in the autumn of 1987, the property market was very buoyant and I suggested to the board that we acquire three freehold shops in Wood Green High Street. They also proved very good business. One unit was occupied by Dixons and two others were vacant units. I had originally thought that we might start a Spurs shop in Wood Green. It didn't quite work out that way, and we let the two vacant units to Adams Children's Wear. In May 1988 we constructed what is called a creative investment, the buyer being a Scottish Investment Company, and then a year later they also bought the Dixons unit with total profit to Spurs of £600,000.

I can understand why the football Press could not always understand some of our business deals. The tabloid Press, in particular, concerned with transfers and the dramas in the dressing-room, have little inclination or knowledge to appreciate what makes a football club tick. But what did surprise me was the criticism we generated as a result of starting Spursline. This was of genuine service to the fans, yet Tottenham was still portrayed as a money-mad club, out only to squeeze the supporters. I can claim little credit for this idea, because it was largely the doing of Mike Rollo. In the summer of 1986 he put forward the proposal of having a special number which the supporters could ring to get daily updates on what was happening at the club. British Telecom had been operating a trial system called Club Call, which marked the introduction of 0898 numbers into the telephone system.

My initial reaction was that I didn't think people would spend their time and money ringing the club, but Mike was convinced and he persuaded me to give it a three-month trial. We had to pay

£5,000 to BT, who would provide us with a number of telephone lines and give us a 50 per cent royalty on all the calls made. We could have signed up with Club Call, which would have cost us nothing, but would also have got us a far lower percentage. However, I agreed with Mike, if we were going to do it we should have our own Spurs Line, which was the name given, and within a few weeks Mike proved his word: we had not only recouped our investment but started making money.

The number of calls we received quite astounded me. If there was a new signing in view, or if we were having a particularly successful time on the field, at times all ten lines would be blocked. Later we expanded this to thirty lines, and yet at times it was difficult to cope, with the result that Spurs were soon making in excess of £150,000 per year in royalty income.

When the programme began Mike acted as a sort of DJ cum producer. He would spend a lot of the time on the training ground carrying out interviews with the Manager and the players, then return to his office, edit the programme and have it broadcast on the lines. But I felt that he was spending so much time on Spursline it was affecting his other duties, and in any case he was not an experienced broadcaster. So as the number of calls rose I persuaded Mike to get his friend John Motson to go to our training ground on two mornings a week to tape the interview for the following week's programme. It proved to be a big success. The quality of the interviews improved significantly, although it was still very much Mike Rollo's baby. In time, Spursline, like other club calls, proved a very useful source for Fleet Street. Football writers got into the habit of ringing the line and picking up on comments made by players and managers. This did inhibit players and managers who were frightened of what the tabloids might do to their comments, but of the success of the idea there can be no doubt. Far from it being a case of grabbing supporters' money, it made a significant contribution to the high cost of running Spurs.

But perhaps the Spurs business that gave me the greatest pleasure was the launch of Cockerel Books and Videos. Ever since Spurs had won the Double I had been fascinated by *Spurs Supreme*, by Ralph Finn, a book that reproduced match reports on every single game played by Spurs in that historic season. It was like a bound volume of what the papers said. As a young boy I must have read and reread it many, many times. In 1985, when English clubs were banned from Europe, it struck me that something similar could be done to chart Spurs' voyage throughout the European competitions since we started in 1961 against Gornik Zabrze in Poland.

About this time I went to a football dinner held by the South East Counties League. I was seated next to an old friend of Bill Nicholson's, who was also at our table. Bill's friend happened to be in charge of a major firm of publishers in the West End. We got chatting, and when I explained my idea to him he suggested that either I take it to a publisher or that the club could publish it itself. That proved a very good tip, and when I went to see him a few days later he provided more helpful hints as to how we might publish such a book.

Clearly a book of that nature meant a lot of research, and I hired Colin Gibson and Harry Harris to edit the book. It was Colin who provided me with the ideal researcher. Alex Bew was then working temporarily at Colin's offices at the *Telegraph*. It was her job to endure many a long day and afternoon at the British Museum and Library at Colindale, going through the old newspapers and photostatting hundreds of match reports, dating back to 1961. An old friend of mine, John Harris, proved a wonderful source of information as well. He is probably the most meticulous Spurs supporter,with leather-bound scrap-books dating back more than thirty years and containing every daily and Sunday newspaper match report on Spurs. Colin and Harry also interviewed many notable personalities who had been involved in Spurs' European exploits. We found a printer in Singapore and finally, in September 1986, the first copies of *The Glory, Glory Nights* were on sale. I knew it would do well, but even I was surprised that the entire print run of 12,000 copies was sold out.

In producing this book I was in a way paying a debt to my old heroes at Spurs. It also satisfied my desire to record and commemorate Spurs' European adventure, which had first fired my interest in Continental football. But the experience also made me think that maybe there was scope for Cockerel Books to become a useful football publisher. Unlike cricket, or even golf, there has been no great market for football books. Football histories of England, of the FA, of the World Cup, have been dutifully produced, and there has been a crop of ghosted biographies of footballers. I saw no reason why Spurs could not produce books not only about their own footballers, but others. Alex, working from my offices in the West End, continued to look at various projects and we signed up Chris Waddle for his authorised biography – written by Mel Stein – and Gary Mabbutt for his book *Against All Odds,* with Mabbutt also doing a coaching book. We cast our net beyond Spurs to make Mark Hughes one of our authors and published *Red Devils in Europe,* a Manchester United version of *The Glory, Glory Nights.*

The Waddle book proved so popular that the print run of 5,000 was completely sold out and, most unusually for a footballer's biography, it went into a second printing. Almost all the Cockerel Books sold very well, in particular *The Gazza Annual,* which brought together Monty Fresco, probably Fleet Street's most brilliant sports photographer, with England's most brilliant footballer. It proved an ideal combination, and since then some of the Monty pictures have been published all over the world, showing Gazza in all forms of fancy dress and bringing out the real clown in him. By 1988 Cockerel Books was quite a little Spurs cottage industry: we had produced a Gazza poster-magazine, another one of the England Team just prior to the 1988 European Championships, a couple of Spurs Annuals and a Spurs Children's colouring book.

By this time I was also heavily into video production. It was while I was in the throes of printing *The Glory, Glory Nights* that I spoke to Brian Moore of ITV about producing a *Glory, Glory Nights* video. He agreed to do the script and suggested Derek Sando as the director. I had already worked with Derek in the winter of 1985, when with TV companies blacking out League football, I had helped him and Lee Walker produce a highlights tape.

Today almost any high-street video shop has a wealth of football videos. In 1986 this was almost unheard-of, and I was later told that we were the first ever club to produce such a video. The main problem was to do it without using the BBC. It was a bit like trying to write a book about cricket without referring to Lord's or the MCC. The BBC has a vast library but is extremely difficult to deal with, and BBC Enterprises, which controls all their video footage, charges very steep rates for using BBC material. We tried to keep this to a minimum, relying mainly on Pathé News, Movietone News and ITN. But in the end we very badly needed a few matches from the Beeb. Eventually, as we were getting close to our deadlines to start studio production, I had to contact the BBC, and decided to get in touch with Bob Abrahams, an old friend of mine and a very good Spurs supporter. I caught him on a rare day off at home, and he was not too pleased with my request, but he understood the predicament and managed to smooth out the odd wrinkles.

If producing Cockerel Books had already made me aware of some of the joys and perils of publishing, in producing the video I realised why so many backup men on television look so exhausted. The only reasonably priced video studio we could get was available between the hours of 7 pm to 9 am, as it was just too expensive to hire video studios during the day, given the competition from film-makers and TV and advertising companies. The studio Derek got was the Molinare near the Palladium Theatre, and that November in 1986 I nearly became a zombie in trying to produce *The Glory, Glory Nights* video. I started work on the Sunday evening, continued on the Monday and Tuesday evenings, and by Wednesday morning was completely exhausted, not having slept very much since Saturday night. I came home that day about ten in the morning, and went straight to bed. That evening, 26 November, we were due to play Cambridge in a League Cup tie, and I drove up there, only to drive back to the studio to work through the night and complete the tape. But the effort was worth it. I had reckoned that we needed to sell 700 copies; in the event we sold many, many more, and even now, six years later, it is still selling.

It proved that there was a market for nostalgia, even among football fans, provided it was presented in the form of videos, and I was determined to exploit it. After many discussions with Brian Moore and Derek Sando, many lunches and much drinking of wine, I suddenly hit upon the idea: why not produce a series of tapes covering Spurs, Manchester United, Liverpool, Everton and Arsenal, each of them called *Six of the Best from the Eighties*? The copyright problem was easily solved with the help of Lee, who constructed a royalty deal whereby the clubs would get an agreed percentage of every video sold. For days I racked my brains about a presenter. Suddenly it came to me: why not Jimmy Greaves, who had become so popular with his Saint and Greavsie programme? His manager, Barry Brown, thought he would agree in principle, and within a few days we had the series all planned: *Greavsie's Six of the Best From the Eighties*. Video Collection were particularly keen to get into the football video market, and agreed to distribute it on our behalf, do all the accounting, invoicing, storage and duplicating, and handle the sort of things that can be a headache but make the difference between success and failure. The first series was four videos on Spurs, Manchester United, Liverpool and Arsenal. One on Everton came about six or nine months later. So far, 125,000 videos covering those four titles have been sold, and Cockerel makes a profit of £4 per video, and that at wholesale prices.

The success of these videos did open the floodgates. We went on to produce, *Six of the Best: Matches from the Seventies*, with Greaves again host; a League Cup Final series; *Gazza, The Real Me* video, of which Woolworths bought 100,000 tapes; and the 1984 Spurs UEFA Cup Final video. I also managed to secure the rights from the Italian League for *110 Goals Italian Style*, for the season 1988/89, and *110 Goals II* for the season 1989/90. With all the insularity of the English football world, it is interesting to note that these last two titles between them have sold over 30,000 copies. Just before I left Spurs I arranged for an annual video tape of the goals Spurs had scored that season plus *Spurs: The Road to Victory*, a video highlighting our successful 1991 FA Campaign, and between them these two videos have sold over 20,000 copies.

Later, when all the newspaper pundits were so sure of how the diversification by the plc had gone wrong and what we should have done, I took comfort from what Douglas Alexiou kept telling me: 'I can't understand, Irving, all this bad publicity, when all the things you've been involved in at Tottenham have actually been profitable, including Cockerel Books.'

The point was that these were diversifications linked closely with football, which was the reason for Tottenham's existence. However, there was one diversification, linked with football, that did go wrong, and showed how easily businesses can turn sour. This, of course, was Synchro Systems.

Soon after we had taken over in 1982, Peat Marwick Mitchell produced a report and recommended that we use the software of Synchro Systems, a company based in Stoke-on-Trent, for our ticketing arrangements. It was then the most modern computerised system being used in football clubs, and by far the best – something that could be tailored to suit individual requirements – and our ticket office manager was extremely happy with it. Derek Peter got to know the two directors who ran it, Charles Howard and Paul Warsop, very well, and everything seemed to be going fine.

At some stage, Howard and Warsop suggested to Derek that while there was tremendous potential in their business for expansion, they felt that they would only do so if they were under the wing of a public company. Would Tottenham be prepared to take them over? Derek was taken by the idea, and sometime early in 1989 he got the board to agree to buy 75 per cent of Synchro for around £120,000. This, on the face of it, seemed a good deal, since they were, I believe, then making profits of £80–100,000. Derek continued to act as their promoter, checking their finances, giving them limits and targets, and also introducing them into one of our board meetings, early in 1989, to explain how their company was doing.

Bob Holt also became a great enthusiast for Synchro, and at one of his first board meetings, on 4 May 1989, he spoke glowingly about how he expected Synchro to make a profit of over £500,000 in the following year. Synchro, he felt, was another successful acquisition, and there were good opportunities to make other acquisitions to add on to its existing business and grow even further. He was very impressed with Howard and Warsop, although he did sound a warning: Warsop was ever the optimist.

It was Warsop's optimism that took Synchro into areas it should never have got into, and encouraged by Holt, it expanded far too quickly. I believe things started to really go wrong when Warsop tried to get Synchro Systems into large events such as the 1990 World Cup in Italy, the Winter Olympic Games and other events. Overdrafts began to rise inexorably, and by May 1990, Holt, having made a glowing profit forecast in the past, now came and told us that the overdraft would peak at £750,000 in the next twelve months. Unfortunately, even this financial information was incorrect. Within six months the overdraft was at £1.5 million, and despite the many questions I asked Holt and the others I could find no credible explanation of how it had all gone wrong.

In fact, the alarm bells should have gone off the year before, when Barclays, who were still our bankers then, had continually complained of the lack of detailed financial information from us. I had seen Synchro as a small subsidiary that would tick over nicely, without making vast profits. It would suit the club, look after our own ticketing facilities – the club membership scheme had been introduced at the beginning of the 1986/87 season and had proved a great success – and perhaps generate a bit of profit with other activities.

But Synchro kept reaching for the stars. They were very

keen to land the National Membership Scheme which was then being touted by the Thatcher government, and in particular the Sports Minister, Colin Moynihan. I was strongly opposed to the ID Scheme, and spoke out against it on numerous occasions, but our ownership of Synchro meant that my words were always treated, at least in some quarters, with a certain degree of suspicion. The feeling was that while I spoke out against the Scheme, Tottenham as a company stood to profit if it ever came about. As we know, the ID Scheme, thank God, never came about, and went the way of all bad ideas, but so did Synchro.

Looking back, it seems a classic case of how things can go wrong when the main company loses control of one of its subsidiaries. Warsop was clearly a bit of a loose cannon. I remember on one particular occasion when he went on a mad, stupid escapade to Russia, trying to sell box office systems to the sports stadia and football clubs there. I said to him at the time: 'What on earth have you wasted that money for? Who gave you the authority?' It turned out it was Bob Holt, but given that the Russians had no hard currency to pay for whatever they bought, the expedition made no sense at all to me. Warsop would have done much better to listen to the one thing that I kept telling him: that with the Taylor Report insisting on all-seater stadia, this provided tremendous potential to sell his box office systems to clubs who had not already become his customers. He only had to read out the roll-call of clubs that used his system – Arsenal, Tottenham, Liverpool, Manchester United, Everton, Glasgow Rangers and other clubs – but he never seemed to get the point.

Holt continued to view Synchro with rose-coloured spectacles. Indeed, throughout 1990 there were numerous offers to buy Synchro, and we could have sold our 75 per cent share, but I'm afraid the board was just a bit too greedy. Having bought Synchro for £120,000, we wanted nothing less than £1.5 million. At one stage in March 1990, Stakis, Wembley and GEC were all interested in buying Synchro. Holt had talks with one which was ready to pay £1 million, and we could have got out of it with profit and none of the trauma we later faced. By the summer of 1990 I myself had spoken to Ticketmaster and their parent company, Associated Newspapers, about selling Synchro, but by then it was clear that it was not likely to meet its profit forecasts. The income it had expected from the Sheffield Games contract had not yet materialised and we were already into a damage-limitation exercise – trying to persuade Howard and Warsop to reduce their running costs to no more than half a million per year and to bring their overdraft down to half a million as soon as possible.

In the end, it ended in tears. After I had left Spurs, Synchro was sold back to its original owners, not for a million but for a pound, with Tottenham keeping the overdraft. As an interesting footnote, Bob Holt, the man who signed the infamous Canvey Island agreement on behalf of Blue Arrow, left Tottenham at the end of June 1990, has since become the Chairman of Synchro, and Derek Peter is involved in doing some accounting work for them.

We have gone ahead of our story, of course. Now let us trace back to the early months of 1989, and examine what was happening at Spurs.

The season, Terry's first full one at White Hart Lane, had been even more dismal than the previous one – if that was possible. We had touched bottom in the League, and although we had climbed up from that, we were still drifting. We had made early exits from both the Milk Cup and the FA Cup. This made a bit of a nonsense of Terry's forecast of the previous summer, when he had launched his spending spree with the boast that he intended to catch up fast with Liverpool. It was a time of reconstruction, both on the field and to an extent off it, and Spurs were going through some major changes.

The purchase of Gascoigne, the previous summer, had already forced a change of bankers. Barclays, our traditional bankers, had told us that they were unhappy about spending £2 million for his purchase. They would only support us if there were personal guarantees by the directors, and while I and Tony Berry were prepared to do so, Bobroff was not. In any case, through his own company Markheath he had got very friendly with Midland, and this was his cue to change the bankers and move from Barclays, who had been our bankers for 100 years and had been very good to us, to Midland. The move would bring dramatic consequences, but that was well into the future.

For the moment Spurs were in a position where the business had not provided a cornucopia of money, but it hadn't hobbled us either, and there was no sign of the storm to come. This was well illustrated when we had a meeting of our board on Tuesday, 7 February 1989. As often, Terry was at the meeting and presented his report on the football club. But before he did so, he asked the board how much money was available to buy players and whether he had to sell them before buying new ones. Bobroff made it clear that in order to keep within the budget Terry would have to sell, and suggested he sell up to £2 million and then spend half of it before the end of the financial year, 31 May 1989, and the remainder in the next season. Terry had already had offers of £600,000 from Manchester City for Walsh, and £325,000 from Luton for Mitchell Thomas, but he had turned them down – Thomas himself had turned down the Luton offer – in order to generate further interest.

Terry now gave the board his valuation of various players, who included:

J. Moncur £150,000
M. Robson £200,000
M. Stimson £125,000
R. Mimms £300,000
G. Mabbutt £600,000
C. Fairclough £500,000
P. Moran £350,000
P. Guthrie £50,000
B. Statham £250,000
D. Howells £250,000
S. Murray £250,000
G. Stevens £300,000

Terry was prepared to sell up to five or six of these players and use the money to buy three players. His first choice was Steve Sedgley, for whom Coventry wanted £1 million but who Terry thought was worth £750,000, although he was prepared to swap him for Paul Allen plus a further £200,000. His second preference was for a left-back, Nigel Worthington of Sheffield Wednesday, who was worth £325,000; his third for another striker, particularly Andy Much at Wolves, valued at around £1 million.

What was really interesting about Terry's thinking was the players he wanted to sell. Who would he like to sell first? He said: one, either Fairclough or Mabbutt; two, Thomas; three, Moran; four, Moncur; five, Walsh; six, Hughton; seven, Mimms and Guthrie; eight, Stevens and nine, Allen, although he said he was particularly fond of this player and didn't want to sell him.

Now, managers wanting to buy and sell players is the common diet of football. However, what struck me about this list was that

Mabbutt was at the top of it. Ever since Terry had arrived at White Hart Lane it had amazed me that he had developed a complex about Mabbutt and would always pick holes in his game. If ever a result went against us, he would always single Mabbutt out for special private criticism. He would complain that when defending Mabbutt would stand too far off the person he was supposed to be marking, and point out that he always seemed to be off balance. Not being a professional footballer I can't tell whether Terry was right or wrong. All I knew was that Mabbutt was the heart of the Spurs defence, and any team without him would be very much weaker.

Terry was always coming to me trying to convince me that Mabbutt should be released, and at one stage he encouraged a great deal of interest from Steve Coppell at Crystal Palace. They had just been promoted to the First Division and were looking for an experienced central defender to act as the linchpin of their defence. Coppell was talking about paying £850,000, and Terry thought this would be a very good price. He was convinced that Gary's diabetes would get the better of him, and told me that his upper body had been getting heavier and was slowing him down a bit. But I persuaded him it would not be a good idea to lose Gary Mabbutt, and he stayed. But the fact that the Manager wanted to sell the captain of the club created a strain which we never quite overcame.

The other significant thing about that meeting was the glow of certainty the plc gave. The interim results for the group for the six months ending 30 November 1988 had shown an increase in profit, before transfer fees, from £244,000 in 1987 to £501,000 in 1988. Every one of the non-football subsidiaries seemed keen to emphasise that their problems were minimal, that the future was rosy. Barry Kennedy of Martex said he had had some manufacturing problems in Indonesia. All that would mean would be a slight reduction in profit. He had already started selling for the autumn 1989 range – remember we are in February 1989 – and received orders to the value of £1 million. He was aiming for sales that autumn of between £5 million and £5.5 million, and expecting to make a profit, if not of £1 million then about £850,000.

John Griffin, who had joined us two months previously in December 1988, to look after Hummel, was reasonably confident that it was perceived as a young, stylish brand. True, his forecasts depended on Hummel International keeping to its scheduled delivery dates – something it hadn't always done in the past – and there was a problem of achieving adequate profits before expenses with Hummel International. Even then he felt fairly optimistic.

Indeed, at this time, despite all the financial pressures that were building up and that were to be shatteringly revealed within a few months, Tottenham, particularly the plc, behaved in an incredibly bullish mood. This was very evident when we met on Thursday 4 May 1989 for yet another board meeting, the one that confirmed the appointment of Bob Holt as Chief Executive of the public company. While Holt was very critical of Hummel, Stenhaag was apparently in dispute with his board and currently working at home, and things were far from well, Holt saw his role as Chief Executive as buying yet more companies. This was no mood of retrenchment, but expansion. Indeed, Holt told us that the only way the group could expand was by making significant further acquisitions. He was looking at Soccer Scene, which had two retail shops, Total Graphics, a small local printing company, a ladies' raincoat company and a clock importer.

However, and this was perhaps the most remarkable part of Holt's announcement, he felt the best way to expand quickly would be if we merged with another major public company. He presented various possibilities: Astra Trust, which owned a company called Splash and was then capitalised around £25 million; Prestwich Holdings, which owned Video Collection; and two other public companies with a capital of £20 million. Merger with a public company was not to the taste of Bobroff, who feared loss of control, and he spent some time at the meeting discussing how we could sell some players. The balance on the account was now more than £1.6 million. The bank was keen that we should reduce it. The bullish mood of the meeting was probably summed up by Tony Berry suggesting that we could sell Martex and Hummel and get anything up to £5 million. Events were soon to show how wide of the mark he was. During 1992 I got Ian Gray to work out how much better off the plc would have been had we not bought Martex and Stumps. The answer was £5 million.

Such optimism was also very much in evidence when we met three weeks later, on Wednesday 31 May, with Holt saying that Martex was likely to make £700,000 profits this year and £1 million the next. Holt felt his main problem would be to keep Barry Kennedy, who ran Martex, motivated. Apart from

Hummel, where Stenhaag had now resigned and things had not improved, similar encouraging noises were made about all the other non-footballing subsidiaries.

For some time before the meeting Terry had been telling me about buying a forward and a midfield player. At the meeting I asked Bobroff whether we would have the money, and he felt that Terry should sell some players before he bought. No conclusion was reached, and we thought our next board meeting would indicate how much we had available. What I didn't tell the board was the name Terry had given me, probably the most exciting forward to come to Spurs since Jimmy Greaves. What I didn't know was that when the next board meeting was convened to approve his purchase, that would reveal the first crack in our crumbling financial edifice.

11 | LINEKER COMES . . . THE CLOUDS GATHER

**'Well all that is fine. But by the way, we haven't got any money.'
– Paul Bobroff, after the board had told Terry Venables he could buy Lineker.**

If there was a moment when I first became aware that the problems looming off the field would affect the team, then it was on a summer Saturday in 1989. It started, as these things often can, with a telephone call that brought joy, but soon set in train a series of events which suddenly brought a great cloud of anguish to blot out the sunny day.

The 1988/89 season had been a rather moderate one. We had been knocked out early in both Cup competitions and had another indifferent League performance. But in every close season hope springs, and this time it positively bloomed.

Sometime in May 1989, a Saturday morning as I remember, the phone rang and it was Terry Venables. He and I had been in very close discussion trying to keep abreast of the Gary Lineker situation at Barcelona. Cruyff, who had replaced Venables at Barcelona, did not hold Lineker in the same regard, had played him out of position on the wing all season, and it was clear he was ripe for a transfer. We felt it might be possible to bring him to White Hart Lane. That Saturday morning I happened to be at the ground, and the news could not have been better. Terry said: 'They are prepared to release Lineker.'

'What's it going to take?' I asked.

'I think they're going to take 1.2 million,' Terry responded.

The figure didn't surprise me. I had always been convinced that Lineker would be available for a reasonable sum and that Barcelona would never hold out for the last penny. I was, of course, thinking Terry meant £1.2 million, when he interjected: 'By the way, it's dollars,' and burst out laughing. It was typical Terry, of course, but it meant Lineker would be available for something like £700,000, which at that price was a steal.

As Terry mentioned the possibility of signing Lineker, I couldn't help recalling that summer day in 1984 when, just as we were selling Steve Archibald to Barcelona, we nearly bought Lineker from Leicester City. Indeed, while the final wording of the transfer between Spurs and Barcelona concerning Archibald was being negotiated in one room, in another I was talking to Terry Shipman, Chairman of Leicester. At that stage Lineker had not yet been capped for England and had been playing most of his football in the Second Division. But Peter Shreeve was very keen on signing him, and our enquiries through a contact in the Midlands had led us to believe that if we paid £750,000 we could buy him.

Shipman wanted £1 million. He was under local pressure, having been on the radio in Leicester to reassure fans that he would not allow Lineker to leave Leicester even though his contract only had twelve months to run. I was prepared to go up to £900,000, but balked at the £1 million, feeling at that time that the sum was immoral. Although at this stage £1 million had been paid for a certain number of players, many of them – though not Trevor Francis – had subsequently turned out to be duff, and their values had fallen dramatically. I did not want to make that mistake, but in the process made a greater one. I should have paid that extra £100,000 to get Lineker in 1984. Now, five years later, we were getting him, and for almost £200,000 more.

We attacked from two sides. Terry dealt with Barcelona FC. The man who deals with all the transfers there is Juan Gaspar, the power behind the throne. He is one of the toughest negotiators in the business. If you ever want to talk about a moving target, then Juan Gaspar is the original moving target. I got on well with him, having dealt with him over Steve Archibald some years before, but I left that part to Terry, as he knew him much better. Also Terry had the task of persuading Lineker that his next career move was to Tottenham. They could talk football in the way I couldn't. I dealt on the monetary side with Lineker's agent, John Holmes. This twin strategy had worked well on previous transfers and made good sense.

Eventually Terry went to Barcelona to tie up the details. At that moment I was in Portugal for a few days. By some curious fate, his room number in Barcelona, which was something like 3864, was exactly the same as mine. This produced some hilarity, and I remember saying: 'Hold on, this could be a lucky omen.' So it proved to be. Terry came back from Barcelona not only with Gary Lineker, but also Mohammed Ali Amar, popularly known as Nayim, a very fine midfielder who had played for the Spanish Under-21 side, for a combined fee of £1.5 million. It was a great coup.

Within a few days, in the middle of June, a board meeting was held to ratify the transfer and I asked Terry to attend. Everything seemed to go smoothly. As Terry put the deal to the directors, Bobroff, who as Chairman of the public company was presiding over the meeting, looked sheepishly round the room and said: 'Yes, I think that's OK. Is everybody agreed?' However, what with our expenditure on the stand, Terry knew that the club was short of ready cash. So it was agreed he would use his best endeavour to try to sell some players to recoup the £1.5 million as fast as he possibly could. Terry was quite happy to go along with this.

But what if he got more than £1.5 million? Well then it was clear that any money over and above that would be given back to him to spend on further acquisitions of players. No one doubted that. Not Bobroff, not the remainder of the board, not Terry. In the light of what happened this was to become a very important point, but at that stage we had no doubts. Not that the £1.5 million for Lineker and Nayim was to be paid in one lump sum. As with all transfers, some money was immediate, £600,000 payable on 1 August, and the balance was due on the following 1 August 1990. Terry left the room quite happy, but no sooner was he out of the door than the first sign of clouds to ruin our sunlit day began to appear, and the cloudmaker turned out to be Bobroff.

The door had barely closed behind Terry when Bobroff turned to the meeting and said: 'Well all that is fine. But by the way, we haven't got any money.' I looked at him in horror and said: 'Look, we've just had the Manager in the room. He's asked you a question. "Can we buy Lineker and Nayim?" You as Chairman have said: "What are the terms?" He's told you. We've agreed. He's gone away to do it. You're now telling us, ten minutes later, that we haven't got the money. This is just not on. I am not going to sit on the other side of the table to Terry Venables and lie and say: "Yes you can," knowing that he can't! I'm sorry, I prefer to be truthful with him and somehow we'll work it out.'

Bobroff now tried to use my own arguments against me. As I have said, I always believed that players under twenty-six should be bought, as this gave time for them to develop. Lineker was soon going to be twenty-nine, and Bobroff said: 'This does go against what you preach about young players. But I suppose you will sell him in another two years for £2 million.' As he said so he smirked, which really upset me. But whatever Bobroff said could not deflect me, and while it was clear we didn't have the money to fund the transfer, in the end I got so frustrated and fed up with Bobroff that I turned round and said: 'Right, we have collectively given our word, I'm not prepared to welch on that. If the money is not available by the first of August, I will personally underwrite the first tranche payment to Barcelona. Then as soon as the money comes into the club from selling any other players, I will get repaid.' This was agreed and minuted. So effectively I underwrote the transfer. Maybe Bobroff was angling for this, I don't know. If he was he certainly got his way.

Even now I was not aware of the full horror of the situation. Perhaps I should have made enquiries, but my hands were full running the football club. The public company was Bobroff's domain, and he had always given the impression he knew what he was doing and was on top of matters.

Not that this was the first time we had run into problems with funding a transfer. As we have seen, Bobroff and I had to guarantee Brazil's transfer, and then there had been problems when we signed Gascoigne. Barclays, with whom we had a long relationship, had expressed concern that they were not getting all the financial information they needed. Bobroff prepared a corporate plan, but Barclays were not prepared to give us more money unless Bobroff, Berry and I provided guarantees. Berry and I were prepared to do so, but Bobroff declined and decided that the only solution was to change our bankers. So at a time when we were entering a financially dangerous period we changed from our long-standing bankers, Barclays, who were also the sponsors of the League, to the Midland. In retrospect it proved not quite as smart a move as Bobroff made out.

Perhaps all this should have made me more alert to Bobroff's words and deeds, but I was then much taken up with the transfer of Lineker. My responsibility was the football club, and Lineker's transfer filled me with great hope, it fitted in so well with my theory about football. The theory is that great teams have at least three world-class players. If you look at the AC Milan team, you see Rijkaard, Gullit and Van Basten, with the others playing around them. During my time at Tottenham I'd never really had a team like that. We'd had some great players, often two at a time, like Hoddle and Ardiles or Hoddle and Waddle, but three world-class players, all at their peak, had never been at our disposal. When we got Lineker, I thought: We've got it. We already had Gascoigne and Waddle. Lineker completed the trinity.

This is it! This is what I've been working for, I thought. To try and assemble something for a really good coach, Terry Venables, to bring the best out of. Now we are really going to go forward. But how quickly dreams are demolished. A single telephone call from Paris changed the whole picture.

We were holding a Press conference on the Friday to announce the signing of Lineker. This was due to start at 10.30 in the morning. Five minutes beforehand, as I was about to leave my room to go to the Press conference, the telephone rang. Would I take a call from Mr Barin? He came straight to the point. 'Chris Waddle?' 'He's not for sale,' I replied. 'Ah,' said Barin, 'but you know, I have a client who is very, very interested.' I said: 'I'm not interested at all, he's not for sale.' Barin wouldn't take no for an answer, and started quoting numbers. 'My client is prepared to offer you £2.5 million.' 'Look, he's not for sale and that's it!' Barin kept saying 'Fine' and offering a higher figure.

By the end of the telephone conversation, which lasted another minute or so, he had upped his offer from £2½ million to £3 million. But I still rejected it. However, before I put the phone down I had got Barin to say who his client was: Marseille.

I went downstairs, and my first stop was Terry Venables's office. 'Terry,' I said, 'you're never going to believe this but I've just had a phone call from Barin. Do you remember Barin?' 'Yes I do,' said Terry. 'Well, Barin's just offered £3 million for Waddle.' 'What did you do?' said Venables. 'I turned it down,' I replied. 'Oh, mmm,' muttered Venables. Then he fell silent for a minute or two before saying: 'You know, he's getting on, isn't he? He's not a spring chicken any longer.'

I knew that Venables was not happy that less than a year ago we had committed the club to signing Waddle for seven years. I did it because I wanted to secure him. As I have said,

I like players on long contracts, but there was a psychological angle to this. I felt the longer we had Waddle at Tottenham, the easier it was going to be to retain Gascoigne. He and Waddle were very close, and Waddle had developed into something of a father figure for Gascoigne.

Clearly Terry didn't see it this way, and just before we went into the Press conference, he said: 'Couldn't we do an Ian Rush deal?'

'What do you mean?' I said.

'Look,' he said, 'if we could get the money now and keep the player for one more year, I think that's a good idea.'

Terry's idea obviously was to get the money and keep the player, so he won both ways. A typical Terry Venables move. I wasn't sure, but he persisted. 'Why don't you ring them and maybe get them over? Then we can talk to them and see how we are going to get on.' There was no harm in that, and I agreed.

With that we marched to the Press conference, presented Lineker to the world and spoke of the glowing future that awaited Tottenham with three world-class players in the side. If later this was painted as a touch hypocritical, then it was not so on my part. The Barin call was no more than exploratory, and I had no desire to see Waddle go.

I had suffered a lot when we first signed him and he struggled to find his feet during his first eighteen months at Tottenham. One particular journalist kept on writing that it was my fault we had signed him, after I'd seen him score an excellent goal for Newcastle against Spurs. I hadn't seen that game, but I was very keen on Waddle and had great confidence in his ability, and I told him so, especially during this difficult period.

Immediately after the Press conference I rang Barin. 'I've spoken to the Manager and it might make some sense, perhaps if you come over tomorrow and we talk it over. But will you bring your client?' He agreed, and we arranged to meet with him and Bernard Tapie, President of Marseille, at the Carlton Tower Hotel at 3 o'clock the next day.

Terry and I met for lunch to discuss our strategy for the meeting. I did not want to sell Waddle, and I asked Terry what his valuation was right then. He said the maximum figure Waddle was worth in his opinion was around £2 million. We ended lunch agreeing that we would put a price tag of £5 million on Waddle. This was clearly way above what he was supposed to be worth, but by pricing it so high I was hoping to scare the French away.

Terry was also thinking about selling Paul Walsh, and he tried to manoeuvre the meeting in such a way that not only were we talking about Waddle, but also about Walsh. Tapie, with refreshing candour, explained why he wanted Waddle. He was then buying several players, including Manuel Amoros from Monaco, and told us how he saw Waddle playing in this new team of his, lifting it to another level. It got to the point where we had to quote a price. I then said: 'Well I think we'd better go outside for a minute.' We got outside the room and I burst out laughing. Terry said: 'You couldn't get the price out could you?' I nodded. 'Well, to be honest, I was a bit embarrassed to say £5 million.' We have to remember that back in 1989 £5 million would have made Waddle, if they had paid it, the second most valuable player in the world, after Ruud Gullit, who went for £5.5 million to AC Milan. But I pulled myself together, we went back in the room and I uttered the words: 'The figure is £5 million.' Tapie said: 'I'll pay you the £5 million for the two players,' meaning Waddle and Walsh.

I could hardly believe my ears. I had expected a dusty *Non*, but here was a full-throated *Oui*, and Tapie had called my bluff. It was my turn to backtrack and I said: 'Well hold on a minute, we can't just agree to this.' I was now beginning to go on the back foot and wanted to delay. Even Terry was a bit shaken. They had never seen Waddle play, and Tapie, by his own admission, didn't know too much about football anyway!

He explained that he had concluded a deal the day before to sell certain television rights for the same figure, and he wanted to give it to us. I've since heard that at half-time, he goes in and gives the half-time team talk, which I find astonishing.

We parted that day with no agreement reached, but it was clear that they were interested, seriously interested. While the sale of Walsh had fallen through, they were prepared to pay above £4 million just for Chris Waddle alone.

Terry's first reaction was: 'Let's try and ring Liverpool and see if we can buy John Barnes.' As he and I sat drinking in my house in Regent's Park, and I can tell you we both needed a drink, we did consider this option seriously. Indeed I tried to ring Peter Robinson, the Chief Executive, but it being a summer Saturday afternoon, he was out at cricket. I stiill couldn't reconcile myself to selling Waddle, but Terry seemed happy. Marseille had made it clear they were not interested in any form of Ian Rush loan for a season. If they were going to buy him they were going to buy him then and there for cash. Terry's view was: 'Look, the player is worth £2 million, we are going to get no less than £4 million – that can't be bad.'

Here we need to understand Terry Venables's mentality. From my dealings with Terry, I learned that he was in favour of releasing players if the Club was offered enough money. He may have developed this outlook when working with Jim Gregory who was famous for the line 'everything is for sale'.

Clearly we had to put the deal to Waddle. These things have a habit of getting out, and it would have been awful if we had tried to keep him in the dark and he got to know of it through someone else. We agreed that I would contact Mel Stein and explain to him that we had a proposal that in principle could be acceptable to the club. I emphasised 'could be acceptable to the club', which meant it had not yet been accepted. I was confident Waddle might reject it, and I said to Terry: 'If any player is likely to turn down a move abroad then Chris Waddle is the player.' Chris seemed to be very happy at Tottenham, and I felt that his 'overseas move' had been moving from Newcastle to London!

I saw Stein on the Sunday afternoon and repeated to him my hope that Waddle would turn around and say No. But when Chris, who was away on holiday, came back a few days later, his reaction was completely unexpected. He spoke about it with his wife, Lorna, and the following morning he told Stein: 'I've been thinking about it long and hard. We'd like to take advantage of it. We are very happy in England, but this is a once-in-a-lifetime opportunity.' The die was cast. Now nothing could stop the Waddle transfer, and it took place a couple of weeks later at £4.25 million.

I could do nothing to stop the deal, but when the final Waddle Press conference took place, I was away. The size of the Waddle fee meant that Terry had money to spend, and he was very keen on signing Steve Sedgley from Coventry City. I had seen Sedgley play in an England Under-21 match at Ipswich a few months earlier, when Terry told me of his initial interest, and I had asked him if he was sure, as he hadn't made a big impression on me. Terry also wanted to buy Pat Van Den Hauwe from Everton. We had to play Everton in the second game of the season, and when we went up there Carter came up to me and said: 'Irving, all this toing and froing, can we agree a deal?' Within a few minutes we'd shaken hands on a deal, with a payment structure that was acceptable.

Acceptable to everyone but Bobroff. He had rung me about a week or two before the Pat Van Den Hauwe transfer and asked what was going on. I told him of the players we were looking at and he said: 'You can't buy that player.' 'Why not?' I asked, thinking that he was perhaps about to venture a football opinion on a player, something he rarely did. But it turned out it was not football but money. 'Well, we haven't got the money.' This shook me. 'Hold on a second, did we or did we not give our word to Terry that he'd get every penny beyond the £1.5 million paid out for Lineker and Nayim?' This meant, I told Bobroff, that: 'There is £2 million left of the Waddle transfer, why shouldn't we spend it?' 'Yes,' he said, 'I agree I did say that, but I didn't think we'd get as much as that for the sale of any player.' 'That's not my problem,' I replied. 'We gave our word and we can't go back on that.' 'You had the money to buy Sedgley, what are you complaining about?' shot back Bobroff.

Bobroff and I had never been on the same wavelength, but this disagreement was something new. Soon after this he went away on holiday, and we didn't speak for quite a few weeks, which was unusual between us. In retrospect it marked the breach between Bobroff and me. His silence could have meant he was sulking, but it soon turned out he was plotting.

Some time in September 1989, when I was in the South of France for a few days, Bobroff rang me. 'Can we meet on Friday, when you're back in London?' 'Sure,' I said, little suspecting what he had in mind. The meeting was at his offices in St George Street in the West End. We had barely exchanged pleasantries before he said: 'I think it would be better if you resigned from the company. Keep your shares of course. I think it is much better if one person runs the business. This split between the plc and the football club is no good. Me as the head of the plc, you as head of the football club, it doesn't seem to work. I think we should have one person in charge of both.'

I was completely taken aback. It truly was out of the blue. After I had recovered from the shock I said: 'Look, I'm going to think about this, but let me tell you my initial reaction is "Get Lost. You're crazy. I can't see the logic." '

Later as I thought about it, it fitted into the pattern of the way Bobroff worked. I believed that everything he did was premeditated and slightly through the back door. It seemed that behind whatever he said there always was an ulterior motive. In many ways, he was quite the most politically motivated person I had met; not party political but he behaved in the way politicians do.

It was clear that he was very annoyed about the purchase of Van Den Hauwe. He wanted the money to go to the plc because the financial position was worse than we had actually been led to believe. But instead of being open about the financial position, he had started intriguing. If we had known the financial position clearly, then would we have even considered buying Lineker? Would we not have actually set out to sell Waddle? Yet during these negotiations Bobroff had given no hint of the problem ahead. Indeed, when I told him that we had an offer for Waddle for £3 million, he said: 'Well you're not going to sell are you?' I was surprised by his seeming reluctance to sell, and of course delighted.

Bobroff had always given me the impression that he saw players as commodities. In 1984, when Archibald had gone to Barcelona and Brazil to Manchester United for a combined sum of £1.75 million and we hadn't actually bought any replacements, he said: 'What we should really be doing is investing this money so we get a return on it for years to come.' To me this was anathema. 'Look, you've got to understand,' I said. 'We're a football club. If we haven't got players, then there's going to be no return on anything. We are there to provide the best players for our supporters and for the club and to try and do our best to win as many matches as we can. The biggest chance you've got of winning as many matches as you can is by having good players.' Bobroff said nothing, but looked at me as if I was demented. Now he had come out in his true colours.

The following day, a Saturday, we were at Aston Villa and I spoke privately to Douglas Alexiou. Over the years Douglas and I had got close, and I felt that I could trust him implicitly. 'Do you know,' I said, 'I have had a very strange meeting yesterday when Bobroff asked me to resign. What a damn cheek!' It was only then that it began to emerge that the meeting with me was part of a Bobroff coup, and that he had been trying to line up the tanks in the boardroom to force me to quit.

A few days before he met me, Bobroff had been to see Alexiou, and he had also seen the other directors, Tony Berry and Frank Sinclair. These meetings were to be a prelude to a board meeting where he could put a vote of no confidence in

me and effectively force me out. He had even had Venables
in his office, saying: 'You find it very difficult to work with
Irving don't you?' What was curious about this was that at
the beginning of the 1988 season, when Terry's multi-million
team including Gascoigne were at the bottom of the League,
Bobroff was one of those urging me to sack Venables. Now he
was a pawn in the game against me. Anyway, Venables told me
afterwards that he was very, very annoyed because he felt that
Bobroff was using him and Terry is not the type of person who
likes to be used.

But like the best-laid plans of mice and men, Bobroff's went a
bit awry. He had begun the intrigue with a series of clandestine
meetings; now a further series of more open meetings made it
clear that the board were not with him. The monthly board
meeting was due in a few days and the showdown would take
place then. As Bobroff arrived at the ground, Berry and Alexiou
took him to one side and said: 'We know what you've been trying
to do. We as a board are not happy about what's going on behind
the scenes. Let's get one thing clear Paul. If it is a choice between
you and Irving, as far as the board is concerned there is only one
choice. It will be you leaving, not him.' Bobroff's only supporters
were Holt and Peter. Berry, Sinclair and Alexiou were with me.

The coup master had been ruffled. His tanks had turned
out to be made of papier mâché. Bobroff was so utterly shaken
by this that the planned board meeting did not take place on
time, although discussions went on between Berry, Alexiou and
Bobroff. But despite being cornered, Bobroff refused to go. 'I'm
not going to resign from this company unless I sell my shares.'
It was one rule for everyone else and another for himself. As
always he appeared interested in number one. Finally, after a
great deal of talk, an agreement was reached. Sinclair together
with me, Berry and Alexiou were going to buy his shares, and
he was going to leave the company.

Bobroff insisted on an agreement being signed there and
then, but I warned I couldn't be included in it. I held 26
per cent, and I was worried that if I was party to that then
it could possibly put me into a position where I would have
to bid for the entire company. Now Bobroff started banging
the table, ranting and raving that he wouldn't sign it unless
everyone else did also. According to the City code, anybody
who buys 30 per cent or more of a public company must bid for
all the other shares. It was possible that quite inadvertently and

with the best of motives we might breach certain City codes. I
kept asking Berry: 'Look, am I breaking any rules by doing this?
Surely it puts me into a position to bid.' But Berry, who signed
the agreement along with Alexiou, reassured me. 'No, no, no, it's
OK.' I'm not a City man. Berry had more experience than anyone
on City matters, having been involved with Blue Arrow. Finally
an agreement was signed that evening that was placed in escrow.
Bobroff resigned, and the board then resolved that I should take
over as Chairman of the plc. As so often in such situations, our
public announcement was short and cryptic. Bobroff had gone
to pursue other business interests, a catch-all phrase meant to
hide a multitude of sins.

I immediately set about trying to find out the full financial
position, telling Holt and Derek Peter that within seven days
I wanted full financial details of exactly where we were. Like
everyone else in the club, Holt and Peter were a bit shaken by
the event, but they promised to provide the details.

Everything seemed settled, then suddenly some time the following week, Bobroff turned up and said that he had got legal
advice. He had turned to his advisers BZW, and they had advised
him that there were certain parts of his agreement which would
not hold. He wasn't just going to sit back and accept it. This led
to another flurry of meetings, and it soon became clear that we
were in a very, very difficult position. For me to buy out Bobroff
would mean having more than 30 per cent. I would then have to
bid for the entire company, which I did not want to do. I did not
have the money for a full bid. Neither Berry or Alexiou were in a
position to bid for the company. We were in a stalemate. Bobroff's
coup had failed, but our revolution could not succeed. The only
alternative was to return to the old regime.

So finally, on the following Wednesday or Thursday, a meeting
took place at Douglas Alexiou's offices at Brook Street, Mayfair.
It was accepted that the agreement would be scrapped, as it was
only held in escrow, and Bobroff would rejoin the board of directors. We would go back to where we were before Bobroff began
his coup. We begged him not to be reappointed as Chairman, as
this would make us the laughing stock of both the football world
and the City. 'Just leave it, and maybe in a few months' time you
can come back.' But he was absolutely insistent. He can be very
dogmatic as a person, and he had even told the bank already that
he was going to be reappointed.

Until now the Press had accepted the story in reporting

Bobroff's resignation. But with his reappointment as Chairman the whole thing began to look very fishy. Even then we might have contained the damage, but there was the inevitable leak. I think I know where it came from. Tony Berry was very friendly with Philip Green of Amber Day, who in turn was chummy with Jeff Randall of the *Sunday Times*. Randall told me years later that Green had spoken to him and he was the source of the story.

Bobroff got wind that the story was coming from his friend Michael Sandler, a City PR man, and got very hot under the collar about that. Football had made me used to this sort of thing – I accepted that there are no secrets in the game. But this was Bobroff's first exposure, and he did not take it kindly. It was also the first time there was any public hint that all was not well at Spurs.

The only good thing was that at last we began to get a much fuller picture of the financial position. Holt had been trying for some time to see if he could get some form of underwriting done. He and Derek Peter were actually investigating the takeover of another public company, Prestwich Holdings, which owned a company called Video Collection and a number of other subsidiaries. They thought it was a good buy, and that the big cash-flow of Prestwich would be of immense help. They also thought that BZW could perhaps finance the purchase, and this would solve many of our problems.

But this proved no solution, and what was worrying me was that Holt and Peter had spent about six weeks on it, leaving Tottenham aside. I must say that I had never had much confidence in Holt in the first place. He used to work at Blue Arrow, and arrived with a reputation for being a real go-ahead operator. I had interviewed him, and then wrote to him offering him the job of chief executive. I heard nothing for two weeks. This hardly suggested much enthusiasm, and so I wrote again saying that since he had not bothered to reply perhaps he was not the right man. Imagine my surprise when I discovered, about a week later, that he had contacted Bobroff directly and been appointed by him. Inevitably this coloured my attitude to Holt, and I never felt he was up to the job.

As time went on it was becoming clear that we needed more money and that some form of Rights issue had to take place. It was about this that one day Holt turned to me and said: 'Look, you know Robert Maxwell. Why don't you contact him?' I thought no more of it at that time, little realising how events would turn out only a few months hence.

Bobroff's coup against me had failed, but this didn't stop his plotting. Now he turned against Tony Berry, whose holding of 8 per cent made him the third largest shareholder after me and Bobroff. Berry's arrival on the board in 1987 shows the curious way football works.

In January 1987, just after we played Scunthorpe in the third round of the FA Cup, I caught a flight to Hong Kong with Peter, at the invitation of Hummel. We had recently agreed with them on the design of the team's new kit, which was due to be launched that summer, and they thought it was a good idea for us to see how their manufacturing operation worked in the Far East.

Also on the flight, in the same compartment, was Philip Green, who was later to become the Chairman of Amber Day. We had known each other for many years by sight. During the long journey, he came over to talk to me, and started singing the praises of a very close friend of his, Tony Berry, pointing out that he was an extremely avid Spurs supporter and would be very useful to Tottenham as a director. His company, Blue Arrow, had an executive box at Tottenham and he was another of the generation touched by the magic of the Double side. In fact he had been a young trialist at the club, but Bill Nicholson had, with brutal honesty, pointed out that he would never be good enough, and whilst it broke his heart, it helped to shape his future.

Up to a few years previously, Berry had worked for David Evans, Chairman of Luton, and had been a director of Evans's Company, Brengreen Holdings. I was later to find out that after nearly twenty years' association, Berry had been sacked on Christmas Eve. Since that time, he had gone into business on his own and had become one of the young entrepreneurs of the soaring Thatcherite Britain of the Eighties. His employment services company, Blue Arrow, was riding high and was a few months away from becoming the largest company of its kind in the world with an audacious takeover of the American Manpower company.

On my return to the UK I arranged to have lunch with Berry, which took place near his offices in Finsbury Square. He struck me as a very down-to-earth, bright and alert businessman, who had a burning passion for Tottenham. He made it plain that he was extremely keen to become involved and felt that his skills and City knowledge would be of great use to Tottenham. This was not all talk: he was prepared to back his enthusiasm with hard cash.

At this initial meeting I mentioned that it was likely that major works would have to be carried out on the East Stand in the near future, and we believed this was going to cost in the region of £4.5 to £5 million. It was agreed that he would arrange for some form of a loan giving us around £3.5 million, a loan for seven years at an interest of between 7.5 and 8 per cent. He also agreed to subscribe to some shares. The company had around 400,000 unissued shares at the time, and whilst the share price in the market was 70p, it was agreed that these would be issued to Berry at £1.10p per share.

A couple of weeks later, the entire board attended a lunch in Berry's private dining room at the Blue Arrow offices, where the board ratified the previous discussion between Berry and myself, and an agreement was struck to invite him to become a director. The idea was that he would be dealing with the company's non-footballing interests. He joined the board in the week the club was preparing to play Wimbledon in the sixth round of the FA Cup at Plough Lane.

After Berry's arrival the share price, which had been in the doldrums ever since we floated in 1983, almost trebled to over £2.50 that summer. At last it seemed Tottenham Hotspur plc was becoming a roaring leisure stock, caught up in the bull market that was then entering its final phase. Berry also introduced other changes, some cosmetic, others crucial. Before Berry, Press conferences announcing the results of the company were usually held in the offices of Streets, a PR company based in Fleet Street and handled by Michael Sandler. Now Berry's own PR man, who as it happens was an Arsenal supporter, took over and our Press conferences began to be held in the Savoy.

A more crucial Berry move was to introduce the board to a friend of his who owned Martex, a women's fashion company. Associated with it was another company, Stumps. Berry proposed we buy these two companies. Now you may wonder what was Spurs, a football club, doing in the women's fashion business? I did. But this was partly the logic of being a plc and hence involved in the leisure sector of the market, and partly the silver tongue of Berry, which at times could prove even silkier than the one Terry Venables possessed.

The proposal to buy Martex and Stumps would cost us £3 million, plus a top-up provision if they made a certain amount of profits in the first year. When it came to the board, I voiced my doubts. 'Are you sure we are doing the right thing? Do we know anything about this business?'

We didn't, but Berry was persuasive. 'Don't worry about it. When we buy it we're going to get the business going, and in two or three years' time it won't really matter because we'll have moved on to other things, expanded and raised sufficient equity capital etc.' I should have backed my doubts by voting against, but when the hands went up in the boardroom so did mine. The deal was approved unanimously, and another silver-tongued man had his way.

There had been a lot of talk about a Rights issue to raise capital that summer, and it was virtually ready to go ahead when the October Stock Market Crash of 1987 happened. This, as it turned out, proved to be Berry's swan-song. The two companies' purchase took place in December, by which time Berry's bubble, along with that of many of the go-go men of the Eighties, was about to burst. The record Rights issue which had funded the purchase of Manpower had run into trouble – although we weren't to know this for some time – and his whole empire was unravelling. Also the crash meant that there was no prospect of raising money, let along £3½ million, from the market. So by the time, in December 1989, when Bobroff launched his coup against Berry, the early promise that had brought him to the board had all but faded, and the venom, at least in Bobroff's mind, had been building for some time.

Bobroff lined up his guns against Berry in much the same way that he had targeted me. At a board meeting held in his office he listed all the anti-Berry points. The Blue Arrow affair, he said, was having an adverse effect on Tottenham, and with Berry still on the board we would never raise the money. Indeed, it was felt that Berry was now on the board under false pretences. 'One of the reasons he came on the board was to produce the £3½ million towards the East Stand, which he never did.' What was worse, the Martex acquisition would cost us £5 million and would prove one of the main reasons for our downfall. But, typical of Bobroff, he made this attack at a meeting where Berry was not present, and I made it absolutely clear that I would not allow anybody to be discussed in their absence. It was bad manners, beside being morally wrong. At least if you're going to discuss some fellow let him have the opportunity of hearing what is said and answering any criticisms that people may have of him. So Bobroff was thwarted, but his venom against Berry was in the open and he had as it were set out yet another marker.

By now, of course, everyone on the board was aware that we faced a critical financial position. In one of our board meetings early in 1990 it had been agreed that we should all look for investors, but this meant me, Bobroff and Berry. In March we again had to approach the bank for an extension of the overdraft limit from £5.8 million to £6.5 million. This they did. However the following month, when we approached them for further funds to make payments to Lelliotts, they refused, and Frank Sinclair and I agreed to lend £350,000 each. Now you cannot just lend money to a public company. It had to be cleared with the Stock Exchange, which Holt did, I believe through Stewart Millman of BZW, the City securities house owned by Barclays Bank. But no lawyers were involved, no formal loan documentation drawn up.

Bobroff had also begun to make noises suggesting that he might be willing to stand down as Chairman. Some time in March or April he told me he felt that it would be best for Tottenham if one person was in charge. 'If you want to be that one person, then I'm prepared to stand down as Chairman. Or if you don't want to take on the job, then I will do so.' I promised to think about it for a few days, and then came back and told him that I was quite prepared, albeit reluctantly, to combine my chairmanship of the football club with that of the public company. I think my reply surprised Bobroff, who expected me to turn down his offer, if that is what it was, but we agreed that Bobroff would resign as Chairman during the next few months. Somehow, he never got round to it, and so we got into a situation where Bobroff had expressed his desire to leave but had not left, and I was sucked in to seeking funds and finding an underwriter.

It was against such a background that the 1989/90 season was played. Not that the players knew or were involved in this, but a pall seemed to hang over the club and our results were again disappointing. We were knocked out early from the FA Cup, and made the quarters of the Littlewoods Cup only to lose to Forest in a game which showed off the skill of Clough's team. Late in the season when there was nothing to play for we did have a great League run, and finished with a flourish in third place, which as so often held out hope that maybe next season it would be better.

It was in the final game of the season that our efforts to find money took on a different perspective. Capital Radio wanted to do an end-of-season interview, and Terry Neill who works for them came to find me. After the interview he suddenly said: 'How would you like a million or more in the club?' 'Terry,' I replied, 'I don't think there's a football club in the country that would say no to that. What have you got in mind?' 'Well,' he replied, 'I've got somebody who is interested in investing in a big football club, and Tottenham seems to fit the bill.' 'OK,' I said. 'Maybe we can talk.' A couple of weeks later we met at my offices in the West End.

The investors were the Mindo Group, a business group from Indonesia keen to tie up with a football club in England. They had already spoken to Queen's Park Rangers, which had come to nothing, but they were still very interested. They had a football club in Indonesia, and they wanted to be able to send out coaching staff every summer to England. We, in turn, would have to send a representative Tottenham team every year to play in a tournament in Indonesia. Terry Neill was clearly interested in his commission, and at a very early stage we agreed that he would be paid 5 per cent of any monies invested.

I was invited to a meeting at their City offices near Leadenhall Market, and the money they proposed investing – £5 million: £3.5 million in shares, the rest in a five-year loan at 10 per cent interest which could be converted into shares – seemed just right. The board agreed I should carry on the negotiations, and soon Holt, Peter, and Finers, the lawyers, were involved in a deal that seemed to make a lot of sense for us. We wouldn't have to sell players, that was always my main aim, and we quickly agreed a deal whereby they were going to underwrite a form of placing at £1.30 per share which would mean holding 20 per cent of Tottenham. In addition they would lend us a sum of money for a period of five years. Their English advisers proposed documents showing how Mindo would make the investment, and for reasons of confidentiality, Tottenham was called London plc. My discussions suggested the Indonesians were very serious. We checked them out, and learned that they had quite a big operation in the City and the money did not appear to be a problem.

There was no doubt we were facing a crunch. On 6 June we had our regular board meeting and Derek Peter outlined the grim situation. We had to pay Lelliotts at the end of June, and there just wasn't enough money to pay them. Bobroff suggested that we look for a one-for-one Rights issue at 60p or 70p a share, but the Indonesian proposals seemed the most attractive. However, what worried me was that details of any funding would leak, and I got the board to agree that I would not come to the board with a proposal unless I was sure that funds were in place. The Michael Knighton saga weighed a great deal with me, and I did not want a repeat.

I was right to be cautious. As I was to discover, talking was one thing, producing the money quite another. After two months of intensive discussions, involving advisers, lawyers and endless meetings, I had still not seen any money from the Indonesians. Eventually they turned round and said: 'We're not going to do that deal but we are prepared to do a slightly reduced deal.' By now I was getting fed up and said: 'Before you do any talking, you prove to me that the money is in London and is available. When it is held in London we can then begin talking to you.' The money never ever turned up.

The unfortunate thing about football, especially when it comes to directors, or would-be directors, is that they've all got very long pockets and very short hands. If you ask anybody, whoever they may be, say a Stockport County fan, does he want to be on the board of Stockport County, he'll say 'Yes.' Then say to him: 'Well, how much are you going to put in?' He'll say: 'Oh, I'm not going to put in money.'

It was while we at Tottenham were in this limbo land, with the Indonesian deal still up in the air, that the 1990 World Cup Finals came. On the field, Tottenham's duo Lineker and Gascoigne helped England to her best World Cup run since 1966, ending in an untimely and unfortunate semi-final defeat by West Germany on a penalty shoot-out. I went to see the Final in Rome on 7 July in a mood where optimism was tempered by sadness at England's defeat.

Rome that day appeared deserted. Everybody was either by their television sets, or those lucky enough to have tickets were making their way to the stadium. There was not a taxi to be had. It was as I was waiting at a taxi rank in a Roman square that an event occurred which was a curious prelude to what followed. Suddenly a car came round the corner. Much to my astonishment I realised that Robert Maxwell was sitting in the front seat of the car. I shouted out to him, but the window was closed and he couldn't hear. Was seeing Maxwell an omen? I do not know. But he had been much in my thoughts. Bob Holt had been suggesting for some time that I should think about approaching Maxwell, and a few days after my return to London I rang him. It was to prove one of the most fateful calls I have ever made.

12 | ENTER THE CABDRIVER

'We must keep this confidential. If the tabloids get hold of it, it will be dynamite.'
– Kevin Maxwell.

I returned from Rome to find that the Indonesians had failed to keep their part of the bargain. I had asked that the funds be placed in escrow, but the money had just not turned up. Now the option proposed of approaching Maxwell became urgent. I knew I had to do something. The performances of Gascoigne and Lineker in the World Cup meant that offers were coming in for them from all over the place. Indeed, during the World Cup, a soccer friend of Terry's based in Italy had already told us that Torino were very interested in signing Lineker.

Lineker still had another three years of his contract with Tottenham, and when this same friend of Terry's, passing through London, met Terry and me for a drink at the Hilton, we both made it very clear that we had no intention of selling. Terry said that if he could get £5 million for him and spend that money on Dean Saunders and Mark Wright then he would let Lineker go. Terry's friend was insistent that Torino would not go above £3.5 million, but said they were prepared to throw in Haris Koro, the Yugoslav international, who had scored against England at Wembley in 1989. Lineker himself put pressure on us, albeit indirectly through his agent John Holmes, who went to Italy to speak with Torino. Meanwhile Lineker was quoted in the press as saying he was very interested in going there. I made it very clear to Holmes that Lineker had had his big-money move abroad, and there was no question of him going.

On top of all this there was also a financial timebomb ticking away under Tottenham. This involved the balance of the money due on the Lineker transfer to Barcelona. By 1 August, less than four weeks away, we had to find £900,000, otherwise the Spanish club could reclaim Lineker and Nayim. That was too awful a prospect even to contemplate. The financial problems I had glimpsed at the time of the Waddle transfer were now becoming a nightmare, and I knew something had to give.

On the Tuesday or Wednesday after the World Cup Final I rang Robert Maxwell's office to fix an appointment and arranged to see him at 10.30 on the following Sunday morning. I had got to know him quite well by now, ever since we had both served on the Football League television negotiating committee back in 1985. For some reason, I don't quite know why, he had taken a shine to me, and most people in football knew that Maxwell and I got on well together. We also did some good football business together. I sold him David Leworthy, which from Spurs' point of view was a very good sale indeed, as we bought him from Fareham Town for £5,000, and sold him to Oxford United two years later for £200,000.

Maxwell was a very powerful man in build, reputation and personality. I had witnessed his overbearing presence reducing even Mirror Group editors to quivering toadies. He was never without an opinion, and felt his opinion was always right. On one occasion he rang me at my office and the telephonist, a young girl, failed to recognise who he was and asked: 'What company do you represent?' 'Fuck off!' roared Maxwell, and slammed the phone down.

I remember distinctly one occasion at the Mirror Building with Ken Bates and myself. I had had an idea for several years of trying to finance ticket sales so that supporters could make a weekly or monthly payment rather than paying for a whole season in advance. I pointed out that the potential market for this could be in the region of £40 to £50 million per year. Maxwell jumped on this at once, and said that one of his companies would be prepared to finance half of it. I looked at him in amazement and asked: 'Can you do that?' He looked back at me and said in his booming voice: 'I can do anything I want.' He burst out laughing as he said it, but he believed it.

I was not privy to Maxwell's business dealings. I saw him in relation to football, and he gave me the impression of being a benevolent dictator, a man who liked the game and was prepared to back it with hard cash. In a game where few people put their money where their mouth is, Maxwell did seem one of the exceptions. He could be charming, and was quite the most astonishing character I have ever met.

On that Sunday morning I was shown into Maxwell's private suite at the top of the Maxwell Communications building in Fetter Lane, and given a cup of coffee. A few minutes later the big man turned up, looking very relaxed in a summer shirt, but holding his back.

'This is too much of playing at bloody football.'

We both laughed. I quickly came to the point. We had been seeking to get a Rights issue away, but had failed, and I was of the opinion that the help of a major investor might do the trick. I also told him about our discussions with the Mindo Group, without naming them. I outlined a proposal for him to underwrite a Rights issue at £1.30 per share, which would have had the effect of injecting £13.24 million cash directly into the plc. I had assessed the company's debts at around £12 million, and if Maxwell provided this money it would clear the slate and help us to go forward.

He seemed reasonably interested, but, naturally, was not prepared to make any commitment. In any case he said: 'I shall have to speak to Kevin before I can tell you my thoughts on this.' Before I left we discussed the immediate advantages of a deal. He thought his coming in as a major shareholder might do a lot of good to Tottenham, and I was thinking of what Tottenham might get from Derby County. 'I tell you what else would be very interesting if we could do a deal. You've got a couple of very good players at Derby County,' I said, meaning Mark Wright and Dean Saunders. Maxwell, who reportedly had lost interest in Derby County, immediately said: 'Well, if you get them, you'd wind up winning the Championship, wouldn't you?' 'That wouldn't be a bad start would it?' I said, and we both laughed.

Gascoigne was fast becoming the 'Gazza' of popular mythology. His well advertised tears at the end of the semi-final against West Germany formed part of modern English football folklore, and at the reception for the team on his return from Rome he had put on large-sized breasts and clowned his way into the hearts of millions. Maxwell asked: 'What about Gascoigne?' I said: 'Yes. We could raise the money by selling Gascoigne tomorrow, but that is not the answer.' He entirely agreed.

Before we parted he gave me his private number and promised to ring me back that evening. I waited by the phone and nothing happened, but on the morning of Tuesday I received a call from Kevin: could he meet me in an hour and a half? Kevin was keen to go ahead, but what worried him was confidentiality. He wanted the discussions to be kept very private and I, aware of the Michael Knighton fiasco, agreed. But I told Kevin that I would have to involve Derek Peter, and he understood that.

My main worry was how Maxwell would invest in Tottenham with his other football interests. He owned Derby County, his family was involved in Oxford and there was also a holding in Reading and Manchester United. Some years before this, Maxwell's attempt to buy Watford from Elton John had led to a major rumpus and was eventually thwarted by the Football League, leaving Maxwell to christen the Management Committee 'the Mismanagement Committee' – a phrase he had borrowed from me. Later, on legal advice, we worked out that the way round this would be to put Maxwell's existing football interests in trust, where he would not be the beneficial owner. Interestingly, the League confirmed that this would have been acceptable.

Maxwell told me that his financial advisers, Smith New Court, would be in touch with me that afternoon to start the paperwork rolling. I left the meeting feeling not a little relieved. I was aware that there were now less than two weeks to raise the money that Barcelona needed in order for us to keep Lineker, but things seemed to be going well with Maxwell and a deal was clearly on the cards.

That afternoon Smith New Court did not ring. And although the next day Stein, after consulting counsel, sent a fax to Kevin Maxwell about a trust scheme, we heard nothing. Seven days passed and there was no word from the Maxwells. It was now 24 July, the Barcelona payment was just over a week away, and I finally wrote to Robert Maxwell: what on earth is going on? Early next morning the telephone rang at home. It was Kevin Maxwell. Could I see him at 10.30?

I could see that Kevin was more than a little flustered. A tall, lean man who has a hungry Cassius look about him, he gave the impression of a man in a hurry. It turned out that Kevin Maxwell had been on holiday, but on receiving my note Robert Maxwell had rung him up and demanded he come back and deal with me. However, Kevin told me, he had to leave the office by 1 pm in order to return to France.

I was just as anxious to get things going. I had cancelled one holiday already, and there was the Lineker payment. Just after our meeting began Kevin rang his advisers, Hill Samuel and Titmuss Sainer and Webb, and asked them to come round immediately. But before they arrived, I outlined the company's current position.

Tottenham had some pressing payments to make. Could the Maxwells make a loan of £1.1 million? 'What security can the company provide?' asked Kevin. 'None I'm afraid,' I replied, 'but I would be quite prepared to give you a personal guarantee for the loan.' 'No, no, we would not be prepared to loan money on an informal basis to friends, and I'm afraid under no circumstances could I accept your personal guarantee,' said Kevin. His answer depressed me terribly. 'But,' he continued, 'I am prepared to consider a strictly arm's-length loan, and on the provision of proper security.'

Soon after this the advisers arrived and provided their own pennyworth of thoughts on the subject. Titmuss Sainer and Webb asked what the rate of interest was. I suggested it should be interest-free, but Kevin Maxwell insisted that there should be a commercial rate. Security was not a problem. My company, the Holborn Property Company, owned a block of shops in King's Road, Chelsea, which was free of any charges. I offered that as security for the loan. Kevin agreed, provided his property people were happy about the value of the security. What we were proposing was a back-to-back loan arrangement. Headington, one of the Maxwells' companies, would be providing a £1.1 million loan to my company, Holborn, and Holborn in turn would provide a loan to Tottenham in order to pay for Lineker and a payment on the Stand.

All this seemed smooth and easy enough. Yet already I had made a big mistake. Earlier in the meeting when Kevin had called in his advisers he suggested I do the same. I turned to Mel Stein of Finers. Football had brought me in close touch with Stein; he had acted on the Waddle and Gascoigne transfers, he had also negotiated the end of the Hummel contract for Tottenham and the joint ventures with Paul Gascoigne and Cockerel Books. Mel had also co-authored the book with Chris Waddle which Cockerel Books had published. I felt I could trust Stein, and this was very important. Robert Maxwell had stressed confidentiality with me, and that morning Kevin had repeated the same message: 'We must keep this very confidential. If the tabloids get hold of this, it'll be dynamite.' I knew from experience that Stein could keep his mouth shut and would not let anything slip out.

But in retrospect the choice of Finers was a mistake. The negotiations were to take me into uncharted waters of the City, its regulations, and the rules that govern the conduct of publicly quoted companies. I knew little about these, and I needed good professional advice which could guide me through the coming rapids. Finers, a fine firm, just did not act as a first-class guide for me.

It has always been my policy to get the best professional advice. There is no point in having a dog and then doing your own barking. Once I had appointed Finers I expected them to tell me whether the course of action being proposed was within the rules, such as the Yellow Book regulations of the Stock Exchange. Although many people at Finers advised me, and that may have been the problem, I felt that I never received the sort of advice I expected from professional advisers.

To be fair, we were working against impossible deadlines. The ticking of the Lineker time-bomb was ever more insistent, and despite our meeting on the 25th, Kevin Maxwell was again proving elusive. Kevin had gone back to France immediately after that meeting, and it was not until 2.30 on 31 July that he finally confirmed that the money was with Titmuss Sainer and Webb. By this time it was very much touch and go whether we could meet the Lineker payment, which was contracted to be made in Barcelona. Finers had to get a bank to stay open late on that Tuesday in order to get a peseta draft prepared. The next day – deadline day, Wednesday 1 August – happened to be a holiday in Spain, and Finers had to make special arrangements with a Spanish legal firm to remain open to accept the money and complete the formalities. An assistant solicitor flew over to Barcelona with the peseta draft.

By this time the Maxwells had also pushed me up against the wire. When I looked at the details of the loan documentation I found that the document I was asked to sign not only had a first charge on the King's Road property but had added a debenture for all the assets of Holborn Property Company and my person-al guarantee. This had never been discussed with the Maxwells and, as we have seen, Kevin had specifically said that he would not accept a personal guarantee from me. I suspect it was one of those things that are now known as Robert Maxwell's tricks. I signed the papers, but with misgivings and a heavy heart.

When the deal came out, it was made to look as if I went to Maxwell for the £1.1 million loan. If that was the only money that Tottenham needed I could have gone to the bank, pledged my King's Road property, and lent the money on to Tottenham. As we have seen, I went to Maxwell because I saw him as a solution to a much bigger problem. The loan was a side-issue which circumstances made into the main issue, and by the time the Barcelona deadline approached, I would not have had time enough to process a loan from the bank. In a way I had boxed myself in, but I had done it in good faith, and what else could I do if Lineker was to be saved? As it was, while the Maxwells had a charge on all the assets of my company, I lent Tottenham the money without asking for any security. Had they gone bust, I was on the hook, not Tottenham.

The next few days were to be tumultuous, and in the light of what happened extremely crucial. Just as Bernstein was flying to Barcelona to make sure we still kept hold of Lineker, I rang Sinclair to tell him of the loan from Holborn to Tottenham. Derek Peter and I held a meeting that day to approve the loan.

It was at this meeting on 1 August that the first of the many problems were created. As Tottenham was a listed public company, any transaction between Tottenham and a director of the company, or a company associated with a director (as Holborn was with me), had to be treated with great care. Section 317 of the 1985 Companies Act provided that a director who had an interest in the transaction must disclose the nature of his interest to the board. Also, the Articles of Association of Tottenham provided that a director who had an interest in a transaction should not take part or be counted in a quorum for the purposes of decisions related to that transaction. This meant that I could not be part of the meeting where the loan had been approved, and therefore the meeting was not proper and the resolutions passed not valid.

As we shall see, a board meeting held two days later would get round this technicality, but there were other problems. As I was to discover later, I was a 'Class 4 party', which sounds vaguely obscene, but turns out to be a technicality with a sting in it. A Class 4 party is any director, substantial shareholder or associate, which also includes a company linked to such a director or substantial shareholder, and the Stock Exchange requires that certain transactions between a listed company and a Class 4 party must be approved by shareholders. Normally a loan given by a Class 4 party to a listed company does not require shareholders' approval unless the company is providing security for the loan. In this case Tottenham provided no security to Holborn – all the security was provided by Holborn (and me) to Headington. However, the Yellow Book, which is the bible of the Stock Exchange, requires the company to keep the relevant Stock Exchange department informed and to find out whether approval is required.

At the time, nobody told me that I should keep the Stock Exchange informed. Finers, as the legal advisers, should have but they didn't. Nor did they tell me the level of discosure I should make about the details of the loan transaction. In fact they drafted the relevant Board Minutes.

As we have seen, Kevin Maxwell insisted on a commercial rate of interest. Finers advised that there should be a half per cent difference between the interest rate paid by Holborn to Headington and the rate paid by Tottenham to Holborn, to ensure that there was a commercial reason for Holborn to enter into the transaction. This half per cent in 'turn' was to compensate Holborn for the fact that it (along with me) was taking on the full risk of Tottenham not repaying the loan, as Holborn received *no* security from Tottenham but gave *full*, security to Headington. Later, much was made of this half per cent 'turn' and the fact that I had not told the other directors about it, including Derek Peter.

At that stage all this was part of the desperate need to get the money to pay for Lineker. I saw these as details, with the legal advisers – and there was no dearth of legal muscle, with Titmuss Sainer and Webb on the side of the Maxwells and Finers on the company's – telling me how exactly these arrangements would be negotiated. I had not made the arrangements in order to make a half per cent turn, or £5,500 p.a. That was quite ridiculous. If getting the money to save Lineker meant making the Maxwell deal, then I was prepared to do it. I felt that Finers' failure to advise me on the formalities I had to observe in order to be, and appear to be, above board caused the problems.

The negotiation of the Lineker loan was, of course, part of the more complex and wider issue of trying to raise money for Tottenham. The Maxwells were to act as underwriters to a Rights issue, but this was not a conventional Rights issue. Normally an underwriter acts as a sort of insurance in case investors do not take up their Rights. In this case the Maxwells were going to take quite a big stake in Tottenham, and some or all of the directors would renounce their rights in favour of them. However, Robert Maxwell made it clear that he did not want all the stocks, and he was also very keen that I should continue to look after the club. 'Uncle Bob', as I had christened him, had told me that he would not have time to involve himself in the company and would not be on the board.

The negotiations for the Rights issue were even more complicated than the loan arrangement. There were four sticking points: the Maxwells wanted a 25.5 per cent minimum holding; they wanted 51 per cent of the shareholders to approve this in advance; they wanted Tottenham to pay the underwriting costs; and they wanted a formula to be worked out whereby if the 25.5 per cent minimum was not obtained it should be made up in some way by me and the other directors.

On the afternoon of 3 August, after I had come back from lunch with a few of the staff at Tottenham, I had a message to ring Robert Maxwell. I explained to him the outstanding points, but he seemed keen to settle them fast and, obviously prodded by him, I worked out a deal with Kevin. It was agreed that the Maxwells would have a 25.1 per cent minimum holding, that they would be happy to go ahead initially with 35 per cent shareholder approval, but that Tottenham would not pay the underwriting costs. As far as I was concerned this was now a firm proposal that could go to the Tottenham board. It was about 5.40 that Friday afternoon, and I wanted a board meeting held as soon as possible.

Derek Peter had already warned the directors that there could well be a board meeting at very short notice and that they should make themselves available some time on Friday evening. A week or so earlier, Paul Bobroff had gone on holiday to the South of France. I knew where he was, and the moment I put down the phone to the lawyers I rang him at his hotel. There was a good chance of getting him: France was an hour ahead of London, it would be twenty to seven, and perhaps he would be in his room preparing to go out to dinner. But there was no answer. I left a message with the concierge. At 7.15 the directors gathered in my office in the West End to consider the proposal. At Tony Berry's suggestion I took the Chair and began explaining what had happened.

'As you know,' I informed them, 'I have been in discussion with a potential underwriter, and I now need your authority to go ahead and sign an agreement which will enable us to receive an offer that the board members can then consider. Of course, a "due diligence" process has to be undertaken, but I must say I see that as a formality, as they have been told the company's financial position. No doubt you will want to know who the underwriter is, and you will know who he is. But at this moment I cannot tell you. The underwriter has requested that his name be kept confidential until he is ready to make an offer for you to consider. At that stage you will have the opportunity to either recommend it to shareholders or not, but until then, I have promised to keep his name confidential. You may think he is being a bit paranoid about confidentiality, but from my experience, particularly of football, I feel there is some merit to what he is saying. So for the moment, I cannot tell you who he is, but once everything is ready for your recommendation to shareholders, then, of course, you will know his name.'

The board heard what I had to say with the sense of relief that the besieged at Mafeking must have felt when rescue came. For months, almost a year, we had struggled with the problems of raising money. Now it seemed that we had at last secured it, there was almost a sense of elation among the board members. True, nobody quite jumped up from their seats and waved their arms as they would have done had Tottenham scored a goal, but all round the table there was that same feeling of relief.

Everyone on the board knew what our financial situation was, and how critical it was to get money to pay Barcelona. But, as so often, none of them had done anything. They had left it to me. The feeling of relief at my success was evident. Later, when the storm blew up and I was painted as the villain, a few of them stepped in to defend me. I was to discover that the board of a company consists of both sheep and lions, and while I would not quite like to say that I am a lion, it is astonishing how many sheep there are.

The board quickly authorised me to pursue a reasonable Rights issue and try and raise not less than £3 million at a share price of not less than £1. So these were bottom-line figures which were more or less plucked out of the blue. But anything lower than that would hardly have been worth doing. In my commitment letter to Maxwell I was, of course, hoping to raise much more, but I did not feel I could tell that to the board at this stage when I was not yet sure that the deal would go ahead. In any case I did tell them that I hoped to have much better terms.

To emphasise the fact that the whole thing was still very much subject to the board's recommendation to shareholders, a further meeting was pencilled in for 29 August. I felt that this would give us sufficient time to get the Maxwells to an unconditional stage, which was when the entire details could be revealed. I had seen the 3 August meeting as one where I was telling the board that I had got the fish on the hook, but that it had not yet been landed.

Just before the board meeting, at about 7.15, along with some of the other directors I had once again tried to get hold of Bobroff. It was a replay of my previous efforts. He was not there, and I left a message with the concierge to ask him to ring me. Now in law I did not have to contact him. More than a century ago the Halifax Sugar Refinery Company Limited v. Franklin case had established that a director who was abroad did not have to get notice of board meetings, unless the articles of the company specifically said so. Our articles did not. In any case at Tottenham we operated a fairly informal arrangement for meetings, but it was always understood that a board meeting would be held on the first Wednesday of each month. Bobroff had gone on holiday knowing that a board meeting would be held on the 1st, so I was in law and in practice quite in the clear.

On Monday 6 August, having signed the commitment letter and the confidentiality letter, something the Maxwells were very keen on, I finally left for Monaco on holiday. It wasn't until that evening that I managed to speak to Bobroff. I immediately sensed from the tone of his voice that he was extremely suspicious and feeling that he had been left out. I explained: 'We had a meeting on Friday and we tried to contact you.' He said: 'I know you did. What's it all about?' It seems that he had discovered about the meeting in rather a curious way. He had been talking to one of his advisers, Stewart Millman at BZW, regarding his own company, Markheath Securities, when he was told that Millman was about to meet Peter and Finers about a Spurs matter. Bobroff immediately telephoned Peter to find out what was happening, and discovered the 3 August meeting.

Bobroff wanted to know from me who I was talking to. This I could not reveal, but at his insistence I agreed to ring Kevin Maxwell and ask whether he would be prepared for me to tell Bobroff their name. I rang Kevin but he would not relent.

Until this point Bobroff had pretty much got nowhere in finding investors to rescue us from our precarious position – let alone to find the money we needed to pay Barcelona for

Lineker. But now he seemed to be a hive of activity. I later learned that two days after our conversation he instructed his lawyers Clifford Chance to advise him about his personal rights and then rang Peter to get a copy of the loan agreement.

I returned from holiday on the 13th to find that the lawyers had got into another mess. The confidentiality undertaking that I had signed along with Peter on the 3rd now had to be redrafted and an amended version was signed. We were now in some considerable stew. Clifford Chance was writing to Peter Jay at Finers expressing Bobroff's concern about what was happening. I myself was not very happy with BZW's involvement. They after all acted for Bobroff, and I felt there was a conflict of interest. Bobroff and I agreed that I would try to get somebody else, and contact was made with Smith New Court. But their Chairman, Michael Richardson, was one of Maxwell's oldest City friends; they advised him on many issues and could not work for us.

In the meantime the deal with Maxwell was going nowhere. On 27 July Finers had received 'due diligence' questions from the Maxwells. These were being processed rather slowly by Derek Peter, who was on the point of leaving and whose father had recently died, but I had made it clear to him that no confidential financial information should be given to the Maxwells until I had the unanimous approval of the board. This, with Bobroff still seeking to shore up his own personal position, was clearly not obtainable.

It was Monday 20 August when Bobroff finally relented and agreed to allow the matter to proceed on a confidential basis. I now felt we could provide the Maxwells with the information they needed so that we could get the deal under way.

But I was to discover during that year that every upswing was countered by a downswing. That afternoon I received a telephone call at my flat in Monaco, where I had gone for a few days, from a secretary at Maxwell's office. She asked me if I had a fax at the flat, as Maxwell wanted to send me a letter. In those days I didn't, and I suggested that she read me the letter over the telephone. She declined. The next morning at about 10 o'clock I received a call from Robert Maxwell. He said: 'Irving, we think that your financial position is a lot worse than you have led us to believe. You won't give us any information to allow us to start our due diligence, and we can only assume that you are hiding something, and therefore unfortunately we are dropping out.'

Both what he said and the tone in which he said it shocked me. Maxwell also spoke as if there was a time limit to the whole thing, but in my mind there wasn't – we had never discussed any dates about finalising the deal, or getting the directors to approve it – and I said: 'Uncle Bob, it is not worse than you think. It's exactly as you have been led to believe, and I am sure that we will be in a position very very quickly to let you have as much information as is possible.' I immediately rang Peter and told him to get the information to Finers so that they could relay it to Titmuss Sainer and Webb. This was done. That afternoon at about 1 o'clock I rang Maxwell to say that he had all the information he needed. He promised to try and reinstate the deal. I heard nothing from him for the next couple of days.

At about 8 pm on 23 August the telephone rang and it was the secretary from Maxwell's office asking again whether I had a fax. They then took down the address of my flat in Monaco and a letter was faxed to Maxwell's office in Antibes. At about 10 pm that evening a lady chauffeur arrived at my flat with two faxed letters from Headington Investments signed by Robert Maxwell dated 20 and 21 August. They confirmed that he was now not willing to proceed with the deal.

True, we had delayed matters – a delay caused by Bobroff's suspicions and what I saw as his desire to protect his own interests. But as I thought about it I began to smell a rat. Something was not right in the Maxwell world. With hindsight I believe the turning-point came on the night of 2 August. That was when Saddam Hussein's troops poured into Kuwait, invading that little country. The invasion of Kuwait led to a deepening of recession, a worldwide phenomenon not merely confined to the UK. Maxwell, already under pressure, was now really under the cosh, and did not dare to be seen, at least in the eyes of his bankers, squandering £13.24 million on what to most people must have seemed a whim.

When I first heard that he had withdrawn, the immediate thought that crossed my mind was that he was in trouble, but at that stage in August 1990, Robert Maxwell in trouble seemed so improbable that I laughed away the thought. Remember, Maxwell was still riding very high, and supposedly was one of the richest men in England. In Maxwell's world, where deals involving hundreds of millions of pounds were commonplace, we were being let down over a deal worth £13.24 million, which I thought was a mere drop in the ocean to him. The previous year, in one of the biggest deals of its kind, he had bought Macmillan, the American publishers, for around $2 billion. With hindsight, that deal was one too many for Maxwell, but that was not apparent to the outside world.

By now the season had started. I travelled with the directors on a flight from Luton to Sunderland for a Spurs away match, and told Sinclair and Berry that we didn't have a deal. A few days later, on 5 September, we had our regular board meeting, and for the first time since Maxwell appeared on the scene Bobroff was present. I'm afraid it degenerated into something of a shouting match. I felt that Bobroff's ambivalence and the spokes he put in the wheel had caused a two-week delay in Maxwell getting the information he wanted. Perhaps, as I said, the Kuwait invasion had destabilised Maxwell's world, and even if we had got the information to him in time, he might still have reneged. But Bobroff's obstructive stance, full of questions and suspicions, had not helped. I told him so at the meeting, and Bobroff accused me of trying to keep him in the dark. The minutes of the 3 August meeting lay on the table without being approved.

The next day Bobroff rang me in some panic. He had heard from his City contacts that our deal with Maxwell was about to be revealed in the *Sunday Times*. Indeed, even as Bobroff and I had argued at our board meeting, on the golf course at Wentworth Jeff Randall, the City Editor of the *Sunday Times*, was being provided with some information that would blow the story about our dealings with Maxwell – and provide him with one of the greatest scoops of his distinguished journalistic career. For weeks I had striven to observe the confidentiality clause imposed by Maxwell: now the world would be invited to witness the drama and the trauma that we were experiencing at Spurs.

13 | WHEN THE UNDERWRITER BECAME THE UNDERTAKER

'Listen, I don't give a shit about the company, I'm only interested in my own position here.'

– Paul Bobroff.

To this day I'm not sure how Jeff Randall got his scoop. Roy Greenslade, who edited the *Daily Mirror* for Maxwell and has written a book about him, suggests that Maxwell sent the story to Randall. Randall denies it and has given me a version of how he got the story. He claims that he had two sources, one the chief executive of a merchant bank, the other a young stockbroker. The chief executive, who apparently owed Randall some favour, told him the story at a cocktail party, and the stockbroker then confirmed the details on the golf course at Wentworth. Not surprisingly, Jeff has consistently refused to name his sources, as any good journalist would, but I wonder if he told me this version in order to remove any suspicions from Philip Green, who, as we have seen, was close to several members of the board and was also close to Jeff Randall.

Before he went to press, Randall did confront Maxwell with the story and confirmed it with him. I believe he had two conversations with him, one on the Thursday and then again on the Saturday morning, when Maxwell is supposed to have said: 'Young man, you've got a notable scoop.'

That very same morning Maxwell had also rung me about a story that had appeared in the *Guardian* that day. Ian Ridley, then working for the *Guardian*, had examined Maxwell's decision to put Derby County up for sale and then speculated on where he might invest. Liverpool, Everton and Arsenal were out, so that left Manchester United and Tottenham among the big clubs. In 1984 Maxwell had intended to buy Martin Edwards's 51 per cent share in Manchester United, and Ridley wrote: 'Tottenham might look a more attractive proposition to him. As they are a publicly quoted company any bids would have to be put before the shareholders.' Then, after mentioning my name and the other major shareholders, Bobroff and Berry, Ridley said: 'While the Tottenham supporters, who own a total of 3 per cent of the shares, might be in principle against Maxwell at their club, an injection of capital for signing new players is especially required.'

Ridley felt that owning Spurs would enable Maxwell to project the sort of pan-European image he was seeking: there was the *European* newspaper that he had founded, and it might also provide an entrée into the Continental superleaguers led by people like Silvio Berlusconi, who owns AC Milan. It was said that Maxwell had recently met Berlusconi.

Maxwell's reaction to the piece was to ask me: 'Irving, have you seen the *Guardian* story? Are you responsible for this leak?' 'Not at all,' I replied. 'Why should I go around telling the *Guardian*, or anyone else, what you are doing?'

Maxwell accepted my assurances, and of course at that stage I did not know about his conversations with Randall. But looking back I can see what Captain Bob was up to. His confirmation had been vital. Without it, I am quite sure, Jeff could not have run such a story. But having provided the legs for Randall's story, Maxwell was now trying to turn the tables and suggest that it was me who had leaked something to the Press.

As it happened, on that Saturday we were playing Derby County at home. By now nearly all the board members were aware that the next day the *Sunday Times* was going to spill the beans about our negotiations with Maxwell. Bobroff had called a board meeting just before the match, and as soon as it began Bobroff laid his cards on the table. He knew that the *Sunday Times* was going to run an article and he knew that the underwriter was Maxwell. I again felt helpless. I was still bound by the confidentiality agreement with Maxwell, and said I could neither confirm nor deny whether Robert Maxwell was the underwriter I was talking to.

The meeting ended inconclusively, barely containing the simmering tensions between Bobroff and me, although the match ended more happily: Tottenham defeated Derby by three goals to nil. The next morning I hurried to get the papers and there, on the front page of the sports section of the *Sunday Times* (a separate section in the pre-recession era), was splashed Randall's great scoop. He had got almost all the details right, except that he did not know why I had had to negotiate alone with Maxwell. The Lineker financial time-bomb still remained a secret – but not for long.

Randall, a West Ham supporter, combined his knowledge of football with his undoubted experience of business to write the classic football/business story, and the *Sunday Times* were smart enough to realise that this was a major piece of news. The papers had barely landed on people's doorsteps that morning when my phone started ringing. And it didn't stop. Amid this flurry of calls there was one from Robert Maxwell. He had no clue as to how Randall had got the story. He was suggesting that perhaps somebody from Tottenham had leaked it, but was still insisting that I was bound by the confidentiality agreement.

I could not help but admire the man's audacity: it was the height of cheek for Robert Maxwell to say that I was still bound by the confidentiality agreement when his name was now known to millions. But at that stage I did not think so. Call it old-fashioned, if you like, but when I make an agreement I honour it, and I did feel honour-bound to Maxwell. What I didn't realise was that the underwriter was threatening to become the undertaker – at least as far as I was concerned.

The *Sunday Times* story changed everything. My years at Tottenham had inured me to the back-page exclusive, but these had been football stories, speculating about a player who might be transferred, or a Manager who might be on the move. Jeff Randall's story was different. It combined football with business, and led to the very heart of the unique structure Tottenham had: a football club that was also a listed company. If Tottenham had been a public company without being a football club then Randall's story would hardly have had the legs to cross the road. But our status as a football club – and one of this country's greatest – gave it a very special emotional charge, and our position as a public company provided the almost maddening complexity. Running Tottenham Hotspur Football Club, I was aware of the pressures of the job, the incessant phone calls, the almost unending demands on my time. But now I was sucked back into the quagmire of meetings, an endless stream of City lawyers, City advisers, City merchant banks, all proffering their advice and all contradicting each other. It was long after that Sunday that I realised that Jeff Randall's story had started my hellish year. And at every turn it seemed Paul Bobroff was waiting.

Even before the Randall story broke, I had been in discussions with the lawyers about Maxwell's failure to proceed with the Rights issue. Finers had asked Michael Crystal and Gavin Lightman, both QCs, to advise, and on Monday morning I went with Peter Jay to have a conference with Lightman. Meanwhile Bobroff was a hive of activity. He had telephoned Jay and insisted on receiving all the information. Finers gave him some details, but not the copies of the loan agreement between Headington, myself and Tottenham. However, that Monday evening when the Tottenham board met, with Finers, Lightman and other advisers present, not only did I confirm that Maxwell was the underwriter but Bobroff was also given copies of the loan document.

Finers, advised by Lightman, also spent some time drafting a letter that I was supposed to send to Maxwell on what we could now do, given that he was backing out of the deal. But the letter was not sent and the consensus of the board was that if we could do a deal with Maxwell we should still go for one. Even Bobroff agreed. I was still aggrieved by his manoeuvring, which I felt had cost us a previous deal, but I was willing to give it a try. At 8 o'clock the next day I went to see Robert and Kevin.

I immediately felt that father and son were not on the same wavelength. While Robert appeared to be still keen on the deal, Kevin was not so sure. The more I looked at Kevin's face and listened to what he was saying, the more keenly I sensed that he didn't want the Rights issue to go ahead. However, I left the meeting on the understanding that if I could get the Tottenham board to agree then Robert Maxwell might still be prepared to go ahead.

I reported all this to the board, which, by now, was almost in continuous session. Having met the previous night it had started another meeting at 11.30 that morning. It agreed that Bobroff and I should form a two-man negotiating committee to discuss matters with Maxwell, with Tony Berry as first reserve should either Bobroff or I not be available.

By now the board was concerned with an even more pressing issue: the requirement that the Stock Exchange imposes on public companies. The fact that Tottenham were negotiating a

Rights issue was not something shareholders should have read with their Sunday morning muesli. Of course, Tottenham as a public company was a bit of a myth. The big financial institutions, the insurance companies and pension funds who own most of the shares in public companies did not own many shares of Tottenham Hotspur, apart from Prolific, which had 4.27 per cent, and Sun Life Pensions with 3.27 per cent. Bobroff, Berry and myself between ourselves owned very nearly 50 per cent of the company. Twenty per cent of Tottenham was held by the public, but these were supporters, most of whom held a couple of shares almost as a souvenir. I had heard stories that when Tottenham had floated some had bought a single share and framed it. This had caused us embarrassment when we declared our first dividend as a public company. Individual dividend cheques were for 4 or 5p, and some of the shareholders returned the cheques saying that the club probably needed the money more than they did. But by law we had to send them out, and the postage cost of sending many of the dividends was more than what the cheques were worth.

However, Stock Exchange formalities had to be met, and the Stock Exchange was insistent that we put out a statement explaining what had been going on. So I spent much of that Tuesday with the board, the lawyers and BZW, trying to draft a Press release which would satisfy the Stock Exchange. The professionals had also been in touch with Maxwell about the Press release and agreed that he would be consulted before we issued it, so that we could agree on the wording. I must say I have never worked harder on a couple of sheets of paper. It was 10 o'clock that night before we had finally got the Press release together. BZW had already alerted the Stock Exchange about what we were going to say, and I returned to my house in Regent's Park exhausted, drained, but pleased that we appeared to have solved one problem.

As I said, though, from now on nothing was going to be simple, and I was soon to realise that.

At ten past one in the morning my telephone rang. It was Isobel Macpherson of BZW, who had been dealing with the Press release.

'I am sorry to disturb you so late, but I'm afraid we've got a problem.'

'What's the problem?' I asked, still struggling to figure out where I was and what the time was.

'I'm afraid Headington are not accepting our wording.'

'What wording?'

'Well, the other side are saying that it is not quite true that the Maxwells insisted on having a confidentiality clause. They are saying that it was you who wanted a confidentiality clause.'

Her words jolted me, and the last trace of sleep now vanished. I had never insisted on a confidentiality clause. Robert had spoken to me about confidentiality at our very first meeting, and Kevin had reinforced it. My recollection of this was later to be backed up by the lawyers from Finers who have all confirmed that it was the Maxwells who had initiated the whole business of confidentiality.

I suppose I should have made an issue of it there and then, but it was ten past one in the morning at the end of a long, tortuous day, and I just did not know what to think. The thought of two conflicting Press releases being issued, one by us and one by Robert Maxwell, seemed too ghastly to contemplate. I knew we had to agree and issue a Press release that night. For the last two days the Stock Exchange had been screaming blue murder at us, and as a public company we just could not hold out any longer. I was also still hopeful of a deal with Maxwell. I did not want to antagonise him. I could not see any other way of raising the money for the Rights issue – money that we desperately needed if we were to get things right at Tottenham. I thought, if we give in to Robert now we can still get help from him at a later stage.

'Oh, really,' I said to Isobel. 'All right. If the Maxwells are saying that I insisted on the confidentiality clause, then agree to it. It is very important we get the Press release out.'

What I didn't realise was that in making this concession to Maxwell, a concession made in the best interests of Tottenham, I was actually digging my own grave. In 1982 I had made a big mistake by not accepting Bobroff's offer to sell his shares to me. Now by publicly accepting the Maxwell lie I was providing Bobroff with a wonderful opportunity to continue his machinations.

Bobroff had already nailed his colours to the mast. On that Tuesday afternoon, in what was to become a famous incident, he had revealed his true feelings. As he and the solicitors from Finers argued about something, Bobroff, in a fit of rage, suddenly turned on them and said: 'Listen, I don't give a shit about the company. I'm only interested in my own position here.'

That expression of feeling came as no big surprise to me. I had worked with the man long enough to know how he saw his position at Tottenham. But Bobroff would still surprise me in the way he manipulated things. This was to become evident within less than twenty-four hours. He had called a board meeting for the next day, a Wednesday, in his office in the West End at 3 o'clock in the afternoon. But when I arrived, along with the rest of the board, there was no sign of Bobroff. He finally arrived at 3.25, along with BZW. As I was walking into Bobroff's office somebody walked past me saying: 'Good luck. You'll need it.' I don't know who he was and I had never met him before, but he must have been privy to the pressures Bobroff was about to exert on me and the rest of the board.

The twenty-five-minute delay was because Bobroff had been meeting with BZW. They had been considering the Press release and the fact that on Maxwell's insistence I had had to change it. They seemed to feel that the truth about the confidentiality clause had not come out: had the Maxwells insisted on it or had I been the instigator? BZW felt that there should be a full investigation into what had actually taken place in my negotiations with Maxwell, and said that they had a very reputable firm of City solicitors, Ashurst Morris Crisp, waiting downstairs ready to start the investigation once the board agreed to it. Bobroff chipped in saying: 'Well, if we don't do this ourselves, the Stock Exchange will do it for us.'

There were not too many around the boardroom table who were convinced by this Bobroff argument, but we agreed that such an investigation could do no harm. My conscience was clear, I had nothing to hide in my dealings with Maxwell or with the board, and I readily agreed that Ashurst Morris Crisp should rake through the ashes and find out exactly what had happened. Bobroff's satisfaction at the board approval for the Ashurst Morris Crisp report was evident.

It was only later that I learned the lengths that Bobroff had gone to in order to get Ashurst Morris Crisp involved. At the board meeting the impression was created that it was BZW, our financial advisers, who were insisting on the investigation. Bobroff, the good conscientious chairman of a public company, was merely heeding the arguments of his financial advisers. But when BZW had to produce the minutes of their meeting with Bobroff it became clear that it was Bobroff who had engineered the idea of an independent investigation. The minutes reveal that Bobroff suggested there should be such a report: he started the move, BZW merely ran with the ball. However, an independent investigation was just the first part of the Bobroff offensive. The next move came the following morning at 8.15.

The phone rang and it was Bobroff. 'Can I come and see you?' he asked.

'Sure,' I said.

Within forty-five minutes he was at my house. We had barely exchanged pleasantries and he had just sat down when he came to the point. 'I think you should resign from the company.'

I was not quite as taken aback by this demand from Bobroff as when he had made it a year earlier after the Waddle transfer. But I was still incensed. 'Why on earth should I resign from the company?' I asked. 'I have done nothing wrong. All I have tried to do is solve the problems and take the company forwards, not backwards.'

Bobroff was adamant. 'I think you should resign.'

It was clear that he saw this as his best chance of getting rid of me. Since the *Sunday Times* story the Press had been full of the problems of Tottenham, speculating that we might have violated not only City rules but also Football League rules, and Bobroff must have felt that he could use the handle of the Ashurst Morris Crisp report to lever me out of Tottenham. But when I refused to resign he finally said: 'All right. I suggest you go and see your solicitors and see what they have to say.'

I saw no harm in that, and that very afternoon arranged to meet a senior corporate partner of Berwin Leighton. His advice was unequivocal: under no circumstances must you resign. Resignation could be an admission of guilt. I did not leave the offices of Berwin Leighton until ten that night, and by then my mind was clear. I might have made some mistakes in my negotiations with Maxwell, there might even have been some technical breaches of City rules, but they had all been done in good faith and with solicitors guiding me. But for my negotiations with Maxwell and the loan, Lineker would be back at Barcelona and Tottenham in an even greater mess. I had nothing to hide and nothing to be ashamed of.

The next day there was to be another board meeting, this time at Douglas Alexiou's offices, which were also in the West End. We all recognised that this was going to be a crunch board meeting. At the Wednesday meeting BZW had told us that if we went against their advice they would resign. So there was the question of whether we would have to appoint new financial advisers. And, of course, there was the duel between Bobroff and me. This time it would be one to the death.

I would not describe anyone on the board as a friend of Bobroff. Douglas, Frank and Tony respected him as a good City operator but had always been wary of him. Now they shared my anger when I told them that the previous day Bobroff had come to my house and asked me to resign. I also decided to make my feelings about the diversification very clear. When we embarked on it, we had told the world that this would be a method of strengthening the football club, providing money so that we could buy players and take Tottenham Hotspur into the big league of the Continental clubs. But now the diversification was draining the life blood out of the team and into the football club without keeping the whole thing together. 'There is no doubt,' I said, 'that the diversification has been a disaster. We have to recognise it and get out of it as soon as possible. We are a football club, that is what we are in business for, so let's concentrate on football and forget about all these other things.'

Even now Bobroff couldn't see, or at least wouldn't admit, that it was the leisure aspects of the public company that had got us into this mess. At times the argument between us across the boardroom had aspects of the classic Hardy versus Laurel scenes, with me as Hardy telling Laurel Bobroff: 'Look at the mess you've got us into,' except that in physical terms I am more Laurel and Bobroff more Hardy. Nor was there any humour in these exchanges. It is quite the most heated meeting I have ever attended. I certainly did not pull any punches.

At some stage I think it was Douglas Alexiou who suggested that it might be possible to have a quick word with Bobroff and get him to go quietly. But clearly this was not on, and eventually we had a short break and Douglas, Tony Berry and I retired to another room. There was no doubt that we could not avoid the Tottenham boardroom split becoming public. We decided to propose a vote of no confidence in Bobroff. We had the votes: although Frank Sinclair was not present he had given his proxy to Douglas, and that meant four in favour against Bobroff's lone dissenting voice. As soon as the meeting restarted a vote of no confidence was proposed and Bobroff, much to his fury, was voted out as Chairman. Douglas took over as acting Chairman, and I felt that at last we were getting somewhere. Eight years before, when I had bought into Tottenham, Bobroff had offered me his shares and I made the cardinal mistake of turning him down. Now he was gone as Chairman, and while he still retained his near 10 per cent, I felt we had a better basis for getting things done on the board. That night BZW resigned, so Tottenham now had to find new financial advisers.

I also still felt that we could do a deal with Maxwell. Call this optimism if you like, call it stupidity, but at this stage in September 1990 Maxwell still appeared to be riding very high. The Mirror Group newspapers had just been floated on the market, and some of the biggest and best names in the City, including NatWest, Hill Samuel and Rothschild, were acting as his bankers and advisers. Finers' preliminary research, when I was talking to Maxwell, had revealed that Headington Investments had uncharged assets of some £80 million, and in the absence of any other fairy godmother Maxwell still seemed the best one around. Nor was he a reluctant bridegroom. Since the first story had broken in the *Sunday Times,* Maxwell had used the *Daily Mirror*, and Harry Harris, to carry on his own propaganda on this issue. It had been done in inimitable Maxwell style, with regular war bulletins printed on the back pages of the *Mirror*, the simple message being: I am prepared to help Spurs, if the Spurs board can get their act together.

Harry, who had been sitting on the story but who had been chained by Maxwell, was now unleashed and Maxwell said: 'I am flashing the yellow card at those involved in squabbles. It is inconceivable that I or anybody else would entertain having discussions about a Rights issue or becoming involved in any way with a club where some of the board are behaving like children.' Harry made it clear that the yellow card was for Bobroff, and Maxwell told him privately: 'I want Bobroff to accept me or I want him out of the way.'

All this meant that the board meeting was one of the most high-profile in Tottenham's history. As I emerged from Douglas's office I could see photographers waiting on the pavement outside, and that weekend the *Sunday Times* carried a photograph of me and another of Bobroff coming out after me. Like all good journalists Jeff Randall had been trying to follow up his scoop – and he had another interesting twist to the story. He had discovered that the loan I had negotiated with Maxwell was for the payment to Barcelona for Lineker. This fact had not come out as yet. I don't know where Jeff got the story, but I'm sure that the phone lines to his offices in Wapping were hot with calls from various people connected with Tottenham. He has since told me that some of the directors at Tottenham were only too eager to talk to him, giving an almost blow-by-blow account of what was happening.

I must say I did speak to Jeff as well, but this was always on the basis of him ringing me up trying to confirm certain things rather than me initiating the calls. I'm not sure other board members were quite so scrupulous. Subsequent to the *Sunday Times* article the Tottenham–Maxwell saga received almost daily Press coverage, much of which, I believe, was fuelled by a source or sources close to the board of directors. Undoubtedly this hindered the company's attempts to address fundamental urgent business issues, heightened the legitimate concern of bodies such as the Stock Exchange, and damaged the company.

We were pitted against Maxwell, who of course liked nothing better than to have his photograph on the front page of every newspaper going, and whose ownership of the *Daily Mirror* ensured that he could have it on at least one of the mass-selling tabloids. Nobody else connected with football has ever, to my knowledge, courted such publicity. But I knew other chairmen had their own means of making their views known to the wider world. Some had close links with journalists, and they used them to feed information not only about their clubs but, often, about their rivals. I had never cultivated the Press. I realised journalists had a function to perform, but the sort of exclusives trailed on the back pages of the mass-selling tabloids often left me cold – not least because there was nothing very exclusive about them, and because they very rarely contained anything that I did not already know.

The only journalist I was close to was Harry Harris. He had been on the local paper at Tottenham and shared my deep love for the club. Almost from the beginning we got on very well. Harry, by this time, was the chief football writer of the *Daily Mirror*, which meant that, like all Maxwell employees, he was at the beck and call of Captain Bob. How Harry balanced Maxwell's diktats with his own journalistic needs is a story that he must tell one day himself, but all I can say is that despite everything I went through with Maxwell and others, my friendship with Harry remained unimpaired. If anything I came away appreciating how well he understood my own, and Tottenham's, predicament.

I suppose at this stage Tottenham must have given the appearance of a beleaguered fortress. Outside, the modern equivalent of Attila the Hun's marauding armies – the journalists and photographers – were clamouring for news and presenting their views on what might happen. Inside there was a great deal of activity. BZW's resignation meant that I had to find a financial adviser. On the short-list were English Trust, Lloyds Merchant Bank, and Brown Shipley. I was much taken by the latter's chief executive, John Van Kuffeler, who introduced me to Jeremy Knight and Roland Cornish. Although Lloyds Merchant Bank and English Trust, I'm sure, could have done just as good a job, on my recommendation the board decided to go with Brown Shipley. The following day we had a home match and Douglas invited John and his wife and daughter to be guests of the board. This augured well, and so it proved to be.

Meanwhile the minions from Ashurst Morris Crisp were floating around trying to piece together what had happened. They were meeting various members of the board and other relevant people and taking long statements. At 11 am on 18 September one of their representatives arrived at my offices at Maddox Street and spent nearly the whole day quizzing me about what had happened: when I had first approached Maxwell, the nature of our discussions, what I had told Bobroff and, of course, the basis of the confidentiality clause. The Stock Exchange had suspended our shares, and Spurs as a public company were in no-man's-land. The Exchange wanted to have a detailed working capital statement from us to show that we had adequate funding facilities in place, but Midland refused to give us a long-term facility. Whenever we asked they kept asking for our plans to reduce the overdraft. This was well over £8 million, and edging towards the double-figure mark.

Peter Robinson of Berwin Leighton was now acting as my personal adviser, and I must say that working with him was one of the few good things to emerge during that bleak period. As meeting followed meeting, some lasting late into the night and one until 3.30 in the morning, Peter guided me through the legal minefield.

One of the things that the legal boffins of Ashurst Morris Crisp were very concerned about was this wretched business of the confidentiality agreement. I and Derek Peter had signed two versions of this undertaking. The first one, signed on 3 August, ensured that we would not disclose details to 'any third party (other than fellow directors of Napoel plc)', Napoel being the codename given to Tottenham. I do not now remember when I signed it: it was either the 3rd or 6th of August. In any case it was replaced by a version signed on 14 August which said that the details could not be disclosed even to the directors.

I had no problem with either version. My understanding was that I had to keep mum about my negotiations with Maxwell until the final terms were ready, and keeping mum meant not telling anybody, even my fellow directors, until it came to a formal presentation to the board. I was not alone in this understanding. It was also the recollection of Derek Peter and, very significantly, of all the solicitors from Finers. With hindsight, and in the light of the constant leakage to the Press from sources very close to the board after the *Sunday Times* exposé, it is clear that – ironic as it may seem – Maxwell was right to insist on complete confidentiality. But hindsight comes after the match.

At that stage, a little over a month after these agreements had been signed, Ashurst Morris Crisp had arrived on the scene, but instead of finding it easy to reconstruct what had happened, they found themselves like archaeologists at a dig, trying to reassemble part of an ancient civilisation. Every fragment of bone, metal or structure suggested a completely new version. As often happens, individuals had different recollections of the same events, and there had been any number of letters, memos, commitment letters and faxes backwards and forwards between Finers and Titmuss Sainer and Webb.

The report was presented to the board in early October. I suspected that Bobroff would have damned me if he could with the report. It did not work out that way. Later on, I was criticised for not fully disclosing to the board details of Maxwell's loan to Holborn and Holborn's loan to Tottenham – the loan that kept Lineker at the club. I was also criticised for not properly disclosing when the various confidentiality agreements were signed, and for signing an underwriting letter with Maxwell without proper authority. However, the two crucial points that were accepted were, first, that all the problems would have been avoided had I received the benefit of professional advice from advisers experienced in dealing with public companies; second, and most important, that I had always acted with the best interests of Tottenham in mind.

The issue of the report did mark a personal nadir in my fortunes. On 19 October, the Stock Exchange suspended our shares, and it was later to censor me for the way I had conducted the negotiations with Maxwell. When the board finally wrote their letter to shareholders trying to explain the events, they felt that several of my actions were 'ill-conceived and inappropriate', but they had to concede that I acted in the best interest of the company and had taken legal advice. Even the DTI got involved in this. Ian Gray, who had taken over as Chief Executive, had a visit from a DTI Inspector demanding a copy of the Ashurst report, but nothing came of this and several months later they wrote to me saying that no action was to be taken.

It was already becoming clear that I could no longer remain a director of the public company. A week after the Stock Exchange suspended our shares, we had another board meeting at the offices of Brown Shipley. Just before that, Van Kuffeler, who had been meeting Douglas, called me in and suggested that I should resign from the public company. He felt that the bank had lost confidence in the company and that my resignation, by indicating a change, might restore some of this lost confidence. Douglas argued strongly that I had done nothing to justify this action, and he felt my departure would mean the loss of the only director capable of bringing money to the stricken company. Van Kuffeler agreed to sleep on the decision for forty-eight hours and let us know on Sunday, when the board was due to meet again. On Sunday, Van Kuffeler still felt I should go, and since this was presented to me as in the best interest of Tottenham, I readily agreed. If anything, I felt a sense of relief, for the plc meant little to me, and I was still Chairman of the football club, which is all I had really cared for.

Curiously, while all this was going on the team seemed to be unaffected. Tottenham, notoriously poor starters under Venables, had made their best start to the season since the Double year. The players seemed to be cocooned from what was going on, and Terry seemed to have got it together. But, as I was soon to discover, the players could not be shielded from these terrible events, and Terry was soon to reveal his great ambitions to own a football club. Tottenham's peril was his opportunity.

14

THE KNICKERS QUEST

'As for Venables, Sugar is the fifth pair of knickers he has tried. And none of them seem to fit.'
— Robert Maxwell on Venables's attempts to buy Spurs.

During the 1988/89 season, when Spurs were going through a most depressing run which included the quite shattering Cup defeat at Bradford, Edward Freedman found Terry in the toilet at White Hart Lane, sobbing his heart out. 'They didn't rate me as a player but I was a good one. They don't rate me as a Manager, but I'm good and I'll prove it. This club has a jinx on me but I'll overcome that.'

His method of doing that was to use his greatest weapon, his silver tongue. Although neither the 88/89 nor the 89/90 seasons had been particularly distinguished – we had been knocked out of the FA Cup in the third round in both seasons, and embarrassingly outplayed by Nottingham Forest at White Hart Lane in the League Cup quarter-final in January of 1990 – Terry deployed a raft of words to skate right over our mediocre performances. There was always the promise of better things around the corner. Every now and again the team would have a little run, only for the corner to turn into a cul-de-sac, but Terry would use the evidence of the run to build up hope. He well knew that football is run on hope and hype, and he was a master in promising the first and using it to sustain the second. Now, as our financial problems worsened, he had the most wonderful of excuses to explain away our mediocre performances in the League.

The 1990/91 season, as I have said, had started well, with

the team unbeaten until 4 November, when we lost 3-1 at home
to Liverpool. After that, results progressively deteriorated, and
Terry pointed to our financial problems at Spurs as the cause.
He said that without the money to buy players he could not rest
key men who were fatigued, or carrying niggling little injuries.
Possibly so, but by this time Terry himself was distracted as never
before by his plans to take over Spurs.

The first public hint of this came when Jeff Randall, who
had continued to lead the field in Spurs stories, had another
exclusive article about Frank Warren being party to a consortium
of overseas investors, including pension funds, with Venables as
their proposed chief executive. I liked the touch about overseas
pension funds, which I thought gave Randall's story away as a
non-starter – Randall initially stood by it, but later admitted to
me that he had been conned – but what it did was put Venables
in the ring as a possible 'saviour' of Tottenham.

There had been no shortage of redeemers, at least on the
telephone and in informal conversations. One of them found
a middleman in Tony Berry, who came to the board in the
middle of December with an approach from a company who
were interested in putting some money into Tottenham. It seemed
they were a group of overseas investors who also wanted to make
Terry the chief executive and use him as the front man.

An appointment was arranged for me to go and see Ted
Bull, who ran a company called Landhurst Leasing and lived
in a large country home near Crawley in Sussex. Earlier in the
year I had met Ted and we had discussed raising money by
creating a leasehold investment out of the boxes at Tottenham,
which would give us a steady stream of income over a period
of time. Like many such discussions during that period it got
nowhere, but I came away with a genuine liking for Ted.
Now, at his home, I found Frank Warren there and we spent
a whole afternoon discussing the Tottenham situation. Ted was
vehemently anti-Maxwell and kept repeating what a disaster it
would be if Maxwell got involved.

What was curious about that visit was that for much of
the time I was there the telephone kept ringing, and Ted would
excuse himself and take the call. I should have been used to such
interruptions. People who have suffered me know my addiction
to the telephone – I was christened 'Busby' by Peter Day when I
first joined Spurs – but the constant telephone calls at Ted's home
had a deeper significance. I got the impression that Tony, who

was in America then, was ringing him. They were, of course, old business friends and my feeling was that contrary to what I had been led to believe, this meeting was meant to pump information out of me: at what price would I sell my stake in Tottenham? Before I went to see Ted I had told Philip Green, who had also got involved in this, that I thought it would be a waste of time, and so it proved to be. I came away with an impression of the nice home he had, the large swimming pool, and flashy cars in the drive, but there was no money for Spurs in leafy Sussex or any real hope of it.

Christmas was fast approaching, our results on the field were very bleak, and Midland had turned the heat on. Our facility was capped at £10.5 million and the account moved from Smithfield to the Midland Bank casualty unit in Cannon Street, and handled by a certain Fred Miller. Since I was no longer on the board of the public company I had little to do with Miller, although I had met him once in October. What continued to sadden me was that despite the grave situation we were faced with, the board continued to bicker. I saw the problem as Bobroff. Sometimes the problems he caused were so trivial that they would have made me laugh, except that in our predicament they nearly made me cry.

We were required by law to hold an Annual General Meeting before the end of the year, when some of the directors would, as is usual, have to retire and offer themselves for re-election. Bobroff had only ever presented himself once for re-election in the seven years since Tottenham had become a plc, and that was when all the directors by law were up for re-election, in 1984. It was natural to assume he would do so again at this meeting. If so, I and the other directors planned to vote him off. But he argued that he had effectively done so in 1988. That was when he should have retired and offered himself for re-election, but although he had not done so he said that he was 'deemed' to have been re-elected in 1988. This was further grist to the lawyers, and we went to Richard Sykes, a leading counsel. His opinion was that Bobroff must offer himself for re-election, but Ashurst Morris Crisp took the opposite view.

On the last day of 1990 the adjourned General Meeting of Tottenham was held, but it only lasted a few minutes. We were still not in a position to present the accounts. I stood at the back of the hall feeling like a fly on the wall, and sympathised with the shareholders agitated by what had happened and by their failure to get answers to questions.

Douglas had presided over the aborted meeting, but Midland had made it clear that we needed a full-time executive Chairman. The problem was finding one. Brown Shipley introduced us to the Chairman of Gestetner, an Australian who had done a major job of refinancing that company. Gestetner had the right local connections – it used to be a major force in the Tottenham area – but it soon became clear that the Gestetner man neither had much interest in football nor was he keen on the job. He would only come on board when the finance was in place. Since the idea of a Chairman was to build up confidence so as to get finance, this was hardly of use to us.

Our ideal Chairman would obviously be someone who cared about the club and had some standing in the City. This is how Nat Solomon came into the picture. He was the ex-Chairman of Pleasurama, and I had first met him in the summer of 1988 when Tony had introduced him as another mad-keen Spurs supporter who might also help in a Rights issue. Nat had taken Terry and me to dinner at a restaurant owned by Pleasurama, and made the fatal mistake of trying to prove that he knew more about Spurs than I did. My second question, 'Which club attracted a record crowd of 75,038 to Tottenham for an FA Cup tie in 1938?', floored him, but I must say he did know his Spurs, and what is more loved the club. (The answer is Sunderland.)

Three years later the big question was: who could come up with the money? Again Nat had no answers, but it was felt he had the right City connections, and Brown Shipley were quite keen on him. I agreed. It was important for us to have a proper Chairman, for I knew we were about to enter perhaps our most critical phase.

Soon after my meeting with Nat I went with the team to Blackpool. The next day we were due to begin our FA Cup campaign there. I was well aware of Terry's dreadful record in the Cup: only one victory in four years as Manager, and that victory leading to the ghastly emptiness of defeat at Port Vale. Blackpool was just the sort of place where we could have another defeat. I was almost convinced we would be beaten when I saw emerging from the tunnel at Blackpool on the day of the match Tony Gubba, the BBC 'Match of the Day' commentator. To my mind he was the kiss of death for Tottenham, having been at Port Vale, and then twelve months later at Bradford.

The one ray of hope was that the year ended in a '1', and what Tottenham fan doesn't know that that means Tottenham will win something that year, usually the FA Cup? We also had some local knowledge about Blackpool: this was Paul Stewart's old club. He not only knew the back doubles, but he illustrated what Italians call the law of the ex: that an ex-player will always score against his old club. Sure enough Stewart did, and brought us victory – a somewhat lucky one after Blackpool, using the typical English seaside wintry conditions, had dominated the early play and even had two goals disallowed.

In any Cup run there is always one game you look like losing. For long periods in the match Blackpool had looked like winning – one of their disallowed goals looked quite all right to me – and I began to believe that maybe the magic of the 1 would work for Spurs again. The Press had been quick to seize on that, and already our FA Cup run was being written about as the only route to salvation. The theory was that if we won the Cup and got into Europe it would provide the money we desperately needed. From now on every FA Cup match was to be like Spurs' own version of the Battle of Stalingrad: victory provided hope, defeat could mean oblivion.

As our Cup run continued, Terry, despite our appalling League record, came to be identified as a saviour. The Press built up the story of our Manager seeking the salvation on the field that we had botched in the boardroom. Of course, not all the supporters believed this newspaper line, as I had discovered the night before the Blackpool match. I was having a drink with Terry and Bob Cass of the *Mail On Sunday* in a bar next to the Imperial Hotel, where we were staying, when through the corner of my eye I noticed a Spurs supporter walk in. I had met him a few months previously just after the Maxwell story broke when, returning from a match at Leeds, he had harangued me about the club, making it clear he did not like any of the players. It seemed none of them could hold a candle to Glenn Hoddle.

But now his moan was about somebody else. 'Is it true what I read in the papers? This business about Terry Venables taking over?'

'Well,' I said guardedly, 'I really can't tell you right now.'

'I don't think it's a good thing for the club,' he said.

'Why do you say that?' I asked.

'He's not a Spurs man is he? They may have a go at you, they may dislike you and think you've done things wrong, but

I'll tell you what. You are a Spurs man through and through, and
that is more important than anything else. Whatever happens you
mustn't leave the club.'

'Well, that's beyond me.'

I never saw this supporter again, but as the hellish year
unfolded I often remembered his words, and again and again
I met Spurs supporters who echoed his feelings.

So far I had had little inkling of how the players felt about
all this. Terry made much of the fact that he shielded them
from the financial problems, but that was not really in his gift,
as a little aside by Gascoigne made it clear. As the team coach
made its way along the front to Blackpool's ground he, in his
inimitable style, took over the microphone and began to give us
a guided tour of the seaside town, a very effective Fred Scuttle
impersonation. Suddenly along a side turning he noticed a club
called 'Rumours' and said: 'On the left-hand side there is the
famous nightclub Rumours and, let's be honest, there's plenty
of those going around Tottenham at the moment.'

The most fantastic rumours swirled round Gascoigne himself.
A few days earlier, on the 1st of January, when we had played
Manchester United – televised live, and a match we lost in the
last few minutes after Gascoigne had been sent off – I had been
interviewed by ITV and asked about the sale of Gascoigne. I had
made it perfectly clear that I didn't want him to leave White Hart
Lane and that if he left, so would I.

But this did little to stop the tabloid Press, who were conducting a virtual public auction of Gascoigne, with just about every
Continental club supposedly willing to bid for him and willing
to pay anything up to £8 million. For some time now, Bobroff
had been coming back with messages from the Midland Bank
saying they wanted a sale of assets, and Gascoigne was clearly
the biggest asset we had.

I could ignore that, but Nat Solomon's arrival as Chairman
changed things somewhat. Although I was no longer a member
of the plc board, Nat had requested me to attend board meetings, and almost his very first words to me were: 'I know how
you feel, but we've got to demonstrate to the bank that we are
actually making some effort to reduce our debts, so we have to
try and get some proposal from an overseas club to show we
mean business.'

What I didn't know, and only learnt later, was that the Midland
Bank had made the sale of Gascoigne one of the conditions of

their continuing to fund the overdraft. They wanted Tottenham to undertake a 'marketing exercise', and Nat in his first public statement as Chairman made it clear that Gascoigne might be sold. I was less than happy about this, as it was plastered on the back page of the *Standard* just hours before we played a League Cup quarter-final at Stamford Bridge, a match in which Gascoigne couldn't play because of suspension.

Nat had more or less confirmed the back-page rumours, and now Gascoigne's possible sale was to become a regular item at Tottenham's board meetings. However, the bank, aware of my opposition, had asked for the minutes not only of the plc but also of the football club. It was clear what the bank was after, but I refused. That day, Tuesday 15 January, a Tottenham board meeting was supposed to be held, and Douglas rang me in some panic saying: 'If you don't go along with it then we've been told by the bank this morning that we'll have no choice but to ask you to leave.' Douglas, like everyone else on the board, not only knew my position but sympathised with it. 'Look,' he said, 'Gascoigne's sale is not definite. We've got time, and if we can come up with an alternative then he needn't be sold. Please think about this, because I think it would be disastrous for you to go. But if you insist on not even discussing his possible sale then you will leave us with no choice.'

I attended the board meeting, but made it very clear that I would be prepared to discuss a possible sale of Gascoigne only on the basis that the alternative would be putting Tottenham into administration or receivership. (The formal minutes didn't record my comment, but when I tackled Ashurst Morris Crisp they said minutes do not record everything, just give the flavour.) If it was a choice of Tottenham going broke or Gascoigne going, then I was prepared to discuss his transfer, although I was still opposed to it and would do everything to stop it.

It is one thing to talk about selling a player, quite another to organise it. Clubs might be interested in a player, but they were hardly likely to pick up the telephone and ring Nat Solomon. He, realising that this was a specialised business, asked for my advice, and I suggested that Tottenham appoint an agent such as Dennis Roach. I knew, liked and had dealt with Roach, but what Nat didn't know was that Roach and Mel Stein hated each other. They had fallen out over Chris Waddle's transfer to Marseille, and things were so bad that Stein wouldn't even sit in the same room as Roach. My thinking, Machiavellian if you like, was that while Roach's reputation as a good agent could not be questioned by the bank or anyone else, if he couldn't sit in the same room as Gascoigne's adviser then how could the transfer details be arranged?

Indeed, I told Roach that I doubted whether this would come off: 'You may be on a wild goose chase, and I want to warn you of that in advance. This is not like a normal transfer, and even if you get a concrete proposal from an Italian club or whatever, there is no guarantee it is going to go through.'

It is not that I was opposed to selling players. I realised we had to sell some, and I was quite prepared to do a deal on Vinny Samways. Doug Ellis had made an offer of £800,000 to buy Samways, which the board had decided to accept. The offer came the day after we had played at Derby County in a League match, producing a rare League victory thanks to Lineker rediscovering his goal-scoring skills in the middle of Derby fans displaying their spleen for Robert Maxwell. The next afternoon Doug Ellis rang me in a rather formal manner and proposed to buy Samways, saying: 'This agreement is between Doug Ellis and Aston Villa and Irving Scholar of Tottenham Hotspur. We offer to pay £800,000 for the player.' I explained to him that we had an important League Cup quarter-final two days later, and with several injuries wanted to delay the transfer until the following Sunday, after our next league match, which he was quite prepared to do.

So, as Chelsea came to play us in the replayed League Cup quarter-final I was confident he would be sold to Villa, and ease the pressure – that was the impression Ellis had given me. Just before the meeting I told Terry about it and explained that we would find it very difficult to turn down the offer, given the pressures the bank was putting on us.

Terry seemed to understand and picked Samways for the match. I could see Samways's every move being followed by the then Villa manager Josef Venglos and his assistant Peter Withe. But Samways didn't have a good game, Terry substituted him after sixty-five or so minutes, and Venglos and Withe disappeared before the end of the game.

This did worry me a bit, but Ellis had been very firm and keen on the transfer. However, the next day when I rang him 'Deadly Doug' flatly denied that we had any agreement on Samways, and when I reminded him of our conversation a few days previously he just said: 'Sorry, we didn't actually have a firm agreement.'

The Samways transfer was to be a recurring theme of that year, with the Nottingham Forest Chairman, Maurice Roworth, expressing interest. At one stage it got to the point where I was on the telephone to him almost every day, and he made an offer to buy Samways for £800,000. But this was subject to Clough's okay, and as, it seems, with everything at Forest, whatever the Chairman proposed, Clough disposed.

I don't suppose I should have been surprised that Maurice Roworth had failed to get his deal through. A ruddy-faced man with crinkly hair, he was one of the most complicated chairmen I had to deal with, and whilst I can understand that he was living under the shadow of Brian Clough, what I could never get over was the fact on two occasions he came across as a bad loser. I remember one match at Nottingham Forest where we won with a very late goal, and as I was leaving my seat and going down the steps, I overheard him on the other side of the gangway saying: 'Bloody fluke. We played them off the Park. They were dead lucky.'

On another occasion, when Spurs had inflicted yet another defeat on Nottingham Forest at their ground, he turned on Doug Livermore, Terry's assistant, with the sort of abusive venom that was really quite amazing. All Doug had said was 'Well played Chairman', but Roworth thought that Doug, who has a very distinct Scouse accent, was taking the mickey and asked him to leave the boardroom, saying: 'I'm the Chairman and no one comes here unless I say so. You didn't ask me. Get out!' I can never understand such behaviour, and I left soon after, after exchanging a few unpleasant words with him. But, when we beat Forest in the 1991 Cup Final, he did have the grace to say: 'Well done, you deserved it. We didn't play today.' I couldn't help telling him: 'Maurice, bearing in mind I thought you were such a bad loser, I thought the least you would be saying is that you thought your team was unlucky!'

Looking back, Terry's decision to take Samways off in the match against Chelsea put a spoke in the deal. He had expressed objections to Samways going, and felt his true value was £1.5 million. Like all managers he liked to have lots of players around him – it seems the presence of physical bodies gives them a sense of security.

As it happens, the night of the Samways fiasco with Villa was overshadowed by a quite unimaginable threat to my own physical security. I had just got into the directors' room after the match when Peter Barnes entered with a tall gentleman in a dark suit. Peter introduced him as someone from the CID, and the stranger spoke perhaps the most chilling words I have ever heard: 'I'm sorry to inform you Mr Scholar that there has been a death threat on you, and we have been told that you are going to be shot as you leave the ground this evening.'

I had seen such incidents in the movies and read them in thrillers, of course, but when you realise that it is happening to you a feeling of unreality sweeps over you. I did not know what to think or say, and while I could not really believe that anybody would want to shoot me, I could not ignore it either. The CID official said: 'If I were you I would take it seriously. There's no point in taking any chances.' It was agreed they would advise me on how best to leave the ground, and escort me on my way home.

I was led through a side exit which comes out opposite to where the ballcourt is and is used on match days as a car park by directors and guests. The police escorted me to my car, and it was decided that an armoured car full of police personnel would follow mine down the High Road. For about twenty minutes they did so, and then they flashed me, pulled up alongside, and said it seemed quite safe now and I could carry on on my own. I reached home safely, and it was only much later, thinking about it, that I realised that the incident was not quite as ridiculous as I had first thought. For all I know there may have been a sniper waiting for me and he may have been deterred by the police precautions. Football is a passionate game, and can generate emotions to a quite extraordinary degree. In the mad year that I was experiencing, a pot-shot at me would not have been that far-fetched.

Gascoigne had returned for the match against Chelsea, and had he earned a penalty in the first few minutes when he was brought down in the box by Cundy, the match might have turned out differently. But he didn't get the penalty and we were mauled 3-0. We were now drifting in the League and out of the League Cup. The FA Cup was our only hope. Others, of course, saw a quick sale of Gascoigne as a way out, and Roach (who was to receive 1 per cent of any transfer fee up to £7 million and 1.5 per cent beyond that) had been busy on the Continent seeking possible buyers. One day he rang me in some excitement to say that Lazio of Rome were very interested, and a meeting was arranged around the first week of February. This was just after we beat Oxford in the fourth round of the FA Cup 4-2, with Gascoigne making two and scoring two, one of them an absolutely magnificent goal. Given that it was Gascoigne's free kick that had led to Paul Stewart's winner against Blackpool, Gascoigne was clearly central to any progress in the FA Cup.

The pattern for the season was now set. On the field, Gazza's brilliance promised to win the Cup; off it, moves to sell him became more and more involved. On 20 February, I met Lazio for dinner at the White House near Great Portland Street, along with Roach. I have rarely gone to a football occasion with greater misgivings or lack of interest. The Lazio officials, led by Calleri their President, were very interested in Gascoigne, but while I made it clear that I was not interested in selling him I was willing to quote a price. Just as I had done with Richard Gough, when I had asked for a stupid price, I valued Gascoigne at £10 million. Lazio responded with £5 million, and I said: 'Thank you very much for your interest. This is certainly not acceptable to me, but I'll report back to the board, although I must tell you that I doubt if the transfer can take place.' My feeling was that this would be the end of Lazio. I could turn round and say that their valuation was way below a realistic price, and kill any talk of Gascoigne going.

I just did not believe that Midland could force us to sell Gascoigne. The board was nervous that they would appoint an administrator, or put Tottenham into receivership or liquidation, but this just did not make sense. Although we owed Midland £10.5 million, Tottenham had assets worth £40 million. Healey & Baker had valued the ground at £19.5 million, and even at the most conservative estimate the players were worth £20 million. In any event, what was in it for Midland if they bust us? As a bank their own performance was under attack in the financial Press – soon they would be successfully bid for by the Hong Kong and Shanghai Bank – and I knew from my contacts in the property world that they were propping up any number of property companies to the tune of hundreds of millions of pounds.

Midland were playing a game of bluff and counter-bluff, refusing to extend facilities or increase them, but renewing the present terms on a monthly basis. When Nat had taken over I had been told that they would not renew beyond the end of February, the date by which the Annual General Meeting was due to be held. But by the time this came round the facilities had been extended until 15 March, a move that more than ever convinced me that they would never actually close us down. At the very worst they may have put the plc into administration but there was absolutely no chance of touching the Football Club. £10.5 million to the possible administrator would have cleared the debt, and anyone doing that would have 100 per cent control of £40 million of assets, not exactly a risky investment. That thought was a powerful weapon in the battle to keep Gascoigne.

However, in order to bring that off, any negotiations about his transfer had to be kept confidential, and this was where the problem arose. My talks with Lazio did not remain secret. It is difficult to keep anything secret in Italy, where there are three daily sports papers with a voracious appetite for sports news, rumour and gossip. Curiously, the initial story was that Roma, the bigger of the two Rome clubs, were interested. It is possible that the leak might have come from other sources. An agent called Mohammed operating from Leeds had approached Nat and offered five or six million without naming the club. He was clearly trying to get his foot in the door and leaked the Roma interest to the Press.

It was the day after this story appeared that the Annual General Meeting was held at the Chanticleer. This was to be a meeting like no other in Spurs' recent history. On the top table sat Nat Solomon with the rest of the board, to the right the professional advisers, and to the left myself with Terry Venables. The Tottenham Independent Supporters Association which had been formed in the wake of the Maxwell revelations were there in force, ready to ask the truckload of questions that had been agitating them.

Many were upset at what they felt was a humiliating position for the club to be in. Our financial position had now placed Spurs, once considered one of the richest clubs in the country, almost on a par with the church mouse. At the turn of the year when we played Southampton there had been adverse comments in their programme about problems with Hummel. In the Chelsea programme Ken Bates had made offensive remarks about our failure to pay for match tickets we had bought. Every now and again I would receive letters threatening legal action if we didn't pay off some debts. None of them amounted to anything, but the Press played up these stories, delighting in knocking the once mighty Spurs.

I had gone into the AGM expecting the worst, given the

way the Press had built me up as a villain, and prepared for the quizzing I received about the Maxwell loan. One shareholder in particular annoyed me by talking of the so-called turn, the interest, I was making on the loan. 'I wouldn't take a penny out of Tottenham,' I replied. 'Not in a million years.'

This seemed to change the mood of the meeting. Everybody burst out into cheers, and I was pleasantly surprised to find the meeting pick on other members of the board, particularly Bobroff, and grill him about the stand and the other problems of the public company which had got us into this mess.

However, in the flood of questions that were asked that day, the most significant thing, like the dog that didn't bark, was the question that wasn't asked. It was now over two months since Jeff Randall had written his speculative story about the Warren bid with Venables as chief executive. Yet nobody at the meeting asked Terry anything about his plans to take over the club, and in a funny way I think that got him on the raw. Of course, as always at the end of the Annual General Meeting, Terry had his own question-and-answer session talking about football. But the fact that even then – and this was the middle of February – none of the assembled shareholders paid any significance to a possible takeover by him was quite interesting.

Just as the meeting broke up, a man and his wife came running up to the table where I was sitting with Terry. The man put his set of accounts in front of me and asked me to autograph it. Then he said: 'A lot of people appreciate what you are trying to do. Please don't listen to those who don't understand.' To say I was taken aback by this would be an understatement. It left me feeling both happy and drained, and then for the next fifteen minutes or so I must have signed almost as many autographs as Terry Venables. In spite of the growing Press campaign against me, it seemed there were ordinary supporters who were willing and able to understand that not all of it was my fault and that I was just as keen to find a solution as they were.

There was no shortage of people willing to offer solutions, at least verbally. They were all keen to tell me how much they loved Tottenham and impress me with their knowledge of its history. Baltic, a small merchant bank which had a box at Tottenham, were talking about a Rights issue at about 50 or 60p. Since the shares had been suspended at 91p, this was like trying to do it on the cheap, and a backdoor takeover of the company.

One evening, after I had been to the Centenary Club, Stuart

Lucas, who worked for Bear Stearns, an American market-maker, spoke to me about his great love for Tottenham and how he felt he might be able to help. He invited me and Ian Gray, Bob Holt's successor, to lunch in the City and we discussed several ideas about raising money. He felt that there was a very strong possibility of doing it successfully. But nothing ever came of this. Almost every member of the board had a proposal from somebody or other that promised to dig us out of the tunnel. Douglas Alexiou was talking to the bankers Hambro Magann, who were masterminding a number of City financial firms in a project called Tarragon to raise some money.

At the same time we were also looking at doing our own Rights issue, and Brown Shipley had been reasonably confident that they could get such an issue away, raising at least £6 million, perhaps even £8 million. Bobroff was convinced that we could get the financial institutions to underwrite it. He was quite dismissive of any Baltic involvement in this, and wasn't sure that Baltic had the money. On the other hand, I wasn't sure that Brown Shipley could perform for us; although I had been quite impressed with the people at Baltic, and on the couple of occasions that I had met them they had not seemed like men of straw. It was not long before I was to meet the first of Terry Venables's men of straw: Larry Gillick.

We were now in early March. There had been a lot of news-paper talk about the consortium that Venables was supposed to be putting together, but I had seen no concrete proposals. Eventually a meeting was arranged between the board, Venables, Peter Earl of Tranwood, a small merchant bank who were acting as Venables's adviser, and Larry Gillick. Tranwood already had financial problems of their own, and these proved to be so ter-minal that they eventually went into liquidation.

But it was Gillick who intrigued me. I had never met him before, and when I arrived at Nat's offices my first impression was that he resembled an out-of-work gangster. Everything from his clothes to his looks suggested that: the dark suit, white shirt, bright fish tie, the very portly thickset appearance with shortish crinkling hair and a thinning, receding hairline. A Scottish news-paper revealed that he had been bankrupt. None of us then knew anything about his background or what he had been doing, and we were a bit surprised that he seemed to be presenting himself as a principal in this deal. This suggested that he had something between £25 and £30 million at his disposal: he was to buy

Tottenham at 90p, which would cost £9 million, plus take on a debt in the region of £12 to £13 million, plus put in, as he said, another £5 million. There are not too many people who emerge from nowhere and claim to have £30 million at their command. Brown Shipley were extremely dubious about this.

However, there were certain reassuring noises he made. He made it clear that he didn't want to sell Paul Gascoigne, which pleased me since I had made that a condition of any sale. And I liked the sound of his putting in another £5 million over the next twelve months. But there was something cagey about all that he said, and he was unwilling to give any details of the backers who were putting up the money.

Gillick did most of the talking, Venables said very little, and eventually we asked them and Earl to wait, while the board conferred. Nobody was quite sure what to make of it. We called them back again with some more questions, but it was clear that some of the board members were not happy with the terms. I turned to Nat and suggested that perhaps I could have a quiet word with Larry Gillick and see what we could do with the offer. Nat quickly agreed.

I took Gillick to one side and said that if he could up his offer to 110p, or even slightly over the £1 at which the issue had been originally floated in 1983, then maybe we could deal. He thought about this and eventually agreed that he could move up to 95p. Bobroff and Berry were willing to go along, and that meant that 44 per cent of the Tottenham shareholders had agreed on a deal.

Venables, Earl and Gillick were summoned back to the meeting, and it seemed that here at last we had our deal. As we were preparing to leave the room I went up to Terry, shook his hand, patted him across the face and said to him: 'Now go and win the European Cup.' It had always been my dream for Spurs. Tottenham had won the European Cupwinners' Cup, becoming the first British club to win a major European trophy, and had won the UEFA Cup. To win the European Cup would mean they would join a very select group. Only one other club had ever won all three major European trophies: Juventus. I wanted Tottenham to be part of that. Indeed my private fantasy had been that the night Tottenham won the European Cup, and as the trophy was lifted in front of the supporters, I would resign as Chairman of the club and walk away. There would be tears in my eyes, but they would be tears of joy, because Tottenham would have achieved what I had always hungered for. I knew I could not achieve that dream. But I hoped Terry could.

I sat in Nat's office that night thinking that all that needed to be done was to get the solicitors and the financial advisers to work out the details of the agreement. We still didn't know exactly who was putting up the funds, but we had parted on very friendly terms and that didn't seem to be a big hurdle. After all, it was three months since the first whisper of a Venables consortium had been heard, and I assumed that in those three months he had got together the money to make a deal. As I was soon to discover, this was only the first pair of knickers that Venables was trying on, and they didn't fit at all.

Five or six days later Tony Berry rang me to say: 'I think you ought to come and meet Larry Gillick, because I think he's got a couple of things to say to you.' I was a bit shaken by this. As far as I was concerned I had shaken on a deal at 95p, but I went along with Tony to the offices of the solicitors who were acting on behalf of Venables and his consortium, somewhere at the bottom of Harley Street. As I walked into the reception I noticed Frank Warren and partner there, and I immediately thought that it wouldn't be long before there would be something about this in the papers. Sure enough, a few days later there was.

Gillick came straight to the point. 'I'm sorry but I am unable to proceed at 95p. But I can offer you 85p. However, in a couple of days I will get a banker's draft drawn on Barclays Bank so that they will have full funds to proceed and satisfy Ashurst Morris Crisp and Brown Shipley that we are making a full offer.' Reluctantly I agreed saying: 'I have shaken hands with you on a deal for 95p. I am prepared to amend it as you request, but this is the last time I'm prepared to agree with you. Don't come back again if you can't do it. I've shaken your hand. The deal is done.'

At this stage he did give some clue as to the money's source. It seemed to be coming from the rulers of Abu Dhabi, though Gillick said that the Sheikh was very loath to have his name mentioned. If at our first meeting I had not known what to expect, now I was wary of everything Gillick proposed. By this time a lot of water had flowed under the Gillick bridge. A Scottish newspaper had run a large exposé on him which was less than flattering. Ashurst Morris Crisp and Brown Shipley had read the Press reports about his wanting to buy Tottenham and they told Nat that in their opinion he was a person of no apparent means.

Our advisers also warned us that more than anything else what might stop it would be the reluctance of the Middle Eastern backers to be named. The Stock Exchange would insist on full disclosures, and they couldn't put out an offer document which did not contain all the information available as to who was providing the funds, where they were coming from, and what sort of people were going to be involved.

Still, Gillick's offer, however flawed, was the only one on the table, and perhaps some members of the board were more impressed with the Gillick-Venables axis than I was. Pressure from the bank was relentless. Nat had gone to see them with Jeremy Knight of Brown Shipley and David Buchler of Buchler Phillips, a very keen Spurs fan who had a long relationship with Midland, particularly in the area of problem companies. Midland were still threatening to pull the plug, and Nat felt that the crunch would come on 31 March.

On the field, of course, the team was facing a different kind of deadline, as every three weeks or so yet another round of the FA Cup came up. I had gone away for a few days' holiday at this time, and came back in time for the fifth round at Portsmouth on 16 February. With Portsmouth leading 1-0 at half-time I could see the photographs in the next day's papers. They would have a shot of me looking haggard and depressed, as Spurs went out of the Cup. In the second half Gascoigne again worked his magic and we won the game 2-1.

At the end of the match, as per tradition, we were entertained by the Portsmouth board, and this gave me a chance for sweet revenge. About a month before this, Tony Berry had told me that Jim Gregory might be interested in buying Tottenham. My first question to him was: 'If he buys, will he sell Gascoigne?' He had replied: 'Probably.' Then I said: 'I'm not interested in talking to him.' Now I told Gregory: 'So you can see why I'm so keen to keep Paul Gascoigne.'

I drove home with a friend, and we stopped off at a country pub which happened to be full of Spurs supporters celebrating the win and talking about Gascoigne. Their admiration for the man was touching, and there was no doubt what they felt about rumours of his possible transfer. One of them came up to me and said: 'Surely you're not going to sell him.' I replied: 'It's certainly something I'm not in favour of. You know that. But this may not be in my hands.' Hero-worship of players I was used to; but this was verging on idolatry.

I was now like a hostile witness in Tottenham v. Lazio in the case of the transfer of Paul Gascoigne. In mid-March I had attended a meeting in Nat's office where Dennis Roach and Gian Marco Calleri, President of Lazio, were present. It was at this meeting that Lazio's interest became a firm offer with a price tag on it. Roach, understandably, was pressing for the deal, and as the figure inched up to and beyond £7 million Nat got very excited. The poor man was under almost daily pressure from the Midland, and clearly this mountain of money was a godsend. Finally Nat and Calleri seemed to be agreeing on a figure of £7.2 million, and I could sense that Nat was about to shake hands on the deal. I could not bear to watch that. There was nothing I could do to prevent Nat from agreeing to the deal, but I could still make my position clear, and just before the meeting ended, and before anything was formally agreed, in the true style of investigative tabloid journalists I made my excuses and left.

At this stage a spoke was put into the deal by Gascoigne himself. In what must be quite the most bizarre transfer that English soccer has ever seen, much was written about how it was done and the people who did the deal. Much that has been written has been misinformed, if not at times malicious. Both I and the other directors were painted as villains who were only worried about the money and not the interests of the club and the player. Yet Gascoigne himself had by now a very shrewd idea of the amount of money he could make both from Tottenham and from Lazio. It was this that caused the problem. Gascoigne knew that he had Tottenham over a barrel – he had to agree to a move before the transfer could go ahead – and suddenly Stein told us that Gascoigne wanted a payment *from Spurs* to move to Lazio. Not just any old payment: he wanted a million net in order for the transfer to go ahead.

Gascoigne's demand led to another meeting with Lazio, the first of two meetings at the Royal Lancaster Hotel, which happened to be the place that Terry always took the Spurs team to before a big match. It was here more than a year later that the historic, infamous meeting of the Premier League was to take place which approved the £304 million deal with BSB. We met in the hotel boardroom on the first floor, and apart from Nat, Dennis and myself there were lawyers from Ashurst Morris Crisp and, of course, a full contingent from Lazio. At this stage I was still not clear what payment Gascoigne wanted, and initially

I thought that he was talking of the usual signing fee that players want when they move. But Calleri made it clear that Gascoigne was talking of a termination payment, although it was some time before Calleri got to the point.

It is always difficult to carry on talking, let alone complex negotiations, when more than one language is involved, but what made this maddening was that Calleri saw himself as some sort of a Roman orator. So instead of having a normal conversation he would go off on monologues for fifteen or twenty minutes at a time, when he would produce a lava of words, few of which meant anything and none of which we were able to stem. Despite such Italian abundance, we finally worked out a solution to Gascoigne's demand. Tottenham would now receive £7 million, and Lazio would look after any payment that Gascoigne wanted.

It was at the second Lancaster Hotel meeting that Lazio came up with a draft contract. Calleri had brought over his lawyer, and we had people from Ashurst Morris Crisp. Despite the presence of lawyers, which meant their expensive meter was on, nothing could stop the flow of words from Calleri. At one stage he spoke for about twenty-five minutes without anybody getting a word in edgeways. We did manage to get away for lunch, and I took Nat and the two representatives from Ashurst Morris Crisp, James Perry and Chris Ashworth, to an Italian place around the corner. The moment we sat down Nat let out an enormous sigh and said: 'Irving, if this goes through you will not be the only one resigning.' I could see Nat was reaching the end of his tether. His life was now divided between listening to monologues from Calleri and then putting up with the demands of the Midland.

Nat was very pleased with the Lazio terms. He had worked out that this was the equivalent of around £8.5 million. Normally in England to buy a player you have to pay at least 50 per cent on signature with the balance equally over the next twelve months. Lazio's original deal had suggested that the payment would be over a two-year period. The final one that Nat had worked out provided for one third to be paid once Gascoigne had cleared a medical – which Lazio anticipated would take place as soon as the contract was signed – and two thirds after completing the transfer sometime in June 1991. This, discounted for cash-flow purposes and with interest added on, came to £8.5 million, and Nat thought that waving this figure in front of the Midland would ease some of the pressure.

The Midland were being just as greedy and nasty as some players can be during their transfer negotiations. They were extending our facilities a month or a couple of weeks at a time, but every time they did so they wanted a commitment fee, as if they were signing a new contract and wanted a signing-on fee. Their latest demand was for a commitment fee of £50,000. At about this time the *Sunday Times* had run a series of articles showing how the banks were squeezing the small companies, and our experience with Midland was showing that the articles were right on the ball. If anything, as time went on the Midland's demands were to grow.

But the Gascoigne transfer still had hurdles to clear. Gillick's offer was on the table, and according to Stock Exchange rules this meant that the fixed assets of the company could not be sold without some form of clearances from the Exchange. I was hoping that this and other hurdles would prove insurmountable, but the advisers quickly got round this. Despite my wishes and efforts, the barriers to Gascoigne's deal were coming down. Mel Stein had already been to Rome to meet Lazio officials and discuss terms, and it was becoming clear to me that unless somebody came up with some real money we couldn't keep the player.

However, I had already scored some success in my campaign to delay Gascoigne's transfer. Calleri had been so infuriated that on 2 April he had written an angry letter complaining that we were dragging our feet. And even if Gascoigne had to go I was keen to make sure Tottenham could buy him back. English players had rarely found it easy to settle in Italy. Jimmy Greaves was one, more recently Rush had come back after a year, and I had suggested a condition saying that if by 31 August 1993 Lazio wanted to sell him back to a British club, Tottenham would have first refusal at a fixed price. Lazio eventually did not agree, but my attempt to insert this condition made Calleri furious, and he spoke of 'surprise innovations' from me that were constantly delaying and preventing the deal.

What made the situation unbearable was that on the field Gascoigne was probably playing his most effective football for Tottenham. The League no longer mattered. All our eyes, and those of the sporting world, were on the Cup. Our quarter-final match was against Notts County at home, and as in the Portsmouth match, we seemed doomed for defeat. Just before half-time they scored, and this time not even I could believe that the Gazza magic could turn the game. He was clearly not fully fit, and his presence on the field was an enormous gamble.

But soon after the restart Nayim scored a goal, and then, in a quite inimitable fashion, Gascoigne burst through and scored the winner to take Spurs into the semi-final. Then we faced Arsenal. We had played them more than a hundred times, but never at this stage of the Cup. They were going for the Double.

The only offer on the table was still the one proposed by Gillick and Venables. However, despite our agreeing to a 10 per cent reduction to 85p, Gillick could neither produce evidence that he had the money, nor even satisfy the regulatory authorities. The board met on 20 March and decided that we could not recommend this offer. Two days later, on the Friday, both Ashurst Morris Crisp and Brown Shipley advised us to issue a statement making it clear that all discussions with the Venables consortium were now over. The next day, just before the home match with QPR, we had a board meeting at lunchtime.

This was the stage when Tony Berry's role began to assume a new and curious shape. On Friday Tony had been present to read the report from Brown Shipley and had voted with the resolution deciding to end the negotiations. Less than twenty-four hours later, as we ate our pre-match lunch, he began to act as a sort of messenger for Venables and Gillick. He spoke of Gillick's disappointment about our decision and said that Gillick still intended to bid for the company, which produced the only moment of mirth in that sombre meeting.

It was during the meeting that I began to sense that Tony was in a very odd position. He was a member of the board and party to our decisions, but he also seemed to have a foot in the Venables camp. I was not the only person to notice this. Nat asked him: 'Are you involved in the consortium?' Berry, keeping a very straight face, replied: 'I am not a shareholder or a lender to the consortium.' The words were carefully chosen. He wanted to reassure us that he was merely acting as a middleman. He did admit that if Venables and his friends succeeded he might be asked to take up shares, but claimed that at this stage he had no interest in the consortium. However, he added: 'If my position makes it uncomfortable for you to discuss the matter in front of me then I am prepared to withdraw.' But we didn't press the matter. In the fullness of time Tony was to find himself in a peculiar situation.

Everybody understood why the first Venables consortium had

failed – everybody it seemed except Venables himself. He used his silver tongue to suggest to the sporting Press that we didn't understand these things and that he was not being given time to develop his plans. It is because we understood how difficult these things were that we had given him time, and three months in Tottenham's position was quite long enough to come up with the money. Now that he had failed to do so, there was no point in pursuing negotiations that were not going to lead anywhere.

Brown Shipley were still trying to carry out some sort of Rights issue, although I'm not sure that they generated a great deal of interest. I also kept hearing from Tarragon, but they too were finding the road rather hard and difficult. At one particular point while the Lazio thing was maturing, only about £1.25 million separated the Brown Shipley Rights proposal from the Tarragon one. But in the end it didn't matter, because neither amounted to anything. Midland had now suggested that we should reduce our debt to £2.5 million, which meant that by the end of March we would have to find something like £7.7 million.

Like a bad penny, the Gillick-Venables consortium kept resurfacing. In the first week of April they came up with yet another proposal, and another price. Having shaken my hand on 95p, then shaken it again on 85p, now they wanted to pay 80p. What was maddening about this was not that the price kept going down but that they never seemed to be able to complete any of the formalities. Nat still did not have a letter of credit in relation to the offer terms, and they still could not satisfy Midland that its loan would be repaid. Then there was the matter of the loan I had provided Tottenham and the money that Frank and I had lent early in 1990. Round and round went the talks, with Gillick and Venables suggesting to the Press that they were doing everything they could to get a deal going when in reality they had neither the funds nor the means to find them.

Midland had now extended our facilities until 30 April, which seemed to bear out my feeling that their attempts to close us down back in February were a lot of hot air. I think what their threats were meant to do was squeeze more money out of Tottenham: we now learned that they were prepared to extend the facilities provided we paid another £50,000 as a commitment fee. However, Buchler's attempts to try and reason with them seemed to be paying some dividends, and Midland said that they would be prepared to listen to any proposals generated by the board. But they still would not commit themselves to a long-term facility, which would remove this month-by-month hassle. It was a few days after this that Tottenham faced perhaps their most important match against their most important rival: the Cup semi-final against Arsenal at Wembley.

I had been away for a few days and had come back on the Wednesday before the semi-final. That evening Tottenham played at Norwich in a match of greater significance than the usual mid-week League fixture. It was only a few weeks since Gascoigne had had his hernia operation, and it was by no means certain that he would be fit for the semi-final. Terry had decided to give him a work-out in this match and I felt very apprehensive. Gascoigne could break down, and that would mean our one trump card against Arsenal would be lost. But he showed such energy, and so many of his old touches, that instead of playing only the first half – as Terry had intended – he did not come off until an hour was up, by which time he had quite bewitched the Norwich defence. Terry's gamble had paid off and proved an inspired decision.

The day before we played at Norwich, Arsenal had played at Southampton, and as I arrived at the match I was very keen to find out how they had fared. That season they seemed impregnable, hardly conceding a goal and always scoring quite a few. I assumed Terry had been to Southampton to see Arsenal play, and I feared his answers about their form. Instead, I learned that he had not gone to see the match, relying on his minions' reports. That was a disappointment, until I realised that Terry rarely went to matches in the way Peter Shreeve and David Pleat did. He felt that he had done it all before with Crystal Palace and Queen's Park Rangers. Not even the prospect of watching Tony Adams, a player that Terry valued very highly, had attracted him to Southampton. Just over a month before, Adams had returned to the Arsenal side after spending some months in jail as a result of a drink driving charge. Even then, Terry seemed happy to hear reports of how he played rather than see him.

All these thoughts faded as the semi-final day dawned. I had told Terry a week or so before that I was not prepared to entertain any further discussions concerning his consortium, and that all attention must be focused on the forthcoming game at Wembley. It was a day of football, a day away from all the traumas of long meetings and vanishing consortiums. To play Arsenal is special, to beat them, and in an FA Cup semi-final at Wembley – the first time a semi-final was to be held on that hallowed turf – would be heaven. As I drove to Wembley I thought that if Tottenham, starting the day as the undermost of underdogs, were still to beat Arsenal it would be the most significant and famous win against the old enemy. As a boy I had always thought that the ultimate would be to play Arsenal in the FA Cup Final, and for Tottenham to score the winning goal in the very last minute of the game, to give them no chance of coming back – exactly as they had done to us in the semi-final of the Littlewoods Cup in 1987.

The match did not quite turn out like that – if anything it was even better. Arsenal that season were to concede only eighteen goals, yet in the first ten minutes they conceded two to us. Both featured Gascoigne: he scored the first from a free kick and made the second with a wonderful bit of magic. When Gascoigne struck the free kick I immediately turned to my son and said: 'That is the best free kick I have ever seen.' It was an astonishing strike, combining power and accuracy. Very few English players can actually strike a ball with such damaging precision. The only time I have seen such free kicks was when I watched Italian football. However, euphoric as I felt about Gascoigne's performance, a small voice inside kept reminding me of the Littlewood Cup semi-final of 1987, and when Arsenal scored just before half-time the past did begin to cloud the future. But for a change the stars smiled on us, and then Seaman made a mistake and Lineker scored the decisive third. Not even in my wildest fantasies could I have imagined beating Arsenal 3-1 in an FA Cup semi-final. In a single match, Tottenham's strikers had scored 20 per cent of all the goals Arsenal were to concede that season.

Victory at any time is a tonic. Those who are not part of the game cannot always appreciate what I would like to call the weekly audit of twenty to five: if at that time on a Saturday evening your team has won then all your problems seem lighter; if they've lost the world appears gloomier. Our victory over Arsenal had come at an odd hour, in mid-afternoon, but the euphoria generated was such that it even, for a time, managed to banish the Monday morning blues. The next day Nat said that Tottenham's position had been fundamentally changed by the semi-final. Now there was no question of selling Gascoigne to Lazio, at least not before the Cup Final, and not at £7 million. Also, it seemed, playing success had led to creating profits, and he was optimistic of our raising capital without any outside help.

After the match I gave Terry a lift from Wembley to a local hotel where he was going to have a celebration with his father. On the way we agreed to meet a couple of days later, as I wanted to discuss his new contract. The negotiations for this had started the previous October. Terry was on £175,000 plus bonuses. I had offered £150,000 plus much larger performance bonuses than normal, which in a good season would have earned him anything between £350,000 and £400,000. I thought that this was more than fair. His basic was only slightly down, and if he did well, won trophies, then he would earn a lot more money. But Terry didn't see it that way. He said: 'I had that when I was at Crystal Palace.' 'OK,' I replied. 'Tell me what you want and I'm sure we can come to some terms. I have made an offer which you have rejected, now it's for you to make an alternative proposal.'

But try as I might, Terry would just not make any counter-proposals. As I had found before in such negotiations, he expected you to make all the running and he would either agree or disagree, but never propose anything. I kept telling him: 'Give me your terms. I'm sure if we spend five minutes discussing it we shall hammer out an agreement.' But while he disliked my proposals he never put a figure on what he wanted. So as we drove back that sunny Sunday from Wembley amidst cheering, euphoric Spurs supporters, I suggested to him that we meet on Tuesday at my office to come to some agreement on his contract. It had been hanging fire for too long. The Press, to whom the story had been leaked, was painting me as the meanest of Scrooges, out to do Venables while he was leading the team's charge to Wembley.

According to the tabloid pundits, if Venables left then Spurs would be dragged into a Bermuda Triangle of no money, no Manager, no team. This was hardly the case. In fact, long before the semi-final I had had approaches on behalf of two leading managers who seemed very keen to come to White Hart Lane. The football grapevine had first alerted me to interest from others in Terry's job as far back as February, almost two months before the semi-final. On 26 February Kenny Dalglish suddenly announced that he was resigning as Manager of Liverpool. He insisted that there had been no disagreements with the board and he just wanted a rest from the tensions and strain of football. Managers have left clubs for various reasons, but this was, for Liverpool, highly unusual. Ever since Shankly had built the modern Liverpool in the Sixties, the tradition of the club had been that disagreements never left the famous Anfield Boot Room, everything seemed prescribed and according to plan, and the succession flowed naturally from one Manager to his groomed choice. So Shankly had been followed by Paisley and he in turn by Fagan and then Dalglish – all emerging from the Liverpool system which every club envied but few managed to copy. The Dalglish resignation started waves of rumours, and speculation about tensions in the Liverpool camp made Anfield look like any other club.

Although, like everybody else, I was surprised by the news, a few weeks previously I'd had some inkling of the tension that was simmering beneath the surface. I had gone to Brighton with a friend to see Liverpool play in an FA Cup replay. David Moores, then a director but since elevated to Chairman, confronted me as I entered the boardroom. He was in a real state, having a go about Dalglish. 'Can you imagine who we've bought? David Speedie? Thirty-one?' I asked him about another recent Dalglish purchase, Carter from Millwall. It seemed an unusual buy for Liverpool, and I wanted to know how he had fared the previous Saturday, as Terry had always spoken very highly of him. 'How did he play?' replied David Moores. 'He played. He was on the park. That's all I can tell you.'

As I drove back to London my friend, who had never been to a boardroom before, was curious to know if all football boardrooms were like this. I had to reassure him that it was very unusual to find Liverpool directors talking in such terms about their team or their manager. Seeing what happened a few weeks later, it seemed to me that boardroom rumblings must have reached the dressing-room, and the ear of Dalglish.

While Liverpool searched for his successor, Dalglish himself was brought to my attention after yet another tale of my contract negotiations with Venables had been leaked to the Press, with the writer speculating that Venables might leave Tottenham. One day I received a call from a man who described himself as a 'friend' of Kenny Dalglish. 'If things don't work out with Terry,' he said, 'Kenny might be interested in coming to White Hart Lane. I have his number, and when you think the time is right give us a buzz and things can be arranged.'

I had no idea whether the friend was acting with the consent of Dalglish or in an entirely freelance capacity. As it turned out it didn't matter, but it illustrates the point that, contrary to Press speculation, Venables's departure from Spurs would not have created a managerial black hole. Football, like nature, abhors a vacuum, and the position would have been filled by a Manager – and one, perhaps, whose pedigree in winning medals and trophies might have been even better than Terry's.

Dalglish's was not the only name to be floated past me. Not long after the first stories appeared I had a call from a man who described himself as a 'friend' of Graeme Souness, who was then the Manager of Glasgow Rangers and seemed very happy in his Scottish lair. This friend said much the same as in the Dalglish contact: Graeme would be 'very interested' if Terry moved on.

An interesting twist came twenty-four hours after Terry and I met to discuss his contract, on 17 April, when Liverpool announced that Souness would be taking over as their new Manager in place of the departed Kenny Dalglish. Some time after that I met Peter Robinson, and expressed some surprise about the hiring. Robinson said: 'We had to, didn't we Irving?' 'What do you mean Peter?' I asked. 'We had heard,' said Robinson, 'that Graeme was interested in going to Spurs, if things didn't work out with Terry Venables.' I must say I never received any direct expression of interest from Graeme Souness, but clearly the whispers reached Liverpool and had an effect.

The Press got no inkling of all this. In any case they were far too concerned with pushing the Venables view of what was happening at Tottenham. If the semi-final victory over Arsenal had made us feel that our name was written on the Cup, it was also the moment when Terry Venables began to use his extensive media contacts to try and undermine my position and that of the board and suggest that while he was riding on a white charger, we, the rest of the club, were trying to stop it, and even to sell Gascoigne. Jeff Powell interviewed Terry Venables and accused me of double-dealing on the Gascoigne transfer: stating the public position that I wanted him to stay at White Hart Lane but actually working behind the scenes to sell him.

I had ignored many previous criticisms, but I felt very hurt and upset by this and was forced to issue a writ for libel against the *Daily Mail* and Jeff Powell. It was a year before the action was heard, but despite Terry giving evidence for Associated Newspapers, the jury cleared my name and awarded me £100,000 in damages.

I was also being accused of trying to save my own skin, retain my position at Tottenham, and prevent a takeover by spinning out the negotiations, putting in impossible conditions, using any excuse I could to delay a final decision on the sale. This was just as ridiculous as the allegation about my double-dealing on the Gascoigne transfer. As we have seen, I had twice shaken hands with Larry Gillick on a deal, only to find that a handshake meant nothing but more words and more promises that were not fulfilled.

What these Press reports overlooked was the fact that Spurs as a public company was governed by complex Stock Exchange Regulations, and the City merchant bankers and solicitors were constantly advising us that before we reached any final decision we had to protect all shareholders. The last thing they and I wanted was another Michael Knighton situation, and I knew how easy it was to talk about doing a deal, how easy to agree terms, but how difficult it was to actually back up the claim with real money. It was about this time that Terry was asked about the availability of cash from his backers and replied: 'I have seen it, I have touched it.' Whatever he may have seen or touched, our advisers and the board could never arrange a similar experience.

The Tuesday meeting did not resolve the contract, and what grated with me was the way Terry spoke about Spurs. He said: 'I'm getting quite fond of Tottenham. Even my daughters quite like it.' 'Quite fond of Spurs' stuck in my throat. I could not help recalling that ever since I had signed Terry I had tried very hard to get him to wear the Spurs tie. It may not be the greatest tie in the world, but it is a symbol, and for me anyone associated with Tottenham ought to have been proud to wear it. But Terry never liked wearing it. He wore it the day he was presented to the Press as Manager, but never again wore it until the semi-final against Arsenal. Of course he also wore it for the Final. But that apart, he avoided it.

After the semi-final Larry Gillick had once again reappeared. Now he didn't want to make a bid for the entire company, but instead to acquire up to 29 per cent of the shares and refinance the Midland loan together with the loan I had given in order to save Lineker. We were still prepared to talk to Gillick, and Tony Berry, as usual, acted as middleman, but by the end of April Terry admitted that his Middle Eastern backers had withdrawn.

Now he had a new proposal. This one was backed by David

Garrard, a well-known property man in the West End of London. It would mean that once Terry had bought the club, he would then do a sale and leaseback of White Hart Lane, and he had already signed a conditional contract to that effect. The deal was meant to raise £11.5 million, with Tottenham paying an annual rent of around £1.5 million and retaining a buy-back provision over a certain period of time. Terry and his new backers had worked over the proposals on the Bank Holiday weekend, staying up until very late in the night.

I had gone to France for a few days, and the first I heard of it was when Bobroff rang me with the news. My first question was: 'Who has actually signed the contract to purchase?' 'Paul Bloomfield,' replied Bobroff. On hearing Bloomfield's name I couldn't help laughing. 'What is it?' asked Bobroff. 'Why are you laughing? What do you know about him?' I had known Bloomfield for many years, as he was a very astute property dealer, though not flush with funds to the level required to fulfil the contract. The other point on the contract was that it stated that 'Time is of the essence.' What this meant was that unless everyone followed the strict timetable written down in the contract, it would be null and void. In a normal contract you have a completion date. If by that time the contract is not met there is normally a period of grace of around fourteen days. It is only if the completion money is not paid after this period of grace that you can sue for breach of contract. However, in contracts which have a 'time is of the essence' clause you have to keep to the exact date and time specified, and if you don't then you can be sued or the contract be terminated.

In this contract something like £1.1 million had to be paid by the Wednesday morning, otherwise the contract was dead. At 9.30 on that Wednesday morning Ashurst Morris Crisp checked with the solicitors for the new Venables consortium and discovered that the deposit had not been paid. Ashurst was very sceptical about the deal, and Tottenham sent the papers to Healey & Baker, a well-known firm of chartered surveyors, whose comments were not very flattering. And all this whilst there were misleading newspaper headlines, suggesting that a takeover was due within twenty-four to forty-eight hours. Many of these stories were being peddled by some of Terry's sycophants, such as Martin Samuel of the *Sun*, Kevin Moseley of the *Daily Express*, and Jeff Powell of the *Daily Mail*.

All through this saga there were other anglers waiting to get their hooks into Tottenham. Round about that time a company doctor type, reasonably well known in the City and connected with the Thompson family which owns Queen's Park Rangers, approached us saying he was confident that the money was available to refinance the club. Old proposals reappeared, like the ghost of Christmas past, and I was back to the grind I'd known since that July day when I approached Robert Maxwell. Maxwell had also reappeared on the scene. At one of the board meetings Nat presented a letter he proposed sending to Robert Maxwell asking whether he would be interested in reviving the proposals we had discussed the previous autumn. This would be a good idea, since we could not afford to overlook any possibility. As one City banker had said, our financial conditions were so desperate that almost anything was worth trying – even another stab at Maxwell.

The euphoria of reaching the Cup Final was slowly disappearing, and the picture hadn't been as dramatically transformed as Nat had imagined on the morning after our triumph over Arsenal. The long-term requirement for money was still very substantial, but the drama of the past few months continued: men with ideas, but not often very much money, met financial advisers with time sheets to discuss yet more proposals about how they could raise money to save Tottenham. Over all this, as ever, loomed Miller and the Midland Bank.

Soon after the semi-final the Midland had given Nat yet another final deadline: there was no question of extending the current facilities beyond 30 April. Tottenham must reduce its overdraft from £10.5 million to £2.5 million – in other words sell Gascoigne.

On Monday 22 April, following our game at Sheffield United, Nat outlined the pressures Midland was exerting, and much against my wishes it was decided that he and James Perry of Ashurst Morris Crisp would fly to Italy the following Thursday to arrange for the sale of Gascoigne. Midland were playing a game of bluff and counter-bluff in which they proposed deadlines only to extract more fees from us. Later, as we shall see, they extended the deadline to 31 May but asked for a facility fee of £¼ million, which was bargained down to £100,000 and eventually agreed at £50,000. But Nat, not perhaps having my penchant for poker, or at least not at these stakes, did not feel able to resist the Midland.

I left the meeting feeling I had left a little bit of myself there. Nat's words and the look on the faces of the directors told me that there was nothing I could do to stop Gascoigne from going to Lazio. Or could I? Nat came back from Italy with a contract which was undated. It was to be dated when the bank guarantee was received, and was conditional upon Lazio and the player signing a contract of employment. Tottenham were to receive £6.7 million, which was less than I had previously been led to expect. I decided to find out what it would take to keep Gascoigne at Spurs. Mel Stein and Len Lazarus had travelled with Nat to Rome, and I met them to ask one very simple question: what would we have to pay to keep Gascoigne at White Hart Lane? Their answer fairly staggered me. If we could come up with a package which provided Gascoigne with £2 million plus salary, and confirm this before the Cup Final, then he would be prepared to stay and not sign for Lazio. Stein and Lazarus knew that we just could not meet these conditions.

After the 22 April meeting, which approved Nat's visit to Rome to finalise the deal with Lazio, I stopped attending the board meetings. I was an invitee to the plc board in any case, and I saw little point in attending the meetings, which took place almost every two or three days. It seemed there were two proposals which promised to provide some of the money we needed. The Venables consortium, in addition to the doubtful sale and leaseback, involved a Rights issue at 60p per share, which roughly meant that the present board would have to concede control but would have to agree to various conditions, some of which were not clear and others not very satisfactory as far as Tottenham were concerned. There was also a proposal by Baltic, which wanted to do a Rights issue at not less than 45p per share and were seeking to appoint three directors including Ray Green, a director of Rosehaugh plc, who was a box-holder at Tottenham, and Michael Goddard, head of Baltic.

Baltic wanted me, Bobroff and Berry to resign. They would not repay the loans that Frank and I had given Tottenham, but they would replace Midland Bank. By issuing seven new shares for every four already held at 45p per share they would raise £8 million. But the Baltic proposal had a problem – with Venables. Ray Green, who was quite well known to me, made it very clear that he did not see any role for Venables on the main plc board. He could have a position on the football club board, but Ray and his friends were not prepared to underwrite a Rights issue with Venables as Managing Director of the entire company. They saw him as a football team Manager and nothing more.

Baltic's proposals did not actually mention Tottenham Hotspur by name. With Nat getting quite paranoid about publicity, their documents spoke about a company called Striker, yet another in the long line of pseudonyms coined by the merchant bank advisers since the negotiations with Mindo in the previous summer.

I was fairly neutral between the two proposals, although professional advice tended to favour the Baltic approach. Brown Shipley had made the point that Baltic's offer had more commercial merit, as it meant we would not have to sell the company's principal property asset, the ground at White Hart Lane. Later, property surveyors Healey & Baker and accountants would confirm to us that such a transaction would be both difficult and not in the company's interest. We also knew that within three years the Taylor Report would mean more money for an all-seater stadium. The sale of the White Hart Lane ground before that might jeopardise any possibility of raising money later on.

But if this made Baltic attractive, Paul Bobroff did not see it that way. He had never much cared for Baltic from the beginning, and now he did not like their proposal, which meant that his shareholding would drop. He did not think that it was in the best interests of the shareholders, and felt it was quite wrong to consider such a proposal when the financial position of the company was still very much in the dark.

In contrast, the great champion of the Venables offer was Tony Berry. Despite the sort of money that I knew Gascoigne wanted to stay at Tottenham, Berry now believed that if we accepted the Venables offer and it went through then we could keep Gascoigne. Indeed, when the board met on 7 May, when both the Venables and the Baltic proposals were being considered, Berry pressed very hard for the Venables consortium to be accepted there and then. But he couldn't convince the other directors. They wanted to receive proper advice on what the sale and leaseback of White Hart Lane would mean.

My problem was that I just could not see where Terry Venables was getting his money from. I had shaken hands with Gillick on 95p thinking the deal was done, and then found myself in a crazy reverse bidding situation, and now I was being offered 60p by a new Venables consortium. Even if the bidding ended here, and my solemn handshakes were translated into legally watertight agreements, what guarantee was there that Venables would produce the money? He had failed to do so in the past, and this failure had become something of a joke, even among the advisers. As we have seen, the sale and leaseback proposal had stated 'time is of the essence' and required the payment of a deposit. But even this payment was three weeks overdue, which under such a contract was quite laughable. We were also waiting for the provision of a comfort letter of bank guarantee from the Venables consortium.

So as Tottenham approached the FA Cup Final the supporters may have felt that all roads led to Wembley, but in the boardroom they seemed to be stuck on a roundabout of fruitless ideas. Ian Gray was having discussions with the National Bank of Kuwait about borrowing £5 million. The lawyers were raising questions about the season ticket sales. Could we take money from the supporters knowing that, technically, the public company might have to be put into liquidation? A public company is covered by certain rules, and at almost every meeting the lawyers would warn us about our duties as directors in this respect.

The only way forward on the roundabout was, curiously, offered by the Midland Bank. Two days before the Cup Final, the entire board, including Jeremy Knight of Brown Shipley and David Buchler, had been to the Midland for a crucial meeting. David Buchler had helped prepare a Tottenham Hotspur plc recovery plan, and the bank wanted to discuss this along with the question of season ticket sales. Paul Bobroff was very confident that the Midland would be prepared to extend facilities on a long-term basis, something we all wanted, as soon as Gascoigne was transferred to Lazio. As we have seen it was Bobroff who had brought in the Midland in place of our traditional bankers, Barclays. He had a very good long-term relationship with the bank as part of his own business activities, and often he seemed to be one jump ahead of the board and all of us in reading the Midland's mind.

The board went into the meeting on the 16th with the express idea of trying to pin the Midland down to giving us a reasonable breathing space, rather than playing this silly bluff and counter-bluff game of extending the facilities every fifteen days or so. Encouraged by Bobroff, the board seemed pretty confident that the Midland would extend the facilities for three months up to the end of August, which would take us into the new season, bringing in season ticket sales and, if we won the FA Cup, opening up the lucrative European route. Which of these factors impressed Midland I do not know, but it was at this meeting, for the very first time, that the bank began to suggest that they might be prepared to grant us the sort of long-term facilities we were looking for. The meeting, in Midland's intensive care unit at Cannon Street, ended with Miller wishing us the very best of luck for the Cup Final. For the first time in almost six months, I began to feel that perhaps there might be some light at the end of this long financial tunnel.

15

SUGARING THE BITTER PILL

'Terry Venables thinks he is an entrepreneur, but I don't.'
 – Alan Sugar describing Venables to Scholar, just before Scholar agreed to sell his shares to Sugar.

After a year of immense tribulations, and against all odds, including the loss of Gascoigne after only nineteen minutes, Tottenham had triumphed. We had kept our date with destiny in the year ending with 1. Now came the cold reality. The day after the Cup Final I rang Jeff Randall. In the months since he had broken the Maxwell story he had followed a fairly consistent line: the only salvation for the club was winning the FA Cup. If that happened Spurs would have their lucrative entry ticket to European football and most of the problems could be tackled without any outside help. Now that we had won the Cup I wanted to know whether he would stick to that line and provide us with some breathing space. But instead of talking to him I listened to his recorded voice and then left this message on his answerphone: 'Just in case you hadn't noticed, Spurs won the FA Cup yesterday, and the only word I've got to say about it is B*******. And by the way that begins with a capital B.' Later I learned that he found this so amusing that he kept the message on the tape for a few days and often played it back to himself.

But a Spurs rescue without help from any outsiders was more than just a joke. After the FA Cup Final it did become a very distinct possibility. Indeed Randall himself would write a story headlined: 'Spurs: No More Bids, We'll Go It Alone.' After a lunch with Nat Solomon and David Buchler, at Nat's Berkeley Square offices, Randall reported Solomon saying that there was 'no financial crisis here', and Nat insisting: 'We can go it alone.' This was not as much of an empty boast as some people made out. The fact was that at no time throughout the difficulties did the Midland Bank ever mention the words administrator, receiver or liquidator. No matter what Fleet Street wrote.

The tide had begun to turn even before the Cup Final, at the meeting with Miller and the Midland Bank on 16 May. And horrific as Gascoigne's injury was, it hadn't cast as deep a shadow as some commentators made out. On the Monday following the Cup Final, Joe Lovejoy in the *Independent* had begun his doom-laden piece: 'Tottenham's insolvency was in question last night, twenty-four hours after they had won the FA Cup, when Lazio called off the 17 billion Lire (£7.9 million) transfer of Paul Gascoigne.' Then after summarising the various problems we faced he suggested that if we could not come up with something in the region of £11 million then Midland would go to the High Court and have the club placed under an independent administrator. Even if Baltic bid for us, he concluded, it would be a case of 'too little, too late'.

True, at our first meeting after the Cup Final, on Wednesday, Tottenham's possible insolvency was again discussed. Should we start selling season tickets? That would mean that we positively expected the company to be trading the next season. David Buchler felt that the directors would be exposing themselves to grave criticism if Tottenham had to go into liquidation after the season ticket money had been banked. But the lawyers, and there were a great many of them around that table, pointed out that in law we could sell the season tickets if we had decided to continue trading.

Also, as Nat pointed out, the deal with Lazio was not completely dead. He had been discussing various ideas with the Italians, one of which was that they would pay a deposit and then Gascoigne would be transferred the following July, or that they would pay a discounted sum now and he would be transferred subject to a medical at the end of the following season. It was when we met again a week later that Chris Ashworth gave the board the discounted price that Lazio was preparing to pay – £4.825 million. The only problem with this was that Lazio wanted repayment of the money plus interest if Gascoigne did not recover from his knee injury. Gascoigne, of course, had been insured before the season began, and if it proved that he couldn't play again Spurs were due to get £5.5 million. Lazio's renewed interest made Nat try to get some form of insurance underwritten so that if Gascoigne failed the Lazio medical and the deal didn't go through, Tottenham would still get the cash.

It was also at this meeting that I became aware that Terry Venables had a new backer. At the previous meeting on 22 May, I had been told that Terry was proposing to buy my shares and Bobroff's. I had assumed that this was still the Gillick consortium. At the 29 May meeting, Jeremy Knight of Brown Shipley told us that Henry Ansbach, who we had been told was representing the Larry Gillick consortium, would now be making a proposal on behalf of some other consortium. I can only assume that this was the start of Alan Sugar's involvement with Terry Venables. I was later to learn that it was Sugar who took the initiative when he rang Venables and offered his assistance.

There has been much speculation as to why Sugar should have got involved, and I know of at least one documentary-maker who has since been trying to prove that Sugar's involvement with Spurs was the result of a carefully laid-out master-plan between him and Rupert Murdoch. Murdoch had been interested in Manchester United, and there had been some plan to buy the club and then show all its matches live on Sky Television. Now, according to very many stories I have since heard, Murdoch encouraged Sugar to buy Spurs as part of a wider strategy which would help Sky to televise Premier League football matches. I doubt if there was any such master-plan. That would have been far too neat and quite impossible. At that stage the Premier League was still some way from coming together, and the televising of Premier League matches way, way over the horizon.

What I do think happened is that Murdoch encouraged Sugar to get into Spurs if only to thwart Maxwell. Maxwell was now busy trying to get rid of his other footballing interests and had once again come into view as a possible saviour for Spurs. Indeed it was at that meeting that Nat told us that a new party had made an approach to him, and asked each director to sign a confidentiality letter before he would divulge that person's name. That person, of course, was Robert Maxwell.

Maxwell's approach did not come as a complete surprise to me. The board had asked both Nat and me to approach Hill Samuel, Maxwell's merchant bank advisers, to see if they had any proposals for raising money. And a couple of weeks before Nat got us to sign a confidentiality letter, I had received an urgent call in Northern France from my office in London saying that Kevin Maxwell wanted to speak to me. When I rang him back it turned out he wanted to speak to Nat Solomon. It was after Kevin and Nat had spoken that I learnt that the Maxwells were now in a position to put forward some form of proposal concerning the underwriting of a Rights issue.

But although Maxwell and Sugar were now in the ring, our go-it-alone strategy still had some mileage. Indeed it was becoming more and more credible as time went on. David Buchler had helped us prepare a Tottenham Hotspur plc recovery plan which actually saw the group making trading profits, in excess of £1.7 million on a pessimistic projection, and in excess of £3.8 million on a realistic projection, for the year to 31 May 1992. The interest charges had been calculated on a bank base rate of 12 per cent, and any reduction on this would improve the profitability even further. All the group's subsidiaries, with the exception of Synchro Systems, were expected to make profits, and even on the most pessimistic assumptions the report estimated that we could by the following year make profits in excess of £4.4 million, with the bank overdraft reducing to £4.7 million by May 1992. We had to raise £5–7 million, but the report considered various ways we could do it:

1 The Gascoigne sale for about £4.8 million. (The report stressed that if Gascoigne could not be sold at 'a significant discount of the price agreed prior to the Cup Final' then the directors would be prepared to sell other players.)
2 The sale of other players.
3 The sale and leaseback of the football ground and related premises.
4 Injection of fresh money through a Rights issue, convertible loan stock or debt conversion.
5 A debenture offer to supporters to raise funds in the fashion that Arsenal had recently done, and Glasgow Rangers earlier.
6 A package of debt instruments secured on the assets of the Group to replace Midland Bank as the debtor.

Naturally, all this depended on Midland continuing to support the club up to 31 May 1992, and the plan was meant to get this long-term commitment from Midland.

Of course today's optimistic profits projection could easily look like tomorrow's stupid losses. Back in November we had been forecasting to break even for the year ended 31 May 1991, and this without selling any players. Indeed the FA Cup run during the year should have resulted in our exceeding the profit forecast by something like £300,000. All this had turned to dust because of Martex, and the professional fees we had incurred during the year. The two together had cost us £1.3 million, so instead of making a profit we had made a loss of £1 million.

However, the recovery plan we had produced was realistic. Midland seemed to think it had merit, and suggested we have it reviewed by Ernst & Young. On 4 June they gave it their seal of approval, saying that the plan 'appears to have been prepared after due and careful consideration by management and appeared consistent with the assumptions used.' But they warned that the club was 'in imminent danger of breaching its current overdraft facilities'. There were a lot of payments to be made both during June and before the new season, as some suppliers were not willing to supply goods to us. This, said the report, was 'restricting the ability of the Group to generate further cash and profits', and the whole thing depended on 'continued bank support.'

This, at last, did seem to be forthcoming. Nat met John Thompson at Midland Corporate Banking on 4 June to go over the proposals of the recovery plan. When times are booming banks can throw money around like confetti. In bad times, or when companies are in trouble, the same banks can adopt a remarkable crablike approach to lending any money. Midland were doing that, but at least they were moving, however slowly, in our direction.

Thompson wanted to know how Midland's overdraft would be affected if Gascoigne was sold, or if he was not sold. Nat assured him that irrespective of whether Gascoigne was sold or not there would still be a Rights issue some time in October to raise £3.5 million, which would give the club £3 million after expenses were deducted. If Gascoigne was not sold then there would be another player-sale, bringing about a million by December. A Gascoigne sale would mean that the Midland debt would fall between £4.7 million and £5.7 million by December and would be between £2.5 million and £3.5 million by next May. If Gascoigne was not sold and it was another player, for a million, then the bank's debt would be somewhat higher – by December at between £7 and 8 million, and falling to between £4.8 and £5.8 million by May. So, as we gathered for the board meeting on 6 June, there was a very distinct feeling of optimism. Not only were Maxwell and Sugar keen to buy into the club, but the bank was prepared to extend facilities for a year and really help us solve our problem.

For me, the crucial question in all this was whether the club would be secure and whether we could somehow still hold on to Paul Gascoigne. I had just walked into the room when Nat came running over to me, holding a piece of paper. He said: 'Irving, look at this.' It was a proposal by Terry Venables and Alan Sugar, but Nat was pointing to a clause in the proposal and I read it with absolute incredulity. It said that the Sugar/Venables offer was conditional on the sale of Paul Gascoigne for a figure of not less than £4.5 million.

After I had recovered from my shock I started laughing. For months now there had been any number of stories in the Press as to how keen Terry was to keep Gascoigne at White Hart Lane, how if he was allowed to take over the club Gascoigne would actually remain in White Hart Lane, and he would do everything in his power to make sure he did. I was painted as the villain of the piece, the man who said he wanted to keep Gascoigne but was secretly planning to sell him. In contrast Maxwell had made it clear to Nat that he would be very unhappy if Gascoigne were sold.

But I suppose that all is fair in love and war – or in trying to acquire Tottenham Hotspur. At the meeting we decided that negotiations with Sugar and Venables must continue: they were looking to make a Rights issue at around 70p per share, and it was agreed to meet in four days' time, on Monday 10 June, to review progress on both the proposals.

When we met that day the situation seemed to have changed even more dramatically. Lazio's lawyers were looking at an agreement produced by Ashurst Morris Crisp which would mean Lazio placing the money wanted to pay for Gascoigne into a London account and the interest going to Tottenham. Technically Gascoigne would still be a Tottenham player, and the transfer would be subject to a medical which, of course, could only take place once he was fit. But it would mean that Tottenham would have something like £5.3 or 5.4 million in its bank.

There is nothing like the prospect of money to make a banker excited, and Midland, which had so long been a tortoise, was suddenly becoming a hare. On 31 May, Miller had written to Nat extending the current overdraft facilities to 7 June. But on 10 June, the day of our meeting, Midland sent a letter agreeing to extend facilities up to 31 May 1992, provided certain terms were met. In effect the bank was prepared to extend a current overdraft of £10.8 million until next May, provided we agreed to reduce some of the overdraft and, of course, pay hefty fees. Interest would be at 2 per cent above the base rate, and the bank would be charging what it called a facilitation fee. We'd have to pay £60,000 immediately, and from 1 October a monthly fee of £5,000 for every tranche of half a million by which the overdraft exceeded £5 million, as well as legal costs incurred by the bank in preparing all the necessary documentation. I knew such legal costs did not come cheap, and the Midland used Allen & Overy, one of the most expensive lawyers in the City. Coincidentally they were also the lawyers used by Lazio to advise on the draft that Ashurst Morris Crisp had presented to them regarding Gascoigne's transfer.

However, stiff as these terms were, they were like manna from heaven. Brown Shipley were so heartened by the letter that they felt that it should be good enough to go to the Stock Exchange and get the suspension of the shares lifted. The crisis was over after six months of torture. All talk of Spurs going bust and being saved from extinction was passé, even though Fleet Street hadn't grasped the point. There were still little niggling matters to be settled, regarding some of Tottenham's subsidiaries and the loans that Frank and I had given to the company. We felt that David Buchler, who had been so instrumental in getting Midland round to our side, could deal with it. Midland's letter had spoken about steps being taken 'to improve the management of the public company and of the club', and we were all very keen to have David in as a director of the company. I fully supported this because, if nothing else, I felt it would lift the tone of our board meetings.

For some time now there had been growing concern about the various leaks from the board. At one stage it got so bad that I believe the Department of Trade and Industry rang Nat up and expressed concern. Nat had got very worked up about this, and at the meeting it was decided that only Nat could speak to the Press, and if any other director spoke to the Press then this would make that person's position as a director impossible. We all approved the resolution, with the exception of Tony Berry.

On the Saturday before our meeting Nat had spoken on the phone to Maxwell pointing out that we had still received no firm proposal from him, although Hill Samuel and Brown Shipley had been in touch with each other and various prices and amounts to be raised had been mentioned. Maxwell, it seemed, was back to his old game. He required unanimous approval by the board, and an exclusive right to negotiate terms with the company. This was clearly impossible, and we decided Nat should tell him that what we were looking for was a one-to-one Rights issue, one new share for every existing share at £1 a share, which would give Tottenham £10.2 million.

Maxwell had forty-eight hours to reach an agreement in principle. We felt that this would give us some indication of whether he was really keen to proceed, and once we got his response we could judge his proposal against that of Venables and Sugar. Now interestingly Alan Sugar had also requested exclusive rights to negotiate, similar in kind to those requested by Maxwell.

Three days later we met again. Over the past few months I had got used to sombre board meetings where lawyers would warn us about continuing to trade while caught in our parlous financial position, and proposals to raise money would appear and disappear like aces in a card-sharp's pack. This meeting was different. Midland were prepared to go public and, in order to further appease them, David Buchler was appointed a director – although he proved to be one of the shortest-serving directors in Tottenham Hotspur's history.

Midland were not the only bank we were talking to. Ian Gray had finally got a letter from the Bank of Kuwait, who were prepared to extend overdraft facilities up to £4.5 million, but it wasn't a formal letter and it contained a great many unacceptable conditions. Also the amount of security they required was far beyond what we could offer. However we decided that we should keep talking to them, and Ian was asked to go back to the bank and get them to make a formal offer. This was also our intention with regard to Maxwell, but here, as ever, the problem was to pin him down. Maxwell had rejected our previous proposal, but he was prepared to negotiate terms provided he had the unanimous backing of the board.

At this stage the big differences between the Maxwell and Sugar proposals were that while Sugar and Venables would have had to let Gascoigne go, it was a condition of the Maxwell bid that he stayed, and Maxwell was quite indifferent to Venables. As we have seen, Terry's contract with the club was about to run out, and Nat and Douglas had had a number of discussions about a new contract. Indeed, Nat was quite in favour of offering him the position of Managing Director, to which Terry's response was characteristic – he would look at all offers, but obviously could not commit himself to it while his own proposal to take over the company was on the table. Knowing Terry as I did, I did not find this at all surprising. He always likes to keep all his options open in relation to everything. He will listen to any offer you make, but will rarely give you a decision unless he gets to the point where he wants to do something. To push him or persuade him into something is very, very difficult.

Incidentally, the revised offer from Sugar and Venables had suggested that Terry should be appointed a director of the club with immediate effect. We decided that would not be a good idea, but continued to pursue both the Sugar and the Maxwell options. Brown Shipley were asked to contact Hill Samuel and see if a firm offer of finance could be raised from Maxwell. We were meeting on the Thursday afternoon, and we wanted Hill Samuel to come back with some figures by the Friday evening, or at the latest by Monday morning.

We met again on Tuesday, 18 June, when we had a further revised proposal from Venables and Sugar alongside an offer that we still expected to receive from Maxwell. Tony made it very clear that he did not want us to have any dealings with Maxwell. In previous meetings Tony's position as director and his declared support for the Venables/Sugar offer had raised the question of conflict of interest. It had been raised by the lawyers, and even been supported by Jeremy Knight of Brown Shipley. Tony kept insisting that he had no financial involvement in the Venables/Sugar offer, and that all he was seeking to do was act in the best interests of the company.

So what were the best interests of the company? This is a phrase often used in such discussions, but for the first time, at least in my experience, I heard a City firm of lawyers provide a remarkable definition of the company's interest. Chris Ashworth pointed out that when we considered the two proposals we should also take into account the interest of the shareholders, employees, and also the supporters, on the grounds that the best interests of the company would not be served by alienating its customers. This was a very novel, interesting point, and I had never heard it put in quite this fashion before.

Tony was very keen to get the Sugar/Venables deal accepted there and then. Indeed he proposed a motion to that effect, but couldn't find a seconder. After a great deal of discussion about the merits of the two offers it was decided that Brown Shipley should try and improve them and that we would meet, yet again, the next day.

For various reasons I did not attend that meeting, but I heard that Brown Shipley felt that the two teams, Venables/Sugar and Maxwell, virtually cancelled each other out: a scoreless draw. The Maxwell offer would have meant injecting more money into the company, but it was conditional, while the Venables/Sugar offer had been improved from 70 to 75p. Bobroff turned up late for the meeting and expressed his support for Venables and Sugar. This was the first time for a couple of weeks that Bobroff had attended a meeting, and at one stage in early June, when he couldn't attend for a couple of weeks, he suggested that I be appointed an alternative director in his absence. When I heard the news, the temptation to resign on his behalf there and then was very strong!

By this time I was reaching the end of my tether. The euphoria of the Cup Final had long since vanished, and I just sought relief from the non-stop Press comment about Tottenham, which was finally getting to me. It had been illustrated a few weeks before, some time in May, when Bill Fox had rung me saying he wanted to buy Paul Stewart or Gary Lineker. He was prepared to offer around £1.5 million for each player, but when I showed no interest he upped the offer to £2 million. I still didn't think that a deal could go through, but felt duty-bound to place it in front of the board and let them take the decision.

Within two hours of putting the phone down on Fox, I noticed on Ceefax an item saying that Lineker had been bid for at £2 million by Blackburn Rovers. I was absolutely incensed and immediately rang Fox back. 'What's your game?' I said. 'This is not my idea of doing business, by immediately talking to the papers. I haven't even had a chance of putting it to the board. In any case I doubt if Lineker, even if we agree terms, would accept this offer in a month of Sundays.' Fox accepted my point, but argued that it was his role to get favourable publicity for Blackburn Rovers, who were just beginning a remarkable spending spree financed by Jack Walker, and that it was his duty to do the very best for Blackburn. However, in my view, doing the best for Blackburn did not mean conducting transfer negotiations through the Press, and I made my feelings very clear on this. I had never thought I would end up shouting at the Chairman of the Football League, but this is what I did and

I had no qualms about it. As it happened the board rejected the offer, after hearing my view that it was very doubtful that Lineker would accept, but the episode just demonstrated that now almost anything concerning Tottenham was bound to be leaked to the Press. This, I was sure, was doing untold damage on the business front, and affecting our supporters, shareholders, staff, players and everybody. I was fed up to my back teeth with all this Press speculation, and as the never-ending saga of bid and counter-bid went on I decided that I would go for a few days to Monte Carlo. I decided to leave on the morning of Friday 21 June, but before I did I spoke to Alan Sugar.

Soon after Alan Sugar had revealed his hand I had arranged to meet him, but although I had specified a private meeting, five minutes later all and sundry had been told about it, so I called it off. This time I did speak to him, and my very first question was: 'What sort of role do you have in mind for Terry Venables?'

'Terry Venables thinks he's an entrepreneur,' replied Sugar, 'but I don't.'

'Will he be in charge of the team?'

'Of course he will,' Sugar replied.

This was just the answer I wanted to hear, and it reassured me no end. Ever since Terry Venables had made a move to acquire Tottenham I had been fearful that this would mean his leaving the dressing-room for the directors' box. I saw, and still see, Terry as a great coach and I thought that would be a great waste. I had worked with him now for four years, and it was clear to me that he was not yet ready to be Managing Director. A Manager may feel that he has the run of a football club, but a football club, especially one like Tottenham, is more than the Manager of the team. A Managing Director's role was something Terry had to grow into. There are a million and one things the MD has to look at and Terry had done nothing since his arrival in 1987 to suggest that he was interested in the club's other activities. Like most managers, he would leave the training ground at about 1 or 1.30, but unlike, say, Peter Shreeve or David Pleat, he would not go to football matches but followed his own freelance activities, went to his club or whatever. At Tottenham we had management meetings on a weekly basis, and I had often invited Terry to attend those meetings, but he never did. Occasionally he would send along Doug Livermore, the assistant manager. So whilst he may have felt in his own mind that he was versed in every aspect of the club, I knew that he didn't know enough about Tottenham to run it. Sugar's words reassured me that if the deal went through, Sugar knew what Terry's proper role in the club would be.

Sugar was also aware that Maxwell was still hovering in the background. He had made noises to the effect that he wasn't going to get into an auction: he had made his offer, and if he didn't get it on those terms he would just go back to selling his electronic equipment.

I still could not come to a decision as to whether I should sell to Sugar, but I told him that I might well support him.

That evening I kept debating the rival Sugar and Maxwell bids, and next morning I awoke with a very clear head and a decision: I would support the Sugar/Venables bid. I had made up my mind some time back that I wanted to leave, and Maxwell had messed me about for far too long. I was completely fed up with him. I could no longer accept his word, or anything he said or promised to do. His promises always turned to dust, or he did something completely different.

On that Friday afternoon I had no sooner settled into my Monte Carlo flat than the phone started to ring. The first call was from Bobroff. He told me he was on his way to attend the meeting at Ansbachers at 3 pm and that he had struck a deal with Sugar and Venables to sell his shares at 75p. Two or three weeks before this, Bobroff had had discussions with Maxwell and agreed to sell his shares to him, with Maxwell suggesting that he might do the deal through a small bank that he owned. But Bobroff had not committed himself to Maxwell, and now he had gone to the Sugar/Venables camp. His thinking was mirrored by the rest of the board, and I was prepared to go along with this.

But I had hardly put down the phone to Bobroff when Harry Harris was on the line trying to persuade me to deal with Maxwell. In that morning's *Daily Mirror* Harris himself had written that Maxwell was withdrawing from the negotiations to underwrite the Rights issue and withdrawing from the entire transaction. This was entirely typical of Maxwell: to say one thing to the *Daily Mirror* and do something different.

Soon after, I got a call from Maxwell himself to ask me what I was doing. I explained that along with Bobroff I was prepared to sell to Sugar and Venables, but I could not hide the fact that I still had doubts about the deal. Maxwell's withdrawal meant that Sugar and Venables had to make an entire bid for the company. They had said that they would have something like £6 million to

£7.5 million to put in the company. An entire bid would mean that nearly all of this money would go to the shareholders, leaving little for Tottenham. Maxwell immediately latched on to this and said: 'How about if I buy your holding, together with Bobroff's? Or if I limit myself to 29.9 per cent, buying 10 per cent of Bobroff and 19.9 per cent from you, so that you would be left with about 6 or 7 per cent. Sugar and Venables can then go ahead with their Rights issue at 75p, this will not eat up all their money, and all of it would be left to be put into Tottenham. Surely this would be the ideal solution. Spurs would have two Sugar Daddies; myself holding 29.9 per cent and Alan Sugar.'

I must say this did make a lot of sense to me. It meant that Tottenham would be guaranteed £7.5 million pumped into the company rather than having it used to pay the shareholders. Maxwell emphasised that he had no real intention of becoming directly involved in running the company. He would stand on the sidelines holding 29.9 per cent, Sugar and Venables could still go ahead with their deal, and it would be far cheaper for them in the long run.

I rang Bobroff at once and told him about my discussions with Maxwell. He also saw the merit of the proposal and was quite happy to follow my lead. Unlike myself, he just wanted the cash and to get out of Tottenham. I rang Maxwell back with the news and told him that my solicitors in London had the power of attorney to agree any deal I approved. But I emphasised to him that the deal had to be unconditional and had to be concluded that day. There could be no further delay, no equivocation, no more being led up the garden path – whether from the various Venables consortiums or from Robert Maxwell.

I should have known, of course, that dealing with Maxwell would never be simple. Unknown to me, at about 5 o'clock, he rang Nat Solomon, who along with Bobroff and the rest of the Tottenham board was at Ansbachers, to tell him that he had agreed to buy 29.9 per cent. I believe he even said he had bought 29.9 per cent, which was a lie but would have been typical of Maxwell. As the *Sunday Times* would later put it, 'Nat went white' on hearing the news. He immediately rang Alan Sugar, who hurried to Ansbachers' office to try and rescue his deal.

They were not the only people rushing to Ansbachers that evening. Maxwell had sent a delegation round which included Jack Dunnett, to act as legal adviser and provide expertise in Football League rules, a representative from his solicitors, Titmuss Sainer & Webb, and Roger Devlin of Hill Samuel. My own solicitor, John Bennett from Berwin Leighton, was also there. Curiously, John had been involved in the preliminary discussions concerning Ashurst Morris back in September, but only for a day, before he had to go away on business and Peter Robinson had taken over. But with Robinson on holiday John was back, so in a curious symmetry he was present at the beginning and at the end.

John also knew something which meant that Maxwell could not possibly fulfil my desire to have an unconditional deal done that very day. Although I did not know this at the time, and John only told me later, he was involved with one of the parties trying to buy Derby County from Maxwell. Maxwell had told the Press, and Jeff Randall had reported on 16 June, that he had sold Derby County, but John knew that the deal had not been completed. Now under the Football League rules he was not free to make a proposal to buy into Tottenham. Of course, this was not the impression he had given Nat, but as the evening wore on Maxwell's Achilles' heel was to be revealed.

But that would take some time, and meanwhile, as I was later to learn, a quite furious battle took place over the next few hours, between Alan Sugar, Maxwell's advisers, and Nat Solomon and the Tottenham board. I had gone out that evening, leaving John Bennett a number where he could contact me. He didn't need to do so, but Bobroff did ring me in some agitation and said: 'It's all right for you, sitting in Monte Carlo. They are all shouting at me here.' It seemed that he had just suffered a very serious verbal attack from Alan Sugar, who had told him in no uncertain terms that he should not deal with Maxwell but instead sell the shares to him.

Soon it became clear that all this was very academic. Sugar was in a position to make an unconditional deal there and then. Maxwell was not. Maxwell kept saying he could enter into an unconditional deal but he had not yet sold Derby County. What he wanted was a further week or ten days until he got the Football League's approval. I was not prepared to extend that time to him. I wanted a deal that day, and for no other reason than my sharp concern about what a delay might do for Tottenham. It was now the end of June, and if for some reason the deal with Terry Venables's consortium fell through, then it was very likely he would not continue as Manager. We would have to find a suitable replacement, and in a few weeks' time the pre-season training would start. To Maxwell these things meant nothing. To me, having run a football club for nine years, they were vital. After all we had gone through the previous year, we could not start a new season, and one which would see the return of Spurs to Europe, in the possible absence of a Manager and with no proper organisation of pre-season training. Harry Harris kept ringing, trying to persuade me to see Maxwell's point of view, but it was too late.

Finally, just after midnight, John Bennett agreed the sale of my shares to Alan Sugar. He had already bought Bobroff's shares. The deal I did with Sugar was a complete and final settlement: the loan the Holborn Property Company had given to save the Lineker transfer was repaid, with the final instalment of the outstanding interest to be settled on the Monday or the Tuesday. In addition, £350,000 I had lent Tottenham a year before was also repaid, along with the dividend cheques that I had not banked in the previous eighteen months to two years. I also resigned as Chairman of the football club, but retained a seat on the board along with Paul Bobroff. Bobroff quickly sensed that this meant nothing, and later that evening he rang and said: 'They've offered you a seat on the board of the football club, but I wouldn't be at all surprised if within six to eight weeks from now that will be withdrawn.' In fact I asked John Bennett to get the offer of a board seat in writing, but Sugar refused to do that.

If this suggests that Sugar was upset with me, he gave no indication of it when immediately after the deal was done I rang him at Ansbachers' offices and wished him the very best of luck for the future.

'Alan, I wish you the very best of luck, and I hope you get as much enjoyment as I did out of it without the aggravation.'

'Don't worry about me,' he replied. 'I will get no aggravation.'

He had accepted my good wishes with grace, but I later understood from John Bennett that he was a little bit peeved that I had thought of selling to Maxwell, creating a last-minute hitch which he felt might have proved disastrous from his point of view.

True, if Maxwell had been able to complete unconditionally that very day, I would have struck a deal with him. But of course what none of us knew was that Maxwell was at that very moment dipping his hand into the pension fund in order to relieve his great financial problems. With hindsight, I am delighted that he was unable to complete the purchase, because I would have found it extremely difficult to have had on my conscience, for evermore, the thought that he had purchased my Spurs shares with what amounted to stolen money. I am very relieved now, looking back, that fate dealt its hand in the way it did.

I went to bed that evening feeling relief that the whole saga was finally over. The nightmare year had ended. Yet I could not help thinking of the problems that lay ahead for the club, and particularly the problems for Terry Venables. I could not figure out how he had got the money to invest in Tottenham. Some months before this I had discussed with Terry on behalf of Cockerel Books that we might buy his video called *The Terry Venables Story* from the receiver of the production company that had made it. When it came to Terry paying his share of £15,000 to finance the video, he asked if I would mind deducting the amount from his salary over the next six months. This made me very sceptical about Terry's involvement in any deal. The public may have wanted it, but did he have sufficient funds? Eventually Terry had to borrow a lot of money in order to invest in Spurs, and by doing that he broke the golden rule of football: never borrow money to buy a football club.

Also some of his ideas did make me wonder. He had tried to do a sale and leaseback on the ground, which was hardly very clever, because it would mean exchanging interest payments for rent. When I had spoken to Sugar earlier I had asked him: 'Are you prepared to do a sale and leaseback?' He answered No, and it reassured me that at least Terry Venables's partner was of the same mind as I was.

But all this was now in the past. I awoke the next morning at about 10 o'clock, and my first thought was to ring Terry Venables at his home. It was 9 o'clock in London, and I woke him up with my call, wishing him all the luck for the future. I had once desired to be Chairman of Tottenham when they won the European Cup, and I now wished Terry the same success. He said he understood my feelings, knew they were genuine sentiments, and we parted on very friendly terms.

On the Sunday after the deal with Sugar went through, Paul Bobroff telephoned me. He asked what I intended to do now. I said I wasn't sure, but after all the trials and tribulations of the last twelve months I needed to relax. Then I asked him the same question. 'Well,' he told me, 'I've got a job to do. I have to get my share price up in Markheath Securities.' The shares in Markheath were standing that day, according to the newspapers, at around 26p. Nearly a year later, when Bobroff left the company, the shares stood at around 14p.

A few weeks after the Sugar sale, I received a letter from Tottenham Hotspur. It informed me that the board of the new plc, led by Alan Sugar and Terry Venables, had met and had accepted a motion that I be removed from the board of the football club. Paul Bobroff's words had come true.

POSTSCRIPT

'Double? What Double? Is that
something from the 1950s?'
      – Alan Sugar when asked about
      the Spurs Double team before
      the start of the 1991/92 season.

It is now fifteen months since I decided to sell to Alan Sugar.
Since then I have been round the world once, and will soon
set out again, catching up on the things I couldn't do while I
was running Spurs. I feel neither anguish nor bitterness about
what has happened. Those of us who are involved in football,
or for that matter in any major sport, tend to get carried away
by hyperbole: tragedy, disaster, desolation, horror, sadness . . .
and all because Liverpool have lost by one goal. I have never
deluded myself that the game was more important than anything
else in life. If there is defeat at four forty-five on a Saturday
afternoon, four forty-five does not mean the end of the world.
Bill Shankly's remark that football is more important than life or
death was the sort of soundbite – and in this respect he could
teach Terry Venables a thing or two – that was always likely to
be misinterpreted. Football may be a metaphor for life; it is not
a substitute for it.

The real tragedy lies in the world outside. Such tragedies
fill our television screen every day: in Bosnia, in Somalia, in
places far and near. Real tragedy is hearing, as I did when I
was at Spurs, that a young player who had just signed for us
was not going to make it: not in football but in life. A medical
team had found that he had a rare blood disease and had only a
few months to live. I remember when we told his parents, how
distressed they were – particularly his father, who refused to

believe that this young boy, full of life, could be at death's door. Eventually he had to accept it, and there was nothing he could do about it. That was tragedy. Not the fact that Erik Thorstvedt, in his first match for Spurs, against Nottingham Forest, let the ball slip through his hands for a goal. Television commentators did use the word 'tragedy', but then they deal in a currency that is always inflating whatever the state of the game or the world.

The tragedy was Hillsborough, a numbing experience which made administrators vow that this sort of obscenity had no place in football. How sad to relate that almost four years later something similar happened in Corsica when the Second Division French club Bastia erected temporary stands to play a French Cup semi-final against Marseille.

I will never forget going to Milan, a few days after the Hillsborough tragedy, to see AC Milan play Real Madrid in a European Cup semi-final. Sixty seconds after the kick-off the referee awarded a free kick. Instead of allowing the players to take the free kick he ran towards the ball, stood still and upright a yard or so away from it, blew his whistle, and everything stopped on the pitch. There was a minute's silence for those lives lost at Hillsborough. On the upper tier of the San Siro stadium is the equivalent of our Kop, and they all raised their scarves above their heads and gave an impromptu rendition of 'You'll Never Walk Alone'. It was as if they were stretching out their hands to the real Kop at Anfield and at Hillsborough and saying: 'It could have been us.' It was quite the most moving experience I've ever had in a football ground, and I cried like a child. To me that sums up the special quality of football, that is what makes a world game, a game which requires no language and where a single physical action can convey the deepest of emotions.

So what happened to me at Spurs was not a tragedy. It made my life miserable for a year, but it still left me with a lot of blessings: health, wealth and wisdom – although some of my friends doubt if I ever had very much of the last, certainly when they hear my football stories. I have two beautiful children and the friendship and respect of many people both inside and outside the game.

Yet I cannot help but feel a certain sadness about what has happened to Spurs and to English football since I've been away. I say this not with any sense of being the king over the water. I've no desire to return to English football, although in recent months several clubs have been offered to me for sale, including Watford and Luton. There is no question of my going to any other club other than Spurs, and I do not hanker or even wish for a return.

What worries me is the way Spurs is changing – a change that I do not think is for the better.The Spurs I loved, and still do love, is the aristocratic Spurs: always having the star players, always playing the most creative football, always behaving in the most sportsmanlike fashion. I shall never forget Danny Blanchflower saying about football: 'The great fallacy is that the game is first and last about winning. It is nothing of the kind. The game is about glory. And about doing things in style, with a flourish, about going out and beating the other lot, not waiting for them to die of boredom.' Spurs to me is about style. Winning every match, playing the offside game in a defensive style, may be all right at other clubs, but not at Tottenham.

The problem is that it is hard to see how the present Tottenham side, with hardly any world-class players, can produce the sort of stylish, open, attractive football that is the Spurs heritage. Whatever else I may or may not have done at Spurs, I always tried to bring the finest players to the club, and it was during my chairmanship that Gascoigne, Waddle and Lineker were signed.

Yet the present Spurs don't seem to think that way. What else can explain the fact that Spurs made no attempt to re-sign Chris Waddle from Marseille? He probably has another three or four years of top-class football in him. I don't know if Chris would have gone back, but the point is that Spurs didn't try. Several clubs were interested in signing him, yet Spurs didn't even pick up the telephone. I believe that Chris is now an even better player than he was when he left Tottenham, and what is more he has tremendous potential as a first-rate Manager.

That is perhaps my other great regret about the way that Spurs are developing. Many of its best sons are in exile: Ossie Ardiles is receiving rave reviews as Manager of West Bromwich Albion; Glenn Hoddle still proving a wonder player – and a very good Manager – at Swindon; and Steve Perryman in command at Watford. Just as the players sold by successive managers to Norwich form a Spurs in exile, these three, and in time Waddle, form a Spurs management in exile. Surely their talents, their expertise, their skills, would be better employed at White Hart Lane? I have nothing against Doug Livermore and Ray Clemence, now the coaching duo managing Spurs, but why should Spurs, whose old boys show such continuing gifts, have to go to Liverpool Old Boys to get their football management input? I just can't understand that.

Of course, all these questions would be irrelevant if Terry Venables had stayed in charge of the team. As I have already said, Sugar's assurance to me on this was one of the reasons that persuaded me to sell to him. I was further reassured when, during his Press conference after the takeover on 22 June 1991, he very firmly stated: 'I will look after the £11 million at the bank, while Terry Venables will look after the eleven players on the pitch.' But within a few days all this had been stood on its head. Peter Shreeve was appointed as the first-team coach, and then eventually Manager, and despite all the assurances I had been given, and the public statements, Terry abdicated his responsibility as team Manager. As I have always said, he is one of the best coaches in the business. His place is in the dressing-room. During the FA Cup run of 1991 he built up a tremendous team spirit, and that is where he was needed most. After all the trials and tribulations of that season, it would have been impossible for anyone new to come in, declare business as usual, and simply carry on.

I really felt for Peter in that season. He just could not win. If he was successful people would say it was Terry's team; if he wasn't, it would be his fault. As we have seen he wasn't, and he was sacked. When one person is buying players and another is coaching them, picking the team and responsible for the results, you have an imbalance. This is football's version of what Rudyard Kipling, in another context, called the harlot's prerogative: power without responsibility. In my experience you should either control all aspects of the team, or none at all.

I wonder if the duality between Terry and Peter was responsible for some of the strange actions of the last season. Having failed to sign Paul Parker from Queen's Park Rangers to bolster the defence, Spurs signed Gordon Durie up front. True, Terry had always admired Durie, but it is curious that having failed to get one of Britain's finest central defenders, he should then go for a forward. In that sense, of course, it was entirely logical for Spurs, having been beaten by Leeds 5-0 in the Premier League this season, to immediately sign another forward: Teddy Sherringham. Of course if Terry was seeking to recreate the old Spurs' philosophy of, 'you'll score five and we'll score six', then I would applaud him. But I doubt if that was his intention.

In many ways my biggest worry is that Spurs are abdicating their position as one of the Big Five clubs of English soccer along with Arsenal, Manchester United, Liverpool and Everton. Their place appears to have been taken by Leeds, both on and off the field, and Spurs seem to be finding a common purpose with the likes of Wimbledon and Crystal Palace. I cannot honestly believe that they have more in common with such clubs than with Manchester United and Liverpool. The danger is that once you switch alliances it is very difficult to switch back – as much in football as in politics.

As far as the team is concerned, some of the players Terry has bought make me think he is trying to create a Crystal Park Rangers. Spurs' traditions are very different, and I am not sure that is what the supporters would like to see at White Hart Lane.

Of course, if such moves help Terry win honours for the club then I shall be the first to applaud him. But I get the feeling that he has got his excuses already rehearsed. I keep hearing and reading that the current 1992/93 season is a transitional one. A transition to what? This is Terry's sixth season at Spurs. It is five years since he proclaimed: 'I've got three years to win the League.' A lot has happened since then – for example he has spent £18 million on players – but as one shrewd Manager observed, it is the third time in the last four years that Spurs has been in transition. Is this Terry's football equivalent of Leon Trotsky's concept of the permanent revolution in politics? I wonder.

That Alan Sugar has turned the business round I do not doubt. He has done so by injecting his money into the company. In early December 1991 Sugar announced a Rights issue to raise £7 million net of expenses at £1.25 per share. This was the first significant share capital to be injected into the company since the flotation, with Sugar himself underwriting £6 million, Terry £800,000, and Frank Sinclair around £400,000. The *Daily Express* financial editor understood what was happening and wrote: 'The turnaround that's coming can hardly be classed as a miracle, engineered by a wizard businessman. Most ailing businesses could be turned round if a rich benefactor came along.' Precisely.

To be fair to Sugar, he made it clear immediately after the takeover that he saw Spurs as a straightforward commercial deal, and almost every action he has taken since then has borne out that view. Never more so than at that historic 18 May 1992 meeting when the twenty-two Premier League clubs decided that they were going to vote for the £304 million Sky deal instead of ITV. The deal has been too well chronicled for it to require elaboration here, except to recall that Sugar made it very clear that he saw no problems in canvassing a deal which would also be of enormous benefit to his company. They obviously took the right decision as far as he was concerned, and I admire his frankness and forthrightness in setting out his goals and objectives. But I do think that was the wrong decision for Spurs, and for English football.

Sugar, of course, is a new kind of football Chairman. I was very interested to read an interview with him, done just before the Charity Shield Match at the beginning of the 1991/92 season, in which a reporter asked him about the Double. Now any Spurs supporter knows that the Double means the Double side of Danny Blanchflower, which won the League and the Cup in 1960/61. Even if a Spurs supporter was not born then, he would have heard of the exploits of that team almost as soon as he could walk. Yet when this reporter asked Sugar about the Double he replied: 'Double? What Double? Is that something from the 1950s?'

I know I was pilloried for my enthusiasm for Spurs and the game, but for my successor, who is the principal owner of Spurs, not even to know what the Double was is quite something. Football is about tradition, history, deeds of the past leading on to the future. I am not given to unbridled nostalgia, but to so disregard the past must tear at the fabric of the club.

I wonder if that indifference explains why one of the first acts of the new Spurs board, after they had taken over from me, was one full of petty meanness. As I have said, when I sold to Sugar it was agreed that I should stay on the board as a non-executive director of the club. Yet less than a month after the takeover I received a letter from Tony Berry stating:

> In spite of the arrangements considered at the time of the takeover, the controlling shareholders now feel that it would be appropriate for you, in conjunction with other non-executive directors, to resign as a director of the football club. This will, of course, not prejudice the rights to receive tickets for all home and away games and to avail yourself of the facilities that would naturally be afforded to a former chairman of the football club.

I must say I was dumbfounded on receiving this letter. I had seen an interview with Alan Sugar in the *Mail on Sunday* where he had said: 'One cannot take away the fact that Irving Scholar was totally devoted to Tottenham Hotspur. He did not do anything bad against the club. He is entitled, I suppose, in an on-going situation, to have some form of recognition. He loves the club, he put a lot of his life and effort into it.' About two weeks later I wrote to Sugar: 'In your letter to me of 11th June, you mention it was not your intention to cause me any discomfort, that I would be able to remain a director of the club until such time as I might wish gracefully to depart. Our agreement was confirmed once again on the night the transfer of shares was agreed, and subsequently mentioned in an interview given by you with the *Mail on Sunday*.'

Despite all this, on 12 September Tony wrote to me saying:

The Board of Tottenham Hotspur Football and Athletic Company Limited were disappointed that you felt unable to agree to their request to resign as a director. As a result, a decision was taken in accordance with the articles to remove you as a director at the special meeting convened on 6th September 1991. Clearly, the relationship between you and the club has irretrievably broken down and as such we do not feel it appropriate to continue with the privileges previously granted to you with regard to match day seats and passes.

'Irretrievably broken down'? I still do not understand what Tony was talking about. Nothing had happened to change the situation since I had done my deal with Alan Sugar. I can only conclude that having taken over, they wanted nothing to do with me. This became ever more evident during the charade the new Spurs management performed with the season tickets that I had in the Centenary Club in the West Stand. For the first few years following my takeover I renewed these seats annually, and finally I let Mike Rollo sell them on an annual basis only with no right of renewal. It was always understood that these tickets would be available for me at any time in the future, and shortly after the Sugar takeover I told Mike that I would be taking them up for the start of the 1992/93 season. At Christmas 1991 I tried to get written confirmation of the renewal price, but Tottenham kept evading me, and it was only in March of 1992 that I heard that they were not going to be made available.

On the last day of the 1991/92 season, I decided to watch Spurs play Manchester United at Old Trafford, in Lineker's last domestic game. After the match I met Terry in the boardroom. He could not have been more affable. I mentioned the season ticket trouble, and he said he was totally unaware of it but assured me that there wouldn't be a problem. I immediately wrote to Mike, and within a few weeks I received a letter saying that they had been sold. I suppose I should not have been surprised. A few weeks earlier, as I was preparing to see Spurs in Holland against Feyenoord, I received a telephone call from a friend. He had been asked to pass on a message from Terry Venables to me: 'You are not welcome in Holland and you are not welcome at the ground.'

So why should Terry Venables not want me to see the side I have always supported? The frivolous answer is that Terry himself is so ashamed of the way Spurs is playing at the moment, in such an un-Spurslike fashion, that knowing me as he does he doesn't feel he could present this product in front of me. Certainly he has done some curious things; for instance his sale of Lineker to Japan. Venables said at the time that there was an agreement with Lineker that he could leave when he wanted to. I must say I was surprised to hear this since I did the original deal with Holmes, Linkeker's agent, and did not know that the deal had been amended. But I detect some deeper animosity in Terry. I can't account for it. After all, I've done Terry Venables no harm. In his dark days, when our results were horrendous, the crowds disillusioned, and even the board grumbling about Terry, I was his most loyal defender, pleading that he should be given a proper chance.

Does this animosity mean, perhaps, that he is uneasy about taking over at Spurs? As we have seen, he borrowed money in order to do so, and in the summer of 1992 he admitted: 'I overstretched myself beyond common sense.' Has he with Spurs bitten off more than he can chew? I think of the many times I discussed with Terry his dream of buying a club. His ideal was to purchase a small club and turn it into a lucrative business by concentrating on recruiting and improving young players, with the aim of selling them on to the bigger clubs: a sort of nursery club that is quite common on the Continent, although rare in this country. Spurs cannot be like that, and his feelings towards me may be linked up with the frustrations he is possibly experiencing at having 'overstretched' himself.

Yet I bear him no grudge, and I still hold to what I told him the morning after the takeover. Go on, go and win the

European Cup for Spurs. That day I will shed tears, tears of joy.

Notwithstanding Terry's feelings, I shall always be loyal to the only football club that has ever meant anything to me. A few months ago, in the summer, my libel action against the *Daily Mail* was finally heard. The jury agreed that the newspaper had indeed libelled me by claiming that I had professed my wish to keep Gascoigne when I really wanted to sell him. Terry gave evidence for the *Daily Mail*, having by this time already sold Gascoigne to Lazio. The jury found in my favour and awarded me damages of £100,000, but the money was unimportant. What mattered to me more was to have retrieved my reputation. At the end of the trial a journalist came up to me and asked how I felt about Spurs. I replied: 'I was born a Spurs supporter and I shall die a Spurs supporter. Nothing will ever change that.'

A great many things have happened in my life. I shall happily have that epitaph on my tombstone.

Monte Carlo, autumn 1992